RENT-A-GiRLFRIEND

VOLUME **10**

REIJI MIYAJIMA

CONTENTS

RATING 77
MY EX-GIRLFRIEND AND MY "GIRLFRIEND" 4..........................3

RATING 78
MY GIRLFRIEND AND MY DREAM DATE 1..................................23

RATING 79
MY GIRLFRIEND AND MY DREAM DATE 2..................................43

RATING 80
MY GIRLFRIEND AND MY DREAM DATE 3..................................65

RATING 81
MY GIRLFRIEND AND MY DREAM DATE 4..................................85

RATING 82
MY GIRLFRIEND AND MY DREAM DATE 5..................................105

RATING 83
MY GIRLFRIEND, MY HOUSE, AND THE KISS 1..........................125

RATING 84
MY GIRLFRIEND, MY HOUSE, AND THE KISS 2..........................145

RATING 85
MY GIRLFRIEND, MY HOUSE, AND THE KISS 3..........................165

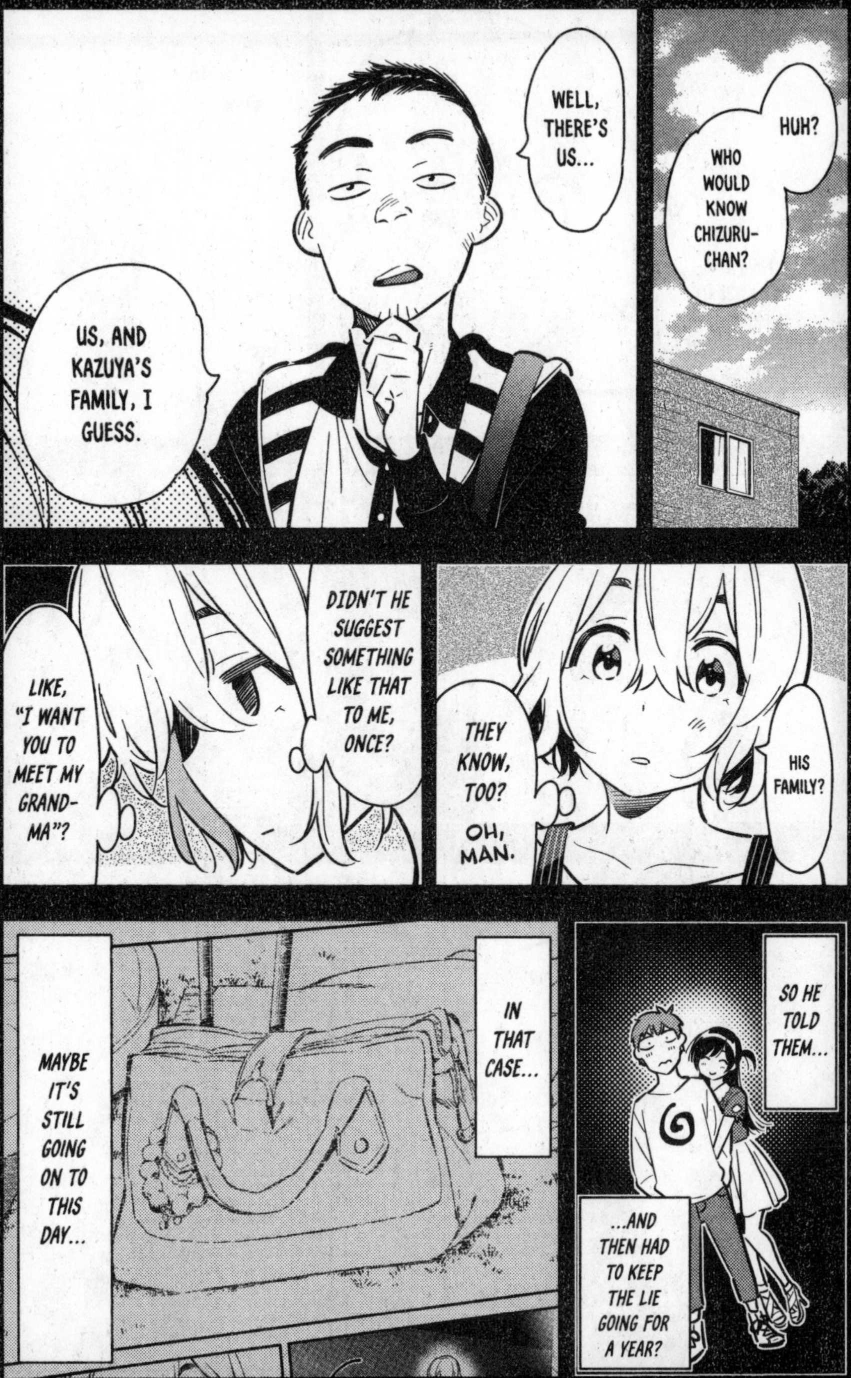
HUH?
WHO WOULD KNOW CHIZURU-CHAN?
WELL, THERE'S US...
US, AND KAZUYA'S FAMILY, I GUESS.
HIS FAMILY?
THEY KNOW, TOO?
OH, MAN.
DIDN'T HE SUGGEST SOMETHING LIKE THAT TO ME, ONCE?
LIKE, "I WANT YOU TO MEET MY GRAND-MA"?
SO HE TOLD THEM...
...AND THEN HAD TO KEEP THE LIE GOING FOR A YEAR?
IN THAT CASE...
MAYBE IT'S STILL GOING ON TO THIS DAY...

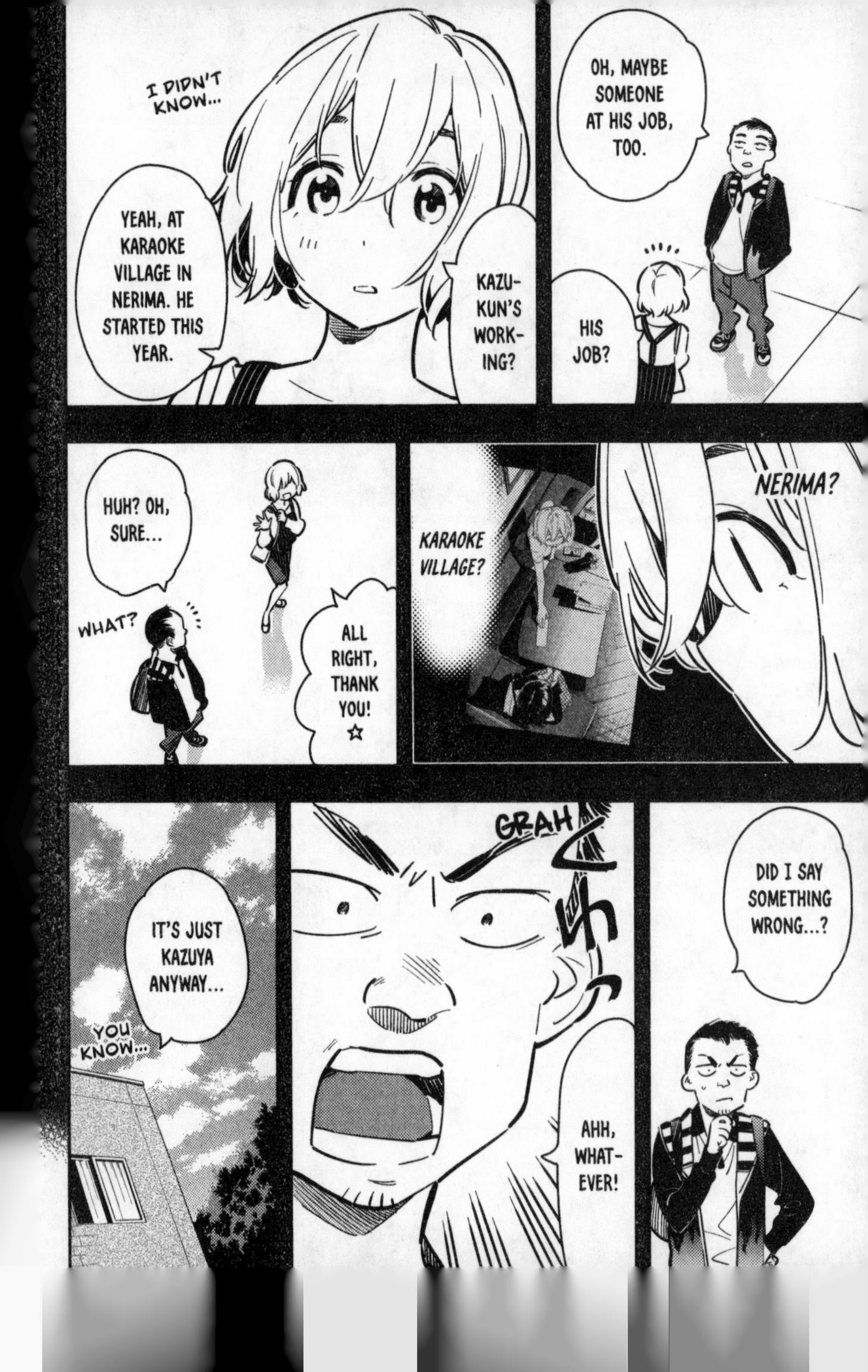
OH, MAYBE SOMEONE AT HIS JOB, TOO.
HIS JOB?
KAZU-KUN'S WORKING?
I DIDN'T KNOW...
YEAH, AT KARAOKE VILLAGE IN NERIMA. HE STARTED THIS YEAR.
NERIMA?
KARAOKE VILLAGE?
ALL RIGHT, THANK YOU! ☆
HUH? OH, SURE...
WHAT?
DID I SAY SOMETHING WRONG...?
GRAH
AHH, WHATEVER!
IT'S JUST KAZUYA ANYWAY...
YOU KNOW...

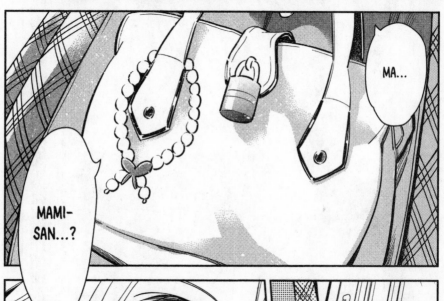

MA...

MAMI-SAN...?

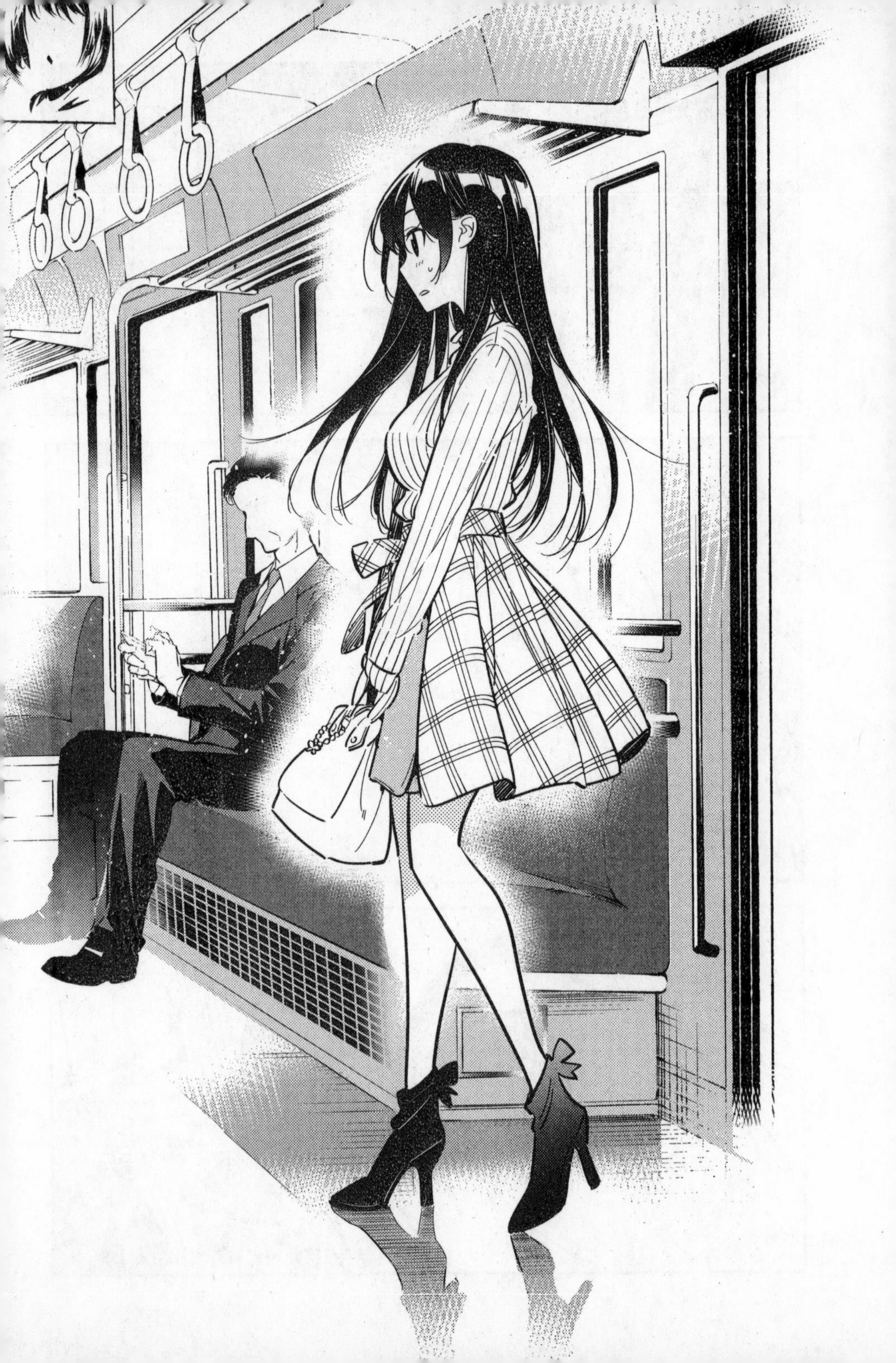

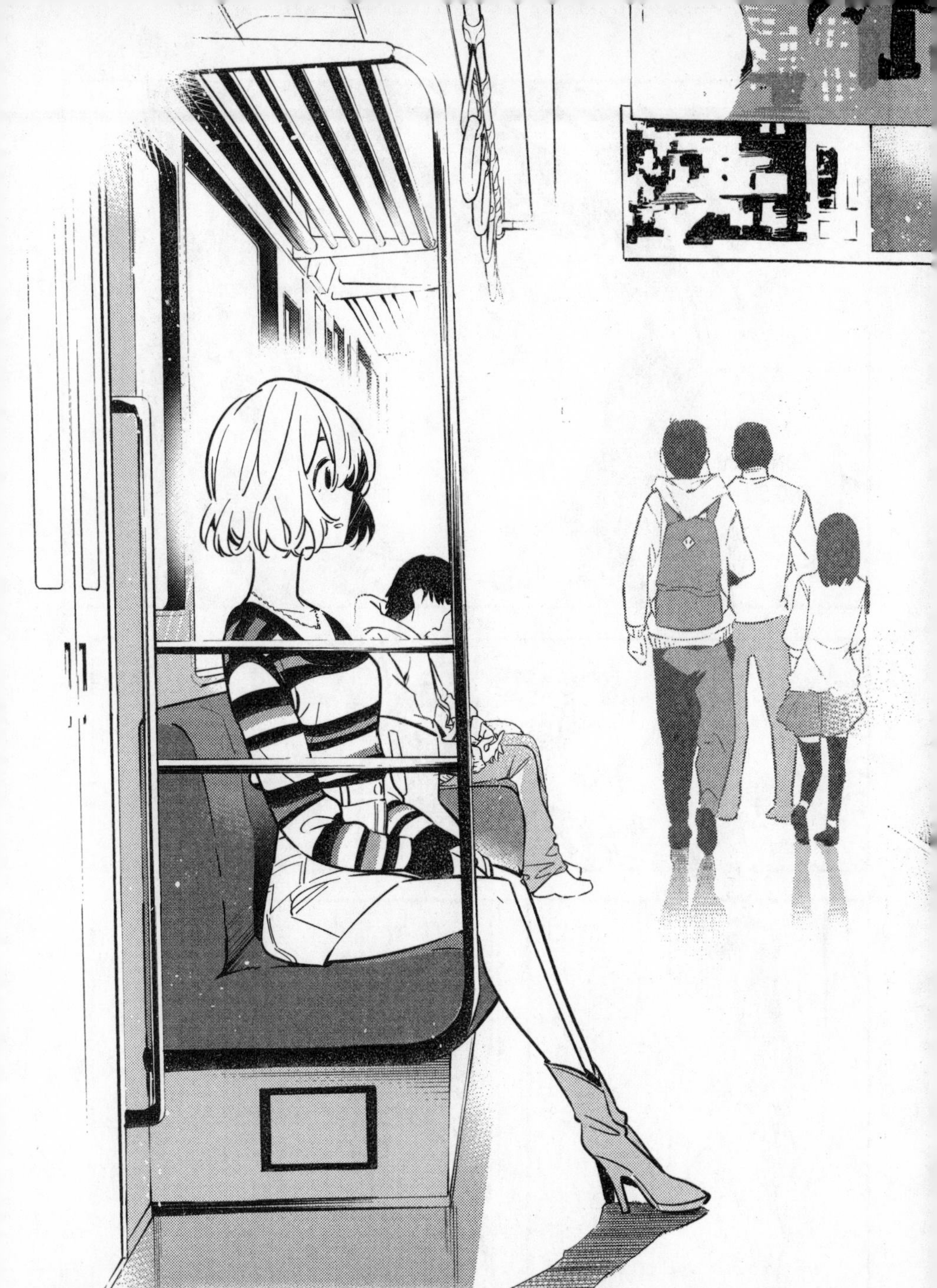

RATING 77 MY EX-GIRLFRIEND AND MY "GIRLFRIEND" 3

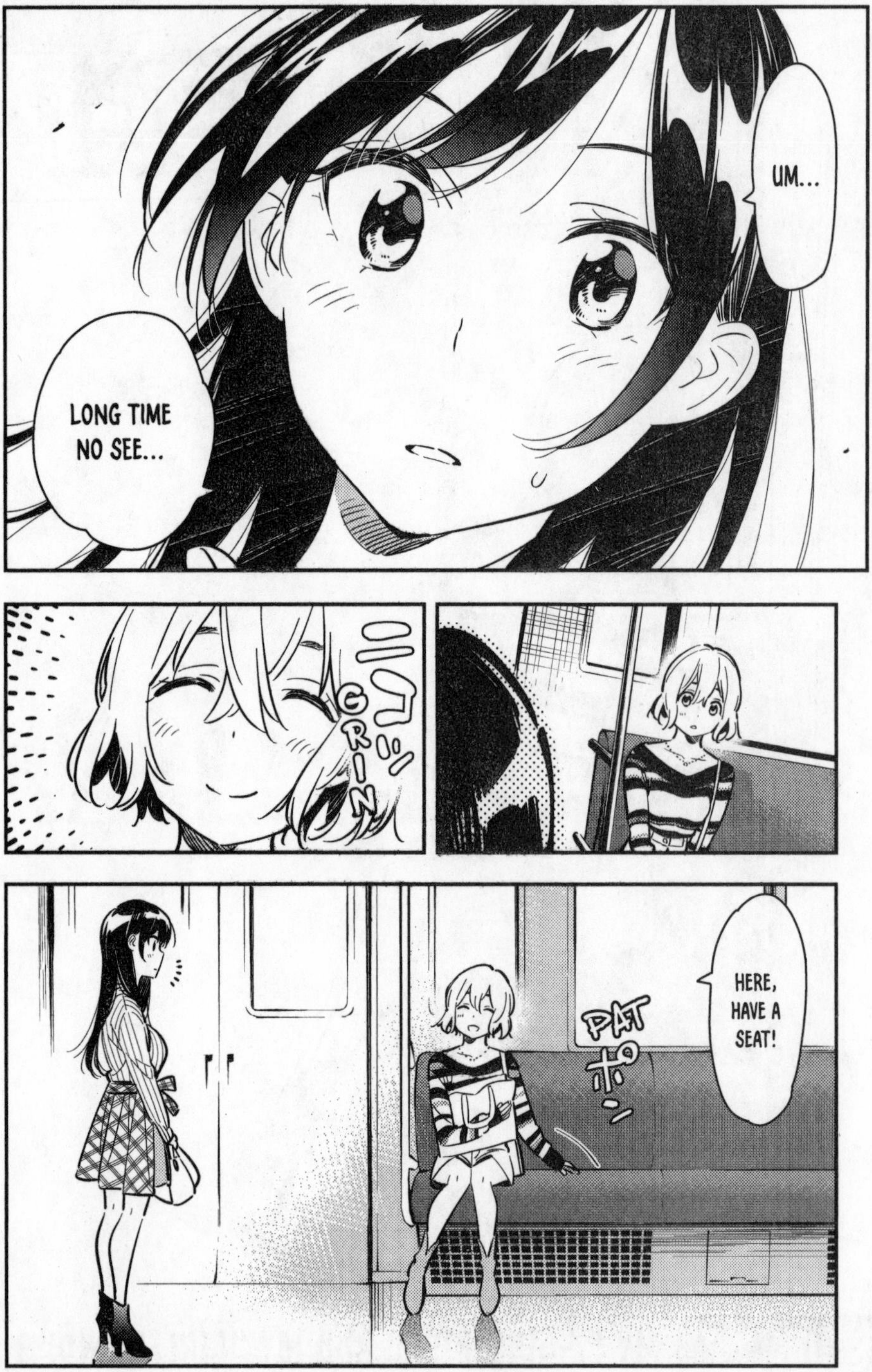
UM...
LONG TIME NO SEE...
ニコッ
GRIN
HERE, HAVE A SEAT!
PAT

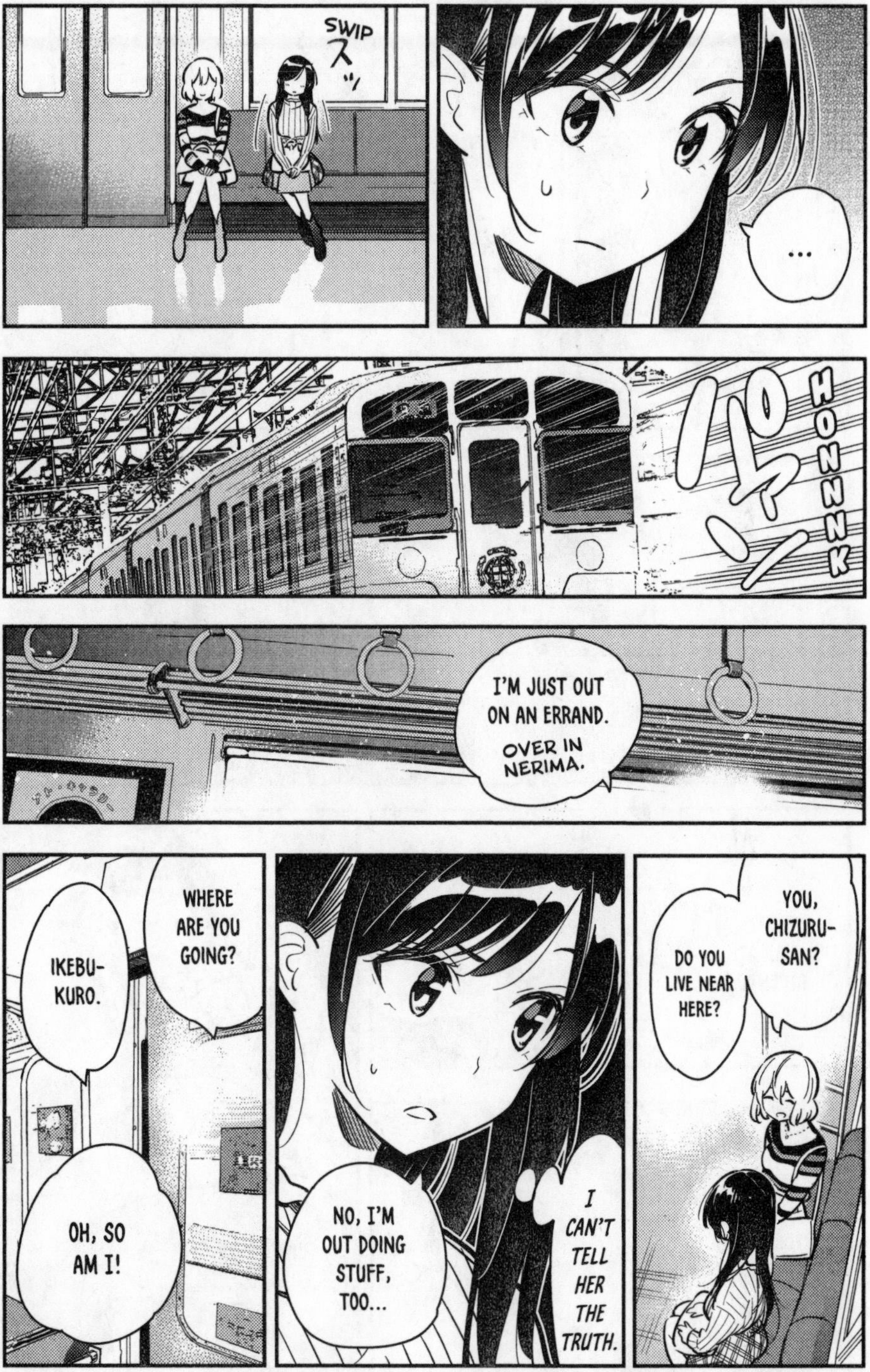
...
SWIP
スッ
HONNNK
I'M JUST OUT ON AN ERRAND.
OVER IN NERIMA.
YOU, CHIZURU-SAN?
DO YOU LIVE NEAR HERE?
I CAN'T TELL HER THE TRUTH.
NO, I'M OUT DOING STUFF, TOO...
WHERE ARE YOU GOING?
IKEBUKURO.
OH, SO AM I!

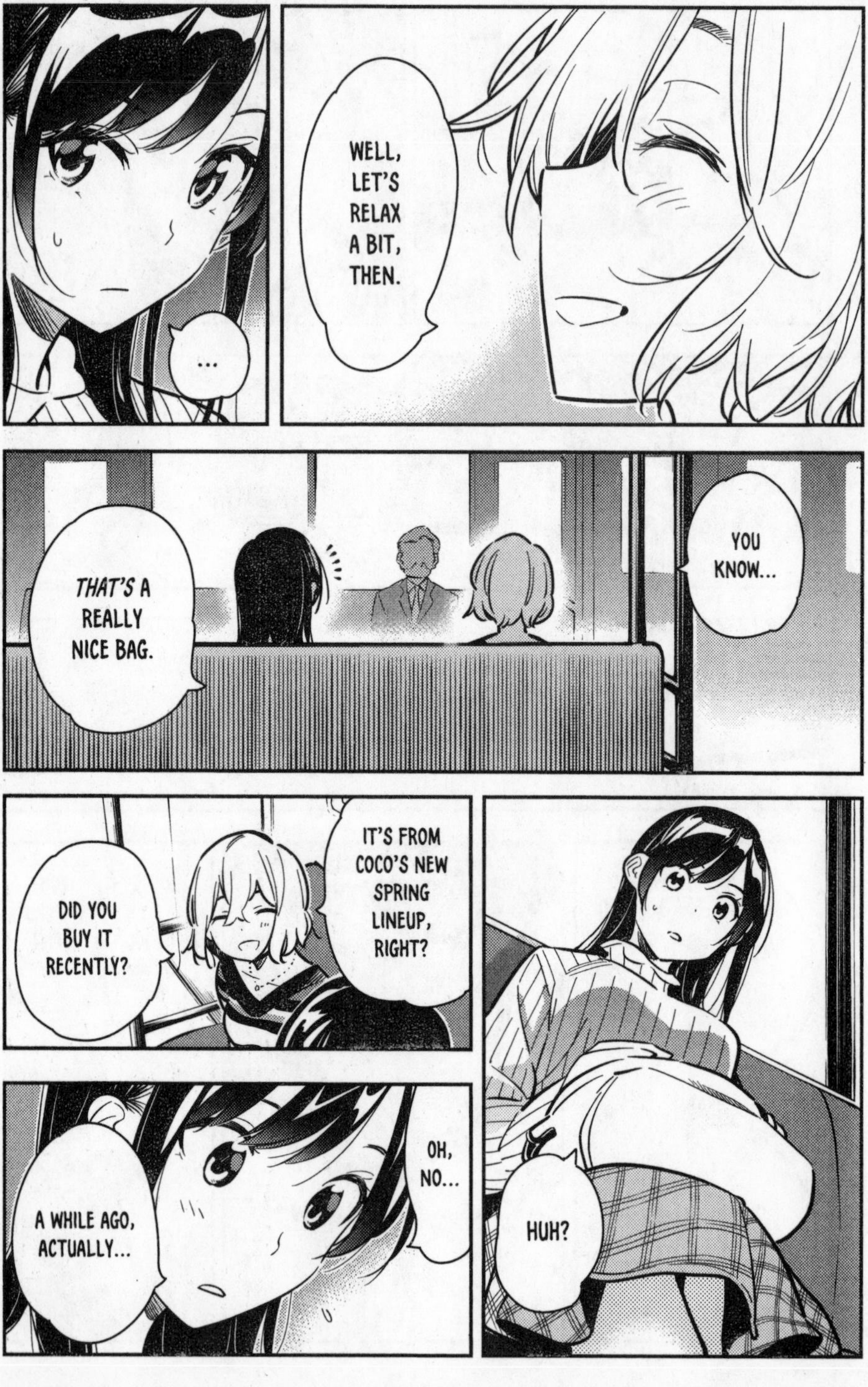
WELL, LET'S RELAX A BIT, THEN.
...
YOU KNOW...
THAT'S A REALLY NICE BAG.
HUH?
IT'S FROM COCO'S NEW SPRING LINEUP, RIGHT?
DID YOU BUY IT RECENTLY?
OH, NO...
A WHILE AGO, ACTUALLY...

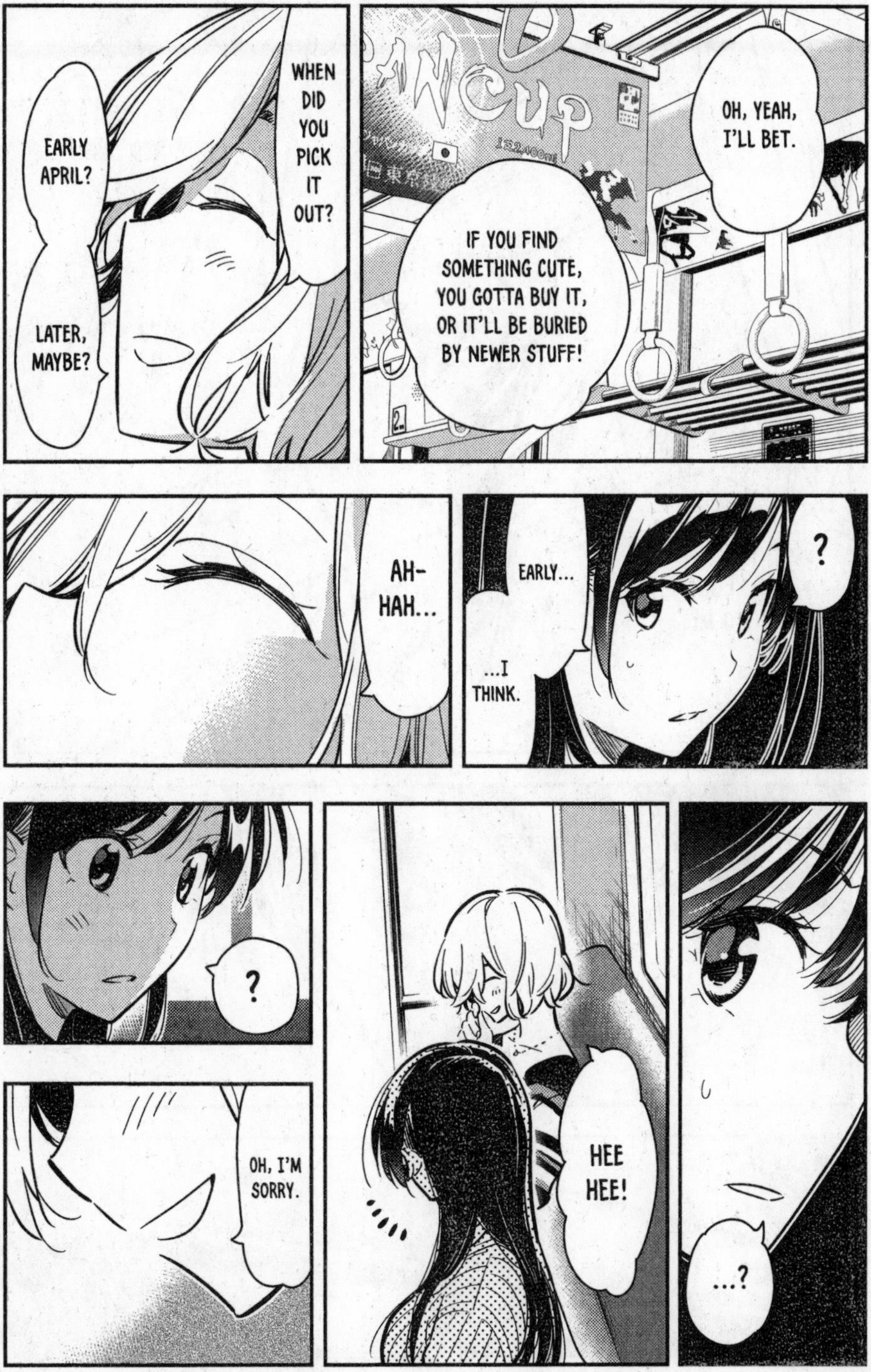
OH, YEAH, I'LL BET.
IF YOU FIND SOMETHING CUTE, YOU GOTTA BUY IT, OR IT'LL BE BURIED BY NEWER STUFF!
WHEN DID YOU PICK IT OUT?
EARLY APRIL?
LATER, MAYBE?
?
EARLY...
...I THINK.
AH-HAH...
...?
HEE HEE!
?
OH, I'M SORRY.

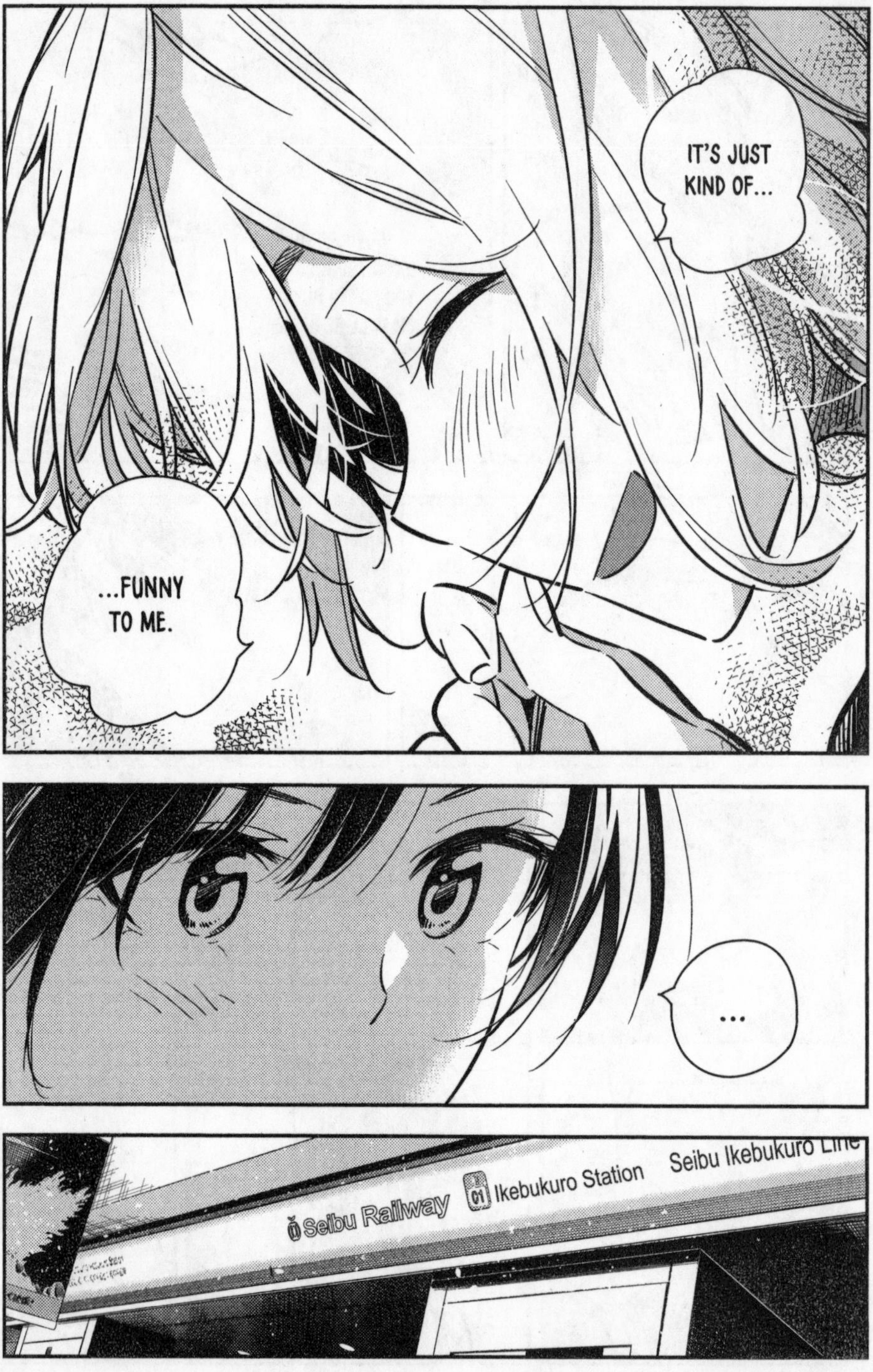
IT'S JUST KIND OF...
...FUNNY TO ME.
...
Seibu Ikebukuro Line
Ikebukuro Station
Seibu Railway

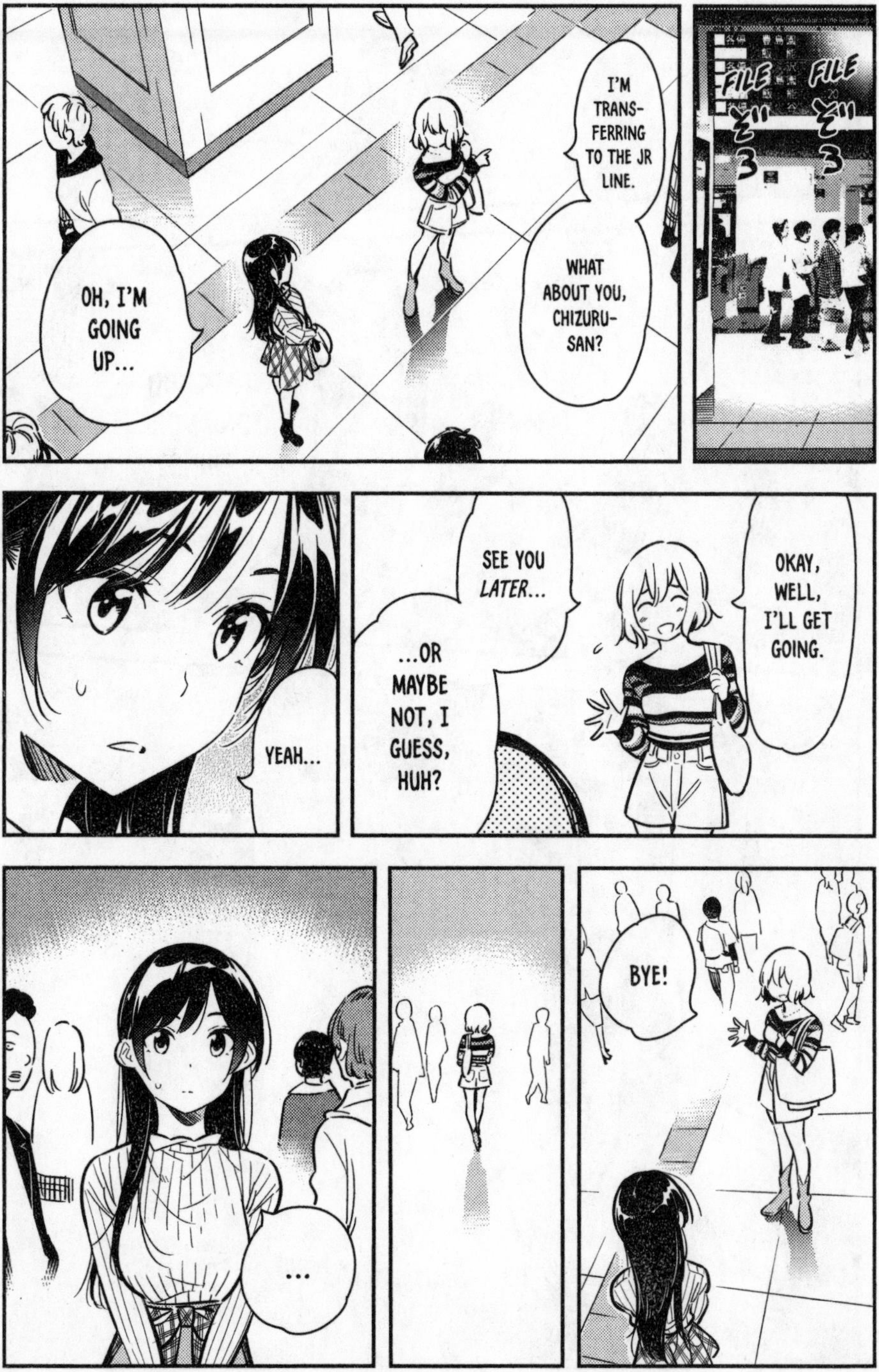
FILE
FILE
I'M TRANSFERRING TO THE JR LINE.
WHAT ABOUT YOU, CHIZURU-SAN?
OH, I'M GOING UP...
OKAY, WELL, I'LL GET GOING.
SEE YOU *LATER*...
...OR MAYBE NOT, I GUESS, HUH?
YEAH...
BYE!
...

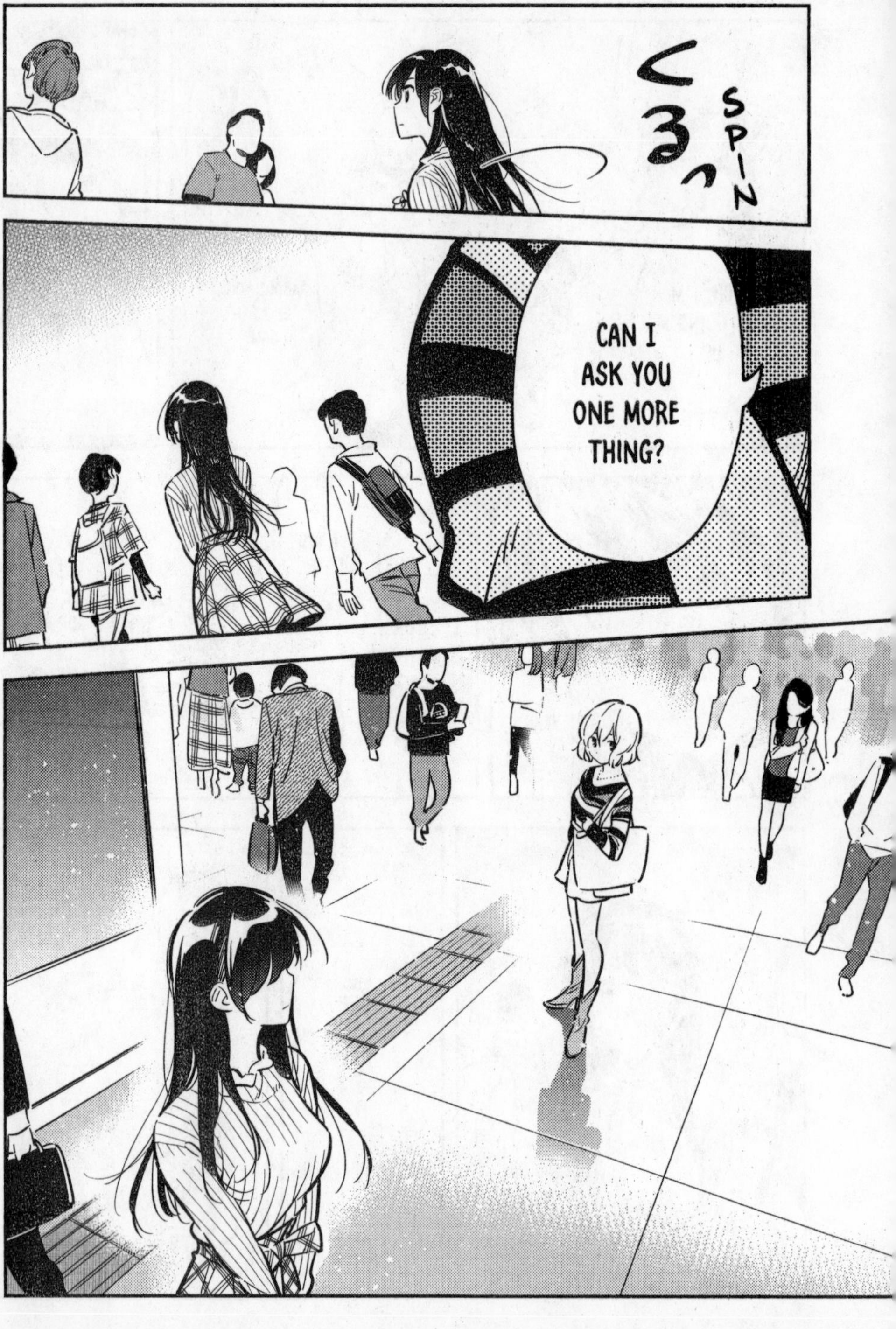
くるっ
SPIN
CAN I ASK YOU ONE MORE THING?

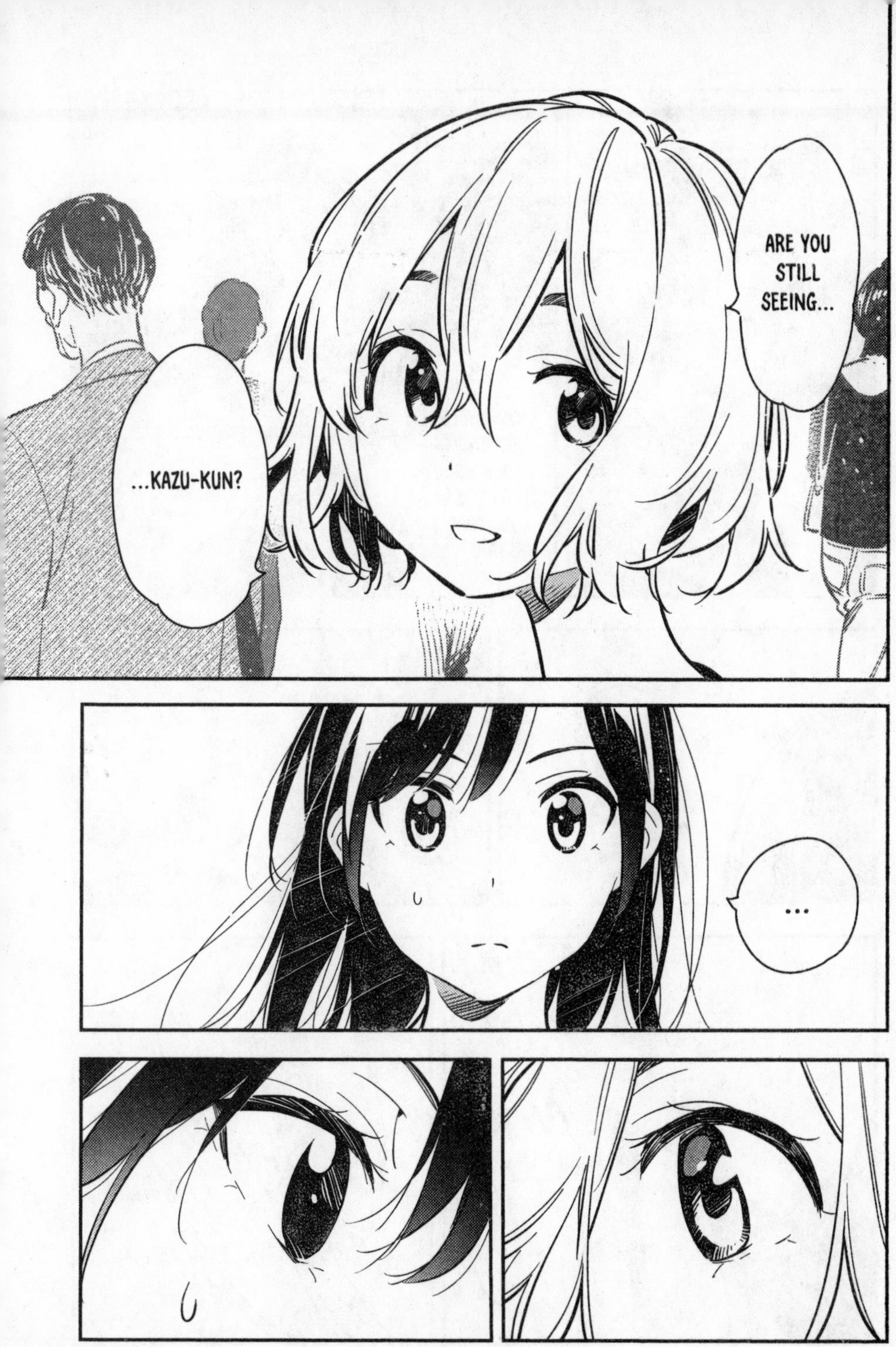
ARE YOU STILL SEEING...
...KAZU-KUN?
...

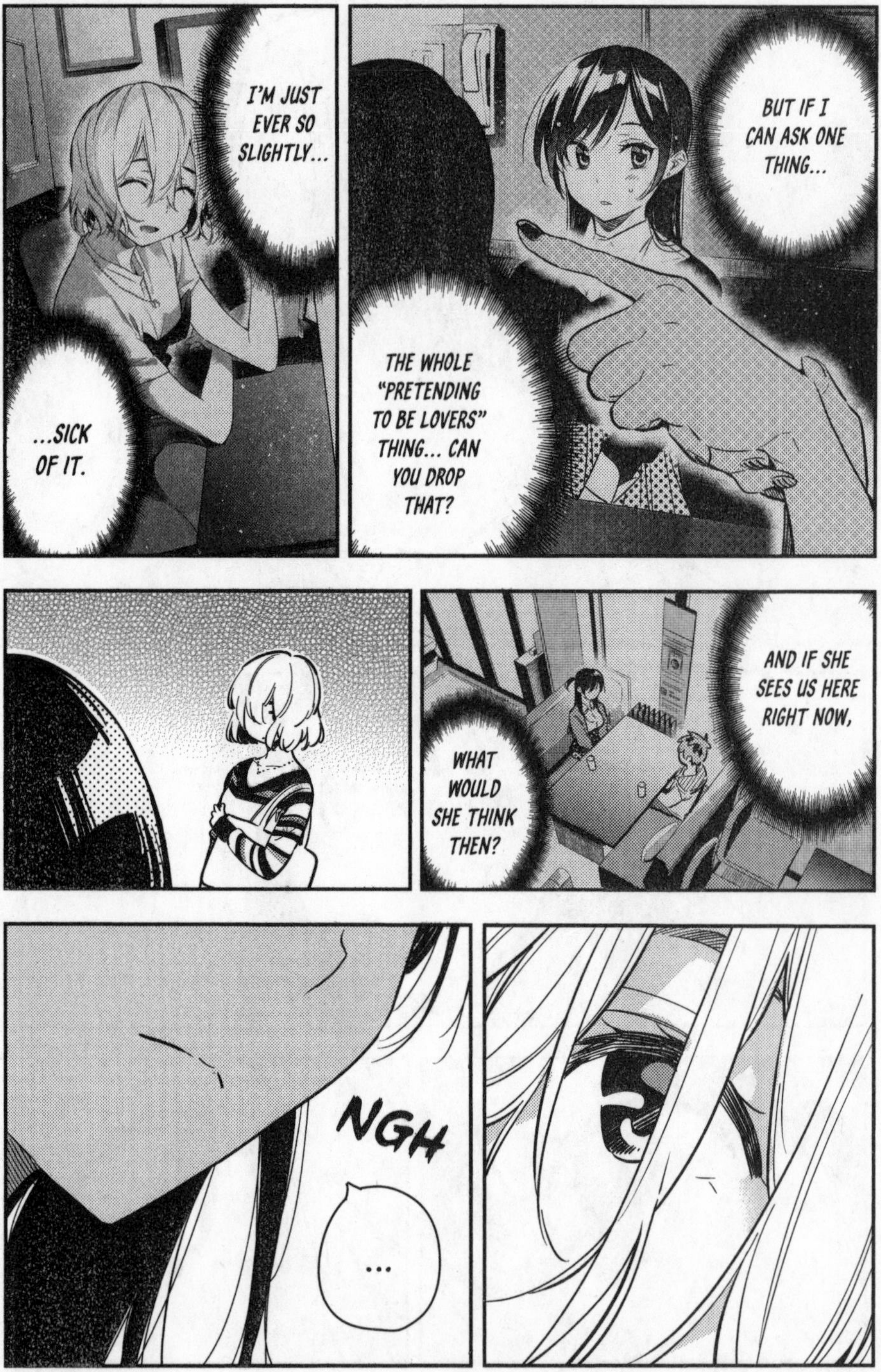
BUT IF I CAN ASK ONE THING...
THE WHOLE "PRETENDING TO BE LOVERS" THING... CAN YOU DROP THAT?
I'M JUST EVER SO SLIGHTLY...
...SICK OF IT.
AND IF SHE SEES US HERE RIGHT NOW,
WHAT WOULD SHE THINK THEN?
NGH
...

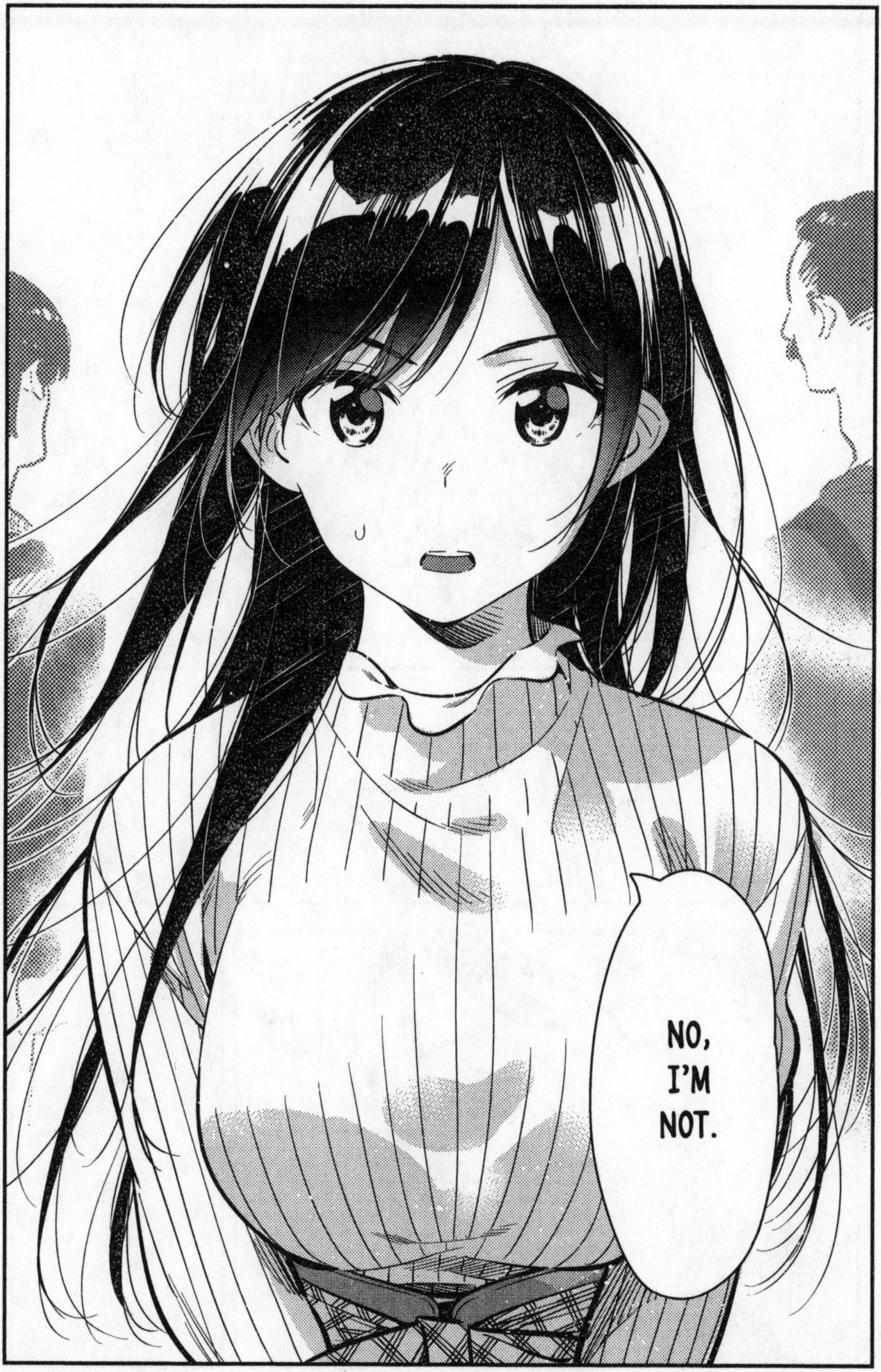
NO, I'M NOT.

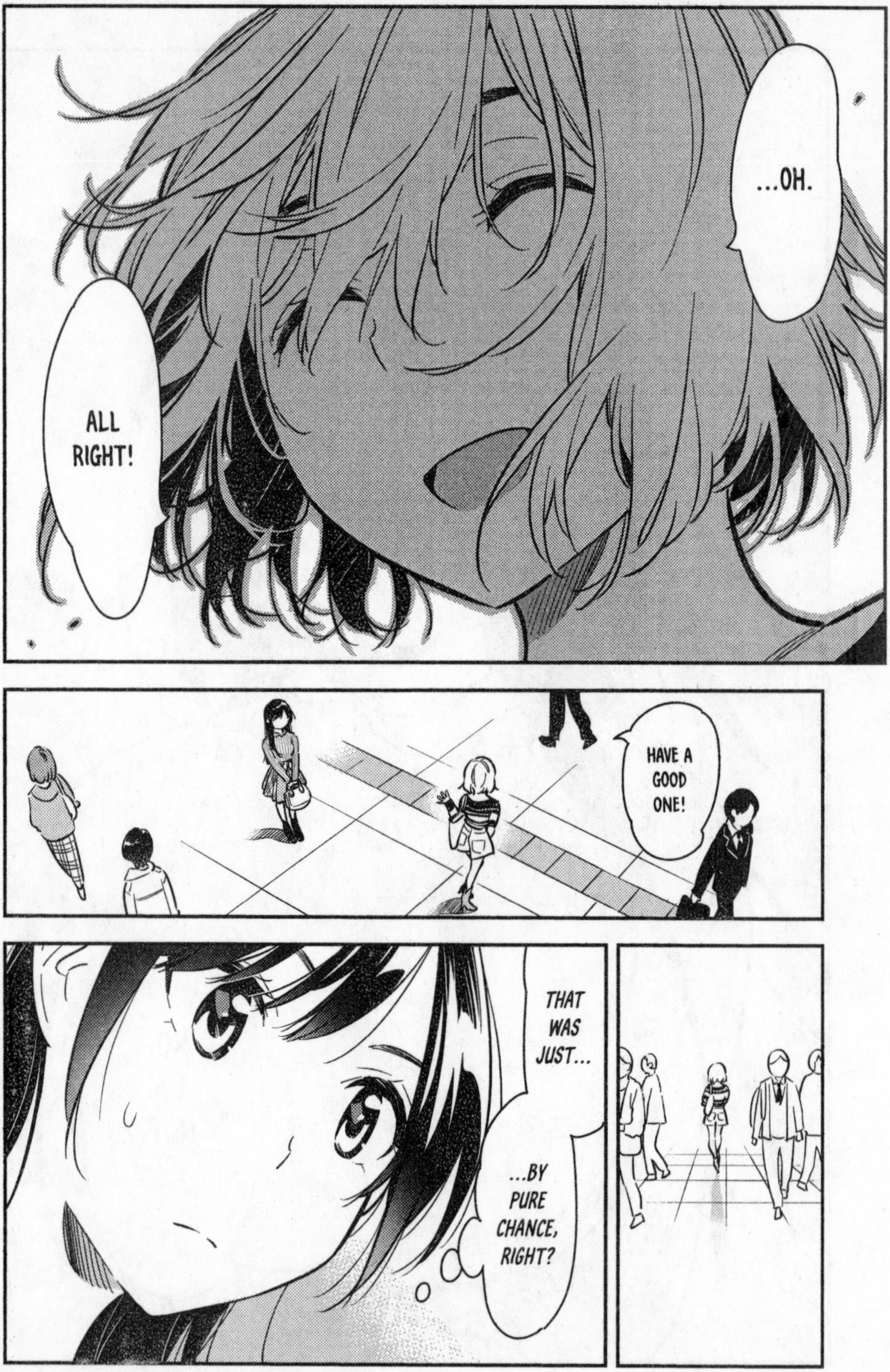
...OH.
ALL RIGHT!
HAVE A GOOD ONE!
THAT WAS JUST...
...BY PURE CHANCE, RIGHT?

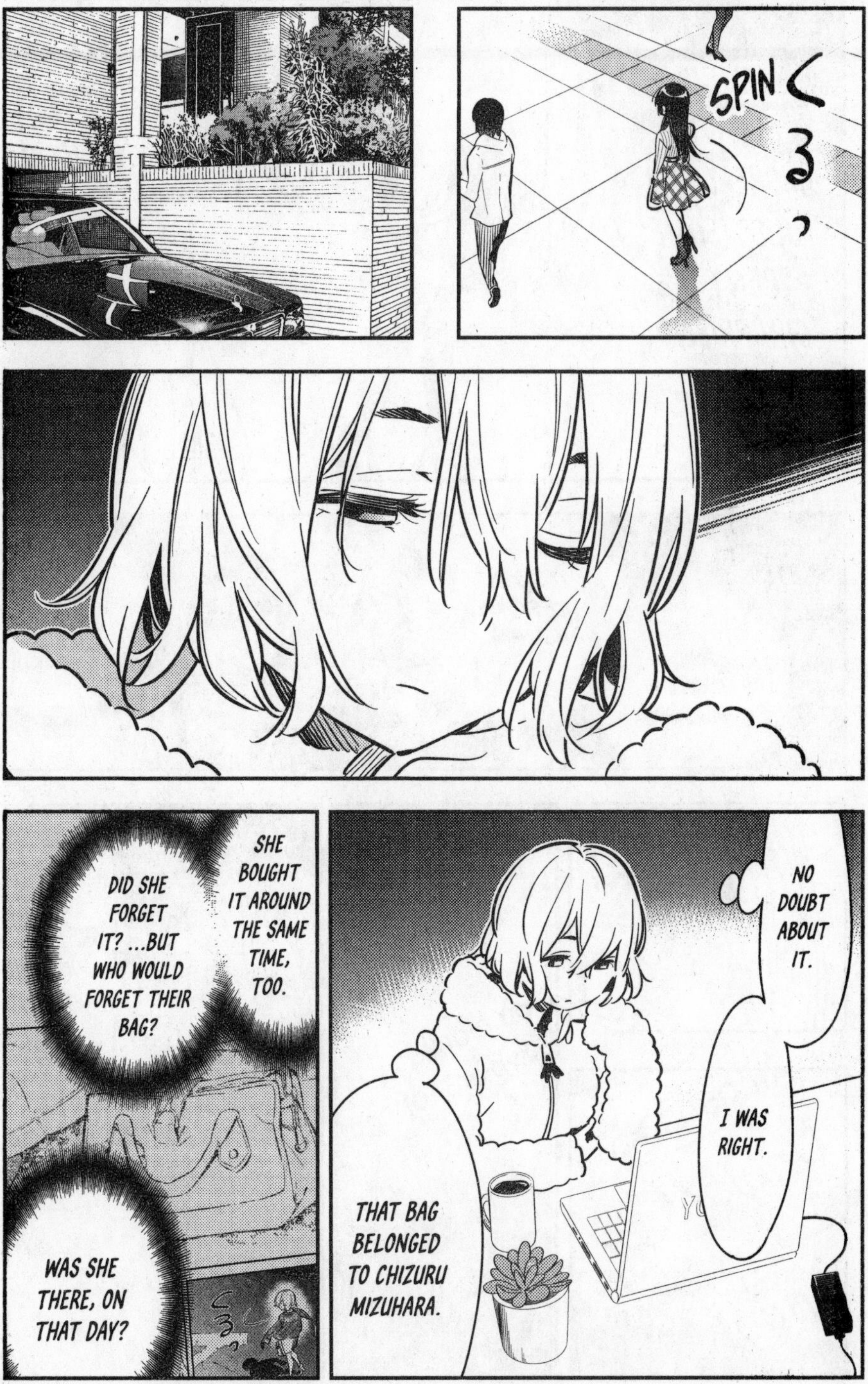
SPIN
くるっ
NO DOUBT ABOUT IT.
I WAS RIGHT.
THAT BAG BELONGED TO CHIZURU MIZUHARA.
SHE BOUGHT IT AROUND THE SAME TIME, TOO.
DID SHE FORGET IT? ...BUT WHO WOULD FORGET THEIR BAG?
WAS SHE THERE, ON THAT DAY?

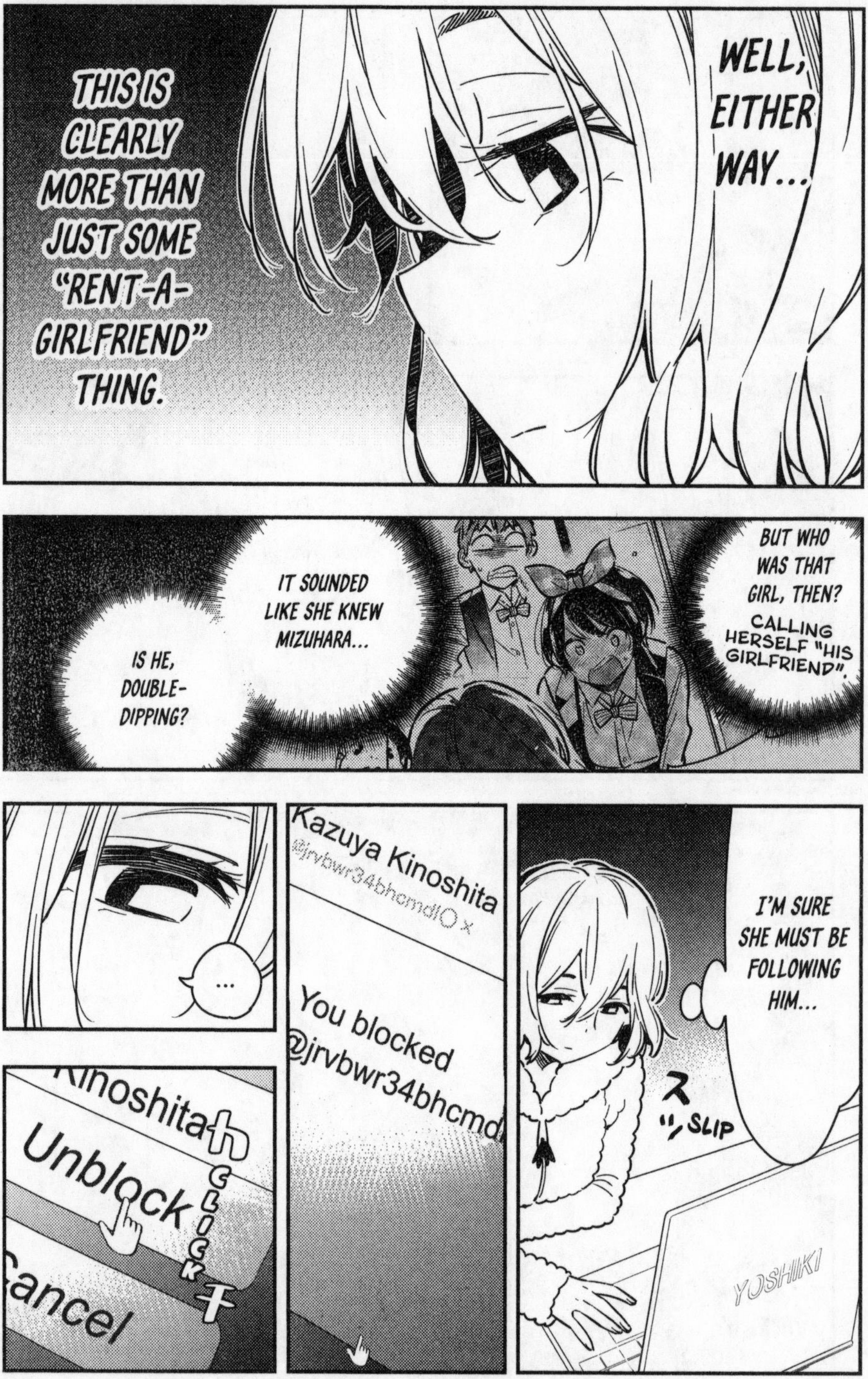
WELL, EITHER WAY...
THIS IS CLEARLY MORE THAN JUST SOME "RENT-A-GIRLFRIEND" THING.
BUT WHO WAS THAT GIRL, THEN?
CALLING HERSELF "HIS GIRLFRIEND".
IT SOUNDED LIKE SHE KNEW MIZUHARA...
IS HE, DOUBLE-DIPPING?
I'M SURE SHE MUST BE FOLLOWING HIM...
SLIP
YOSHIKI
Kazuya Kinoshita
You blocked
@jrvbwr34bhcmd
...
Kinoshita
Unblock
CLICK
Cancel

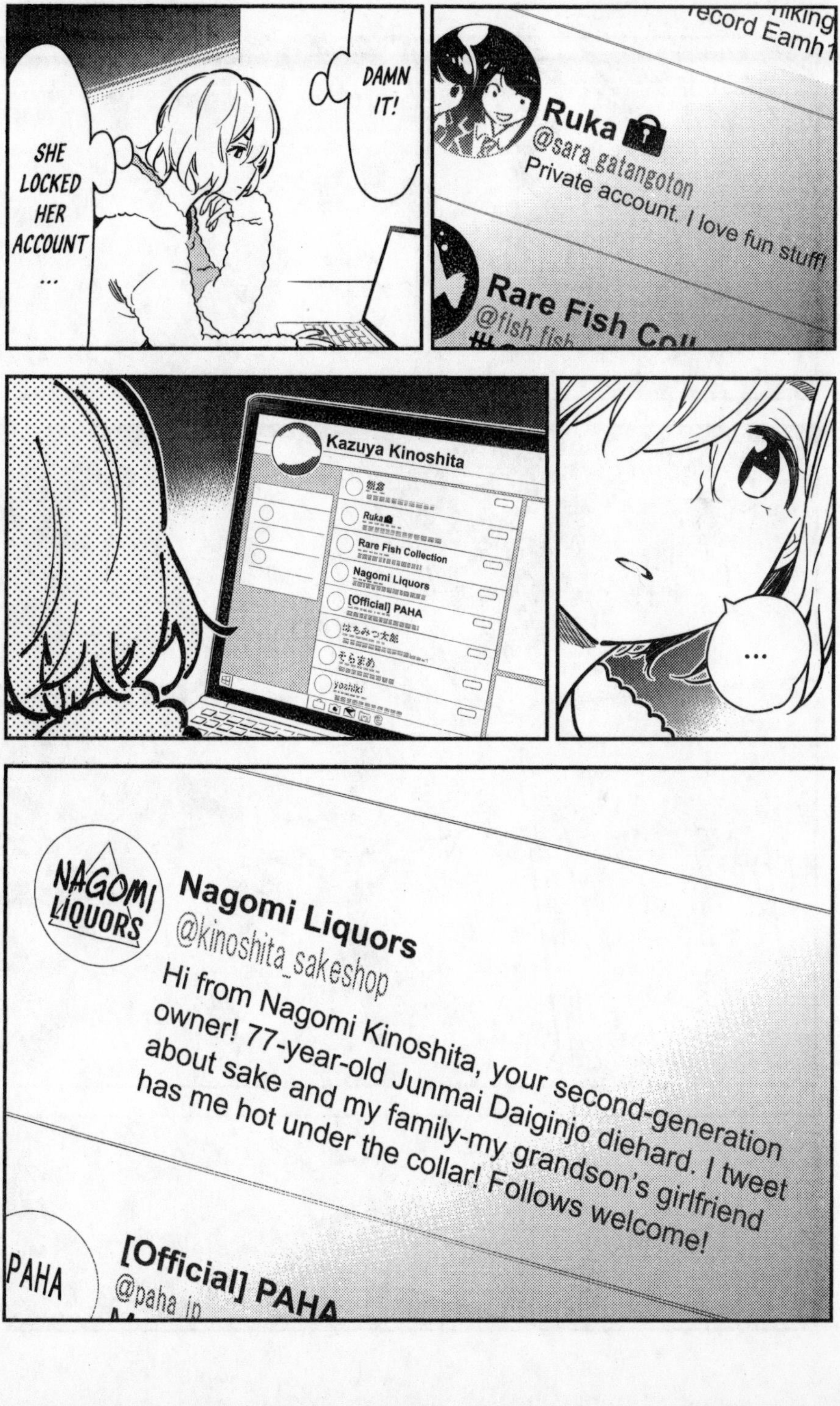
Ruka
@sara_gatangoton
Private account. I love fun stuff!
DAMN IT!
SHE LOCKED HER ACCOUNT...
...
Kazuya Kinoshita
Ruka
Rare Fish Collection
Nagomi Liquors
[Official] PAHA
はちみつ太郎
そらまめ
yoshiki
NAGOMI LIQUORS
Nagomi Liquors
@kinoshita_sakeshop
Hi from Nagomi Kinoshita, your second-generation owner! 77-year-old Junmai Daiginjo diehard. I tweet about sake and my family-my grandson's girlfriend has me hot under the collar! Follows welcome!
PAHA
[Official] PAHA
@paha_jp

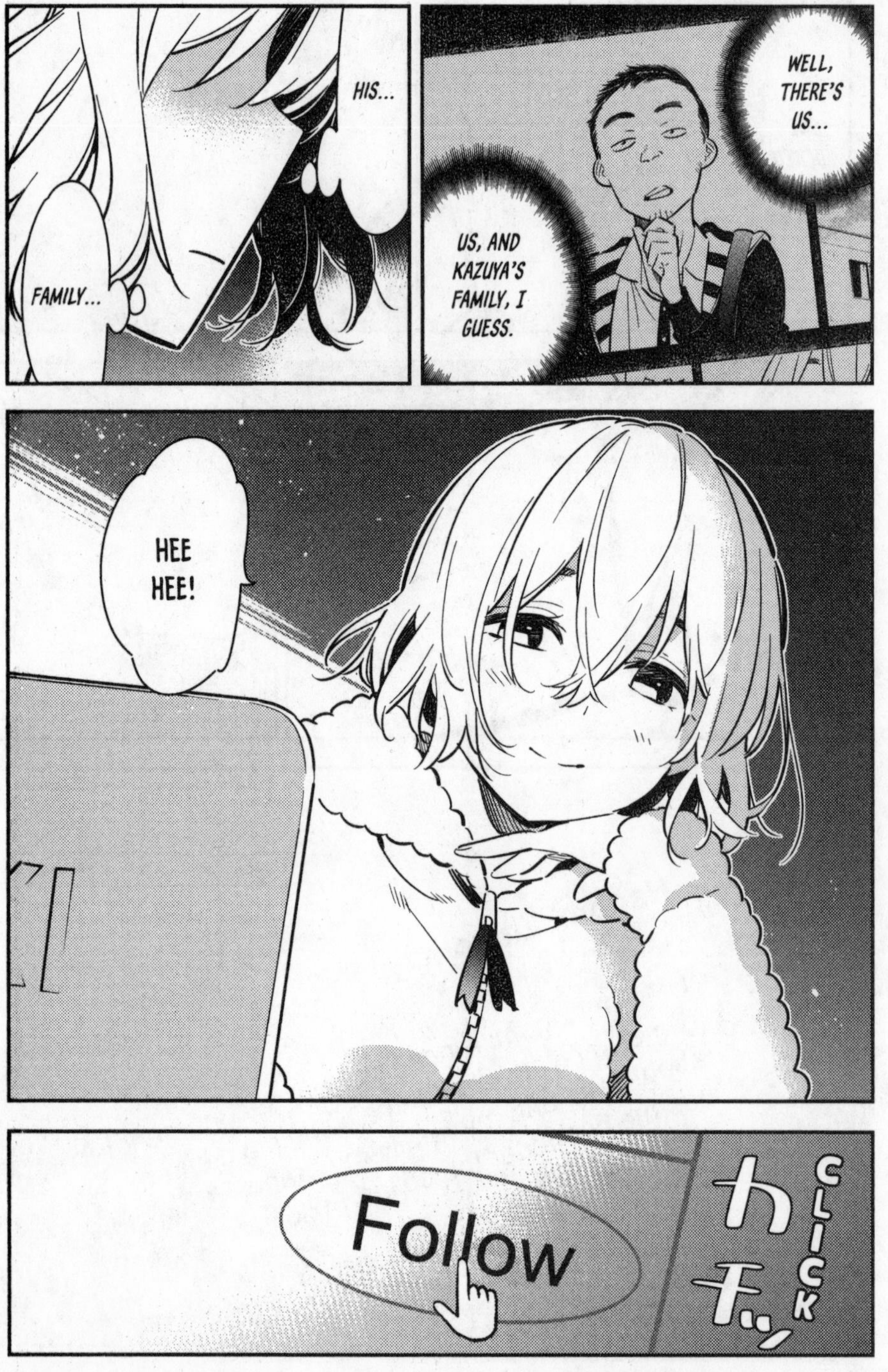
WELL, THERE'S US...
US, AND KAZUYA'S FAMILY, I GUESS.
HIS...
FAMILY...
HEE HEE!
カチッ
CLICK
Follow

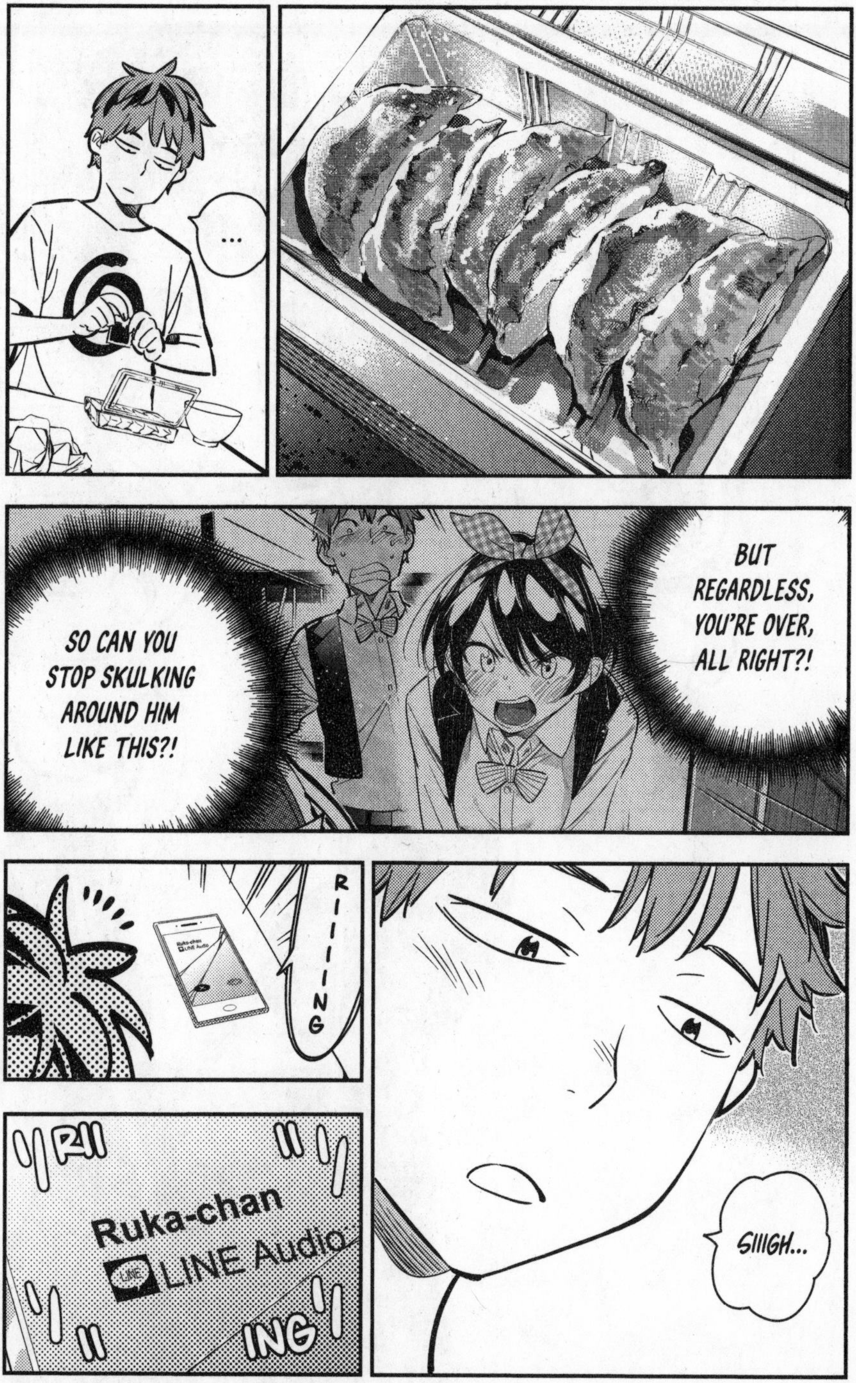
...
BUT REGARDLESS, YOU'RE OVER, ALL RIGHT?!
SO CAN YOU STOP SKULKING AROUND HIM LIKE THIS?!
SIIIGH...
RIIIING
RII
Ruka-chan
LINE Audio
ING

RATING 78 MY GIRLFRIEND AND MY DREAM DATE 1

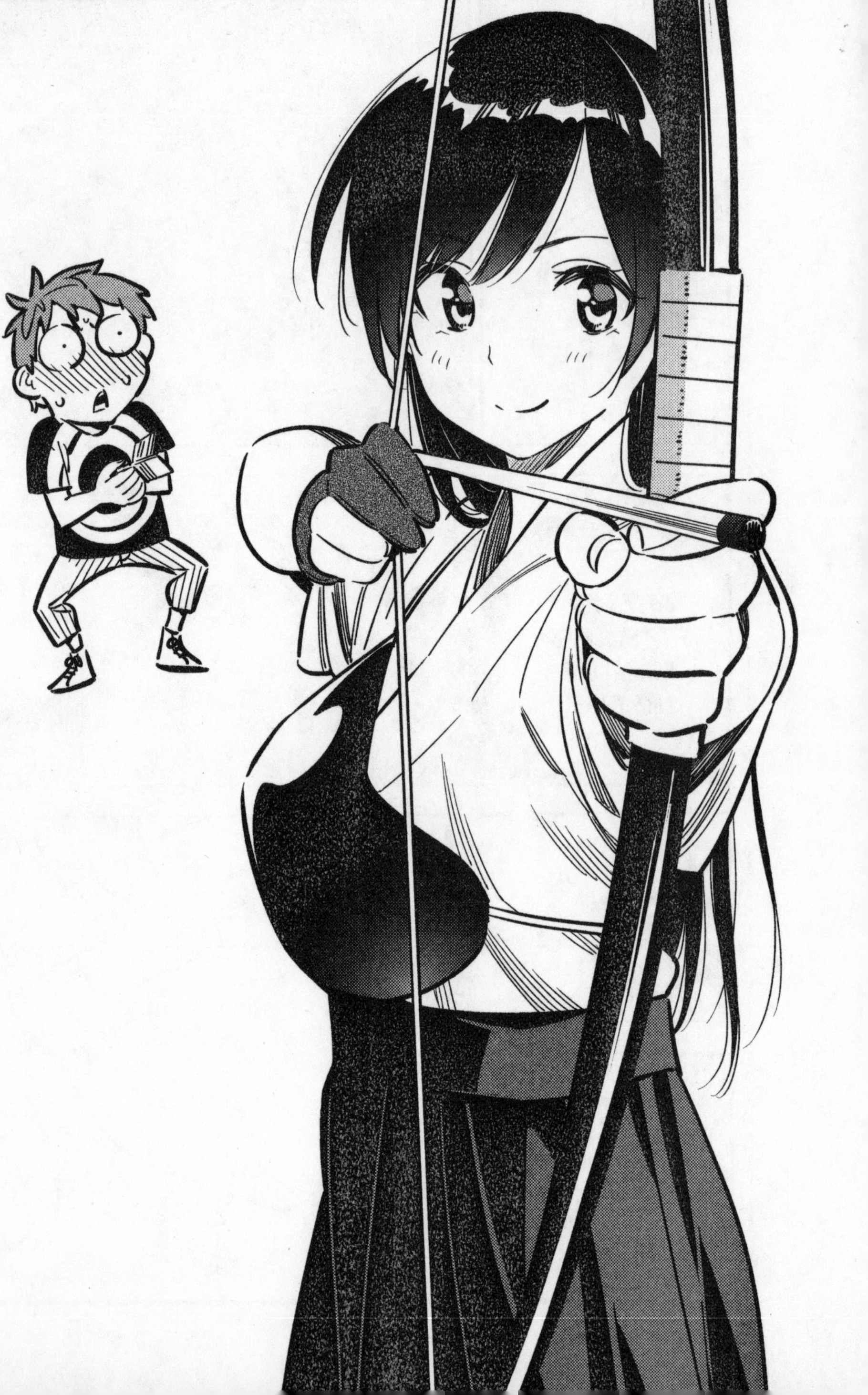

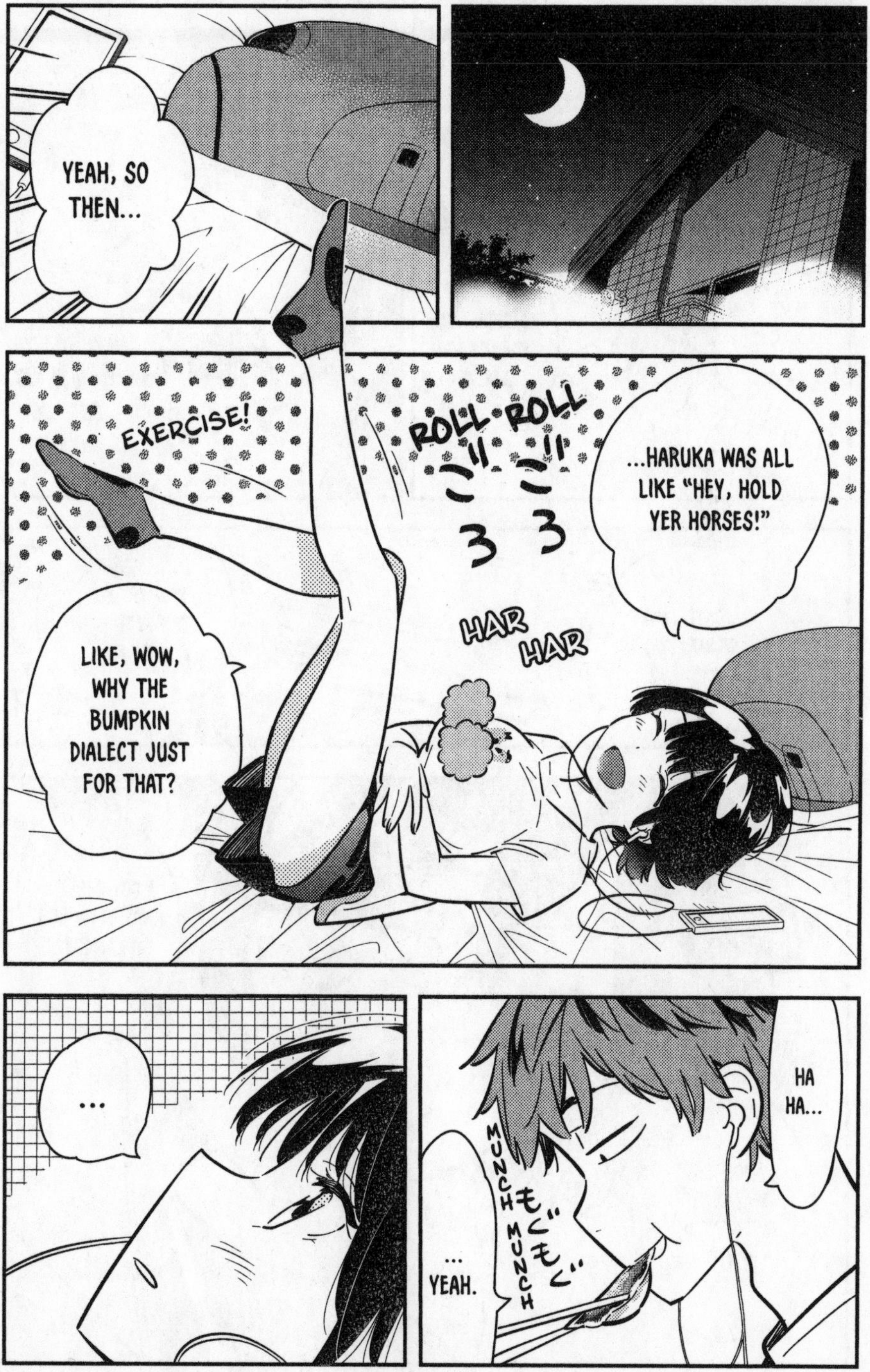
YEAH, SO THEN...
...HARUKA WAS ALL LIKE "HEY, HOLD YER HORSES!"
ROLL ROLL
ごろごろ
HAR HAR
EXERCISE!
LIKE, WOW, WHY THE BUMPKIN DIALECT JUST FOR THAT?
HA HA...
MUNCH MUNCH
もぐもぐ
... YEAH.
...

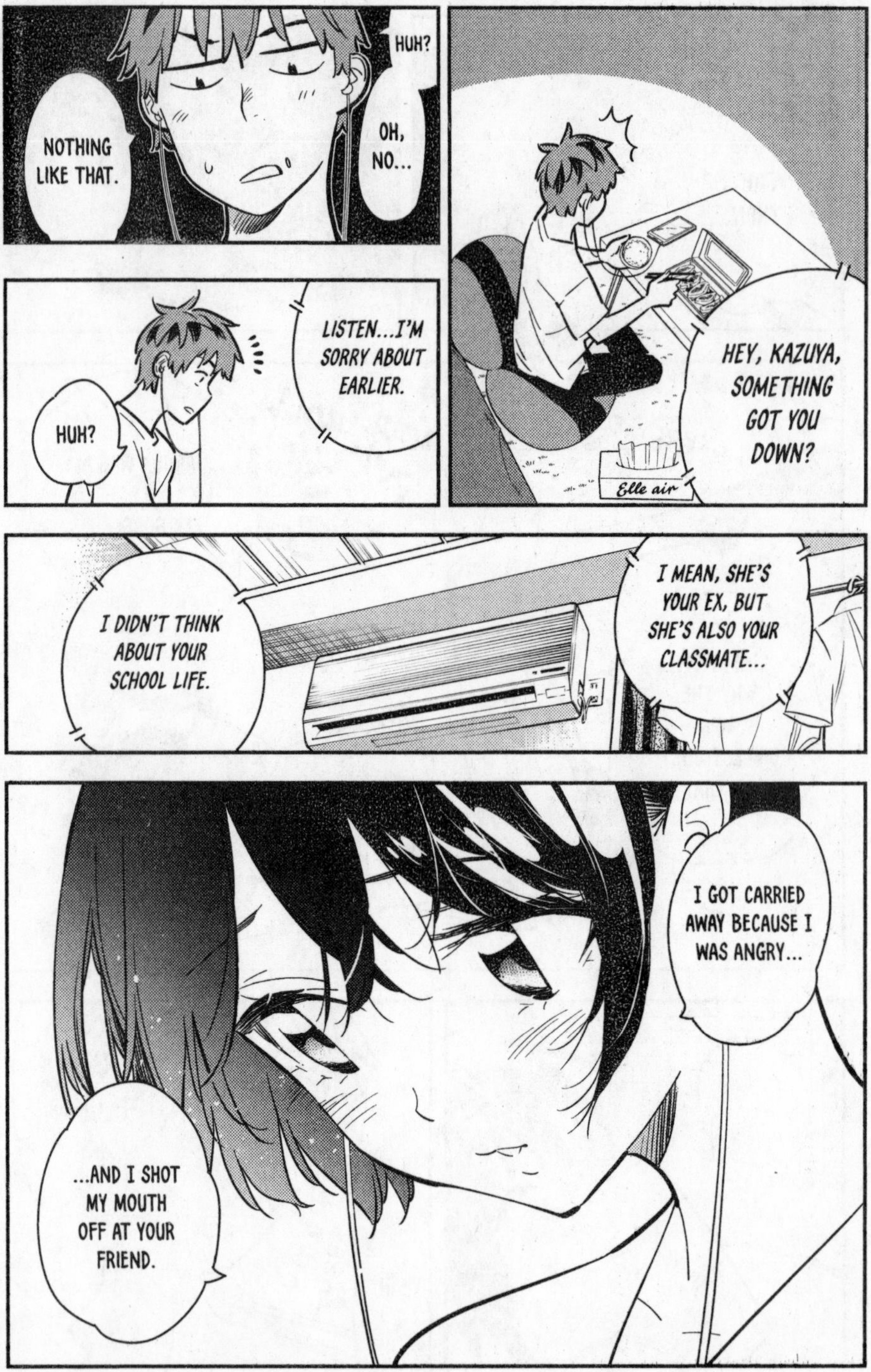
HEY, KAZUYA, SOMETHING GOT YOU DOWN?
Elle air
HUH?
OH, NO...
NOTHING LIKE THAT.
LISTEN...I'M SORRY ABOUT EARLIER.
HUH?
I MEAN, SHE'S YOUR EX, BUT SHE'S ALSO YOUR CLASSMATE...
I DIDN'T THINK ABOUT YOUR SCHOOL LIFE.
I GOT CARRIED AWAY BECAUSE I WAS ANGRY...
...AND I SHOT MY MOUTH OFF AT YOUR FRIEND.

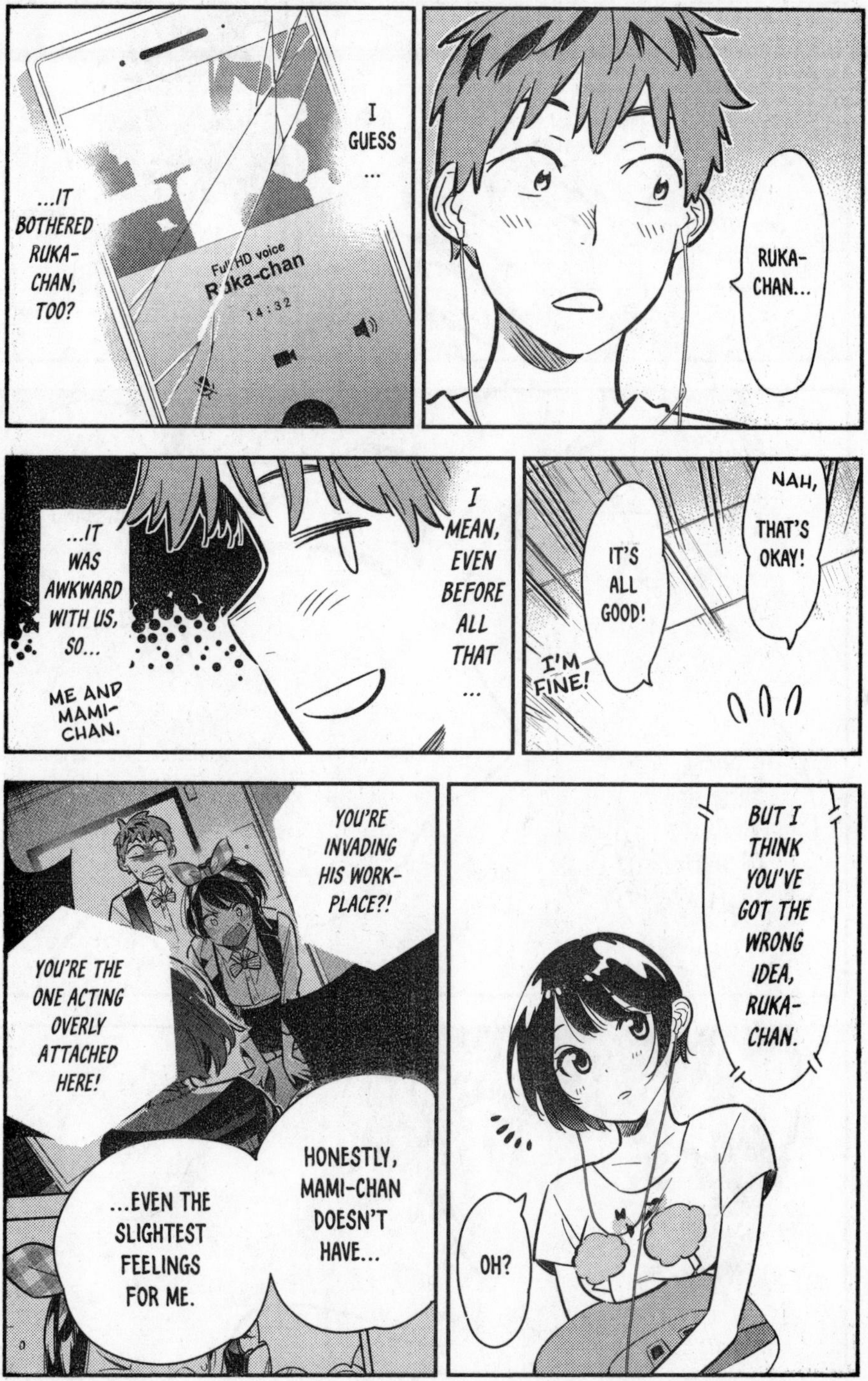
RUKA-CHAN...
I GUESS...
...IT BOTHERED RUKA-CHAN, TOO?
Full HD voice
Ruka-chan
14:32
NAH, THAT'S OKAY!
IT'S ALL GOOD!
I'M FINE!
I MEAN, EVEN BEFORE ALL THAT...
...IT WAS AWKWARD WITH US, SO...
ME AND MAMI-CHAN.
BUT I THINK YOU'VE GOT THE WRONG IDEA, RUKA-CHAN.
OH?
YOU'RE INVADING HIS WORK-PLACE?!
YOU'RE THE ONE ACTING OVERLY ATTACHED HERE!
HONESTLY, MAMI-CHAN DOESN'T HAVE...
...EVEN THE SLIGHTEST FEELINGS FOR ME.

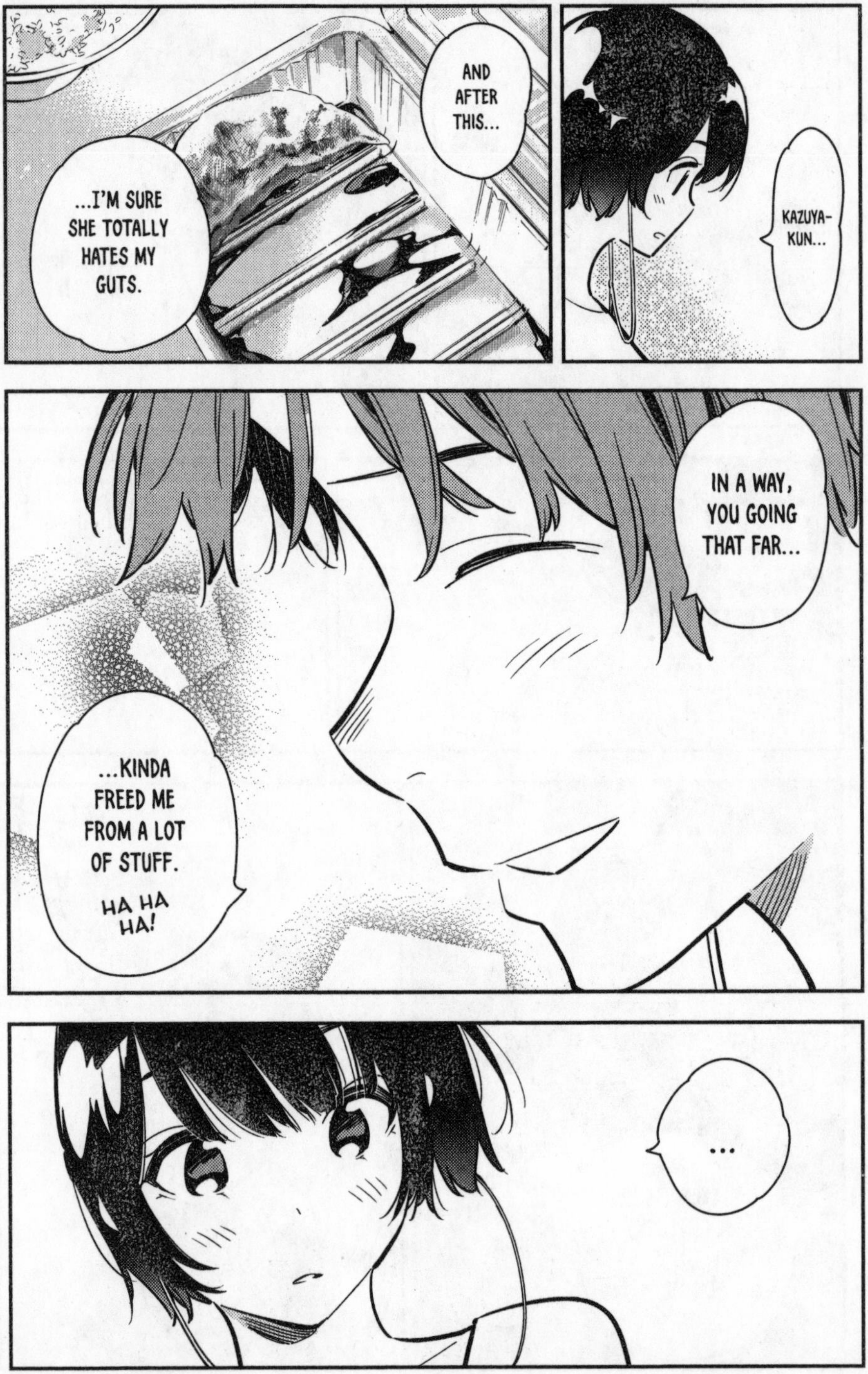
KAZUYA-KUN...
AND AFTER THIS...
...I'M SURE SHE TOTALLY HATES MY GUTS.
IN A WAY, YOU GOING THAT FAR...
...KINDA FREED ME FROM A LOT OF STUFF.
HA HA HA!
...

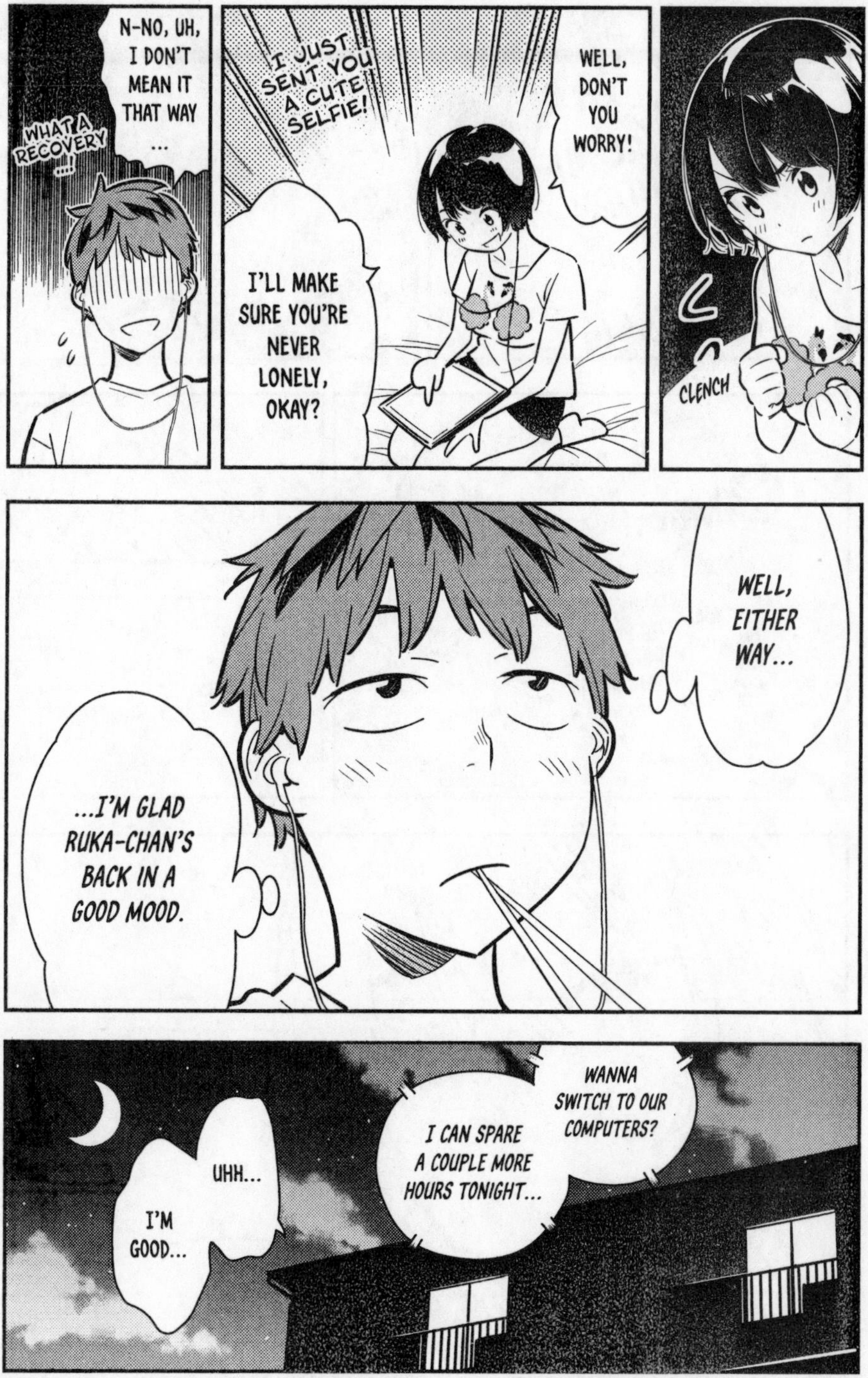
CLENCH
WELL, DON'T YOU WORRY!
I JUST SENT YOU A CUTE SELFIE!
I'LL MAKE SURE YOU'RE NEVER LONELY, OKAY?
N-NO, UH, I DON'T MEAN IT THAT WAY ...
WHAT A RECOVERY ...!!
WELL, EITHER WAY...
...I'M GLAD RUKA-CHAN'S BACK IN A GOOD MOOD.
WANNA SWITCH TO OUR COMPUTERS?
I CAN SPARE A COUPLE MORE HOURS TONIGHT...
UHH...
I'M GOOD...

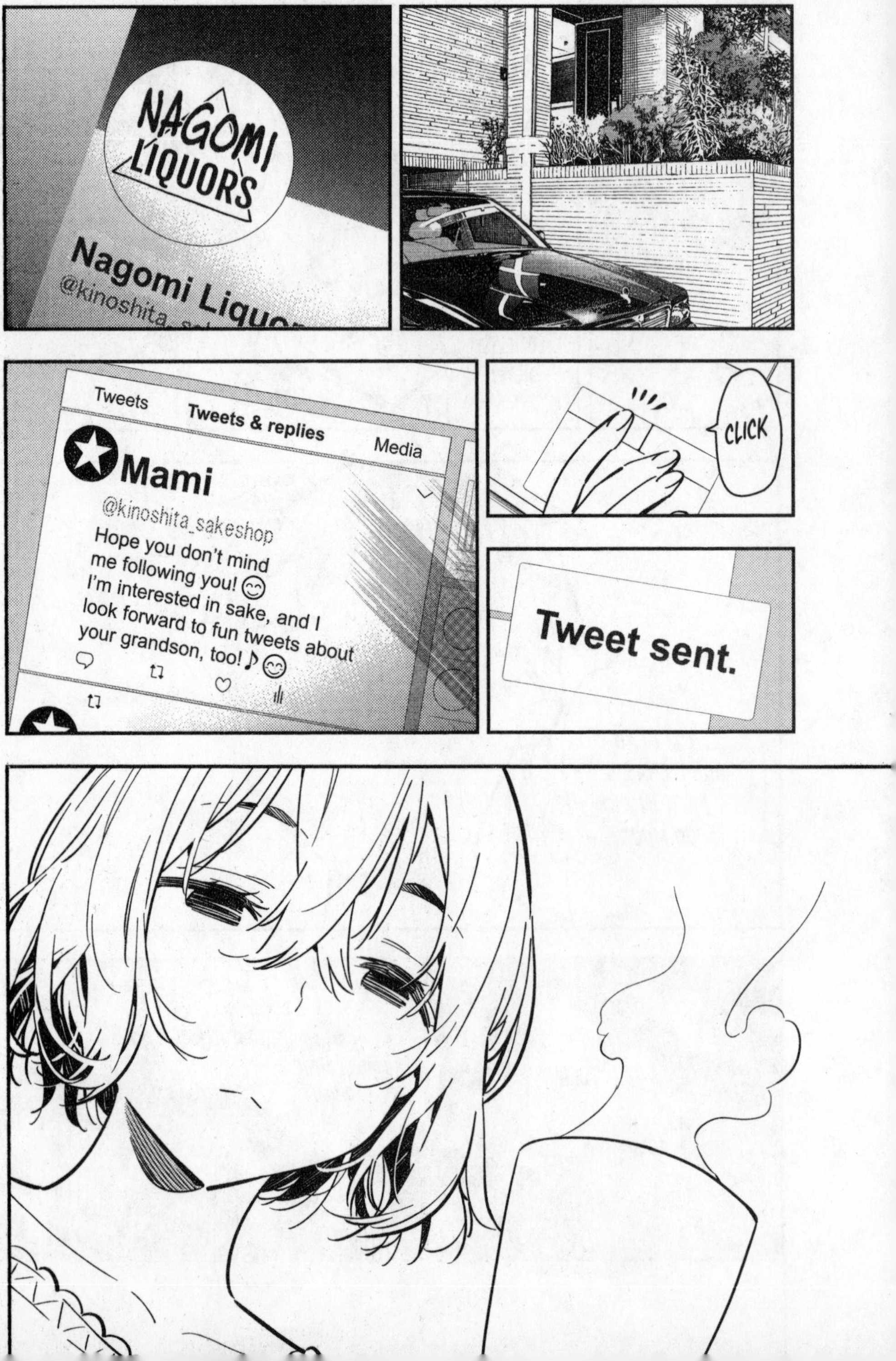
NAGOMI LIQUORS
Nagomi Liquo
CLICK
Tweet sent.
Tweets
Tweets & replies
Media
Mami
@kinoshita_sakeshop
Hope you don't mind me following you! 😊 I'm interested in sake, and I look forward to fun tweets about your grandson, too! ♪ 😊

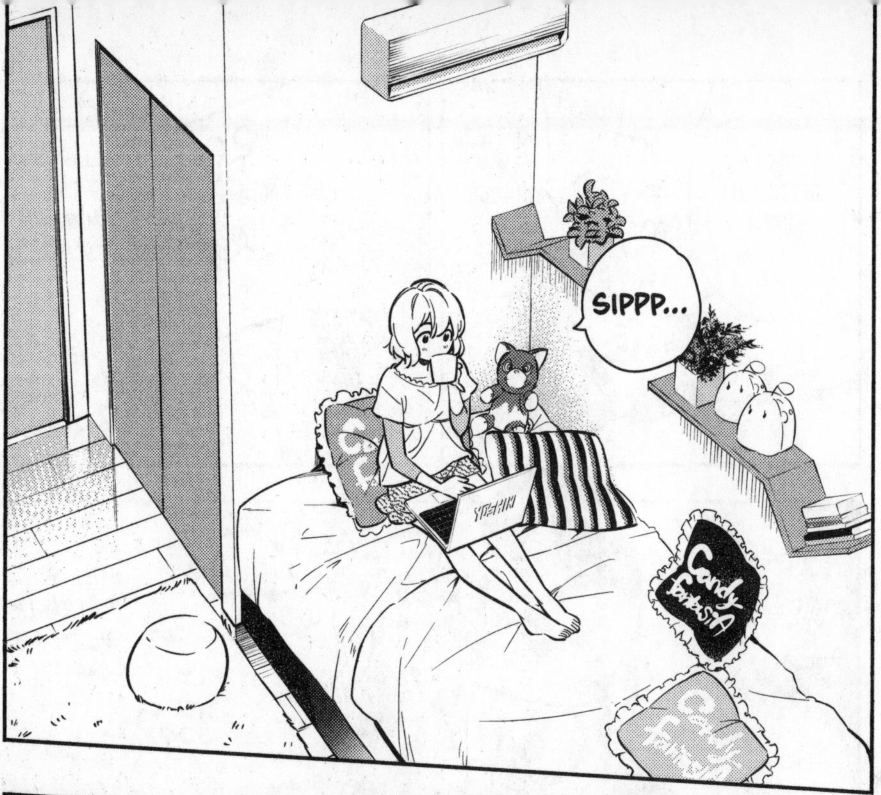
SIPPP...
Candy fantasiA

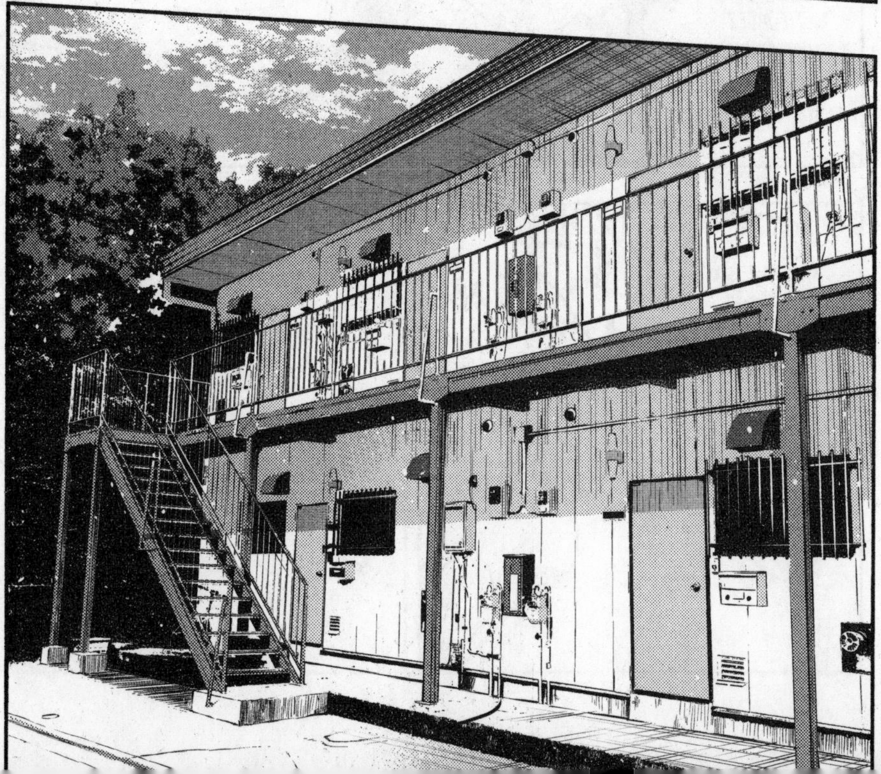

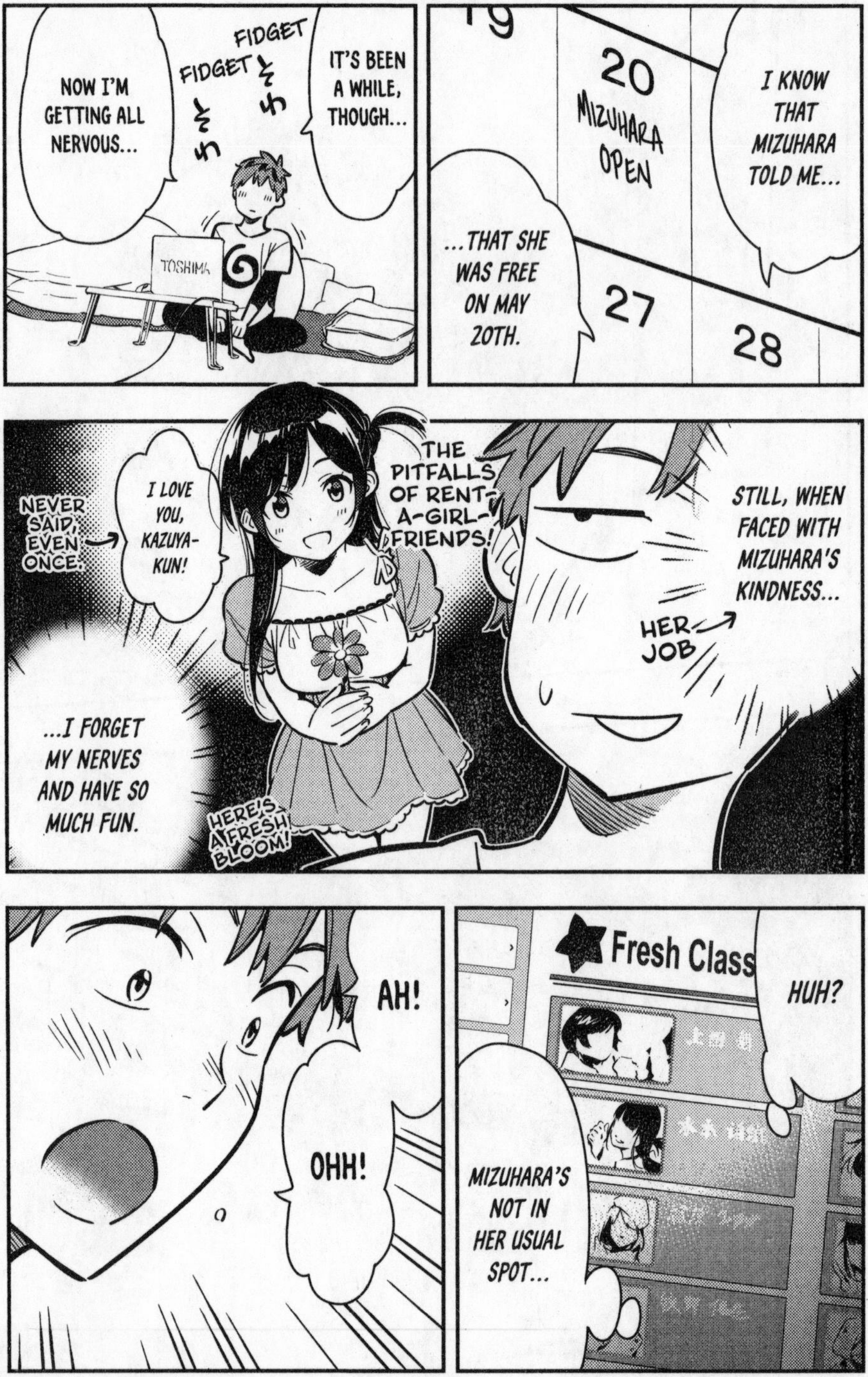
I KNOW THAT MIZUHARA TOLD ME...
19
20
MIZUHARA OPEN
27
28
...THAT SHE WAS FREE ON MAY 20TH.
IT'S BEEN A WHILE, THOUGH...
FIDGET
FIDGET
NOW I'M GETTING ALL NERVOUS...
TOSHIMA
STILL, WHEN FACED WITH MIZUHARA'S KINDNESS...
HER JOB
THE PITFALLS OF RENT-A-GIRLFRIENDS!
I LOVE YOU, KAZUYA-KUN!
NEVER SAID, EVEN ONCE.
...I FORGET MY NERVES AND HAVE SO MUCH FUN.
HERE'S A FRESH BLOOM!
Fresh Class
HUH?
MIZUHARA'S NOT IN HER USUAL SPOT...
AH!
OHH!

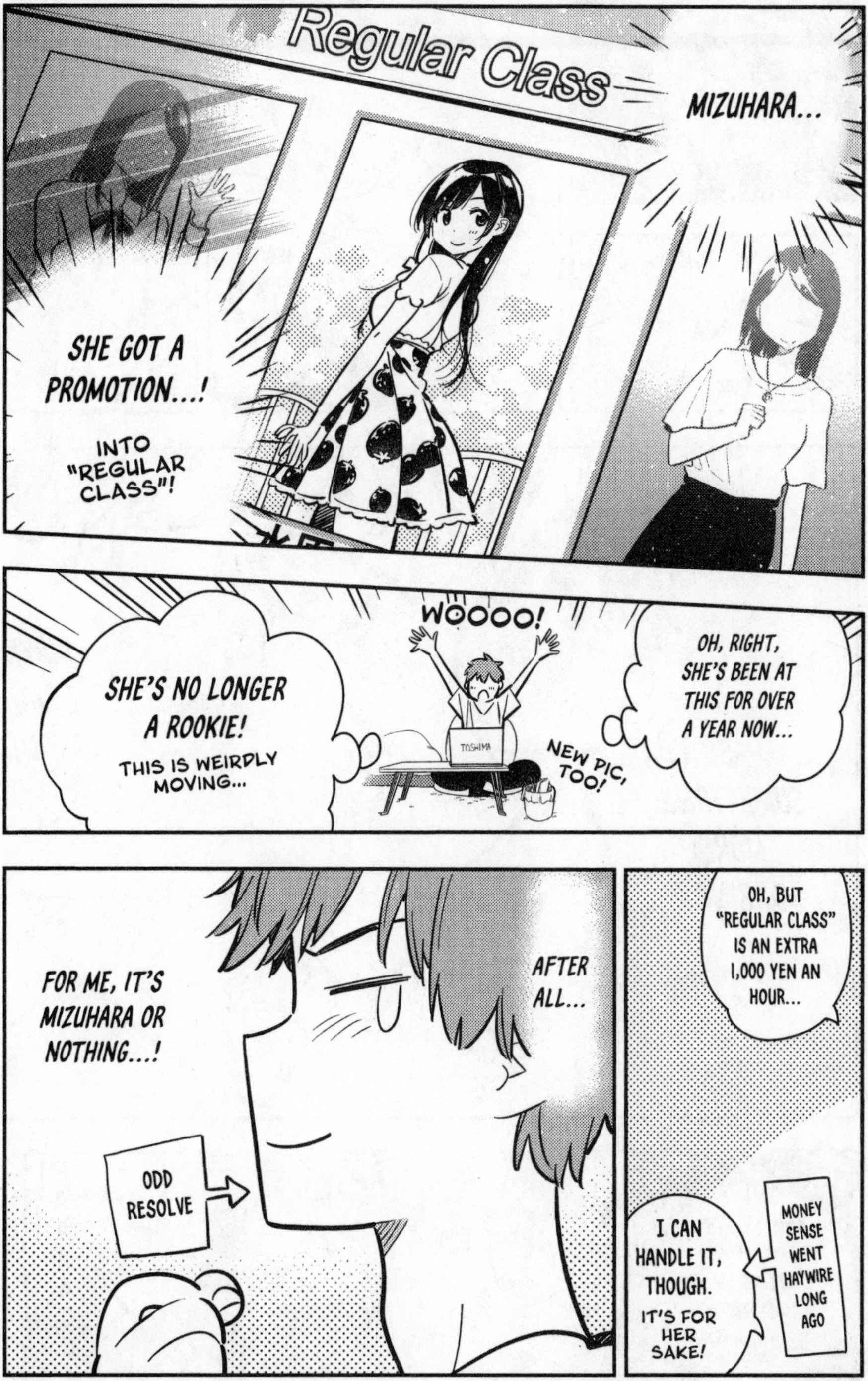

Regular Class
MIZUHARA...
SHE GOT A PROMOTION...!
INTO "REGULAR CLASS"!
OH, RIGHT, SHE'S BEEN AT THIS FOR OVER A YEAR NOW...
WOOOO!
NEW PIC, TOO!
TOSHIMA
SHE'S NO LONGER A ROOKIE!
THIS IS WEIRDLY MOVING...
OH, BUT "REGULAR CLASS" IS AN EXTRA 1,000 YEN AN HOUR...
MONEY SENSE WENT HAYWIRE LONG AGO
I CAN HANDLE IT, THOUGH.
IT'S FOR HER SAKE!
AFTER ALL...
FOR ME, IT'S MIZUHARA OR NOTHING...!
ODD RESOLVE

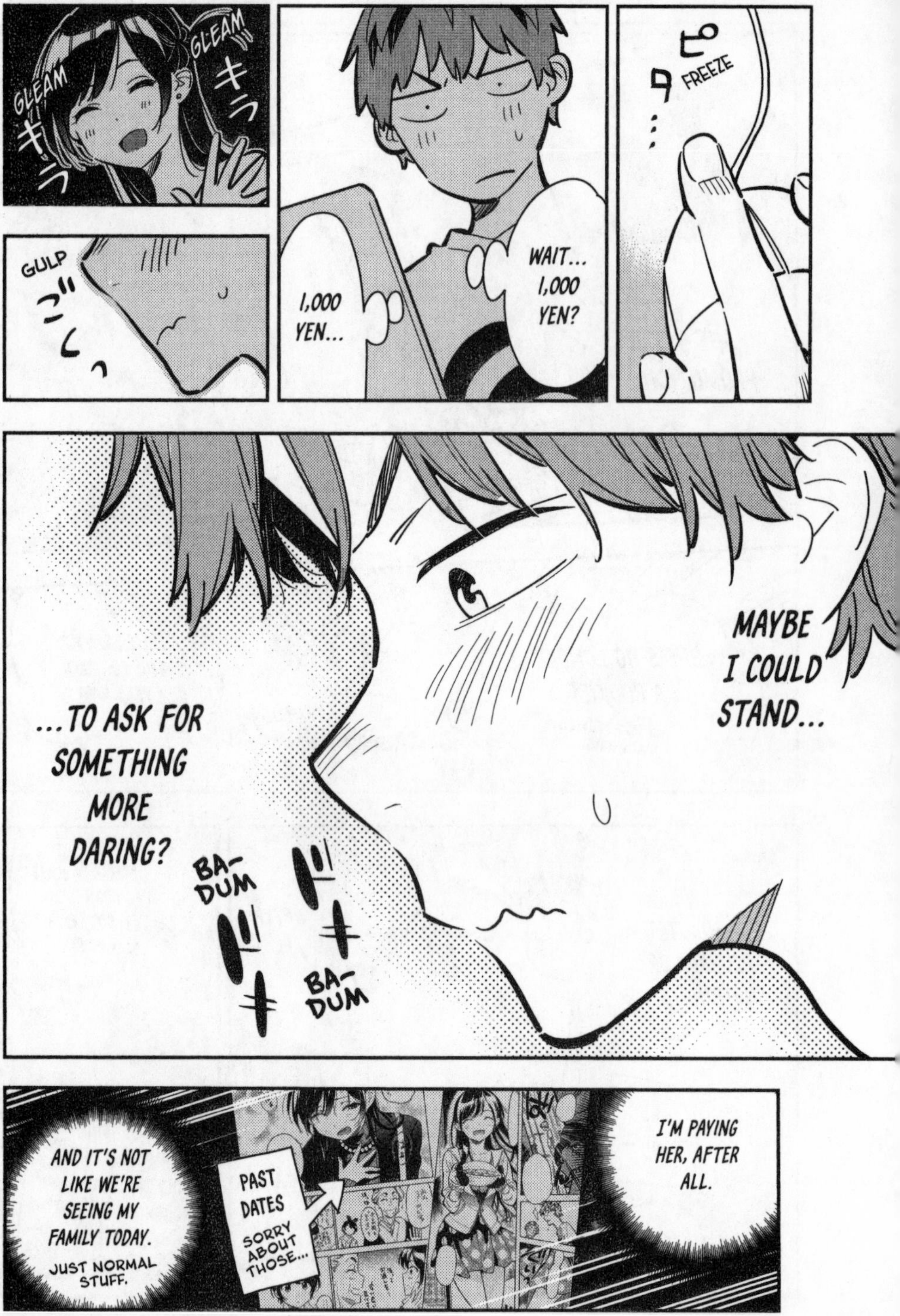
FREEZE
WAIT... 1,000 YEN?
1,000 YEN...
GLEAM
GLEAM
GULP
MAYBE I COULD STAND...
...TO ASK FOR SOMETHING MORE DARING?
BA-DUM
BA-DUM
I'M PAYING HER, AFTER ALL.
PAST DATES
SORRY ABOUT THOSE...
AND IT'S NOT LIKE WE'RE SEEING MY FAMILY TODAY.
JUST NORMAL STUFF.

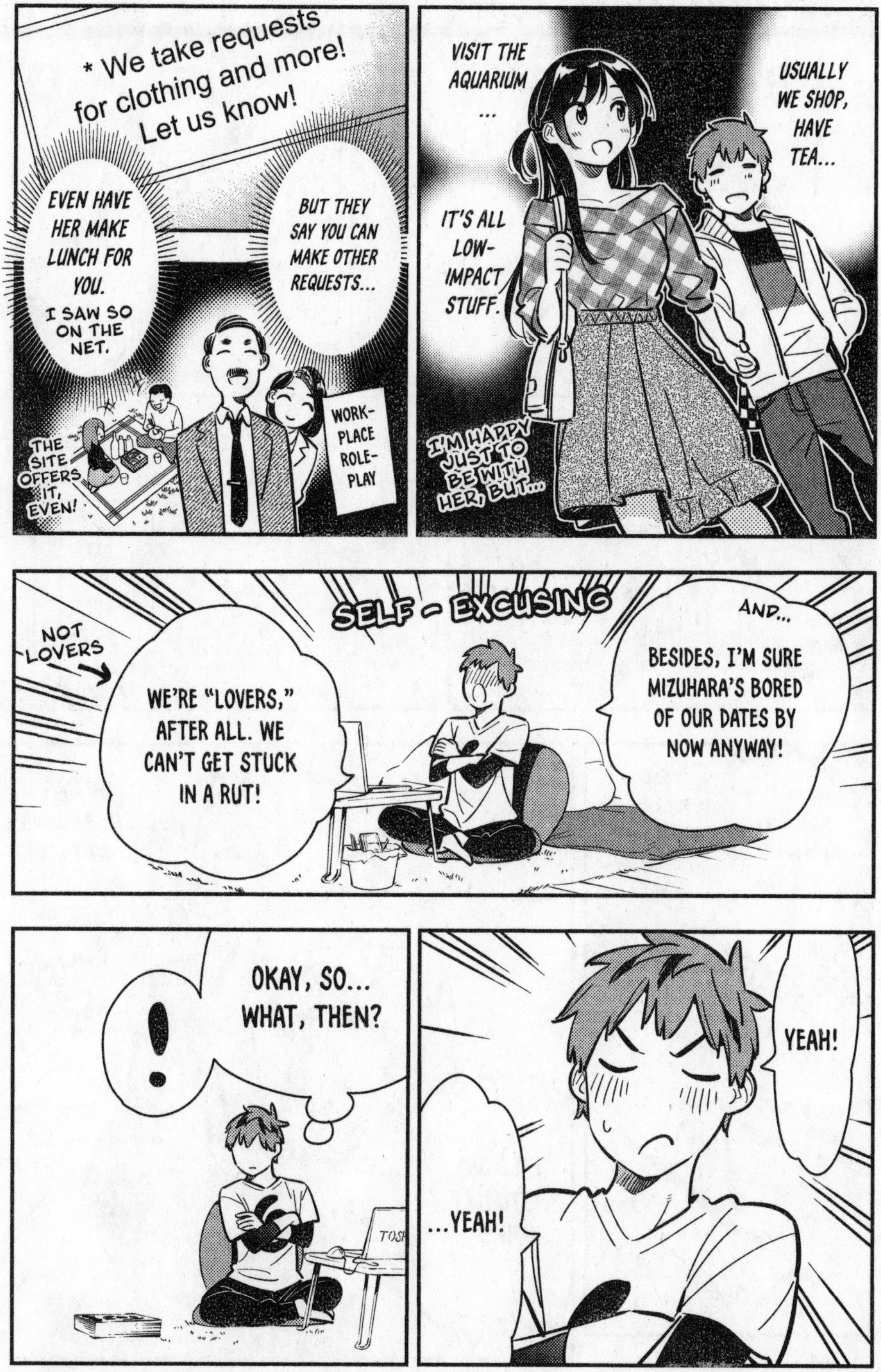
USUALLY WE SHOP, HAVE TEA...
VISIT THE AQUARIUM ...
IT'S ALL LOW-IMPACT STUFF.
I'M HAPPY JUST TO BE WITH HER, BUT...
* We take requests for clothing and more! Let us know!
BUT THEY SAY YOU CAN MAKE OTHER REQUESTS...
WORKPLACE ROLE-PLAY
EVEN HAVE HER MAKE LUNCH FOR YOU.
I SAW SO ON THE NET.
THE SITE OFFERS IT, EVEN!
AND...
BESIDES, I'M SURE MIZUHARA'S BORED OF OUR DATES BY NOW ANYWAY!
SELF-EXCUSING
WE'RE "LOVERS," AFTER ALL. WE CAN'T GET STUCK IN A RUT!
NOT LOVERS
YEAH!
...YEAH!
OKAY, SO... WHAT, THEN?
!

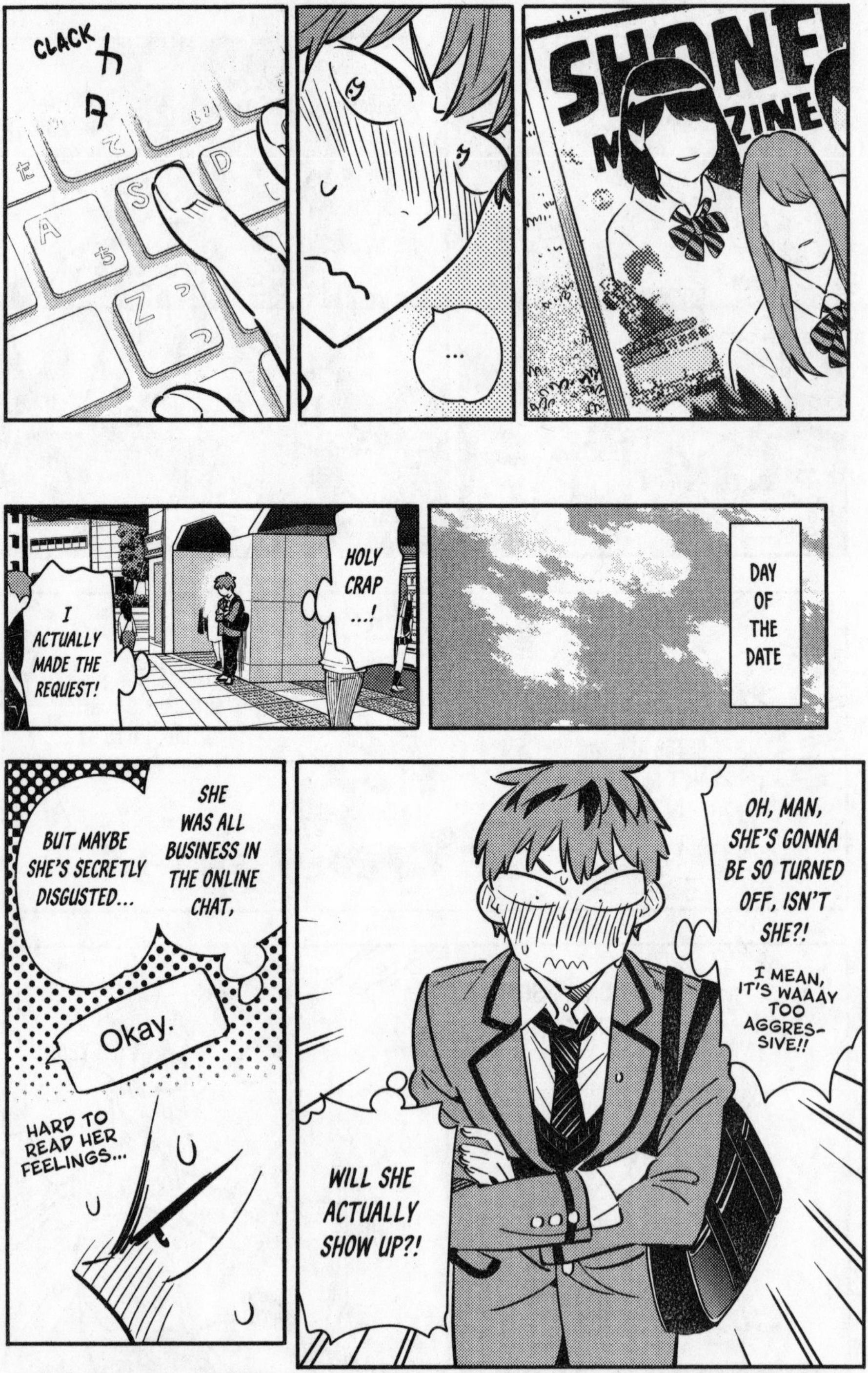

...
CLACK
DAY OF THE DATE
HOLY CRAP ...!
I ACTUALLY MADE THE REQUEST!
OH, MAN, SHE'S GONNA BE SO TURNED OFF, ISN'T SHE?!
I MEAN, IT'S WAAAY TOO AGGRES-SIVE!!
WILL SHE ACTUALLY SHOW UP?!
SHE WAS ALL BUSINESS IN THE ONLINE CHAT,
BUT MAYBE SHE'S SECRETLY DISGUSTED...
Okay.
HARD TO READ HER FEELINGS...

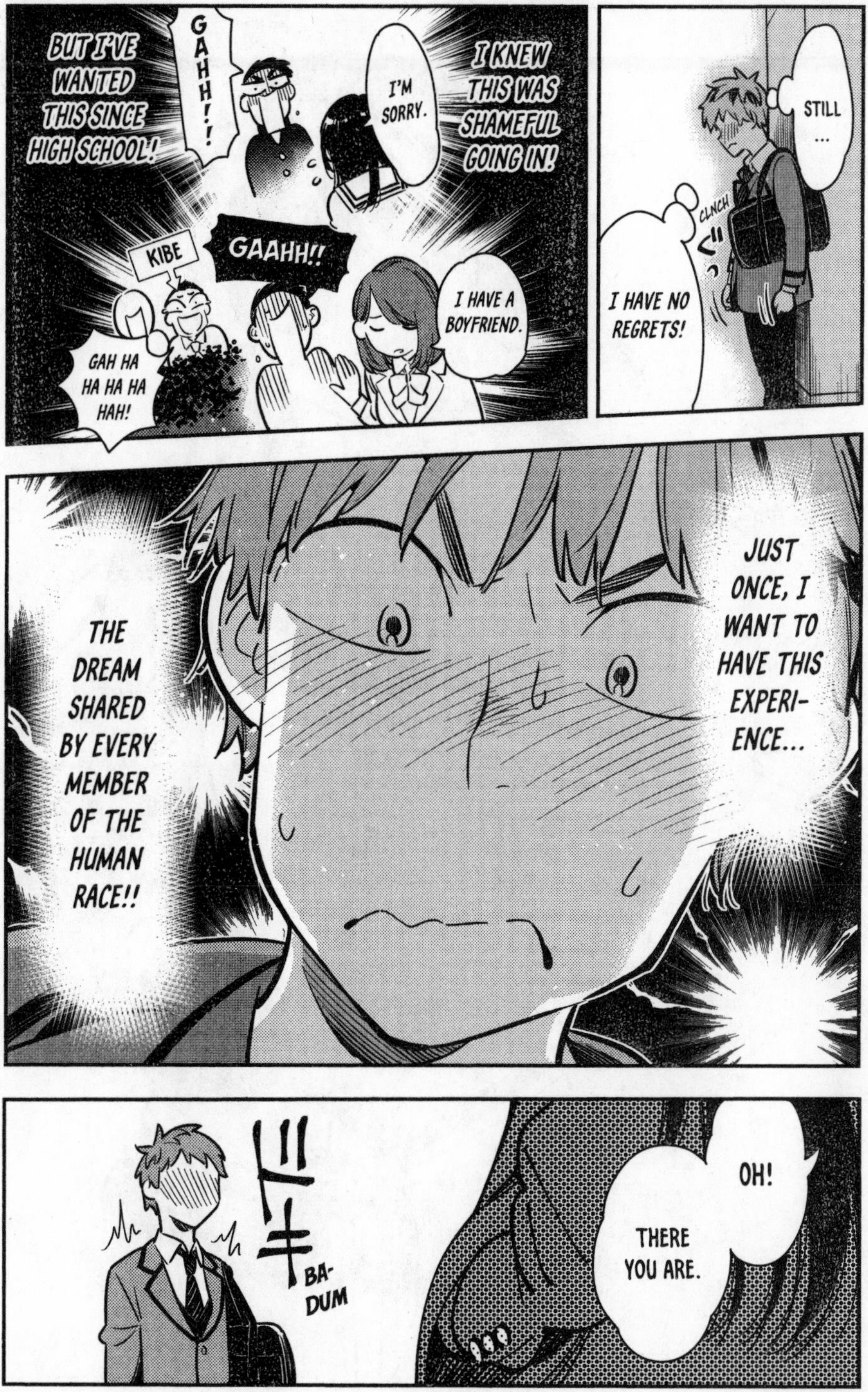
STILL ...
CLNCH
I HAVE NO REGRETS!
I KNEW THIS WAS SHAMEFUL GOING IN!
I'M SORRY.
GAHH!!
BUT I'VE WANTED THIS SINCE HIGH SCHOOL!
I HAVE A BOYFRIEND.
GAAHH!!
KIBE
GAH HA HA HA HA HAH!
JUST ONCE, I WANT TO HAVE THIS EXPERIENCE...
THE DREAM SHARED BY EVERY MEMBER OF THE HUMAN RACE!!
OH!
THERE YOU ARE.
BA-DUM

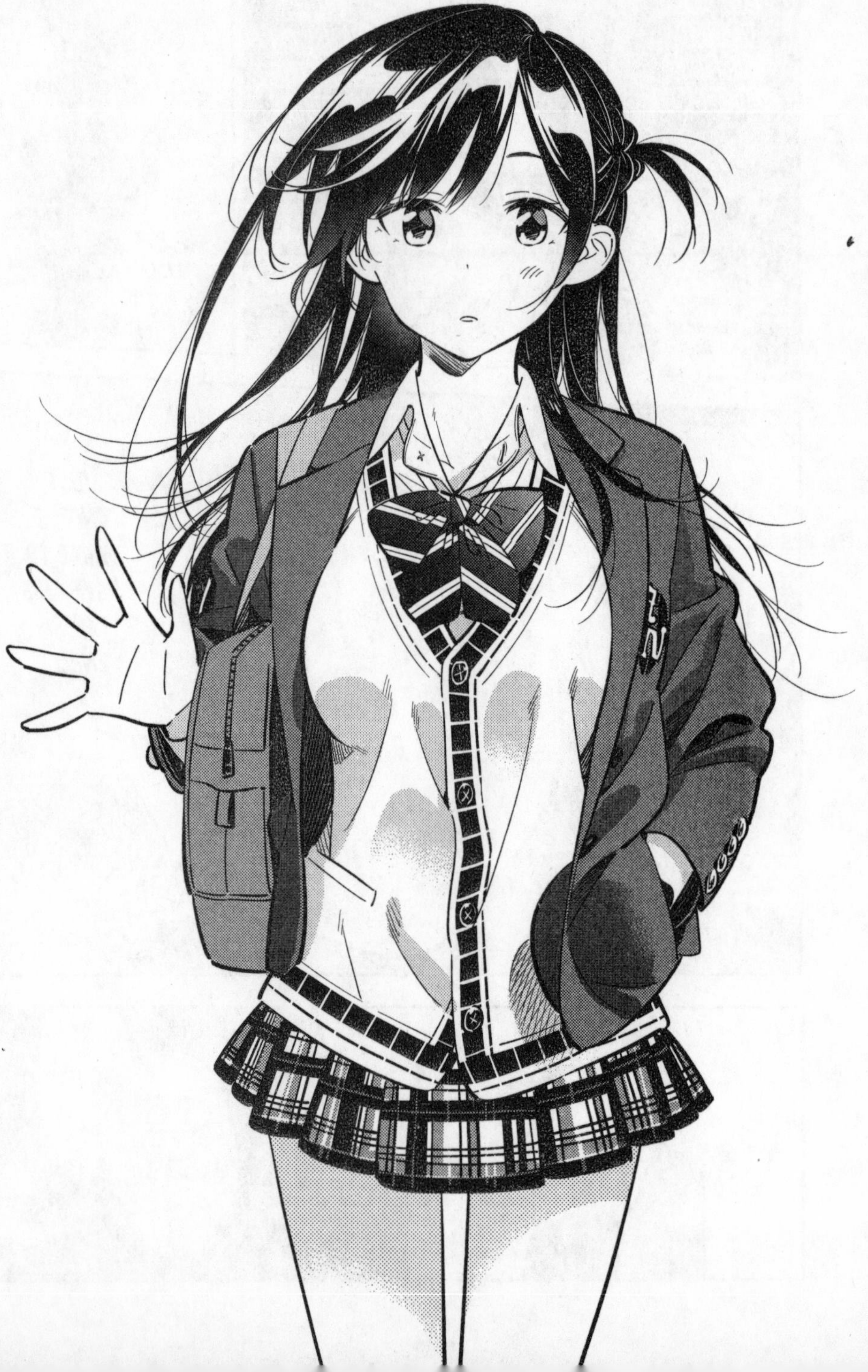

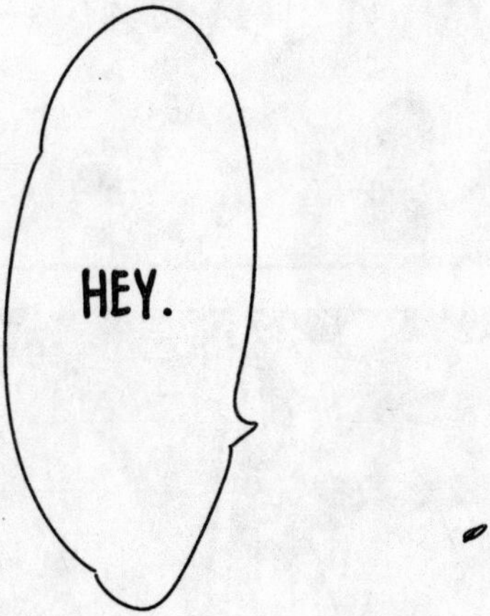
HEY.

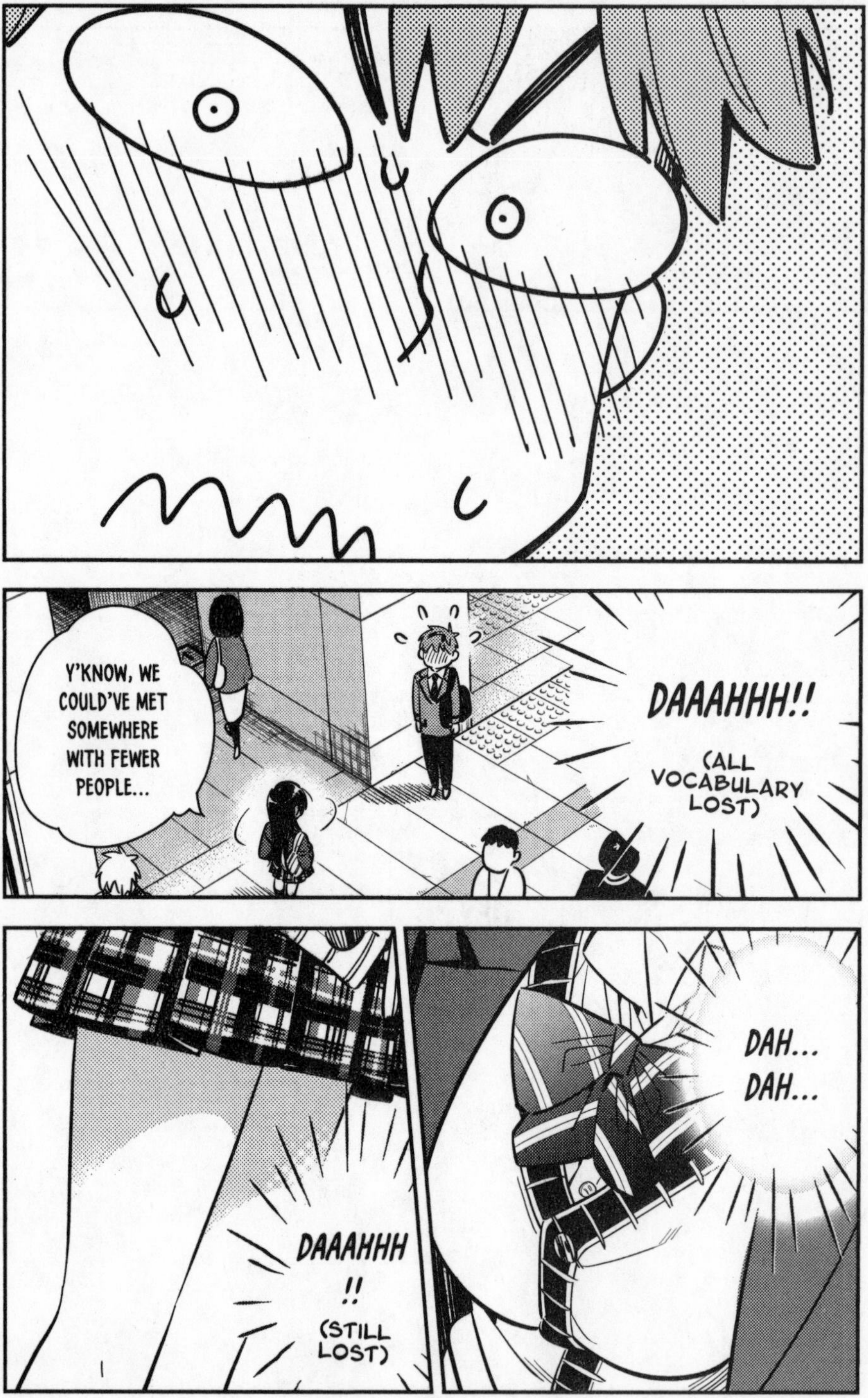
DAAAHHH!!
(ALL VOCABULARY LOST)
Y'KNOW, WE COULD'VE MET SOMEWHERE WITH FEWER PEOPLE...
DAH... DAH...
DAAAHHH !!
(STILL LOST)

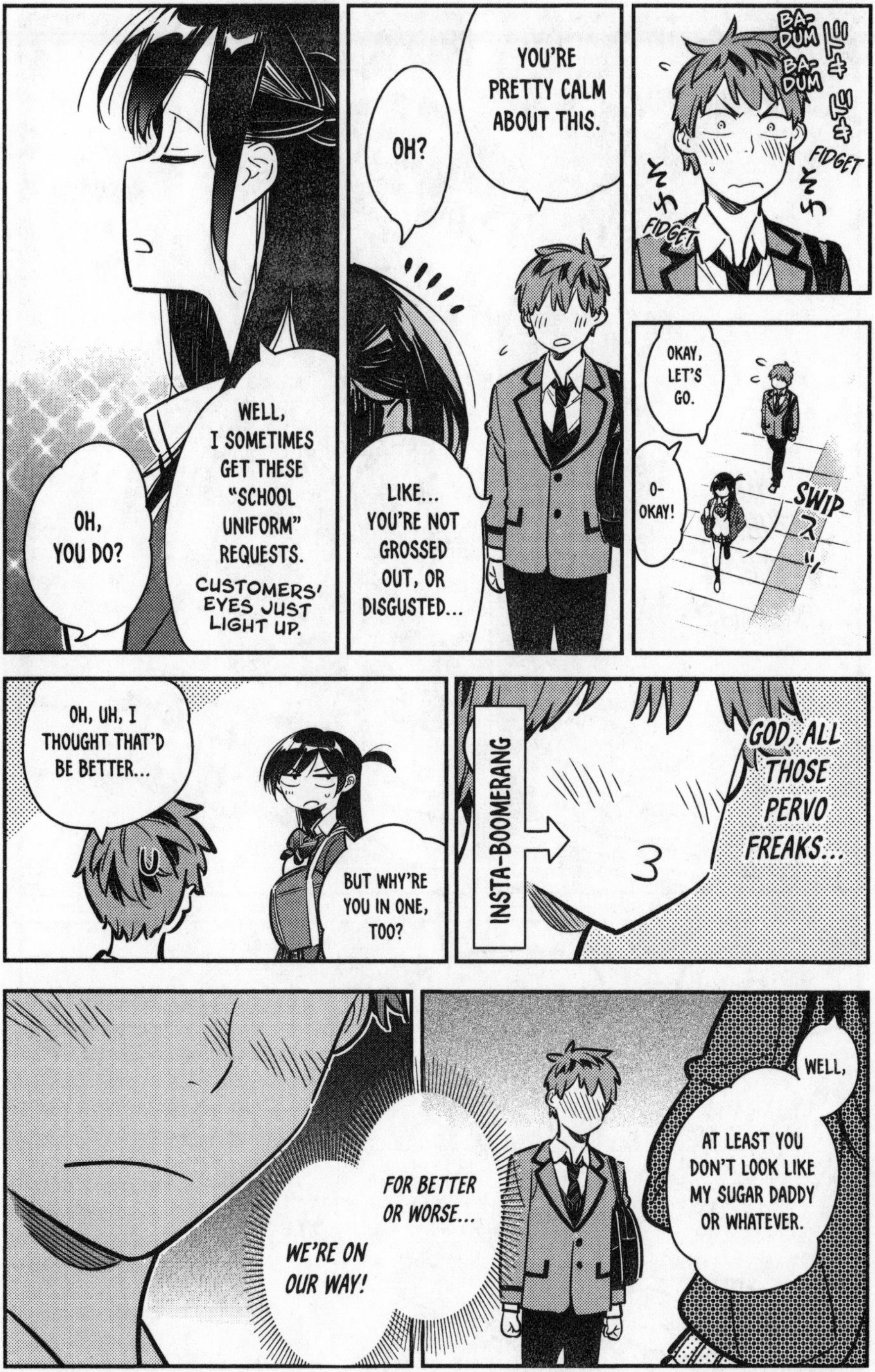
BA-DUM BA-DUM
ドキドキ
FIDGET
そわ そわ
FIDGET
OKAY, LET'S GO.
O-OKAY!
SWIP
スッ
YOU'RE PRETTY CALM ABOUT THIS.
OH?
LIKE... YOU'RE NOT GROSSED OUT, OR DISGUSTED...
WELL, I SOMETIMES GET THESE "SCHOOL UNIFORM" REQUESTS.
CUSTOMERS' EYES JUST LIGHT UP.
OH, YOU DO?
INSTA-BOOMERANG
GOD, ALL THOSE PERVO FREAKS...
BUT WHY'RE YOU IN ONE, TOO?
OH, UH, I THOUGHT THAT'D BE BETTER...
WELL,
AT LEAST YOU DON'T LOOK LIKE MY SUGAR DADDY OR WHATEVER.
FOR BETTER OR WORSE...
WE'RE ON OUR WAY!

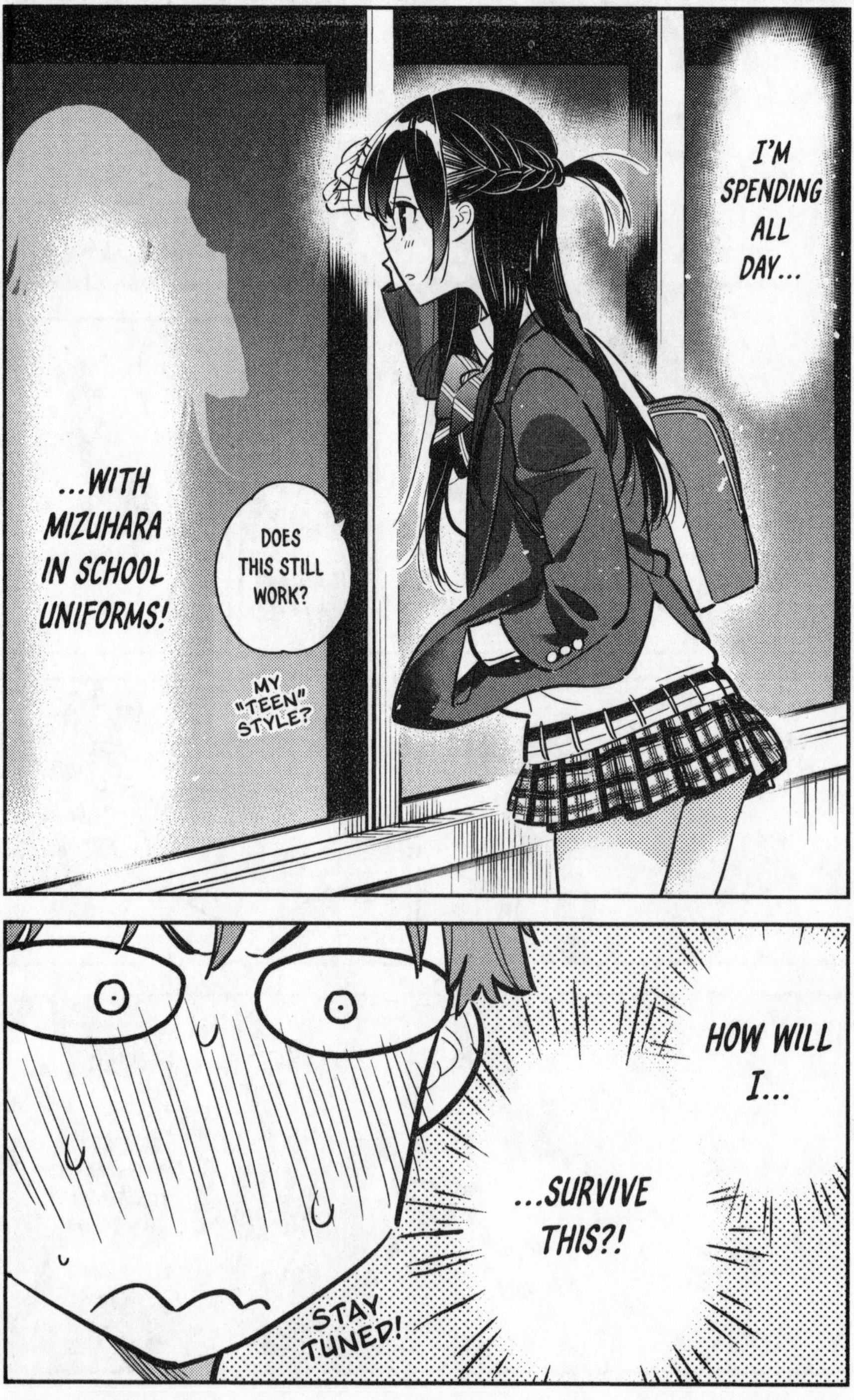
I'M SPENDING ALL DAY...
...WITH MIZUHARA IN SCHOOL UNIFORMS!
DOES THIS STILL WORK?
MY "TEEN" STYLE?
HOW WILL I...
...SURVIVE THIS?!
STAY TUNED!

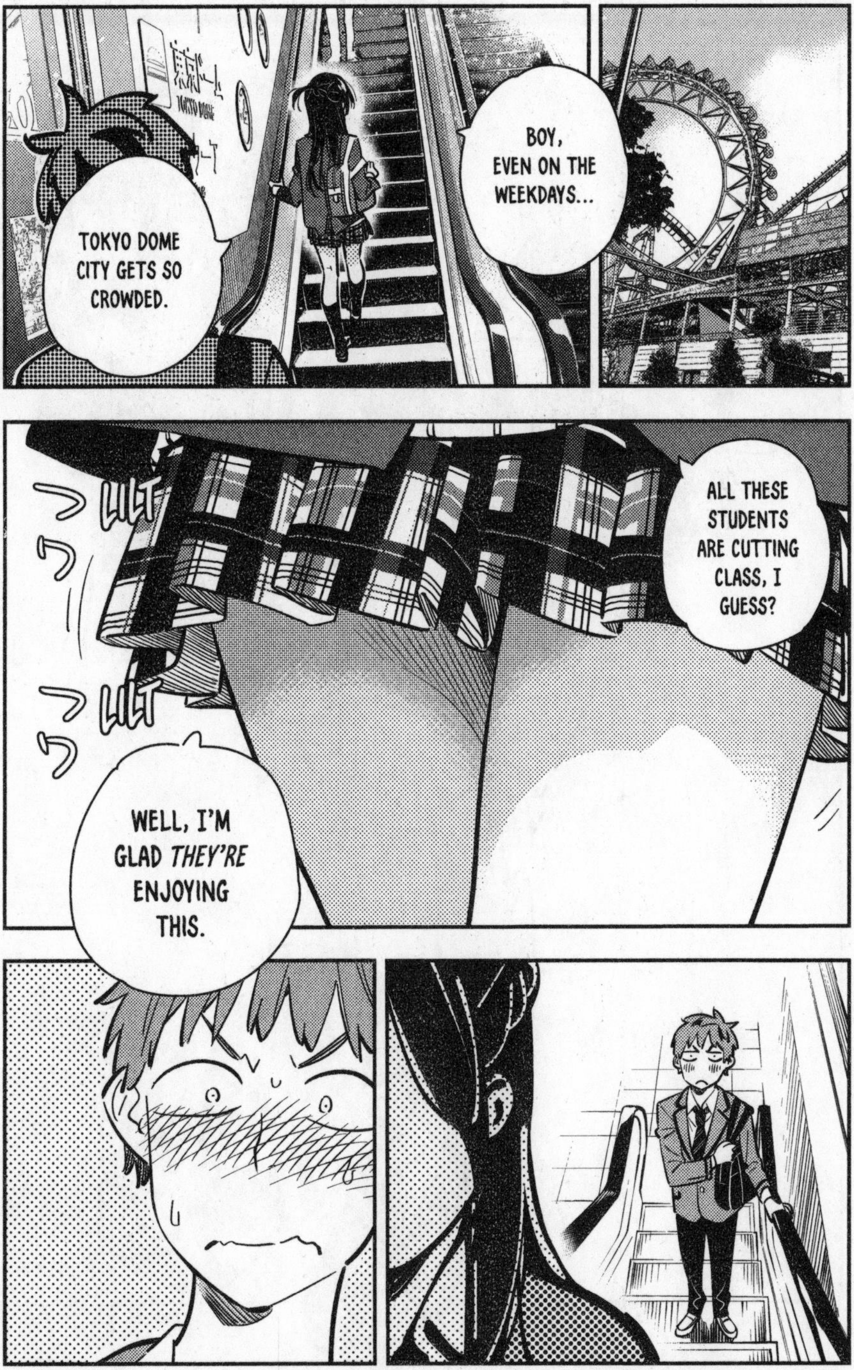
BOY, EVEN ON THE WEEKDAYS...
TOKYO DOME CITY GETS SO CROWDED.
ALL THESE STUDENTS ARE CUTTING CLASS, I GUESS?
LILT
LILT
WELL, I'M GLAD *THEY'RE* ENJOYING THIS.

RATING 79 MY GIRLFRIEND AND MY DREAM DATE 2

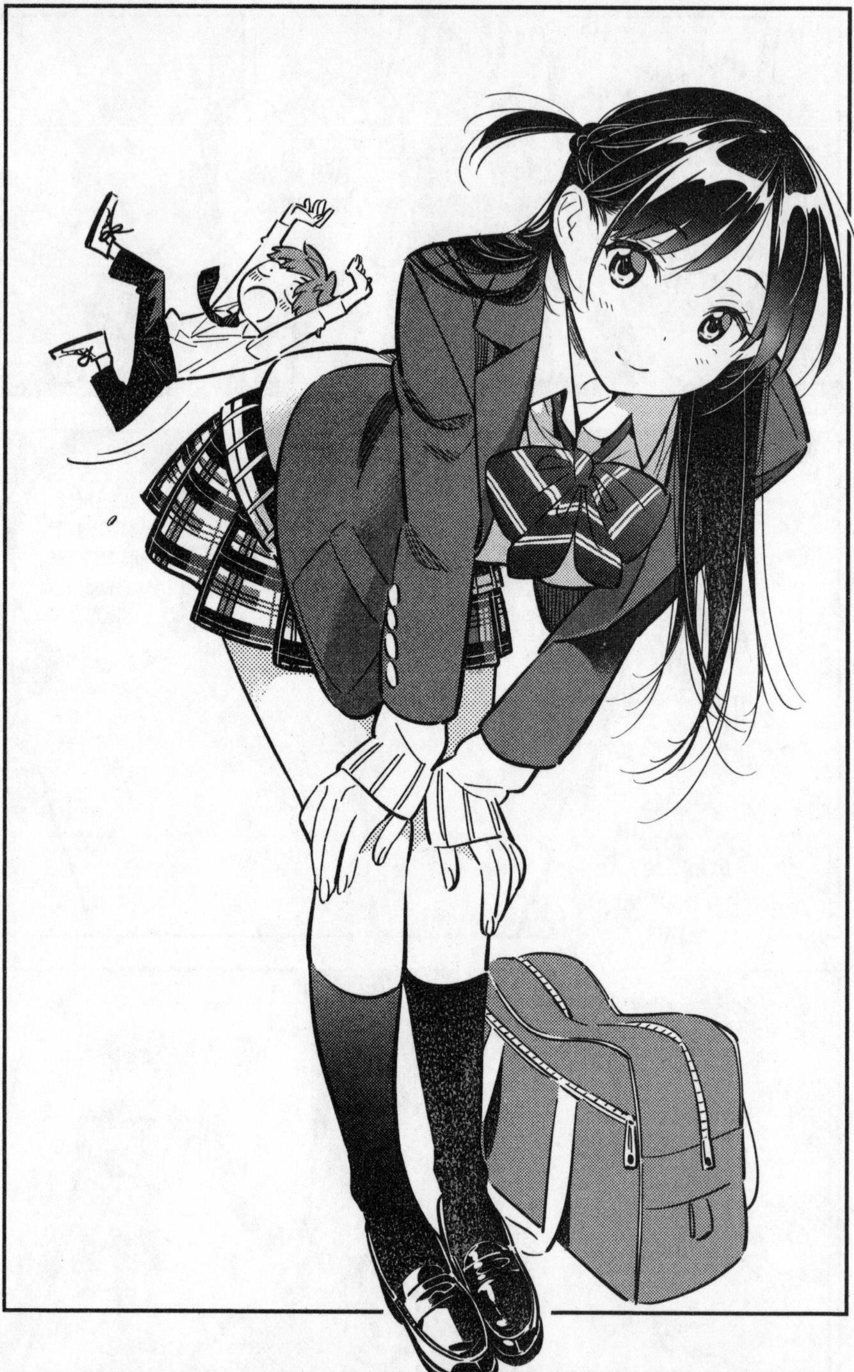

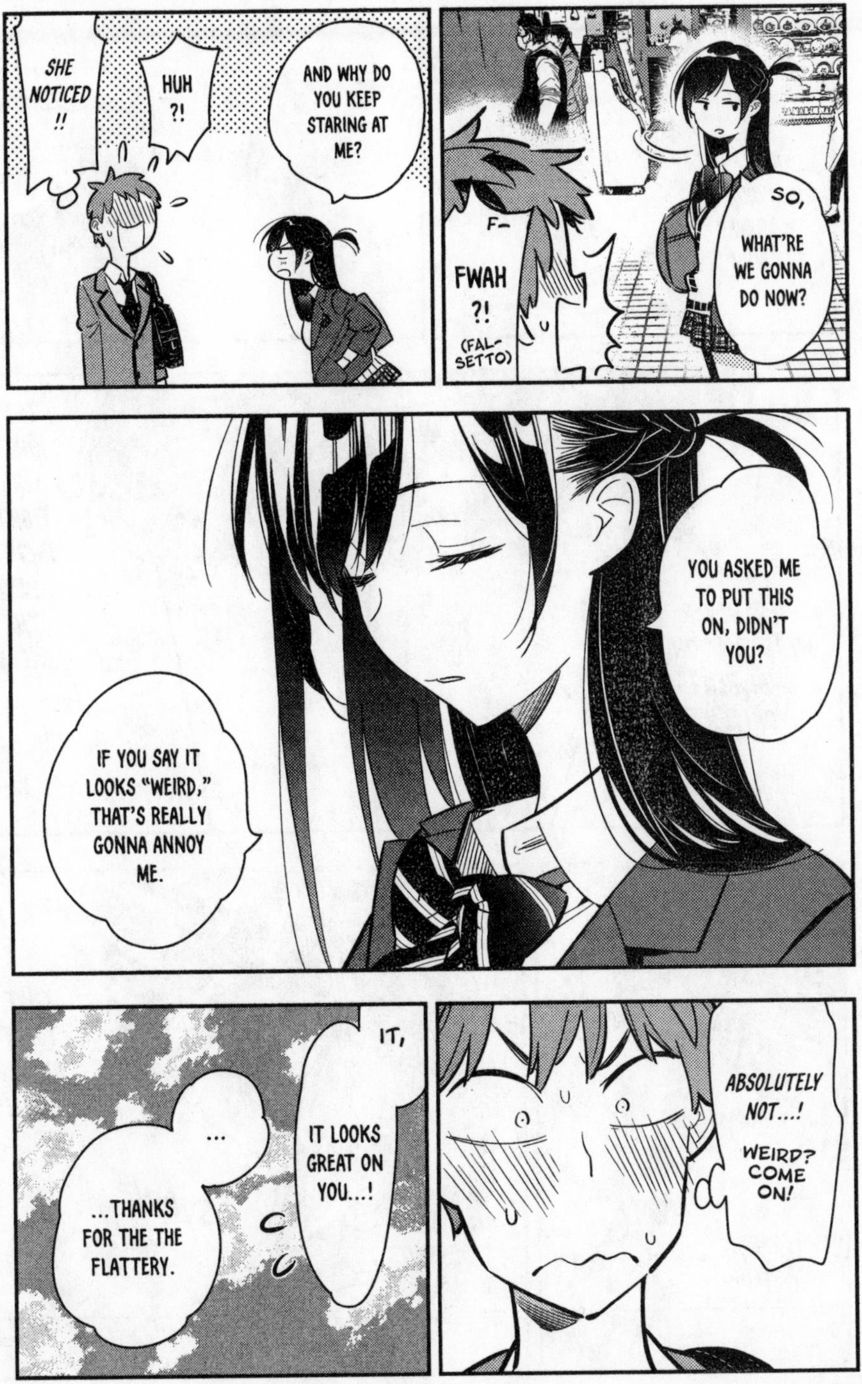
SO, WHAT'RE WE GONNA DO NOW?
F— FWAH ?!
(FAL-SETTO)
AND WHY DO YOU KEEP STARING AT ME?
HUH ?!
SHE NOTICED !!
YOU ASKED ME TO PUT THIS ON, DIDN'T YOU?
IF YOU SAY IT LOOKS "WEIRD," THAT'S REALLY GONNA ANNOY ME.
ABSOLUTELY NOT...!
WEIRD? COME ON!
IT,
IT LOOKS GREAT ON YOU...!
...
...THANKS FOR THE THE FLATTERY.

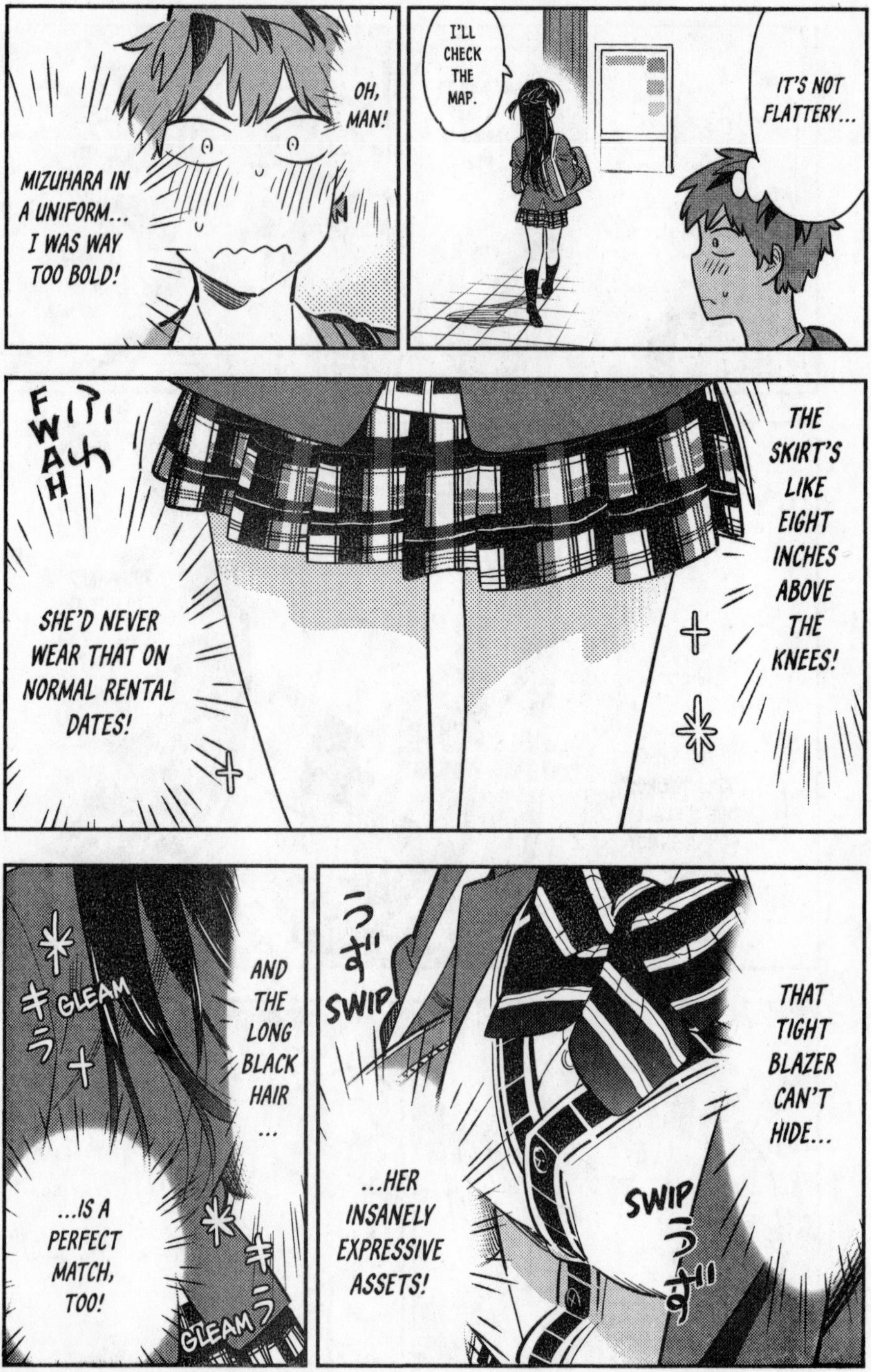
IT'S NOT FLATTERY...
I'LL CHECK THE MAP.
OH, MAN!
MIZUHARA IN A UNIFORM... I WAS WAY TOO BOLD!
THE SKIRT'S LIKE EIGHT INCHES ABOVE THE KNEES!
SHE'D NEVER WEAR THAT ON NORMAL RENTAL DATES!
FWAH
THAT TIGHT BLAZER CAN'T HIDE...
うず SWIP
SWIP うずっ
...HER INSANELY EXPRESSIVE ASSETS!
AND THE LONG BLACK HAIR...
キラ GLEAM
...IS A PERFECT MATCH, TOO!
キラ GLEAM

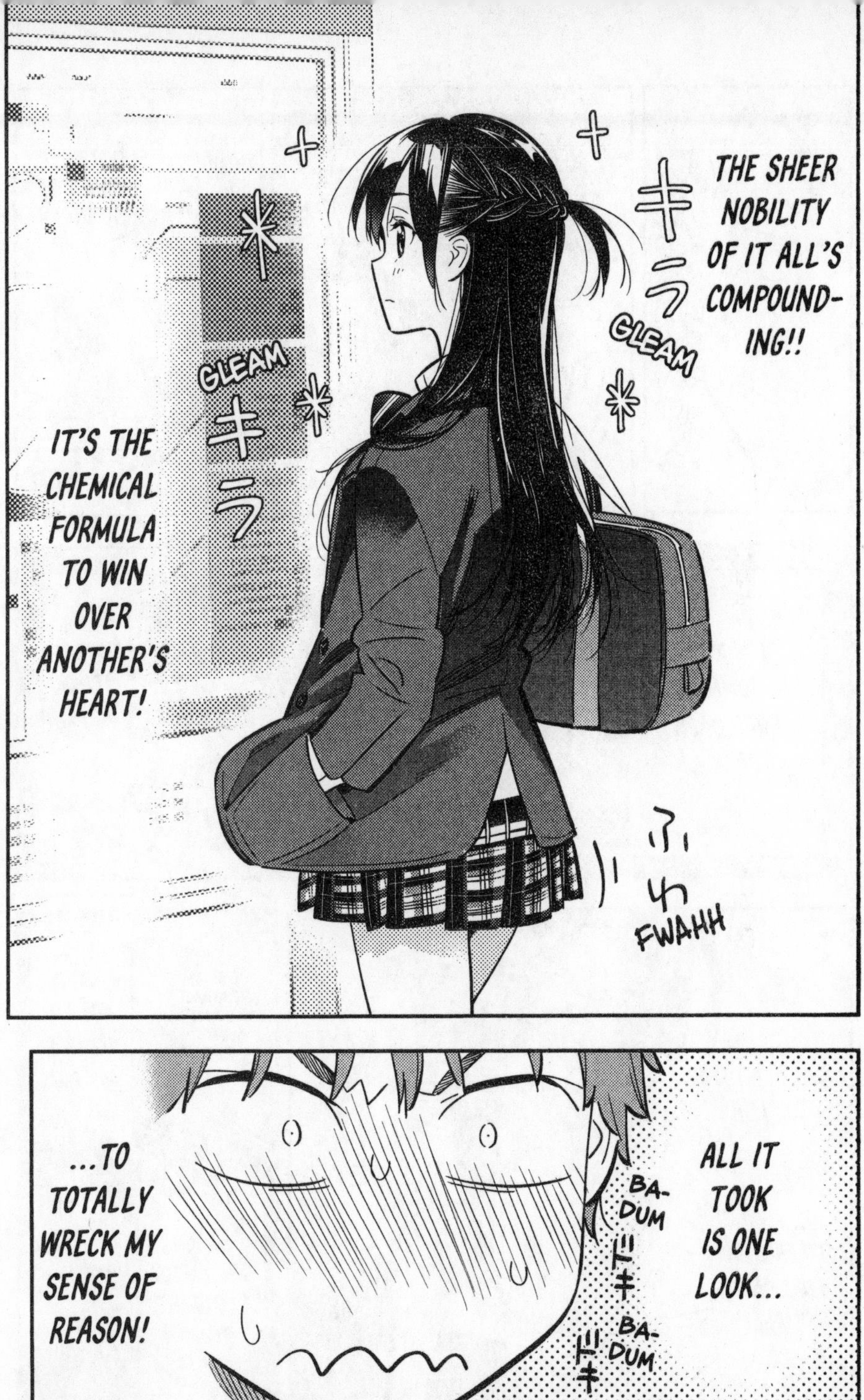
THE SHEER NOBILITY OF IT ALL'S COMPOUND-ING!!
キラ
GLEAM
キラ
GLEAM
IT'S THE CHEMICAL FORMULA TO WIN OVER ANOTHER'S HEART!
ふわ
FWAHH
ALL IT TOOK IS ONE LOOK...
BA-DUM
ドキ
BA-DUM
ドキ
...TO TOTALLY WRECK MY SENSE OF REASON!

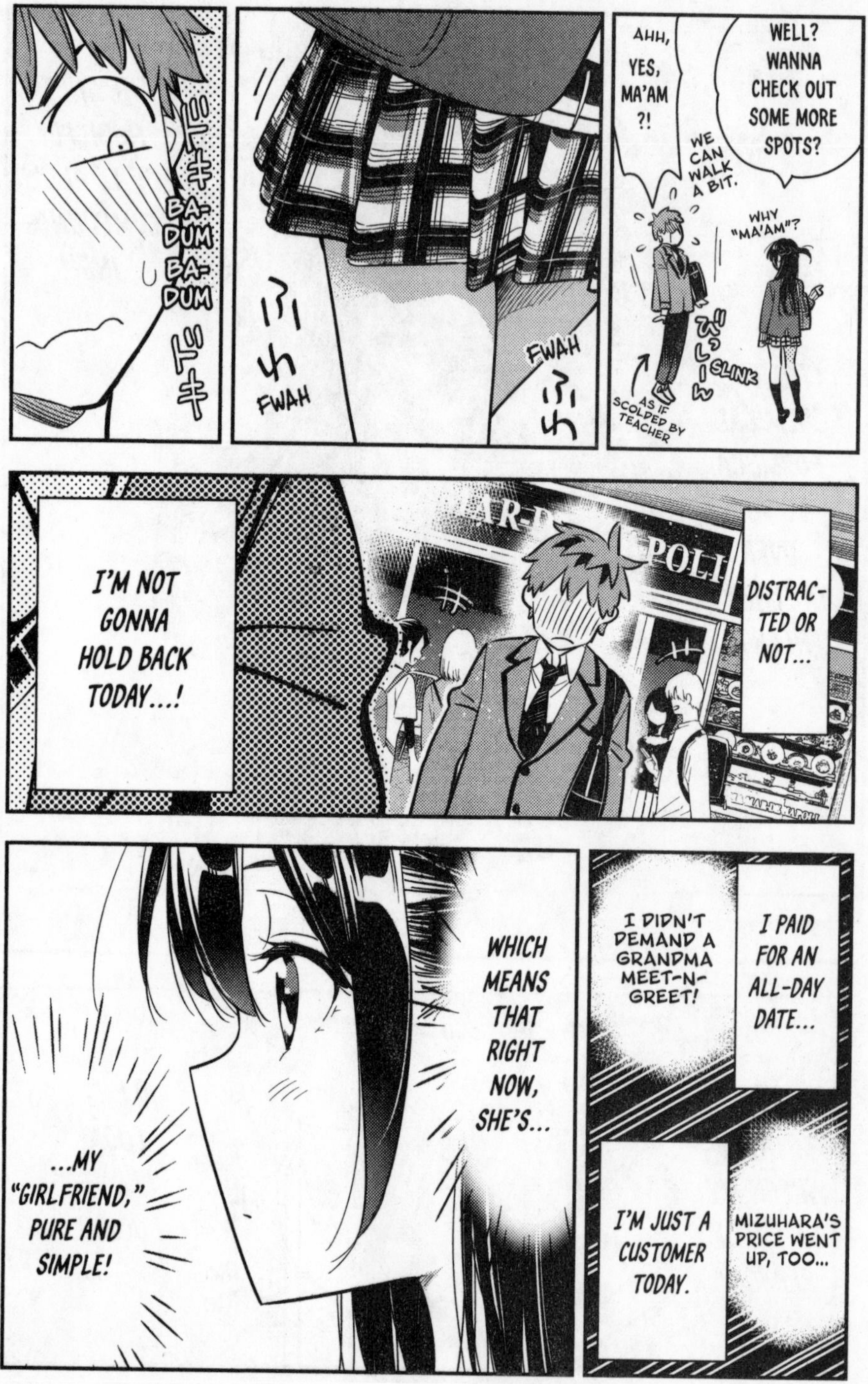
WELL? WANNA CHECK OUT SOME MORE SPOTS?
WE CAN WALK A BIT.
AHH, YES, MA'AM?!
WHY "MA'AM"?
SLINK
AS IF SCOLDED BY TEACHER
ふわ
FWAH
ふわ
FWAH
ドキ
BA-DUM BA-DUM
ドキ
DISTRACTED OR NOT...
I'M NOT GONNA HOLD BACK TODAY...!
I PAID FOR AN ALL-DAY DATE...
I DIDN'T DEMAND A GRANDMA MEET-N-GREET!
MIZUHARA'S PRICE WENT UP, TOO...
I'M JUST A CUSTOMER TODAY.
WHICH MEANS THAT RIGHT NOW, SHE'S...
...MY "GIRLFRIEND," PURE AND SIMPLE!

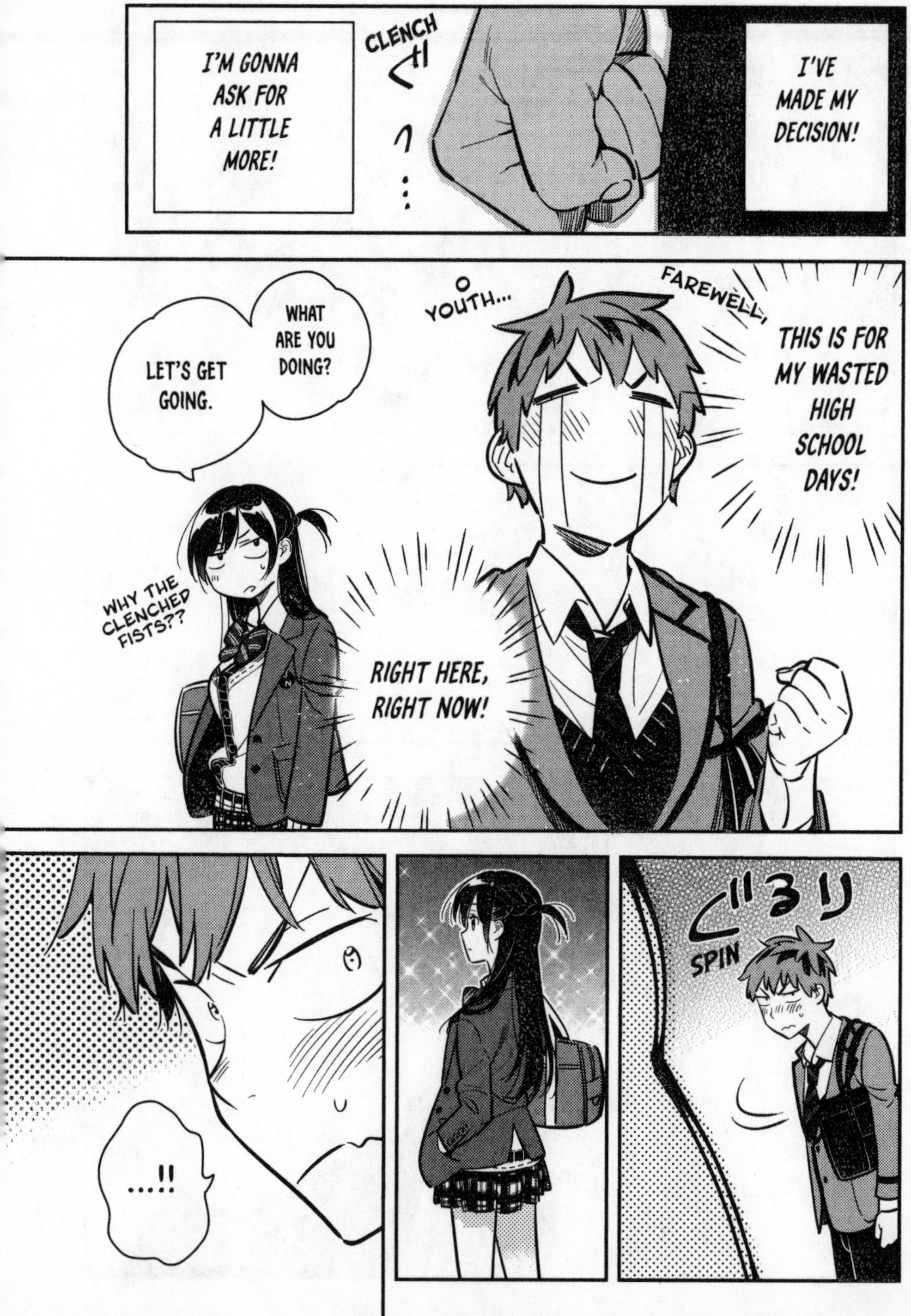
I'VE MADE MY DECISION!
CLENCH
I'M GONNA ASK FOR A LITTLE MORE!
FAREWELL,
O YOUTH...
THIS IS FOR MY WASTED HIGH SCHOOL DAYS!
RIGHT HERE, RIGHT NOW!
WHAT ARE YOU DOING?
LET'S GET GOING.
WHY THE CLENCHED FISTS??
SPIN
...!!

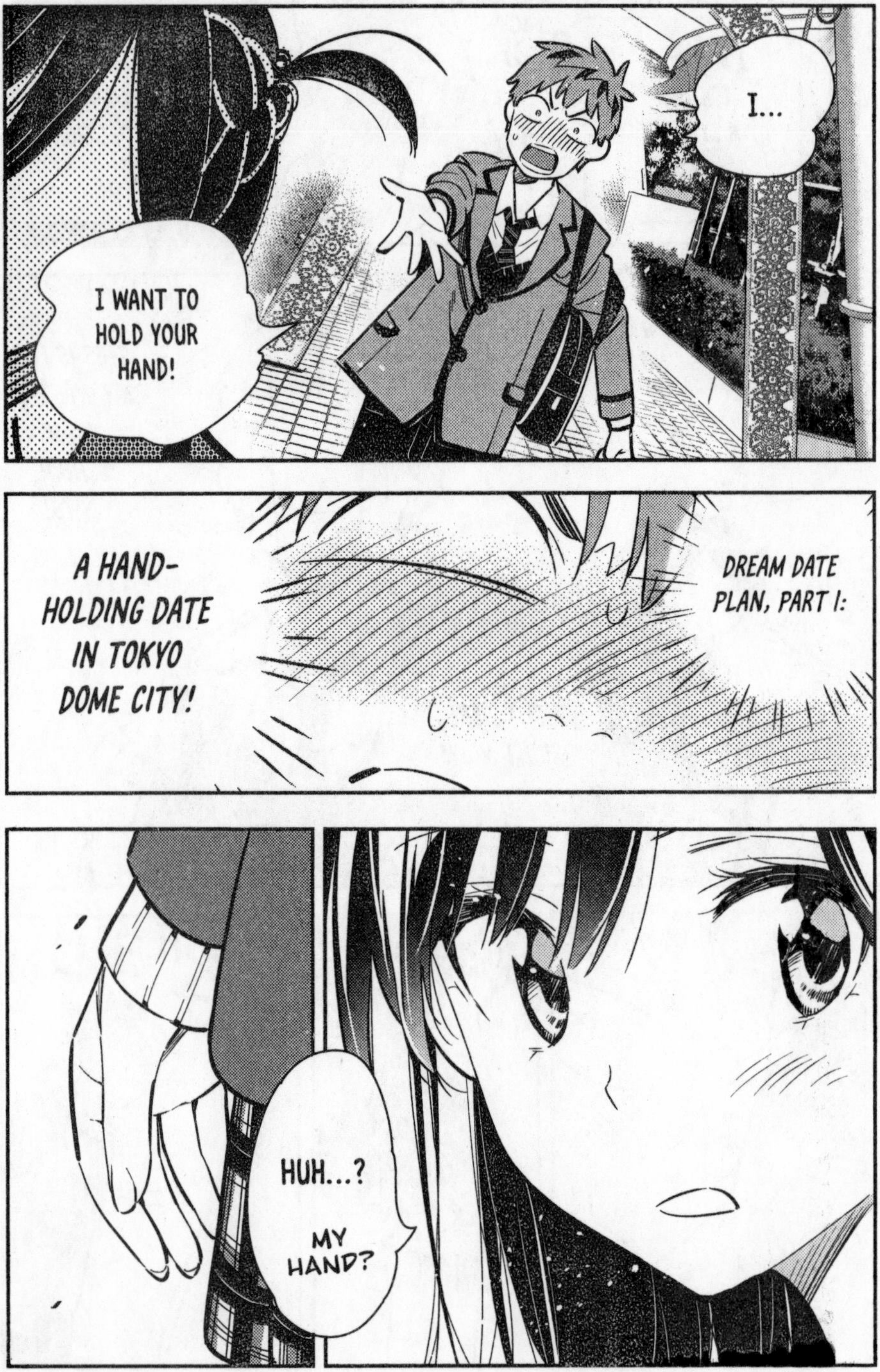
I...
I WANT TO HOLD YOUR HAND!
DREAM DATE PLAN, PART 1:
A HAND-HOLDING DATE IN TOKYO DOME CITY!
HUH...?
MY HAND?

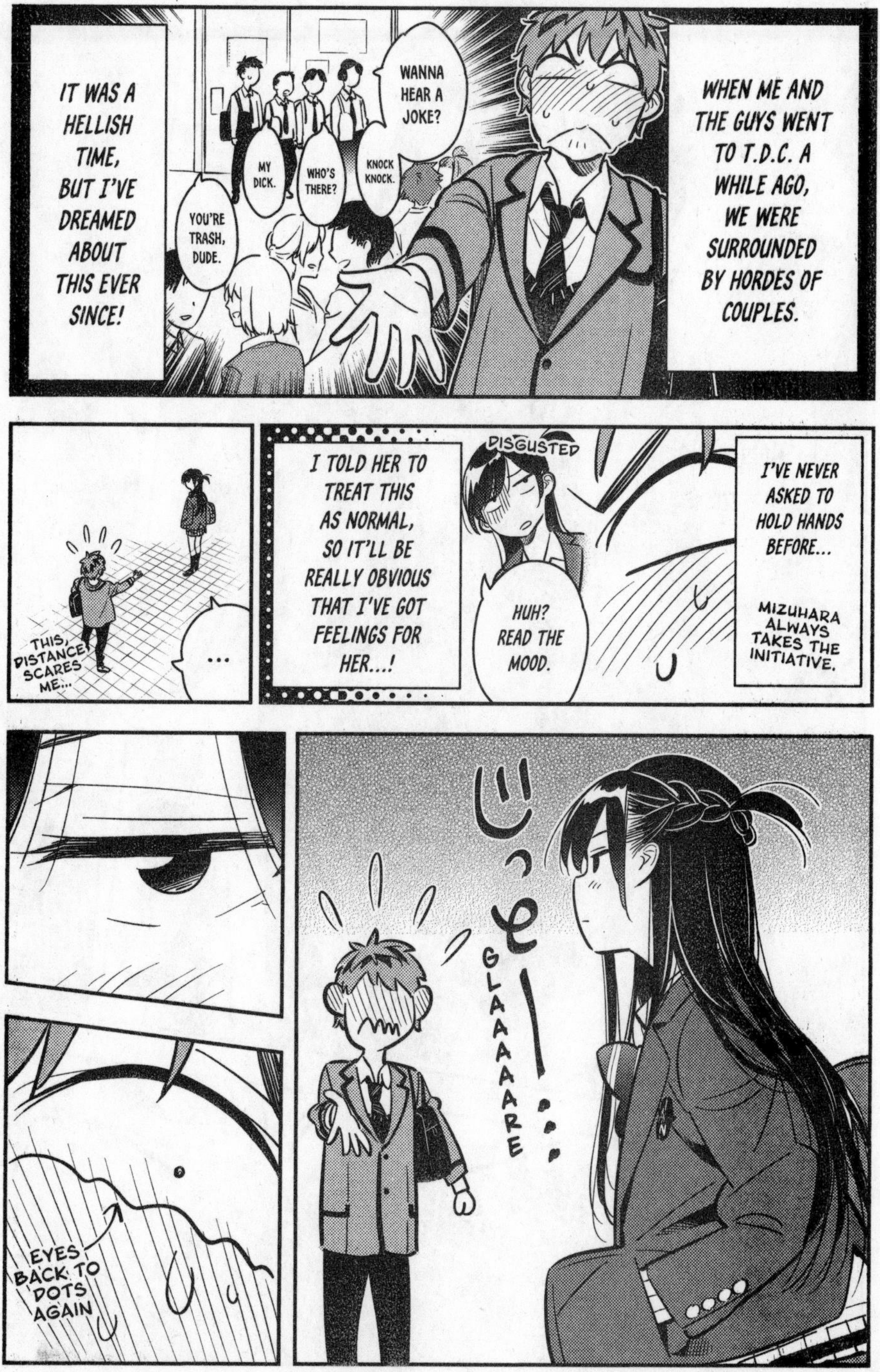
WHEN ME AND THE GUYS WENT TO T.D.C. A WHILE AGO, WE WERE SURROUNDED BY HORDES OF COUPLES.
WANNA HEAR A JOKE?
KNOCK KNOCK.
WHO'S THERE?
MY DICK.
YOU'RE TRASH, DUDE.
IT WAS A HELLISH TIME, BUT I'VE DREAMED ABOUT THIS EVER SINCE!
I'VE NEVER ASKED TO HOLD HANDS BEFORE...
MIZUHARA ALWAYS TAKES THE INITIATIVE.
DISGUSTED
I TOLD HER TO TREAT THIS AS NORMAL, SO IT'LL BE REALLY OBVIOUS THAT I'VE GOT FEELINGS FOR HER...!
HUH? READ THE MOOD.
...
THIS, DISTANCE SCARES ME...
GLAAAAARE
EYES BACK TO DOTS AGAIN

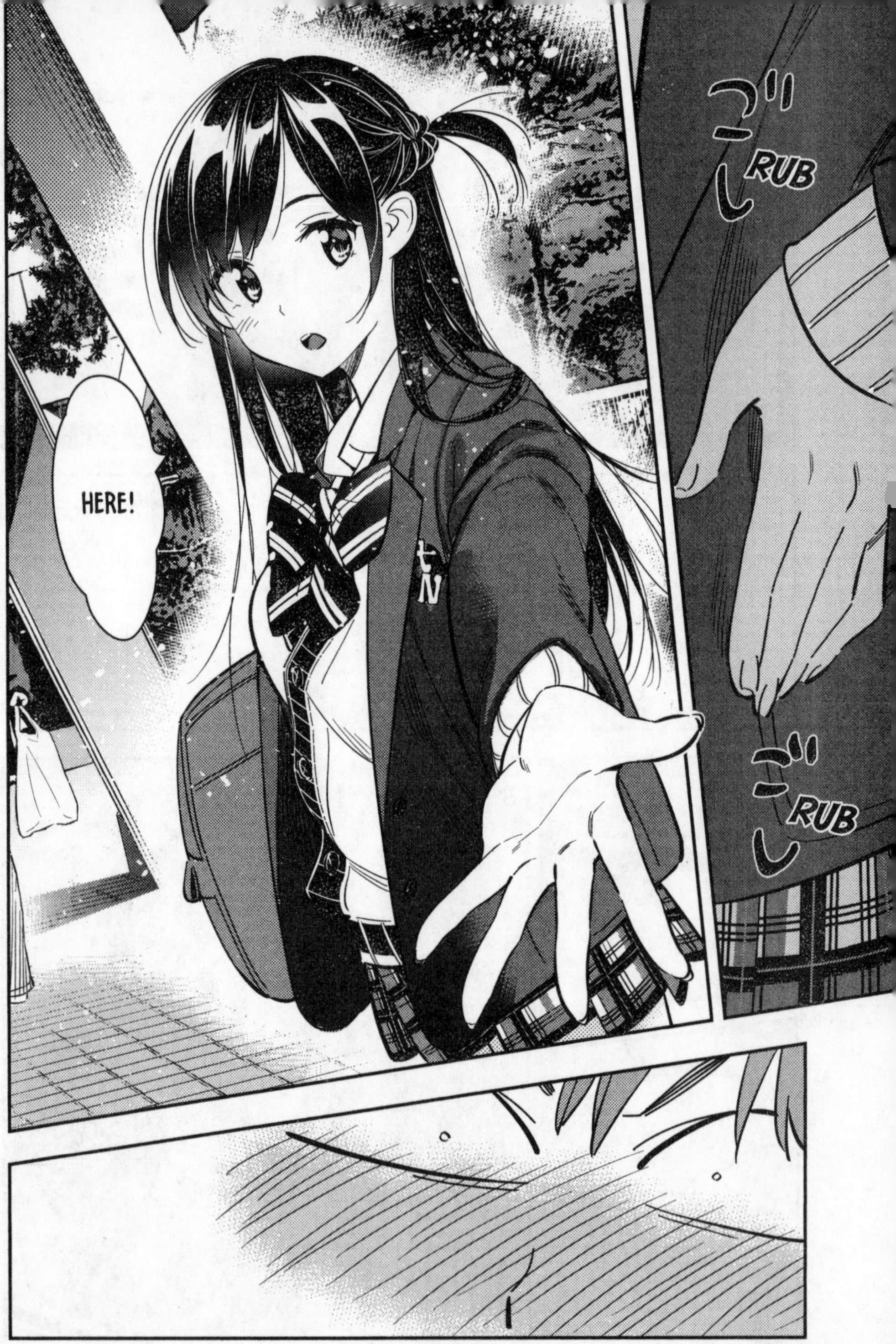
ごし
RUB
ごし
RUB
HERE!

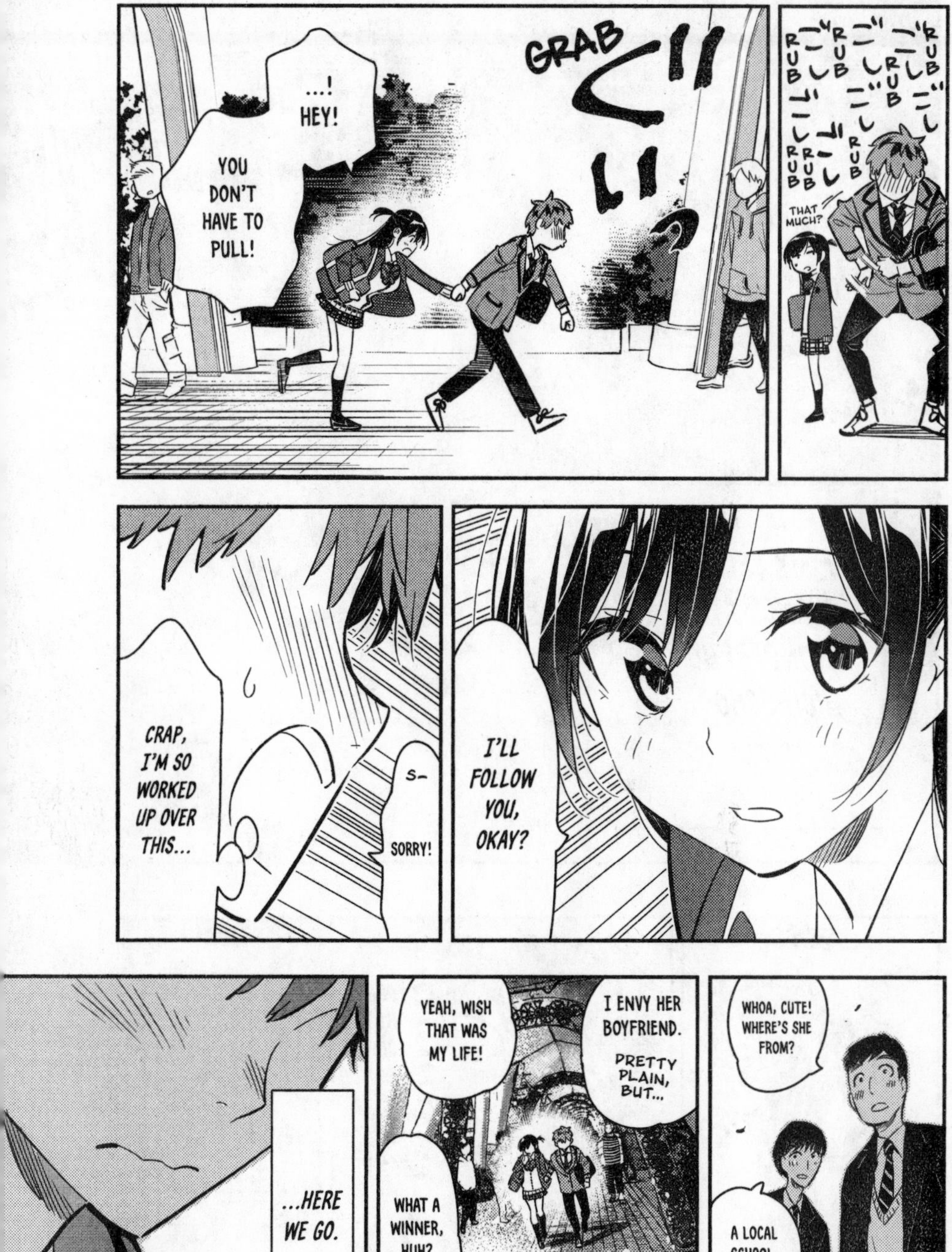

RUB RUB RUB RUB RUB RUB
THAT MUCH?
GRAB
...! HEY!
YOU DON'T HAVE TO PULL!
I'LL FOLLOW YOU, OKAY?
S- SORRY!
CRAP, I'M SO WORKED UP OVER THIS...
WHOA, CUTE! WHERE'S SHE FROM?
A LOCAL SCHOOL, MAYBE?
I ENVY HER BOYFRIEND.
PRETTY PLAIN, BUT...
YEAH, WISH THAT WAS MY LIFE!
WHAT A WINNER, HUH?
...HERE WE GO.

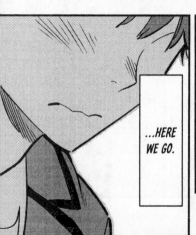

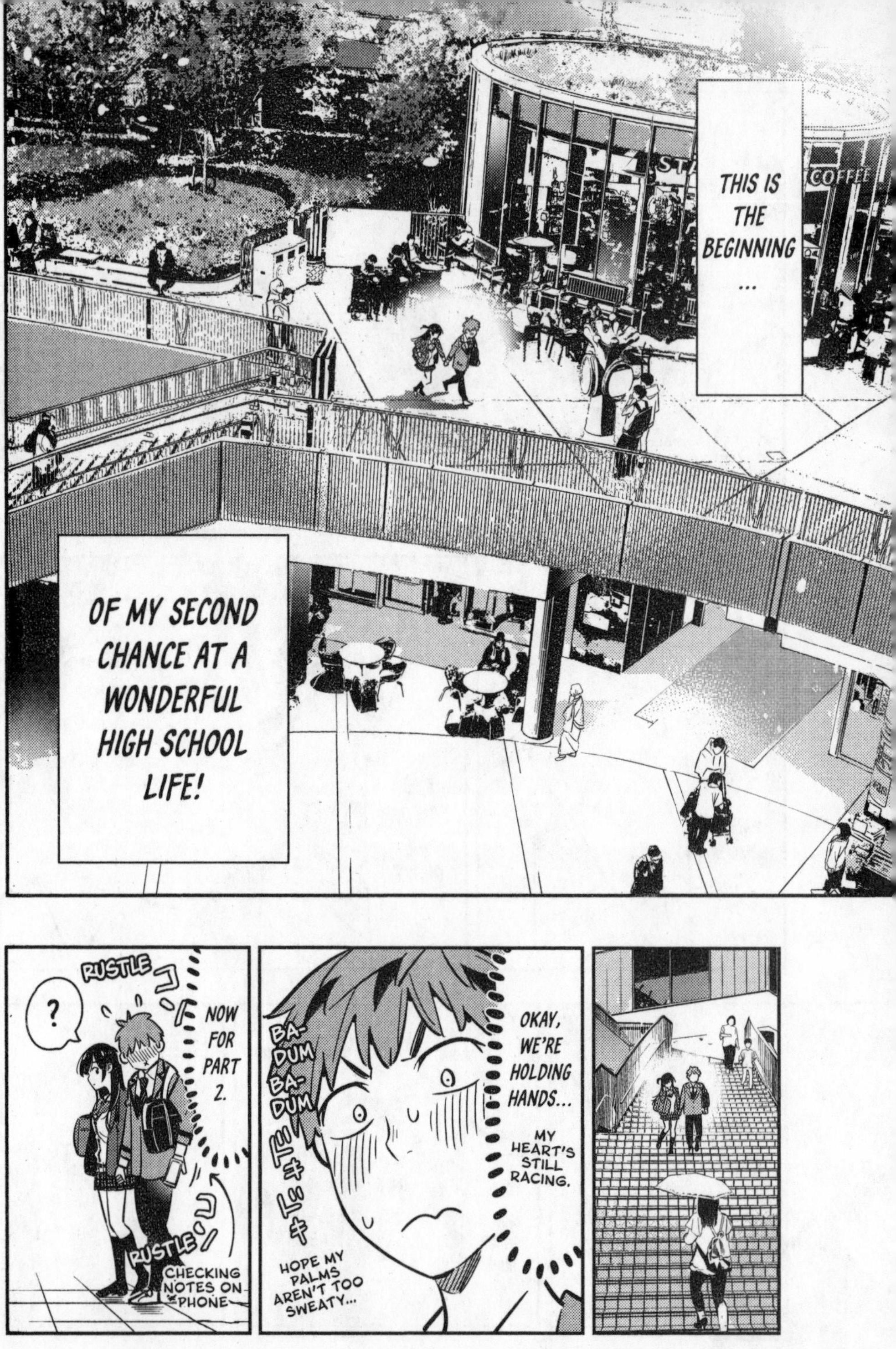
THIS IS THE BEGINNING...
OF MY SECOND CHANCE AT A WONDERFUL HIGH SCHOOL LIFE!
OKAY, WE'RE HOLDING HANDS...
MY HEART'S STILL RACING.
BA-DUM BA-DUM
HOPE MY PALMS AREN'T TOO SWEATY...
NOW FOR PART 2.
?
RUSTLE
RUSTLE
CHECKING NOTES ON PHONE

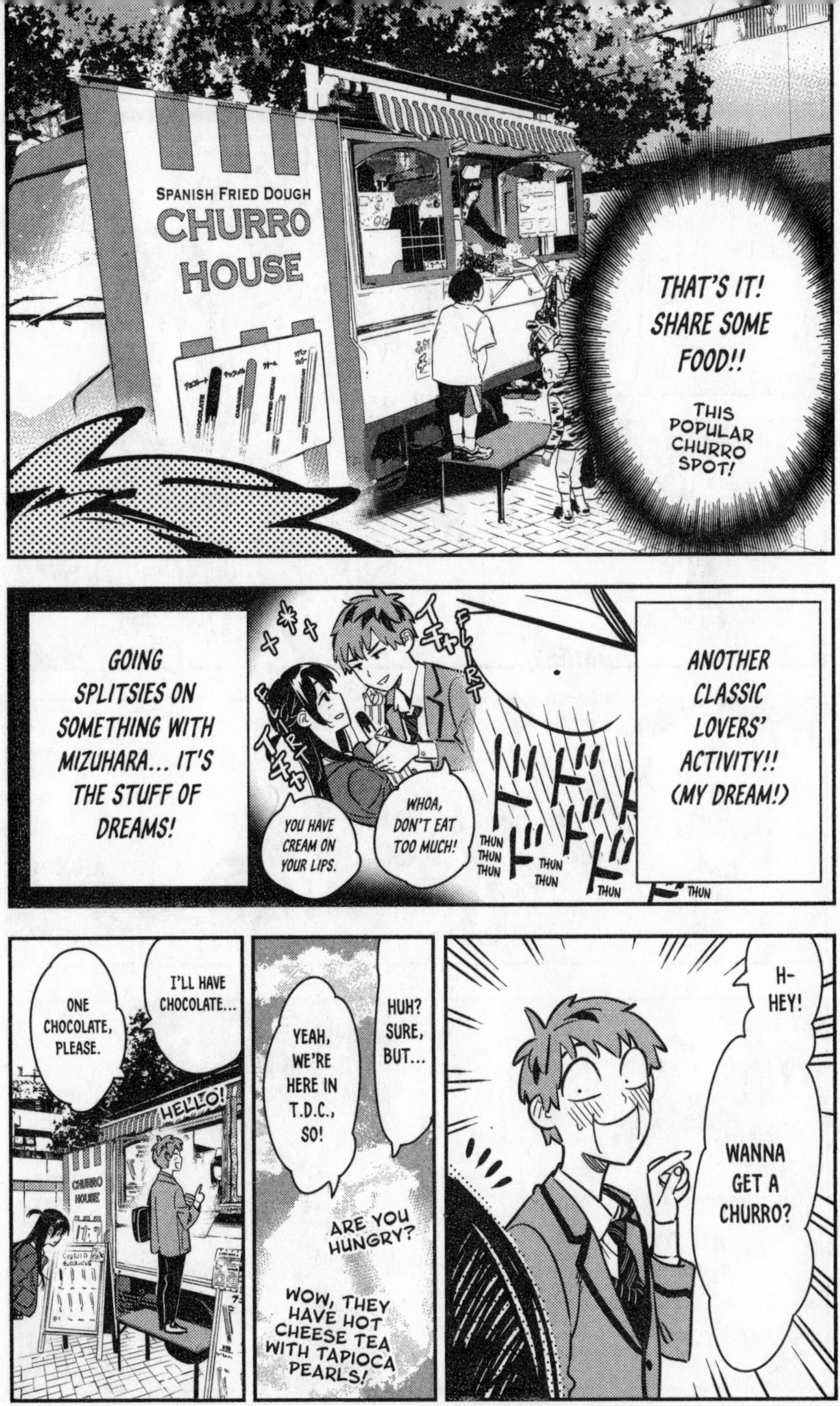
SPANISH FRIED DOUGH
CHURRO HOUSE
THAT'S IT! SHARE SOME FOOD!!
THIS POPULAR CHURRO SPOT!
ANOTHER CLASSIC LOVERS' ACTIVITY!! (MY DREAM!)
FLIRT
WHOA, DON'T EAT TOO MUCH!
YOU HAVE CREAM ON YOUR LIPS.
FLIRT
THUN THUN THUN THUN THUN THUN THUN
GOING SPLITSIES ON SOMETHING WITH MIZUHARA... IT'S THE STUFF OF DREAMS!
H-HEY!
WANNA GET A CHURRO?
HUH? SURE, BUT...
YEAH, WE'RE HERE IN T.D.C., SO!
ARE YOU HUNGRY?
WOW, THEY HAVE HOT CHEESE TEA WITH TAPIOCA PEARLS!
I'LL HAVE CHOCOLATE...
ONE CHOCOLATE, PLEASE.
HELLO!
CHURRO HOUSE

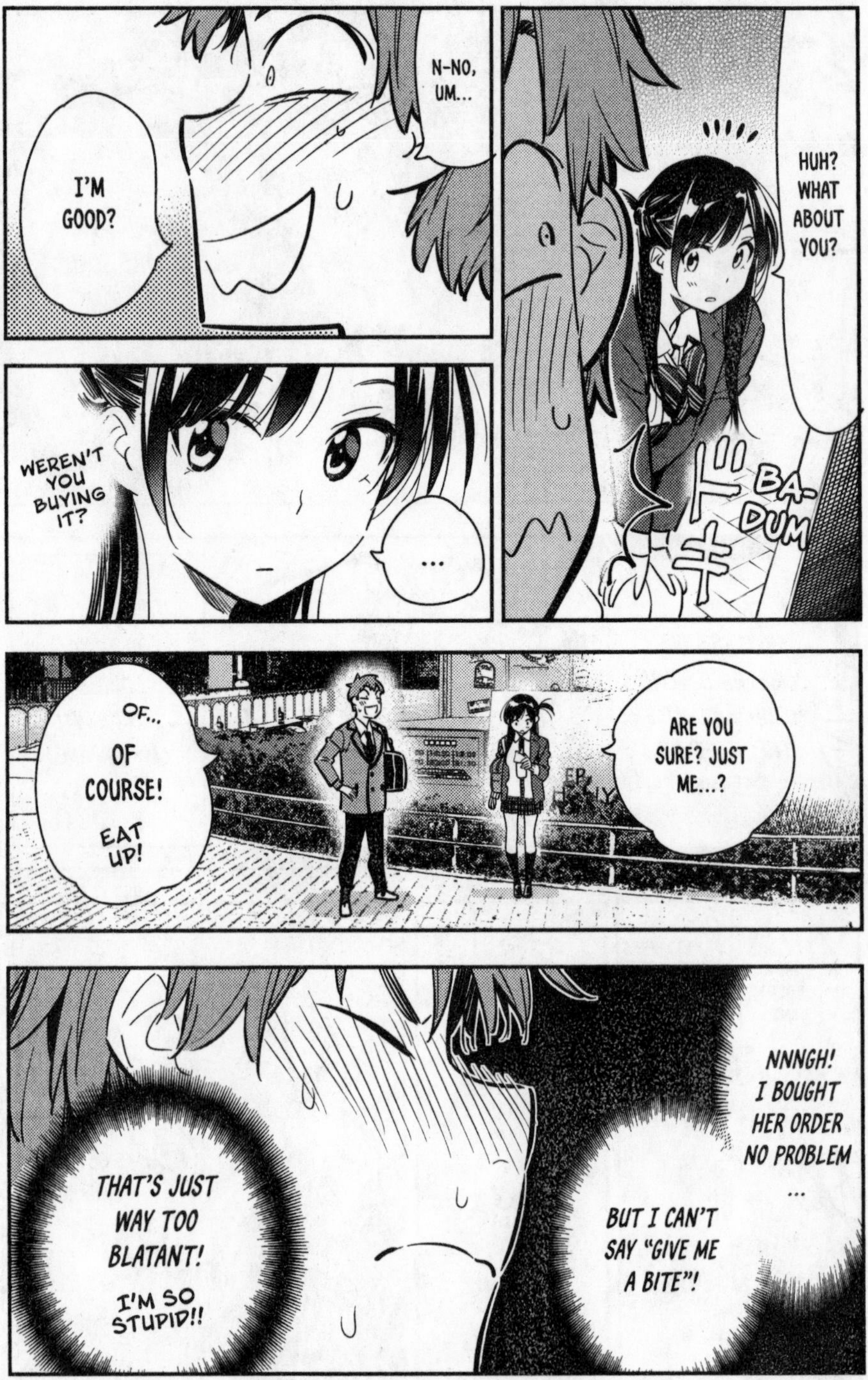
HUH? WHAT ABOUT YOU?
BA-DUM
N-NO, UM...
I'M GOOD?
WEREN'T YOU BUYING IT?
...
ARE YOU SURE? JUST ME...?
OF...
OF COURSE!
EAT UP!
NNNGH! I BOUGHT HER ORDER NO PROBLEM ...
BUT I CAN'T SAY "GIVE ME A BITE"!
THAT'S JUST WAY TOO BLATANT!
I'M SO STUPID!!

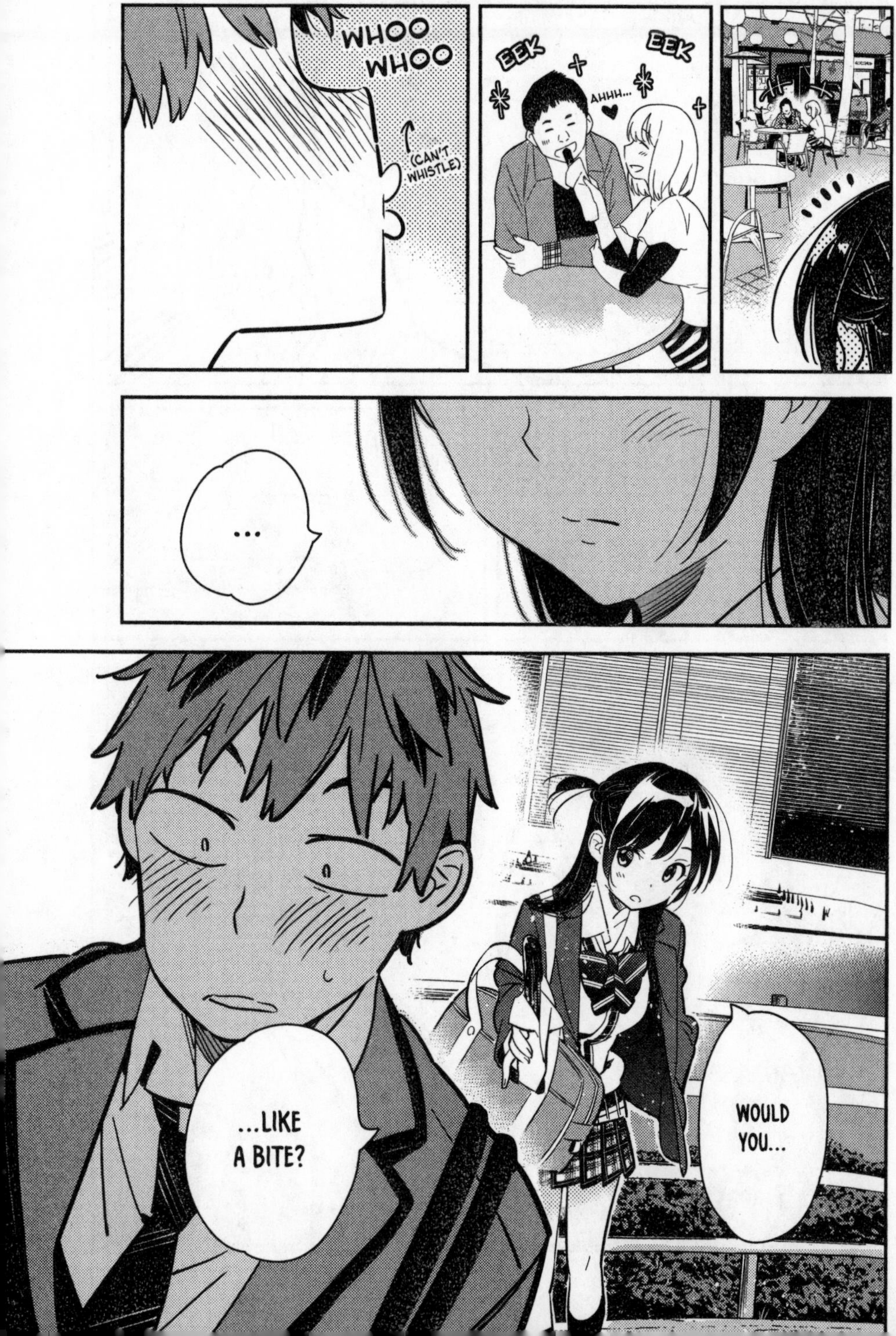
....
EEK
EEK
AHHH...
WHOO WHOO
(CAN'T WHISTLE)
...
WOULD YOU...
...LIKE A BITE?

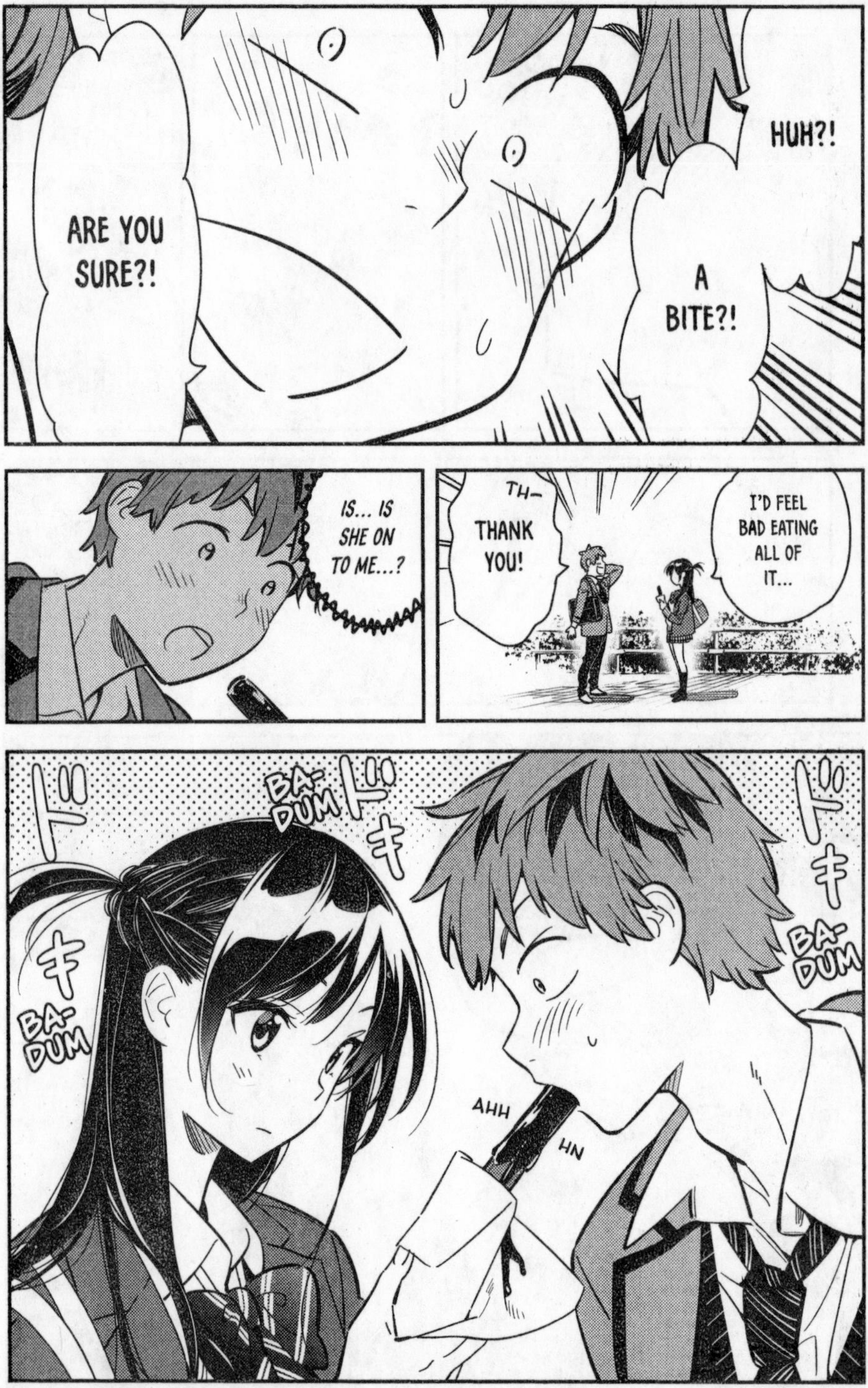
HUH?!
A BITE?!
ARE YOU SURE?!
I'D FEEL BAD EATING ALL OF IT...
TH— THANK YOU!
IS... IS SHE ON TO ME...?
ドキ
BA-DUM
ドキ
BA-DUM
ドキ
BA-DUM
AHH
HN

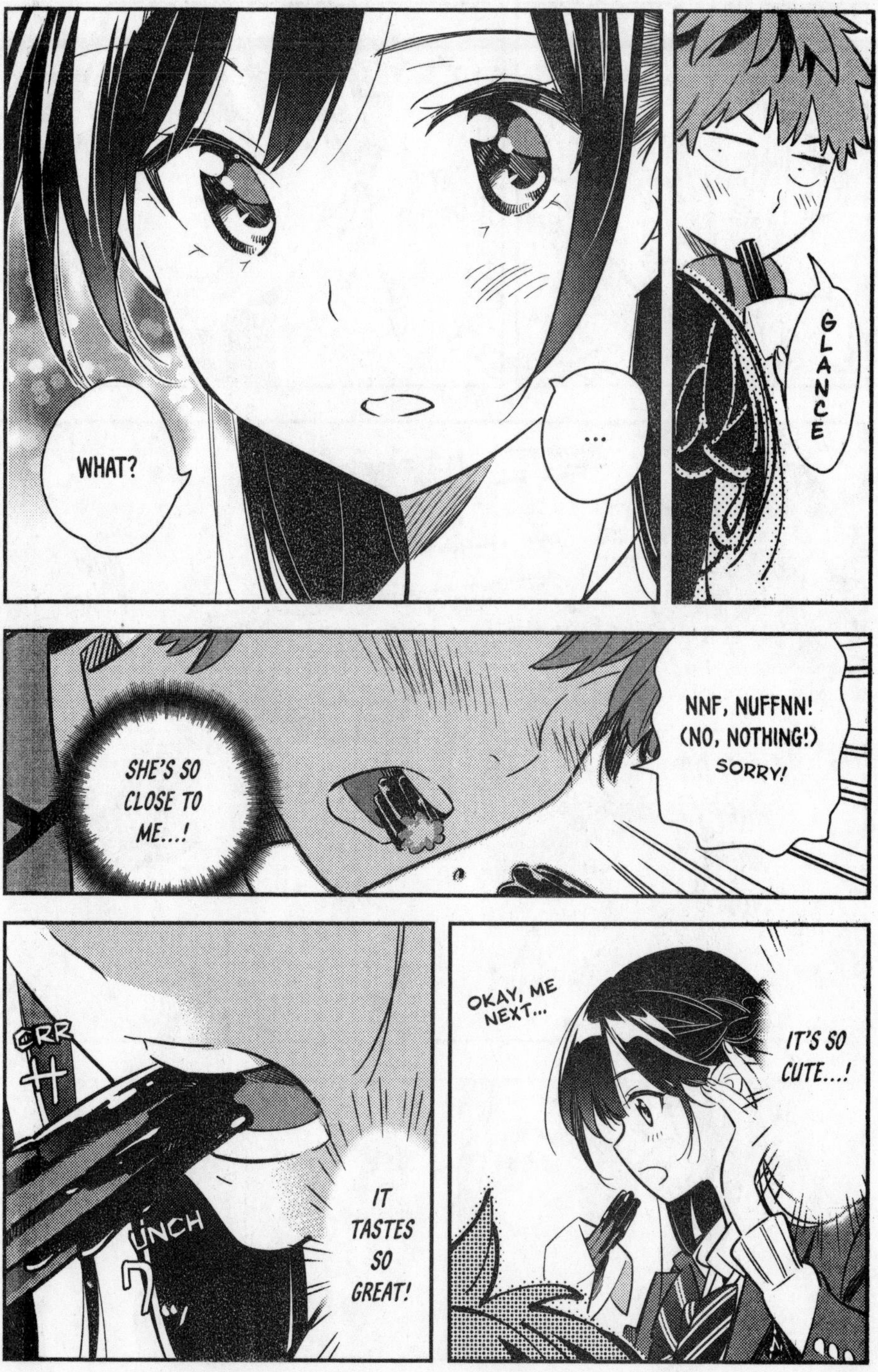
GLANCE
...
WHAT?
NNF, NUFFNN! (NO, NOTHING!) SORRY!
SHE'S SO CLOSE TO ME...!
IT'S SO CUTE...!
OKAY, ME NEXT...
CRR
UNCH
IT TASTES SO GREAT!

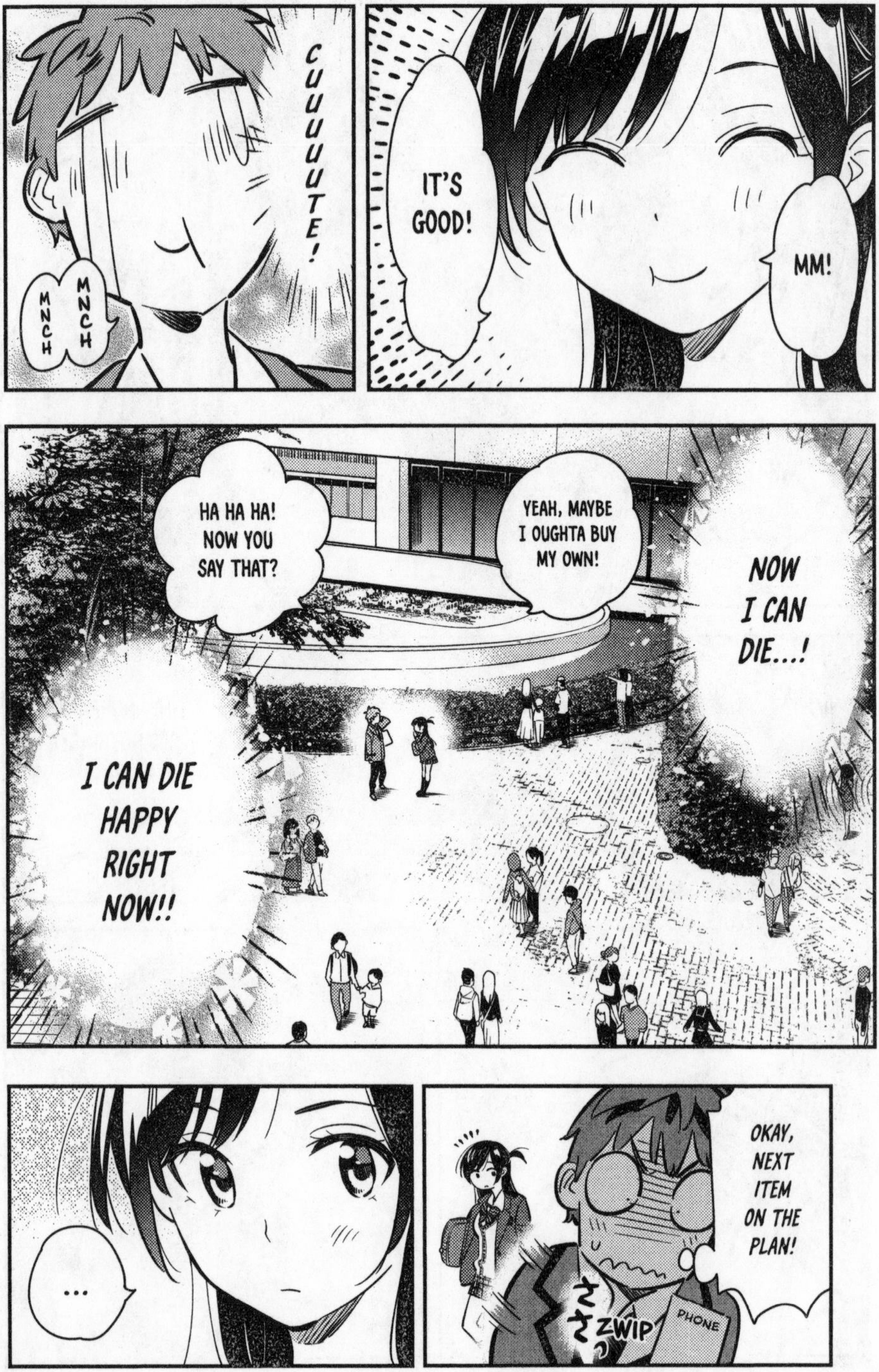
MM!
IT'S GOOD!
CUUUUUTE!
MNCH MNCH
NOW I CAN DIE...!
YEAH, MAYBE I OUGHTA BUY MY OWN!
HA HA HA! NOW YOU SAY THAT?
I CAN DIE HAPPY RIGHT NOW!!
OKAY, NEXT ITEM ON THE PLAN!
PHONE
ZWIP
ささっ
...

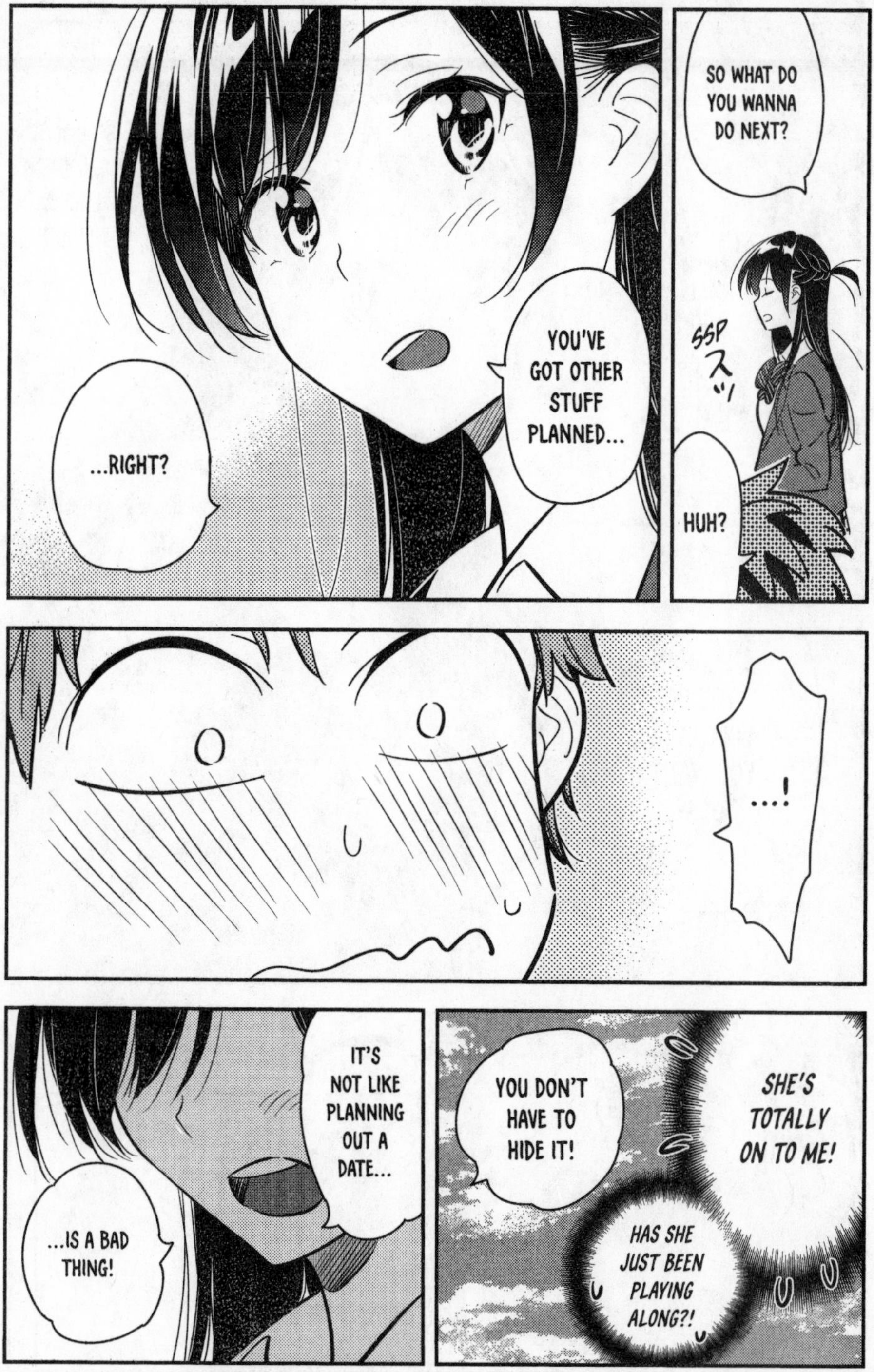
SO WHAT DO YOU WANNA DO NEXT?
SSP
スッ
HUH?
YOU'VE GOT OTHER STUFF PLANNED...
...RIGHT?
...!
SHE'S TOTALLY ON TO ME!
YOU DON'T HAVE TO HIDE IT!
HAS SHE JUST BEEN PLAYING ALONG?!
IT'S NOT LIKE PLANNING OUT A DATE...
...IS A BAD THING!

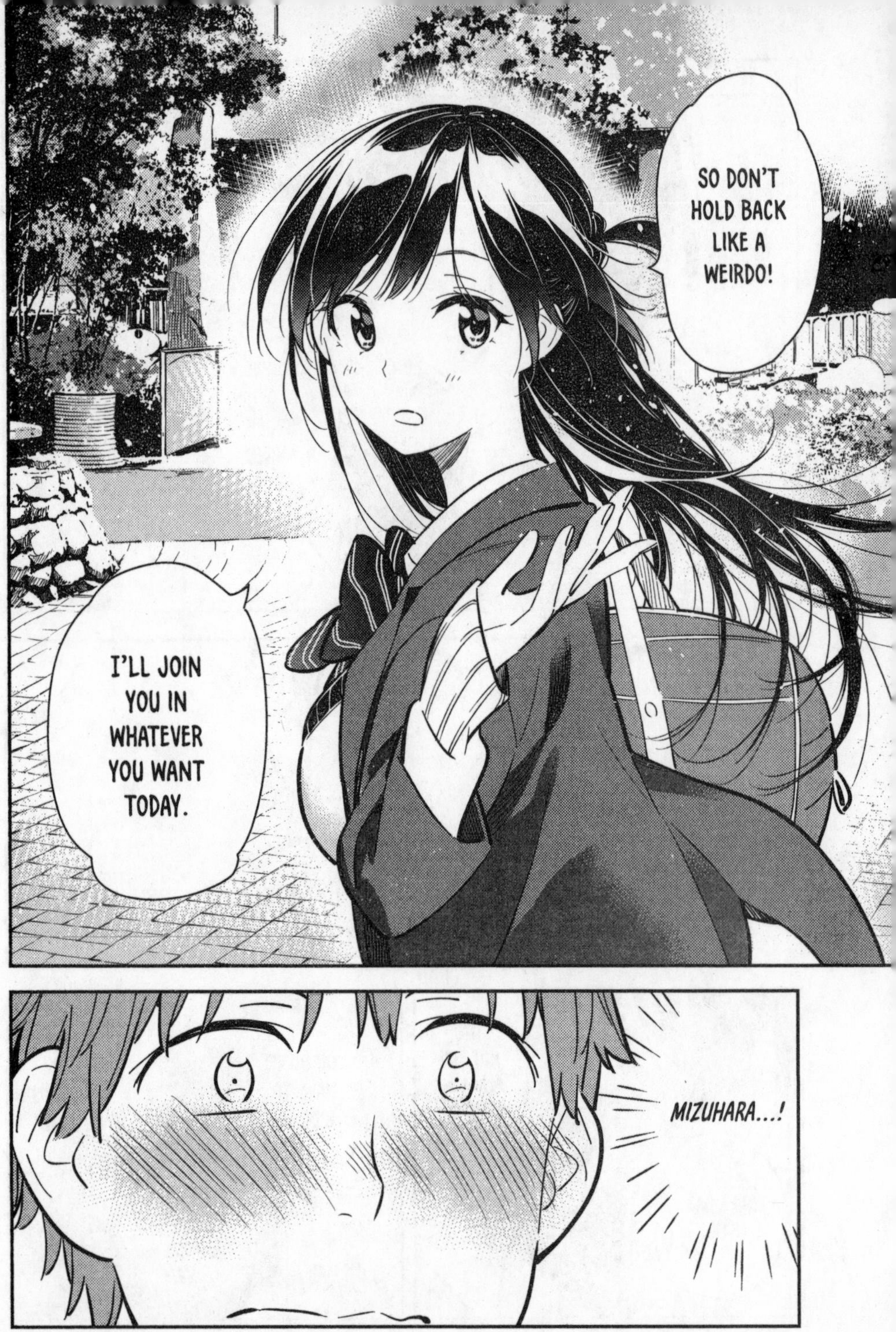
SO DON'T HOLD BACK LIKE A WEIRDO!
I'LL JOIN YOU IN WHATEVER YOU WANT TODAY.
MIZUHARA...!

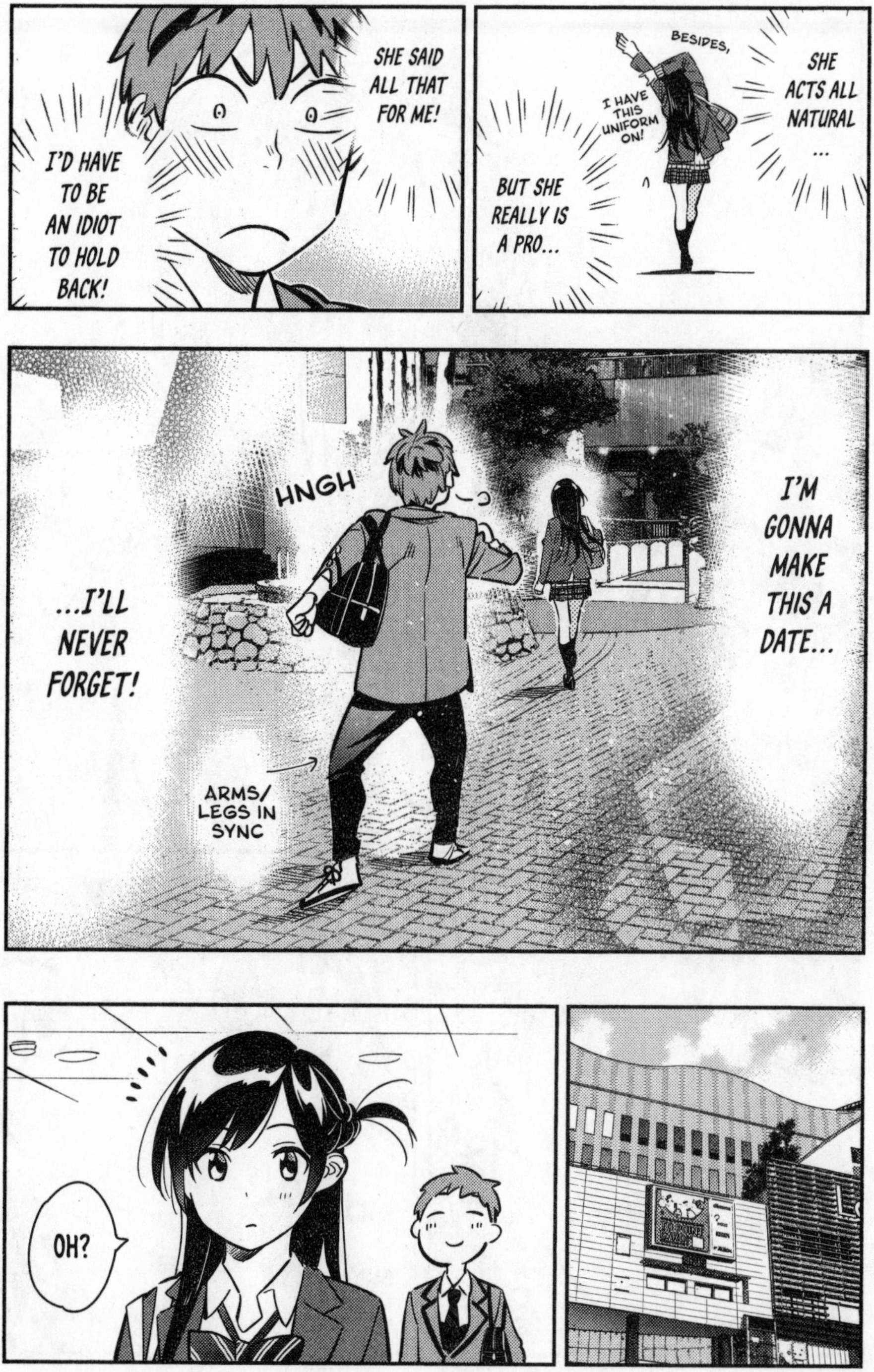
BESIDES,
I HAVE THIS UNIFORM ON!
SHE ACTS ALL NATURAL ...
BUT SHE REALLY IS A PRO...
SHE SAID ALL THAT FOR ME!
I'D HAVE TO BE AN IDIOT TO HOLD BACK!
I'M GONNA MAKE THIS A DATE...
HNGH
...I'LL NEVER FORGET!
ARMS/ LEGS IN SYNC
OH?

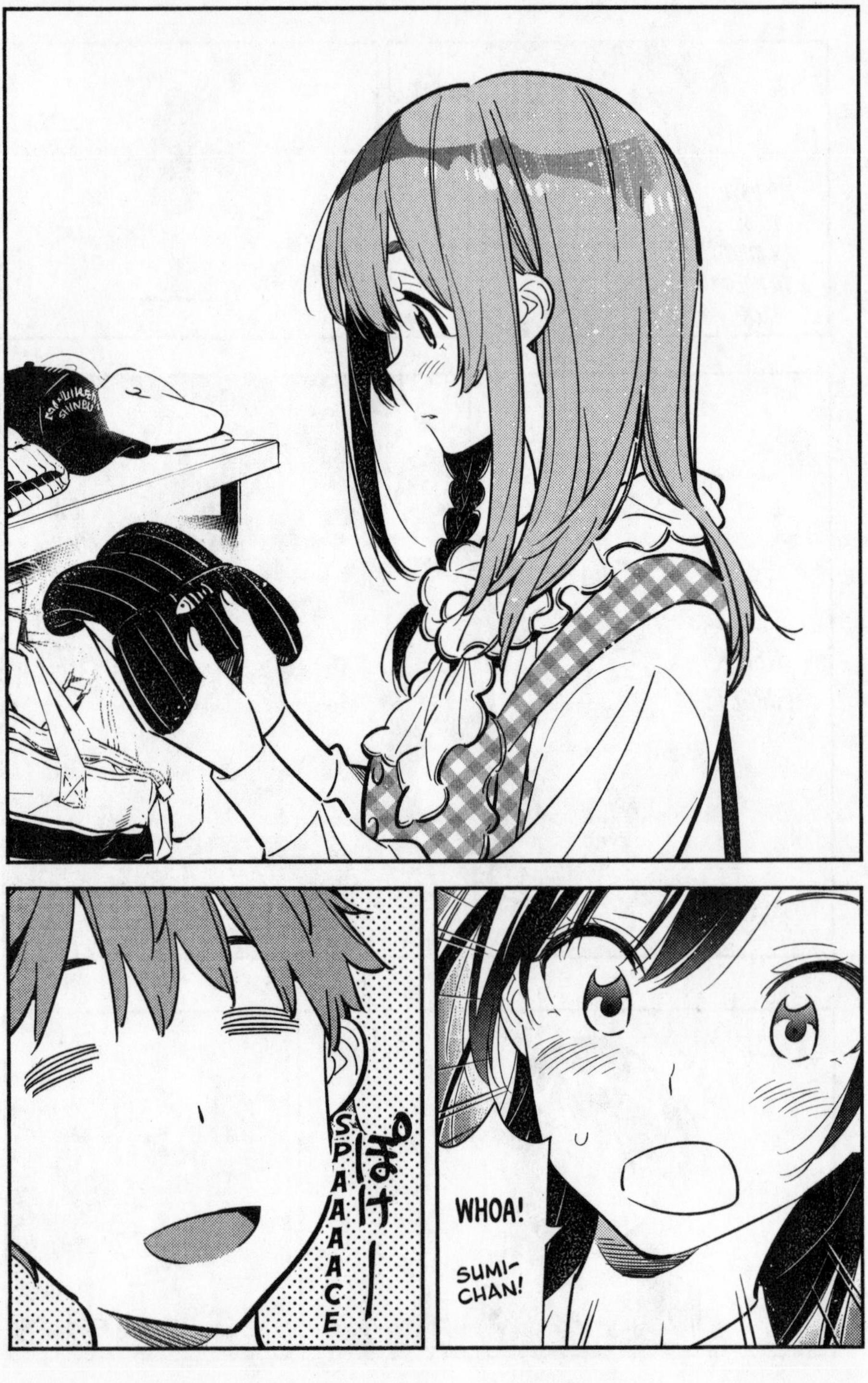
WHOA!
SUMI-CHAN!
ぽけー
SPAAAACE

RATING 80 MY GIRLFRIEND AND MY DREAM DATE 3

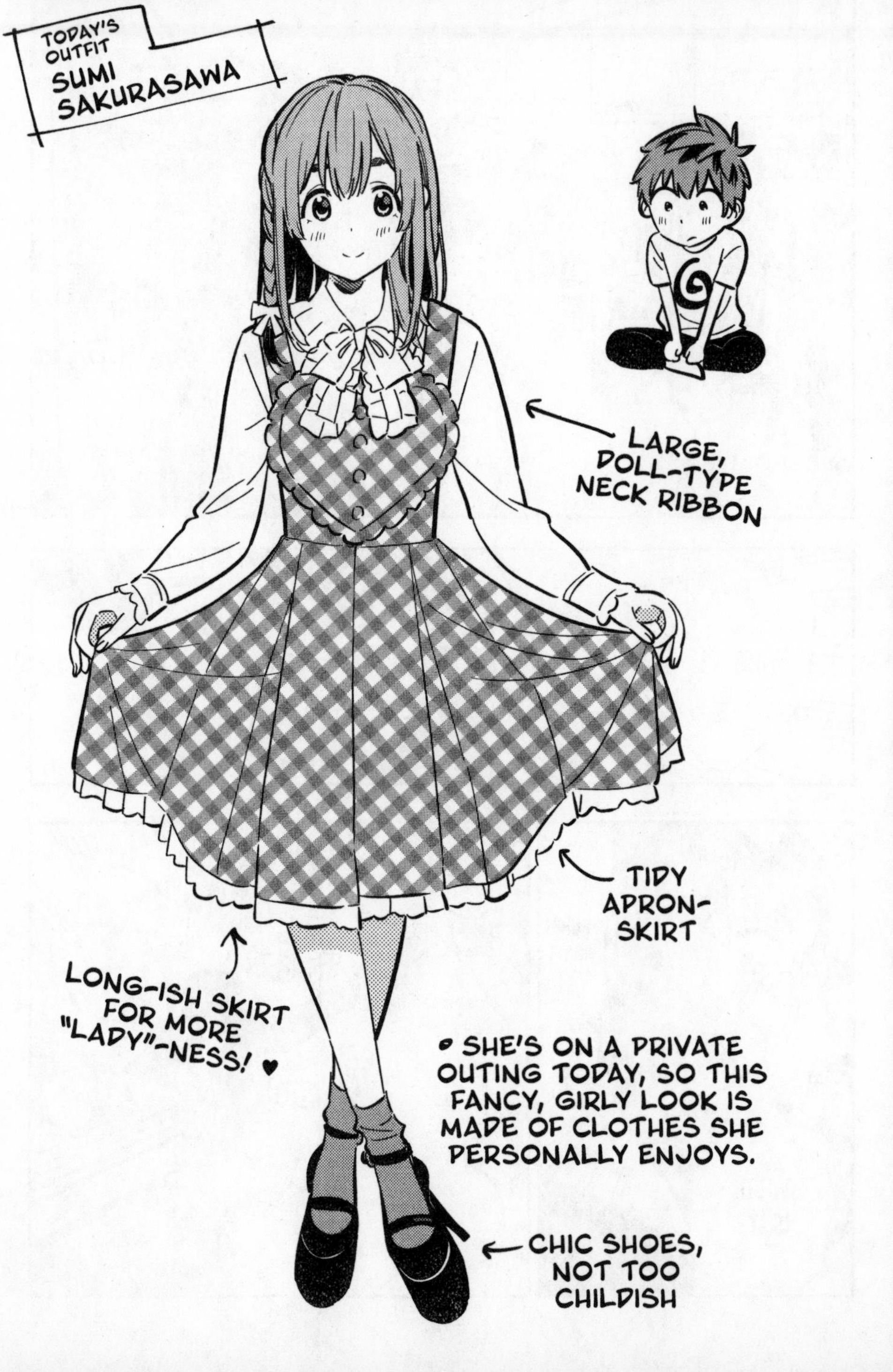
TODAY'S OUTFIT
SUMI SAKURASAWA
LARGE, DOLL-TYPE NECK RIBBON
TIDY APRON-SKIRT
LONG-ISH SKIRT FOR MORE "LADY"-NESS! ♥
• SHE'S ON A PRIVATE OUTING TODAY, SO THIS FANCY, GIRLY LOOK IS MADE OF CLOTHES SHE PERSONALLY ENJOYS.
CHIC SHOES, NOT TOO CHILDISH

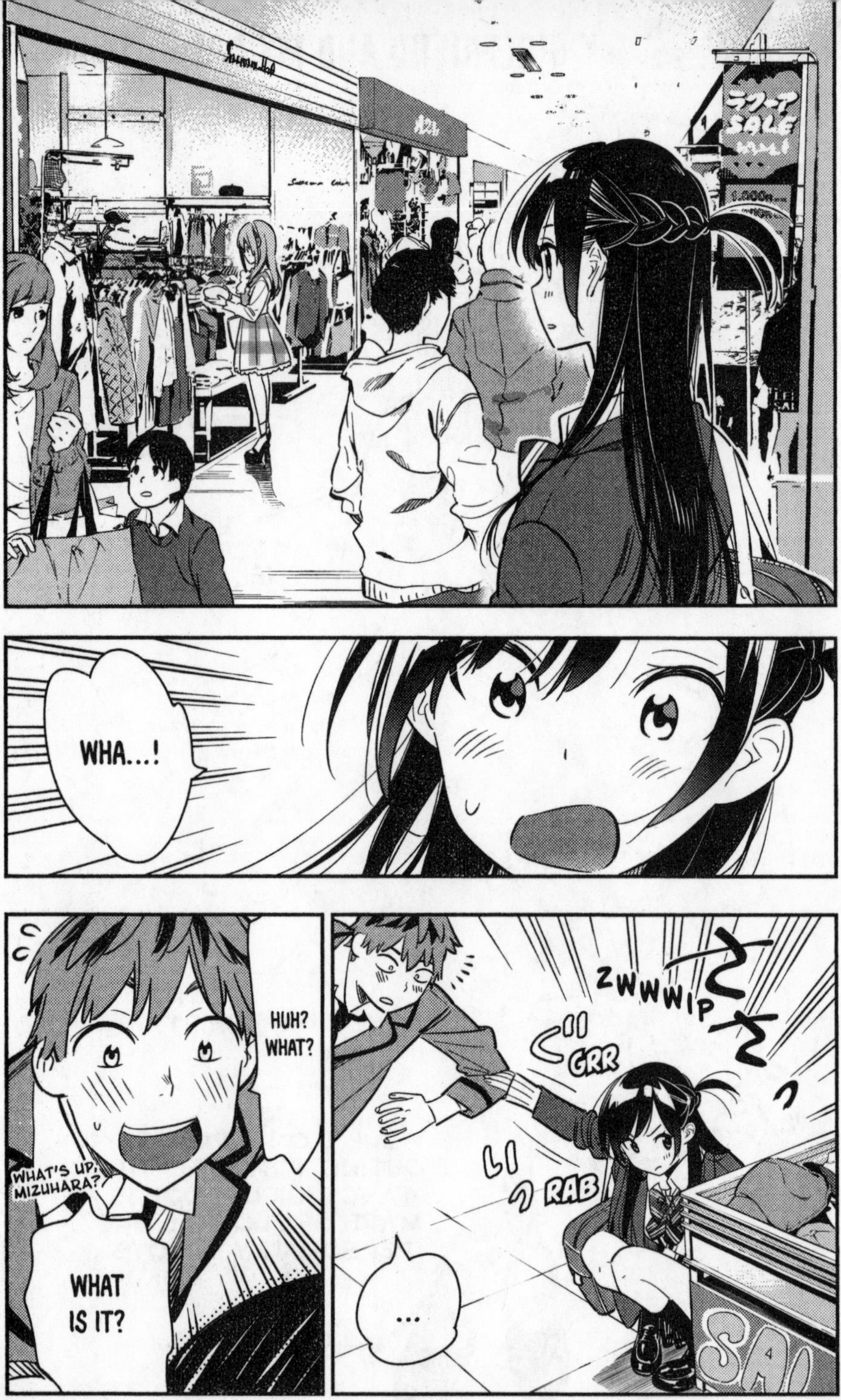
WHA...!
ZWWWIP
GRR
RAB
...
HUH? WHAT?
WHAT'S UP, MIZUHARA?
WHAT IS IT?

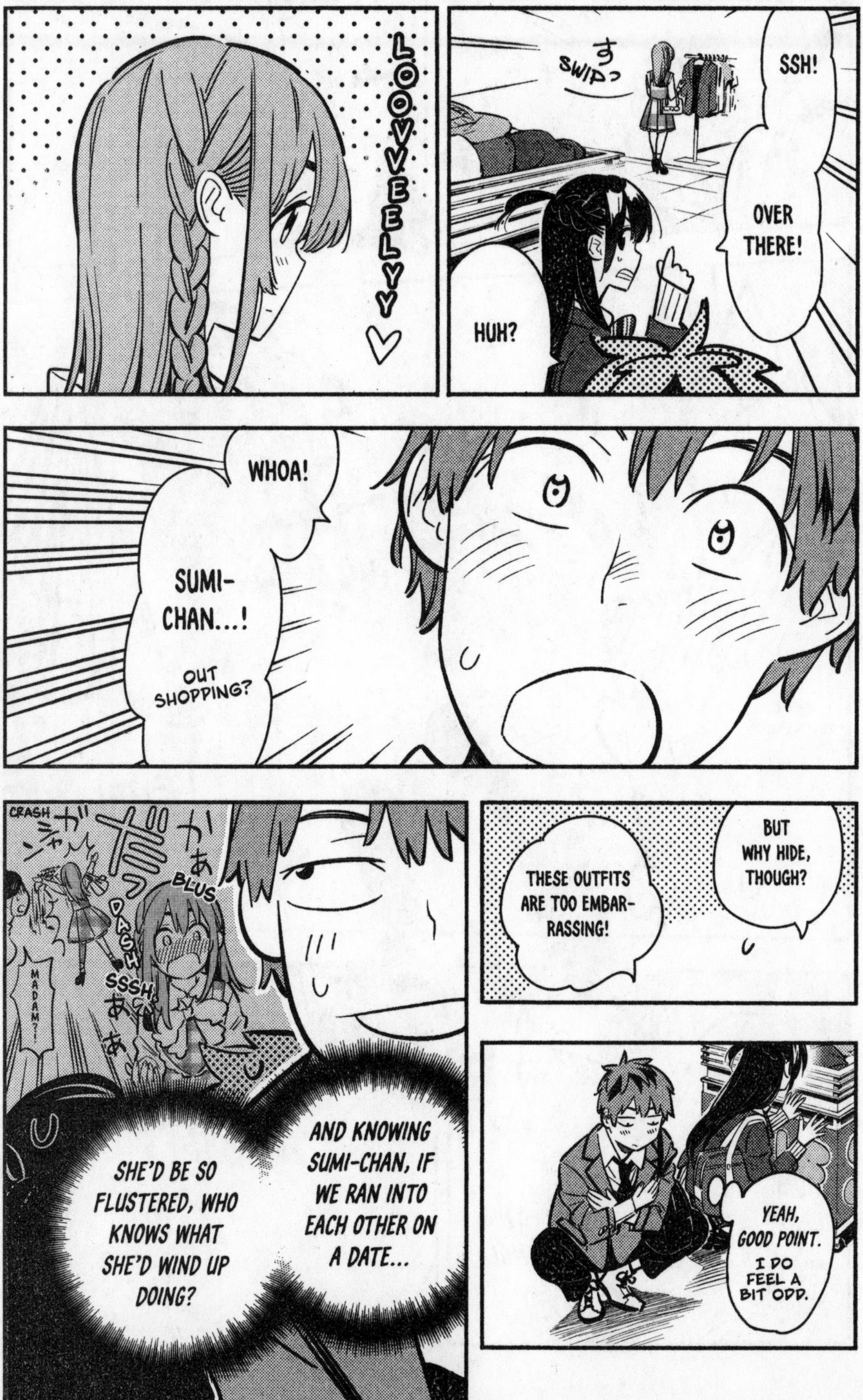
SSH!
OVER THERE!
す
SWIP
HUH?
LOOVVEELLYY ♥
WHOA!
SUMI-CHAN...!
OUT SHOPPING?
BUT WHY HIDE, THOUGH?
THESE OUTFITS ARE TOO EMBARRASSING!
YEAH, GOOD POINT.
I DO FEEL A BIT ODD.
AND KNOWING SUMI-CHAN, IF WE RAN INTO EACH OTHER ON A DATE...
SHE'D BE SO FLUSTERED, WHO KNOWS WHAT SHE'D WIND UP DOING?
CRASH
BLUS
DASH
SSSH
MADAM?!

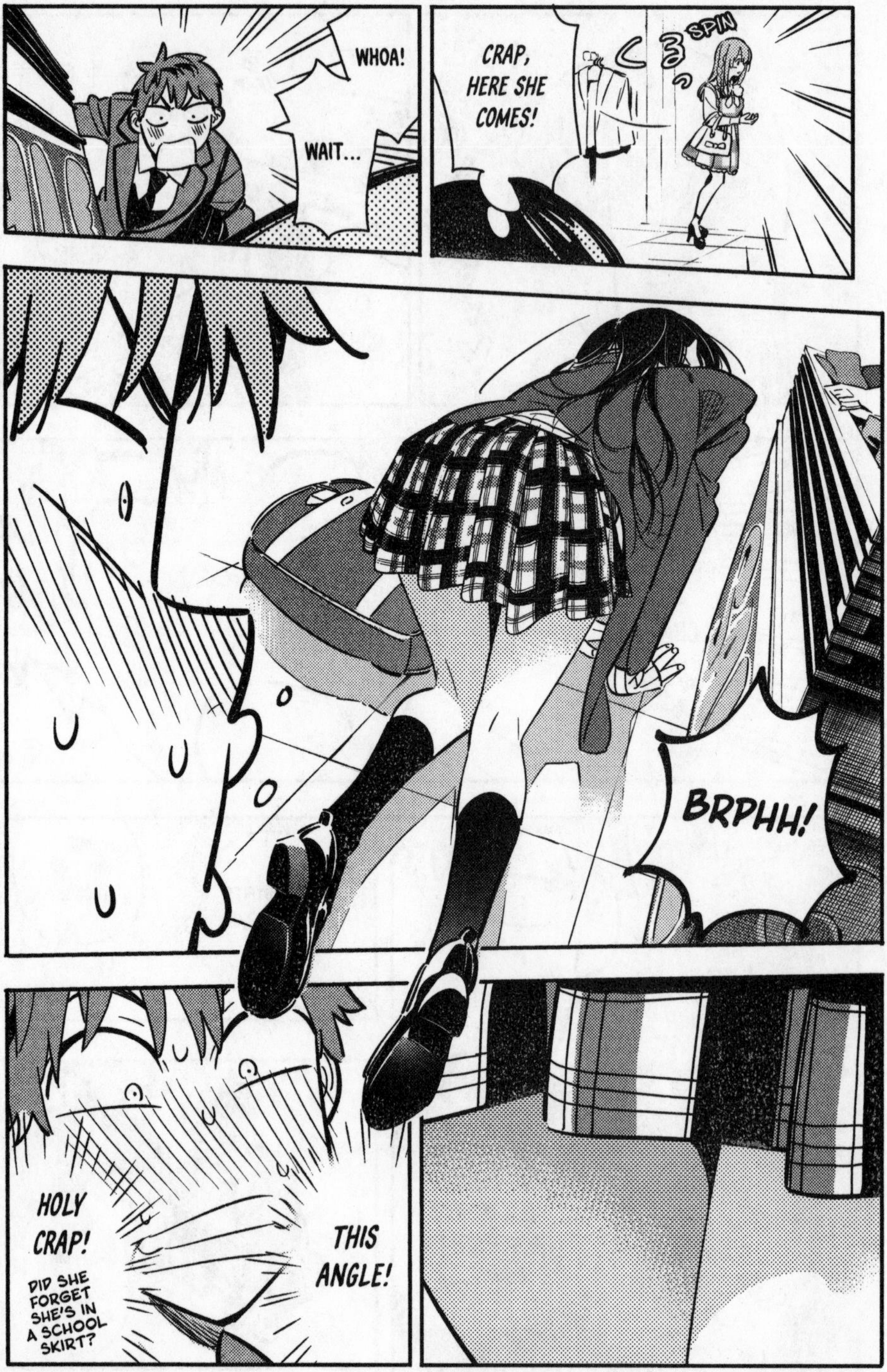
SPIN
くるっ
CRAP, HERE SHE COMES!
WHOA!
WAIT...
BRPHH!
HOLY CRAP!
THIS ANGLE!
DID SHE FORGET SHE'S IN A SCHOOL SKIRT?

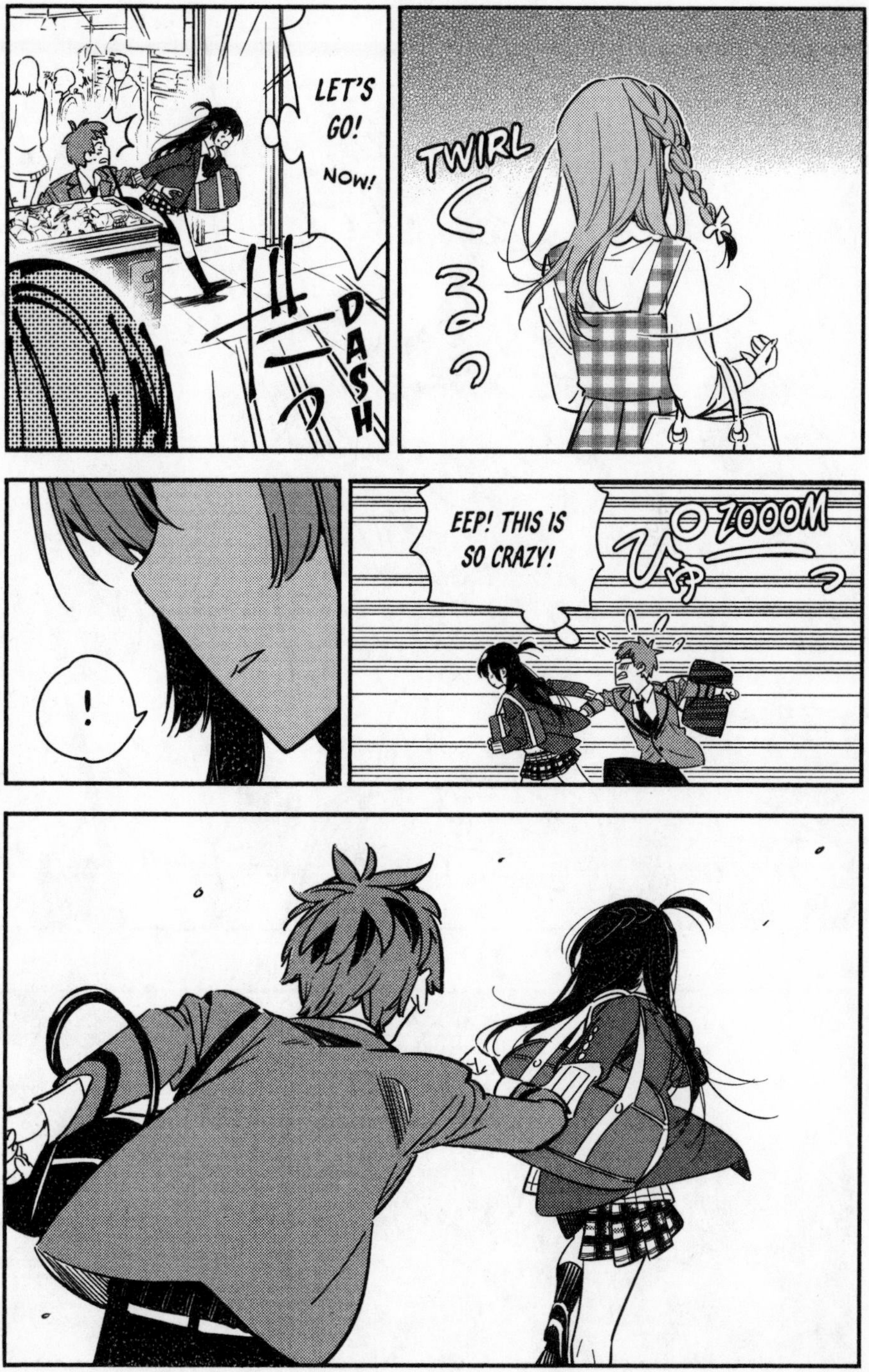
TWIRL
くるっ
LET'S GO!
NOW!
DASH
ダーッ
EEP! THIS IS SO CRAZY!
ZOOOM
ひゅーっ
!

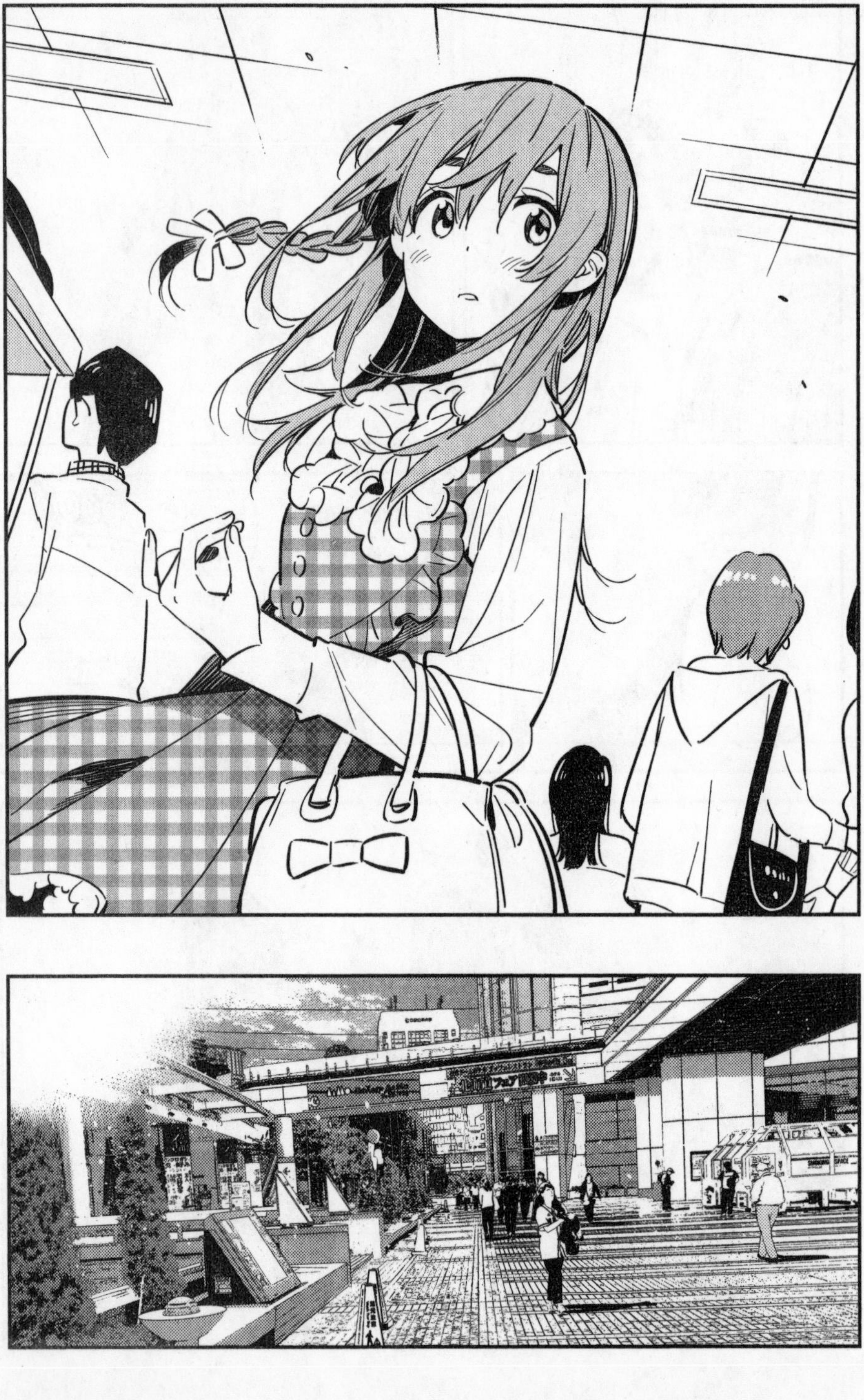

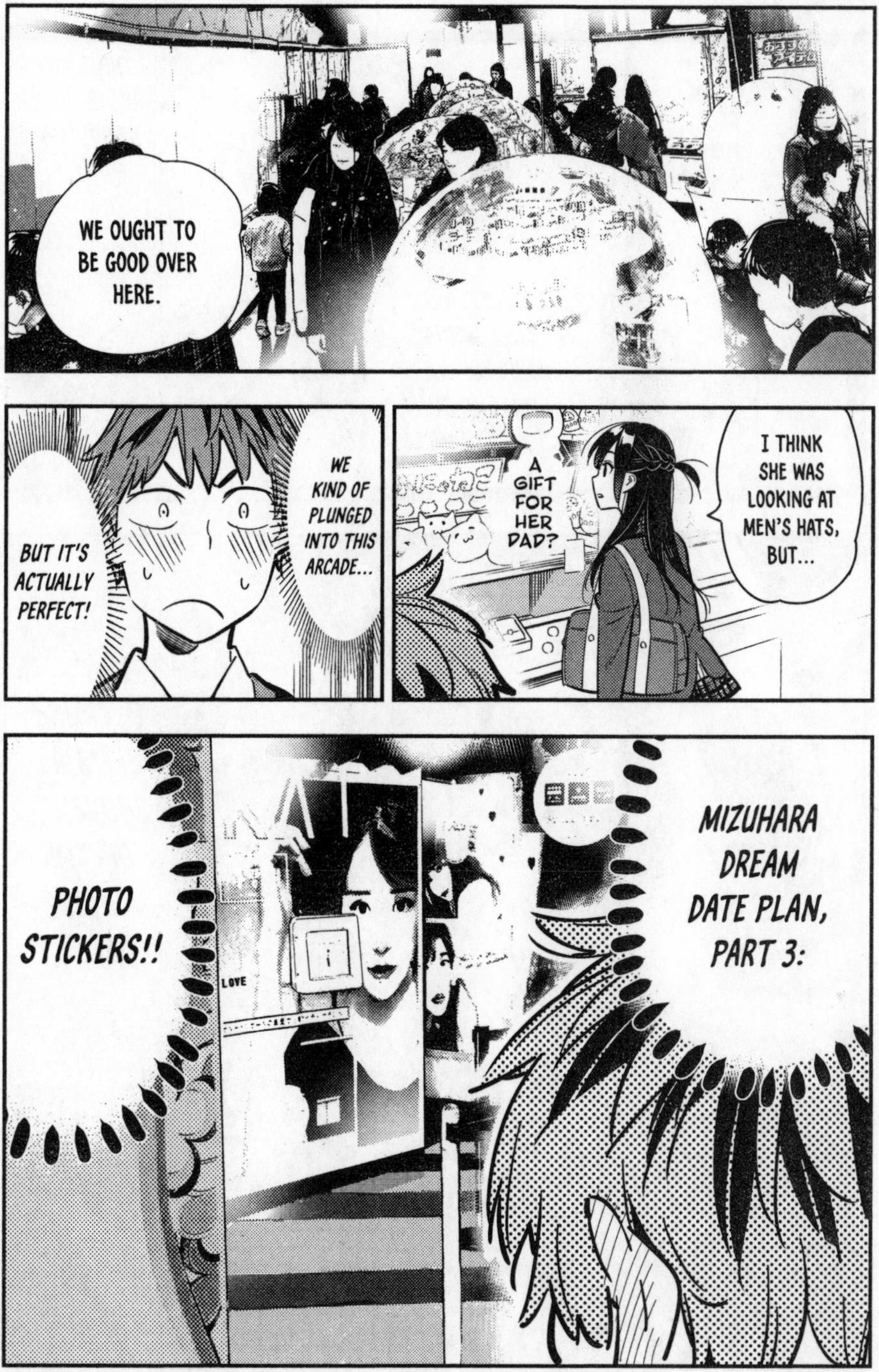
WE OUGHT TO BE GOOD OVER HERE.
I THINK SHE WAS LOOKING AT MEN'S HATS, BUT...
A GIFT FOR HER DAD?
WE KIND OF PLUNGED INTO THIS ARCADE...
BUT IT'S ACTUALLY PERFECT!
MIZUHARA DREAM DATE PLAN, PART 3:
PHOTO STICKERS!!

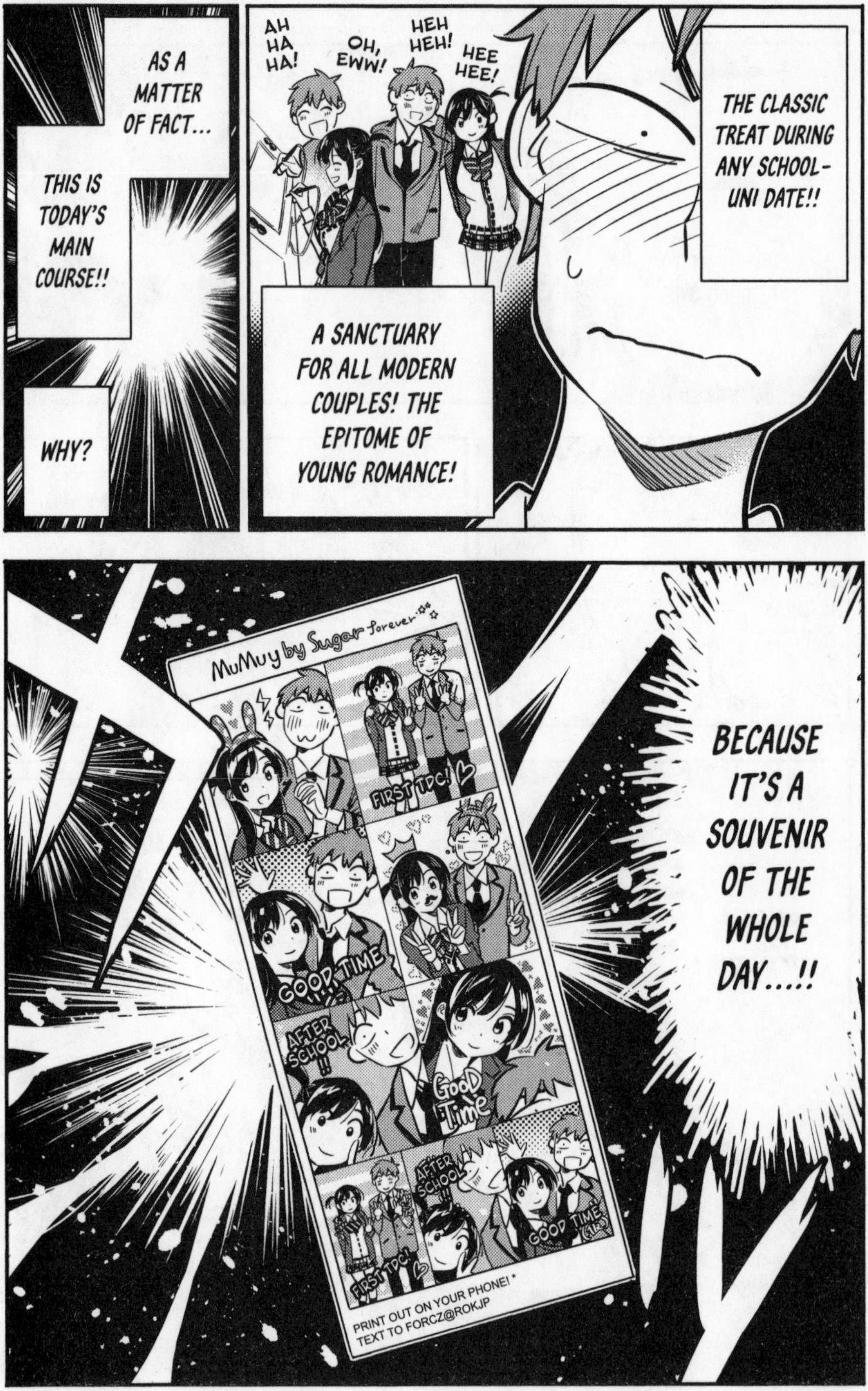
THE CLASSIC TREAT DURING ANY SCHOOL-UNI DATE!!
HEE HEE!
HEH HEH!
OH, EWW!
AH HA HA!
A SANCTUARY FOR ALL MODERN COUPLES! THE EPITOME OF YOUNG ROMANCE!
AS A MATTER OF FACT...
THIS IS TODAY'S MAIN COURSE!!
WHY?
BECAUSE IT'S A SOUVENIR OF THE WHOLE DAY...!!
MuMuy by Sugar forever
FIRST TDC!
GOOD TIME
AFTER SCHOOL!!
GOOD Time
AFTER SCHOOL!!
GOOD TIME
FIRST TDC!
PRINT OUT ON YOUR PHONE! *
TEXT TO FORCZ@ROKJP

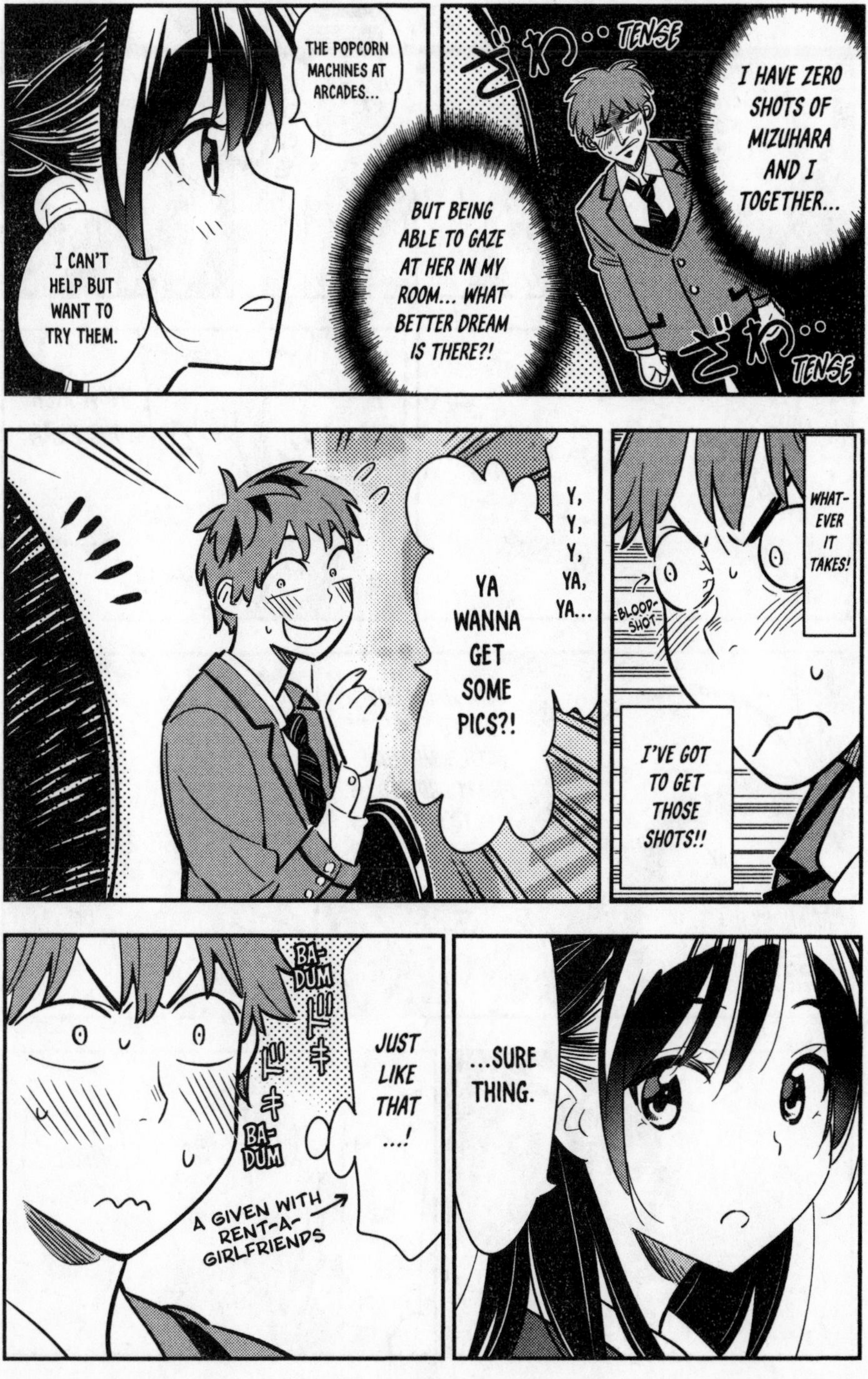
I HAVE ZERO SHOTS OF MIZUHARA AND I TOGETHER...
ざわ‥ TENSE
BUT BEING ABLE TO GAZE AT HER IN MY ROOM... WHAT BETTER DREAM IS THERE?!
ざわ‥ TENSE
THE POPCORN MACHINES AT ARCADES...
I CAN'T HELP BUT WANT TO TRY THEM.
WHAT-EVER IT TAKES!
BLOOD-SHOT
I'VE GOT TO GET THOSE SHOTS!!
Y, Y, Y, YA, YA...
YA WANNA GET SOME PICS?!
...SURE THING.
BA-DUM ドキ
JUST LIKE THAT ...!
ドキ BA-DUM
A GIVEN WITH RENT-A-GIRLFRIENDS

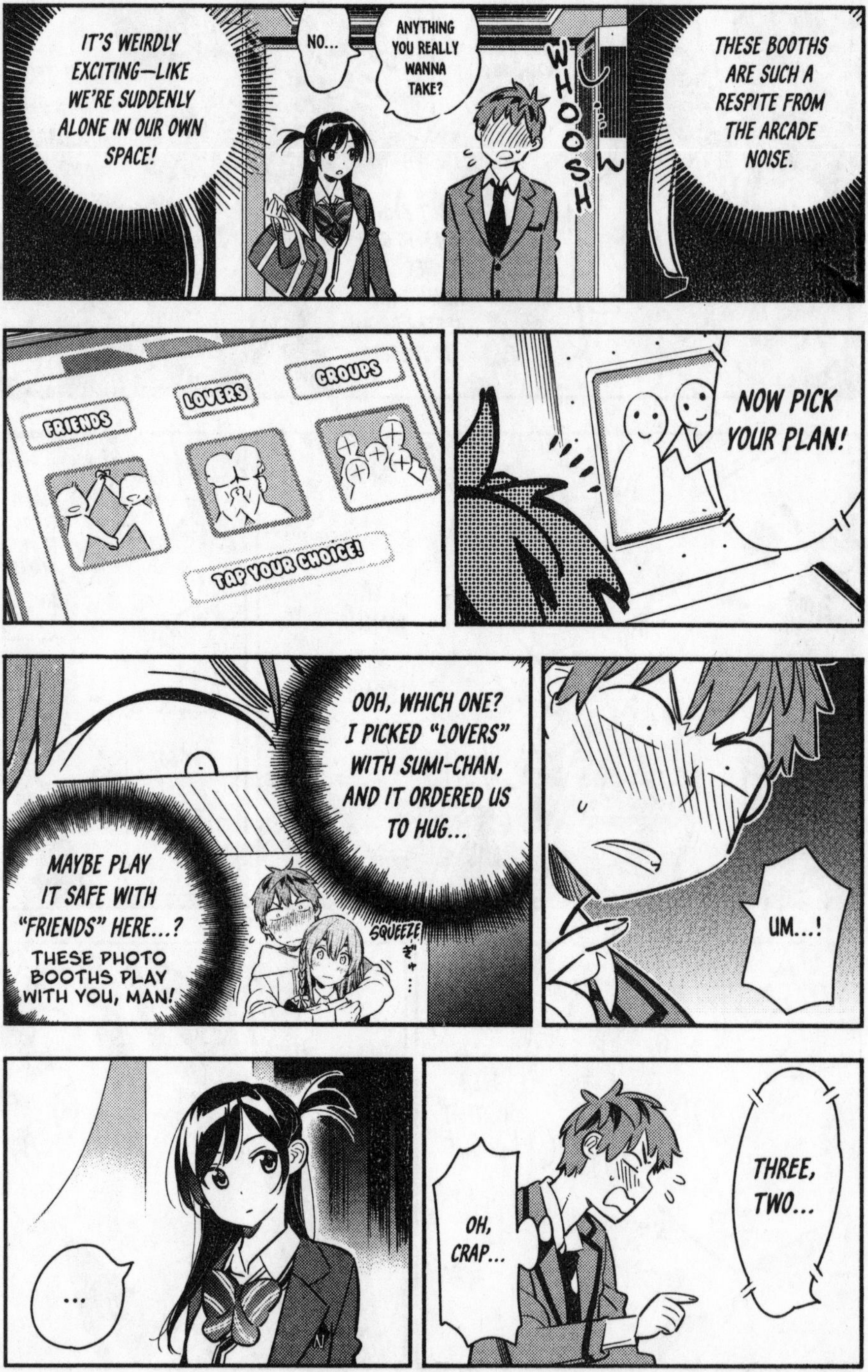
THESE BOOTHS ARE SUCH A RESPITE FROM THE ARCADE NOISE.
WHOOSH
ANYTHING YOU REALLY WANNA TAKE?
NO...
IT'S WEIRDLY EXCITING—LIKE WE'RE SUDDENLY ALONE IN OUR OWN SPACE!
NOW PICK YOUR PLAN!
GROUPS
LOVERS
FRIENDS
TAP YOUR CHOICE!
UM...!
OOH, WHICH ONE? I PICKED "LOVERS" WITH SUMI-CHAN, AND IT ORDERED US TO HUG...
MAYBE PLAY IT SAFE WITH "FRIENDS" HERE...?
THESE PHOTO BOOTHS PLAY WITH YOU, MAN!
SQUEEZE
THREE, TWO...
OH, CRAP...
...

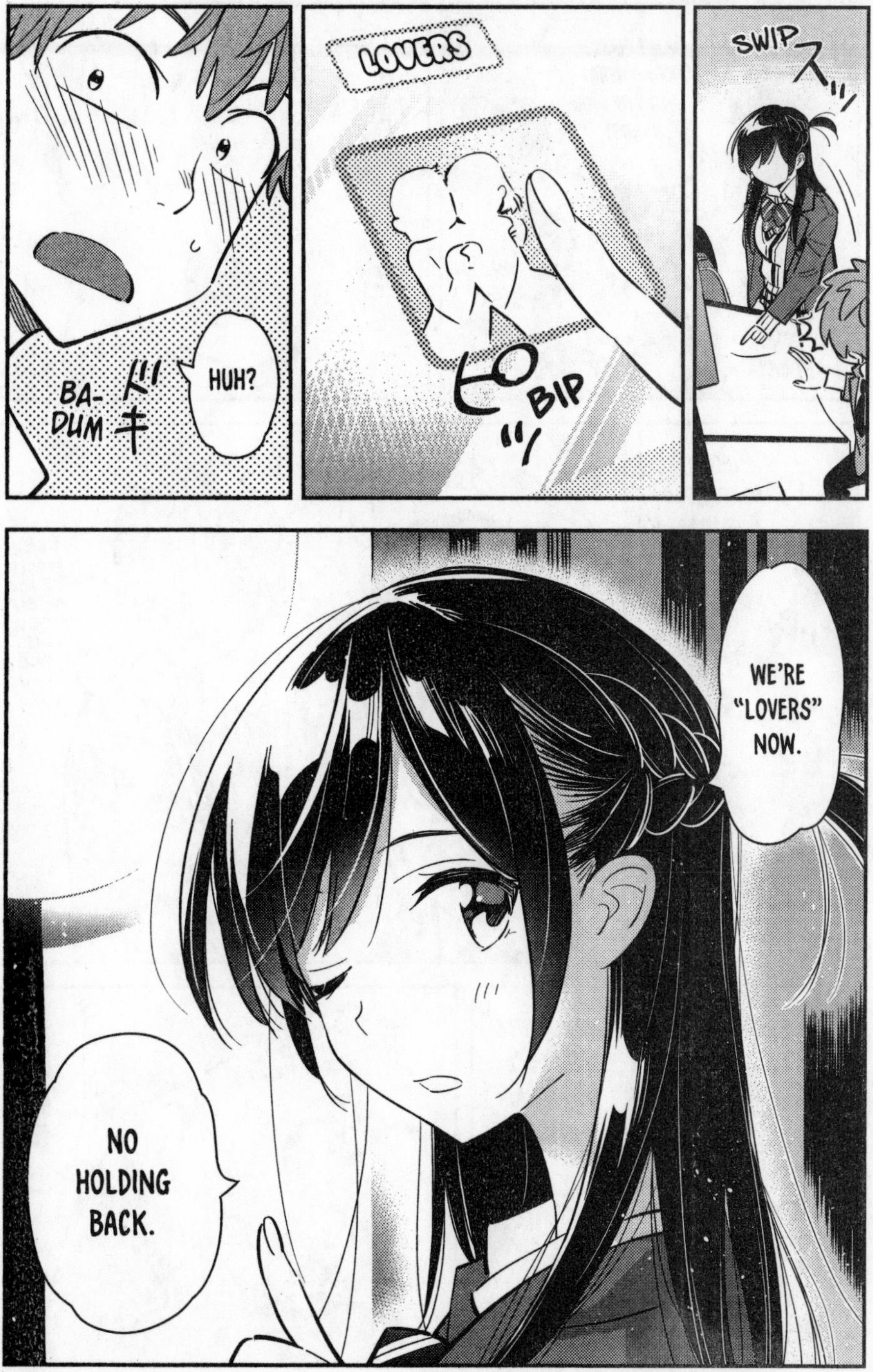
SWIP
LOVERS
BIP
HUH?
BA-DUM
WE'RE "LOVERS" NOW.
NO HOLDING BACK.

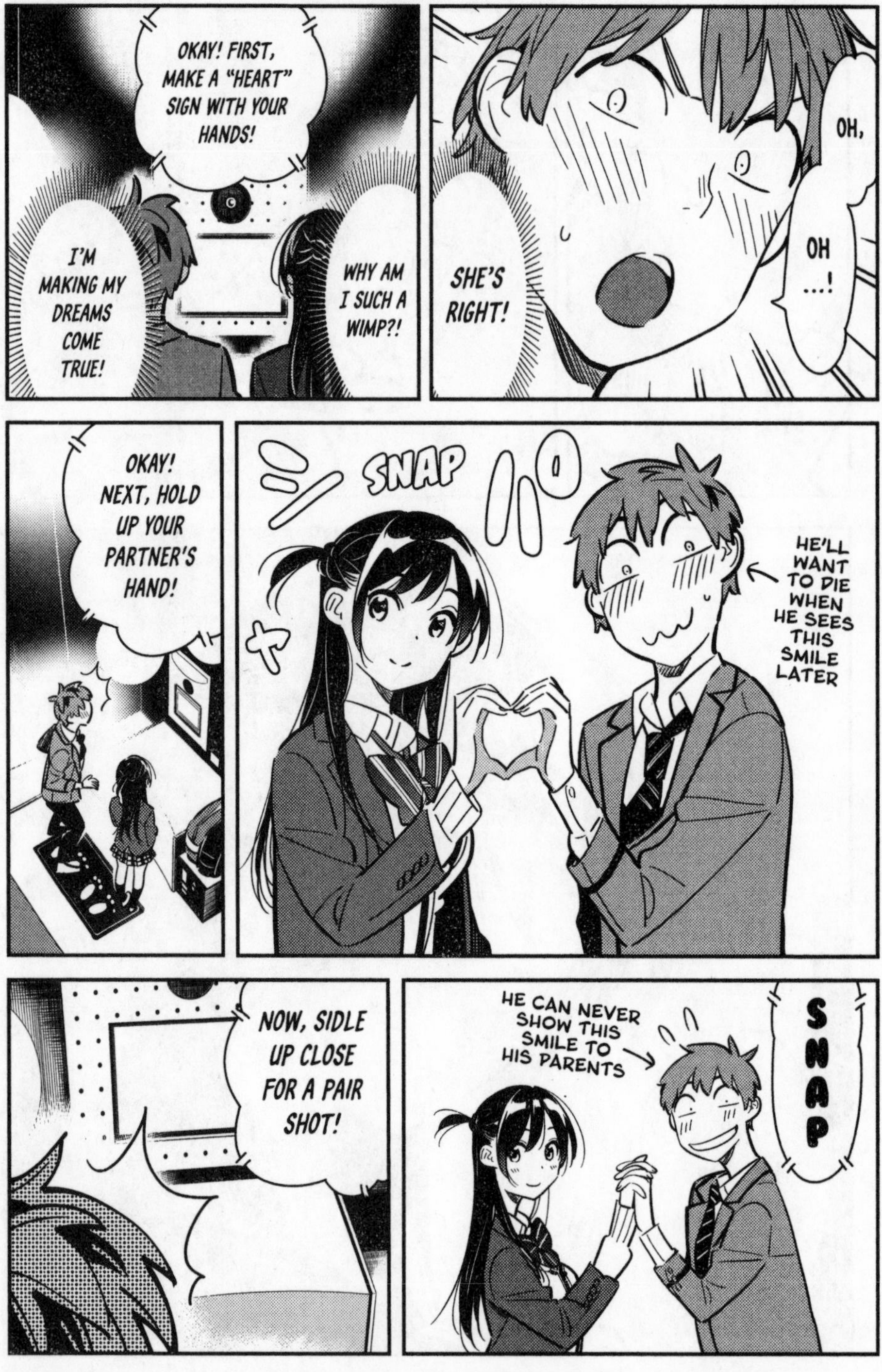
OH,
OH ...!
SHE'S RIGHT!
OKAY! FIRST, MAKE A "HEART" SIGN WITH YOUR HANDS!
WHY AM I SUCH A WIMP?!
I'M MAKING MY DREAMS COME TRUE!
SNAP
HE'LL WANT TO DIE WHEN HE SEES THIS SMILE LATER
OKAY! NEXT, HOLD UP YOUR PARTNER'S HAND!
SNAP
HE CAN NEVER SHOW THIS SMILE TO HIS PARENTS
NOW, SIDLE UP CLOSE FOR A PAIR SHOT!

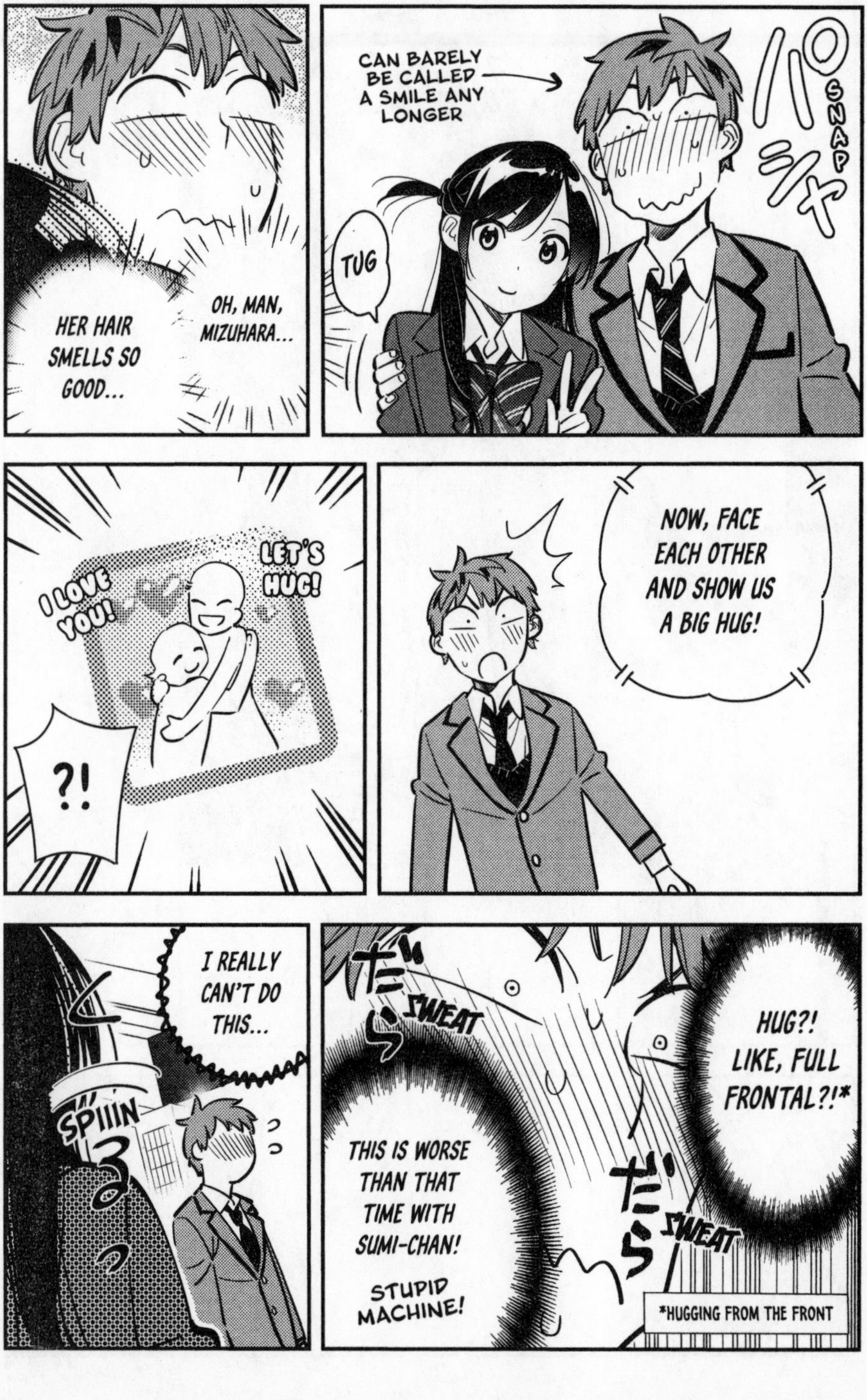

パシャ
SNAP
CAN BARELY BE CALLED A SMILE ANY LONGER
TUG
OH, MAN, MIZUHARA...
HER HAIR SMELLS SO GOOD...
NOW, FACE EACH OTHER AND SHOW US A BIG HUG!
LET'S HUG!
I LOVE YOU!
?!
だら
SWEAT
HUG?! LIKE, FULL FRONTAL?!*
THIS IS WORSE THAN THAT TIME WITH SUMI-CHAN!
STUPID MACHINE!
だら
SWEAT
*HUGGING FROM THE FRONT
I REALLY CAN'T DO THIS...
くるっ
SPIIIN

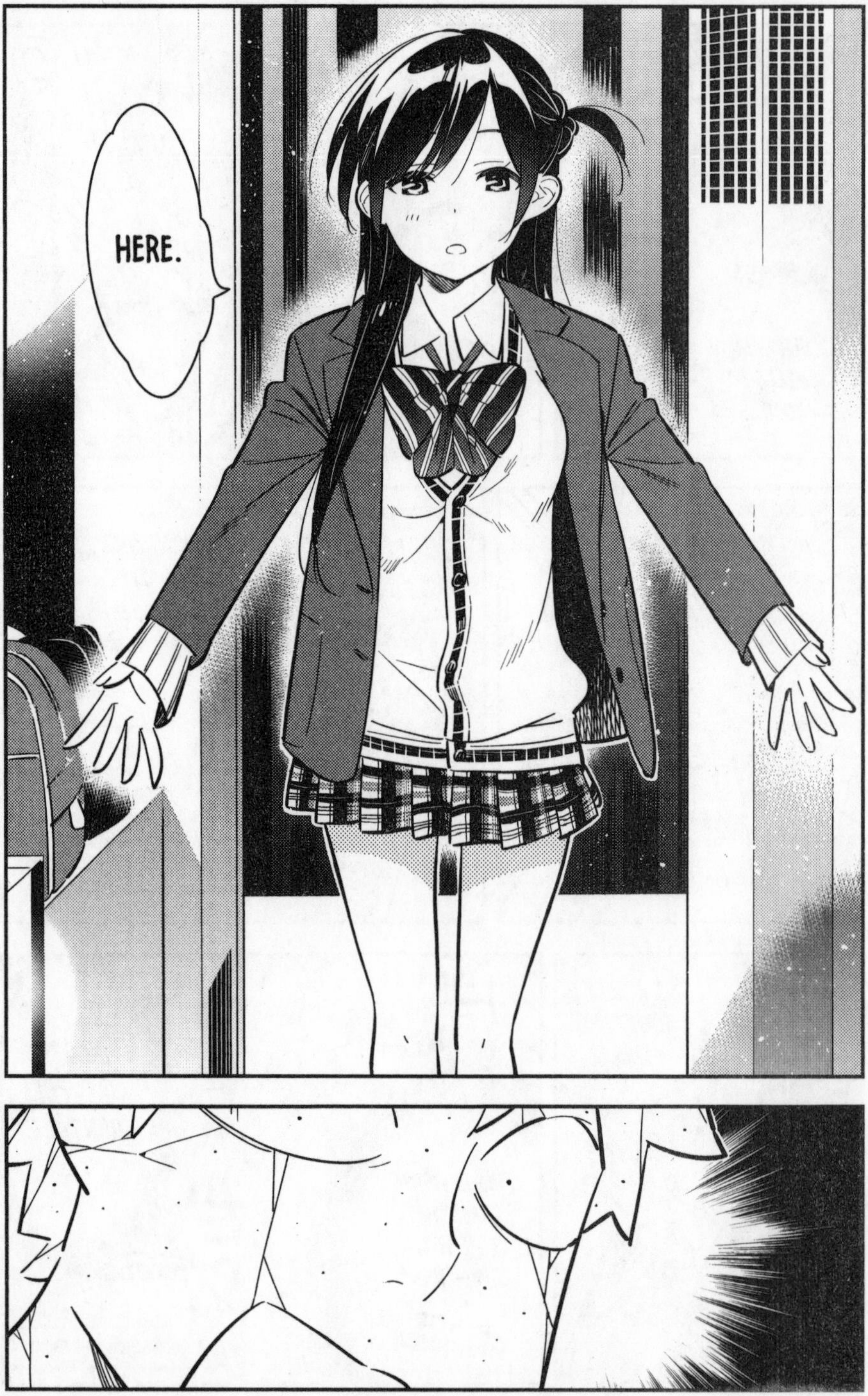
HERE.

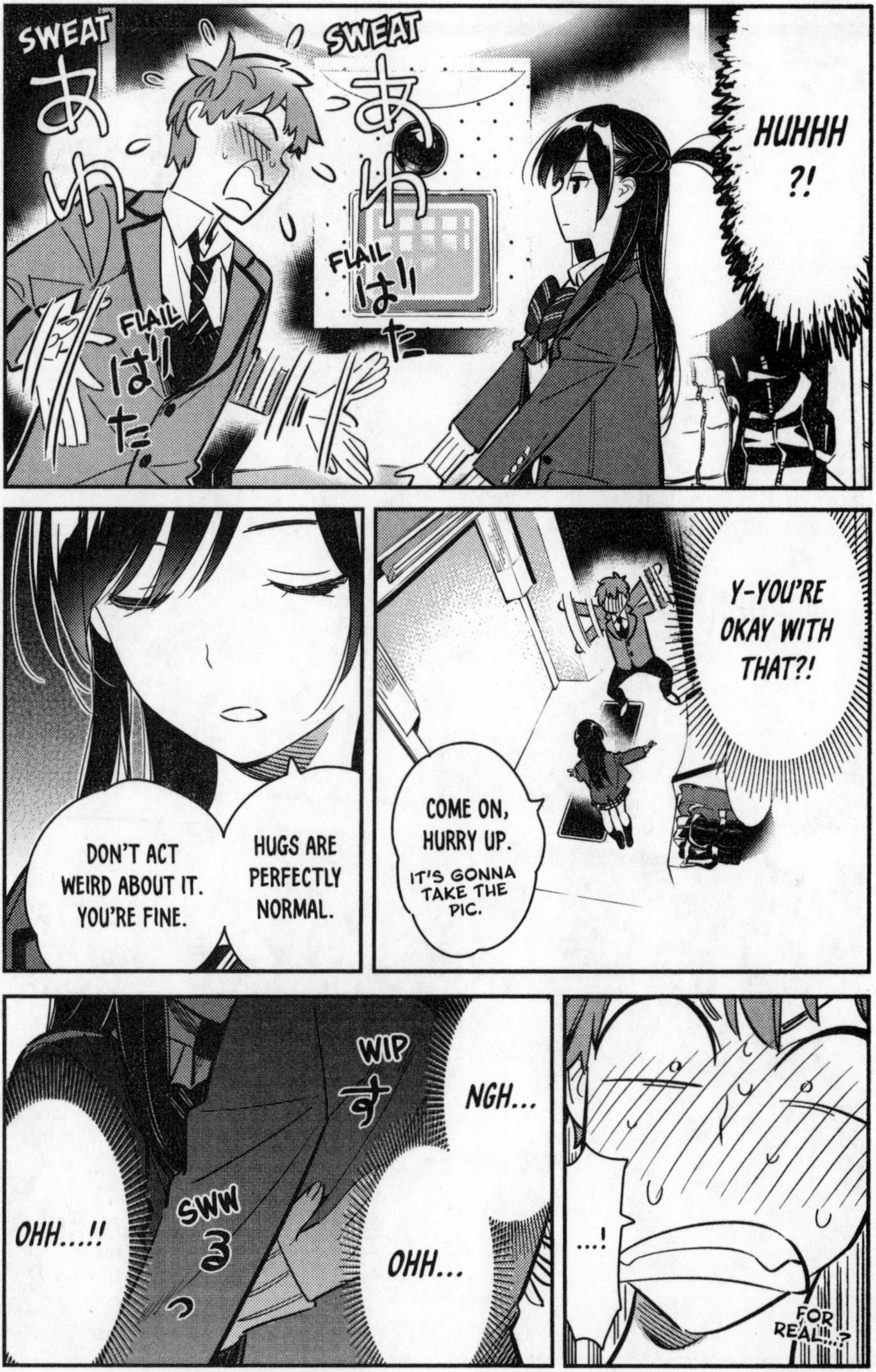
HUHHH ?!
SWEAT
あわ
SWEAT
あわ
FLAIL
ばた
FLAIL
ばた
Y-YOU'RE OKAY WITH THAT?!
COME ON, HURRY UP.
IT'S GONNA TAKE THE PIC.
HUGS ARE PERFECTLY NORMAL.
DON'T ACT WEIRD ABOUT IT. YOU'RE FINE.
...!
FOR REAL...?
NGH...
WIP
す
OHH...
SWW
るっ
OHH...!!

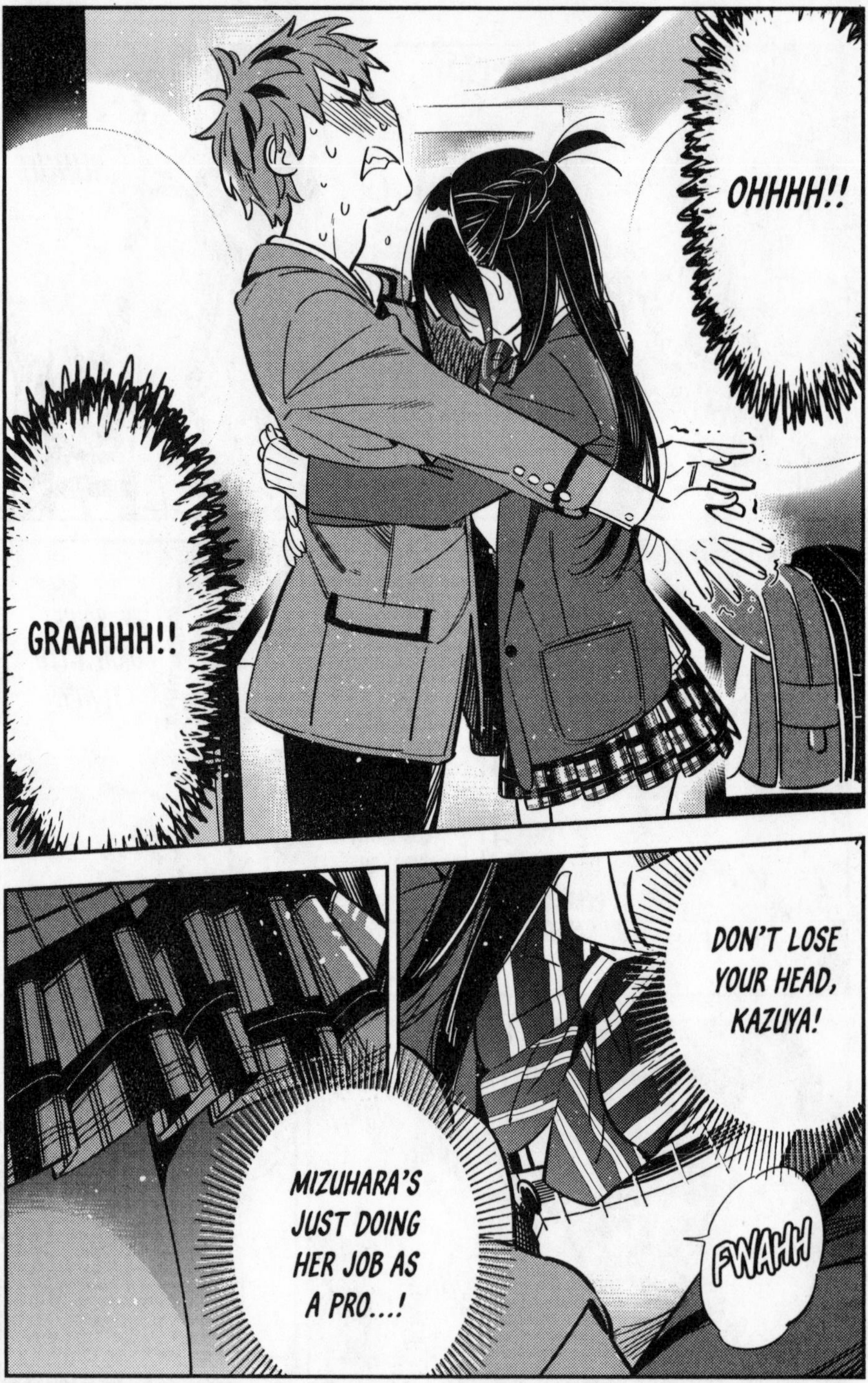
OHHHH!!
GRAAHHH!!
DON'T LOSE YOUR HEAD, KAZUYA!
FWAHH
MIZUHARA'S JUST DOING HER JOB AS A PRO...!

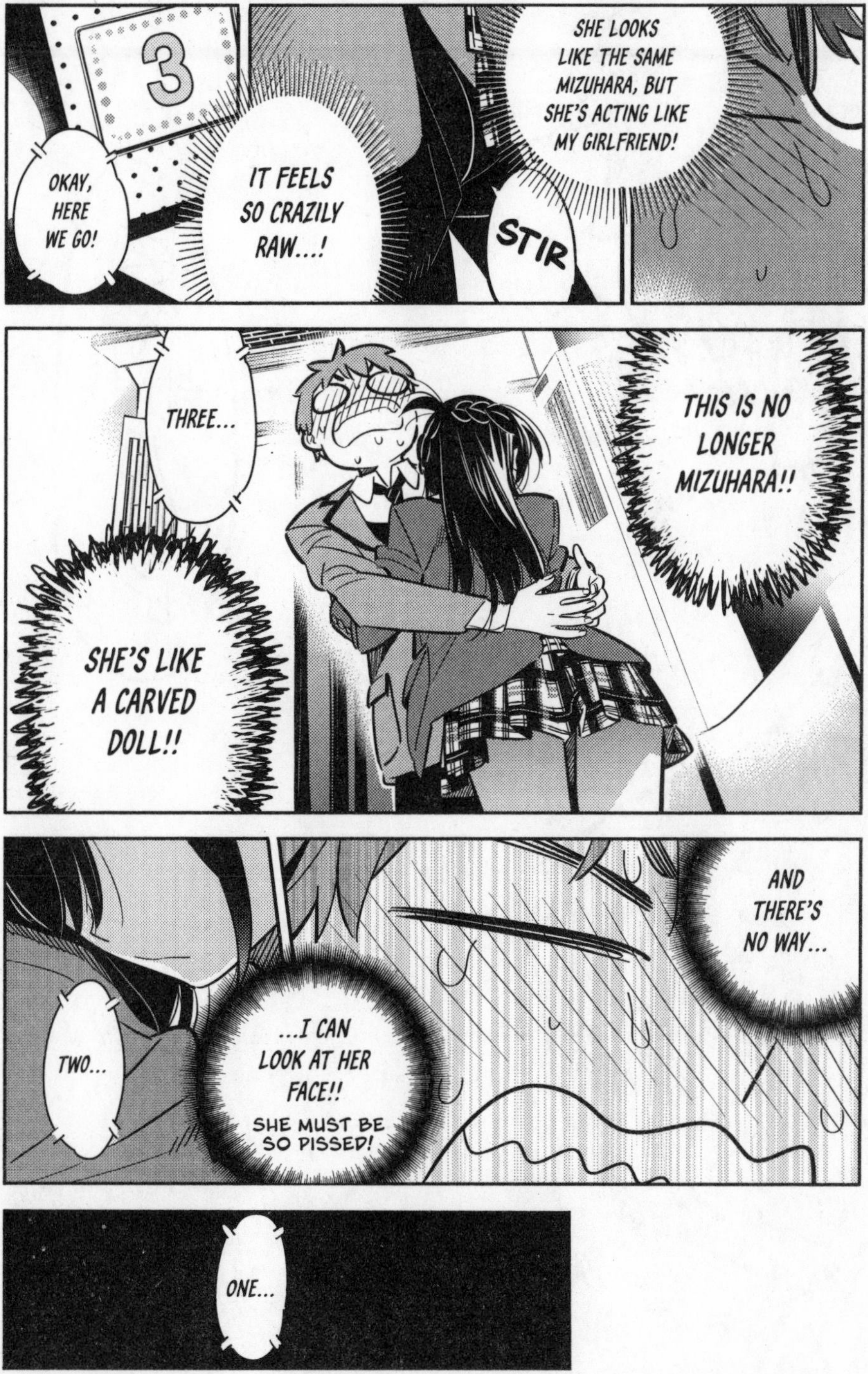

SHE LOOKS LIKE THE SAME MIZUHARA, BUT SHE'S ACTING LIKE MY GIRLFRIEND!
STIR
IT FEELS SO CRAZILY RAW...!
OKAY, HERE WE GO!
THIS IS NO LONGER MIZUHARA!!
THREE...
SHE'S LIKE A CARVED DOLL!!
AND THERE'S NO WAY...
...I CAN LOOK AT HER FACE!!
SHE MUST BE SO PISSED!
TWO...
ONE...

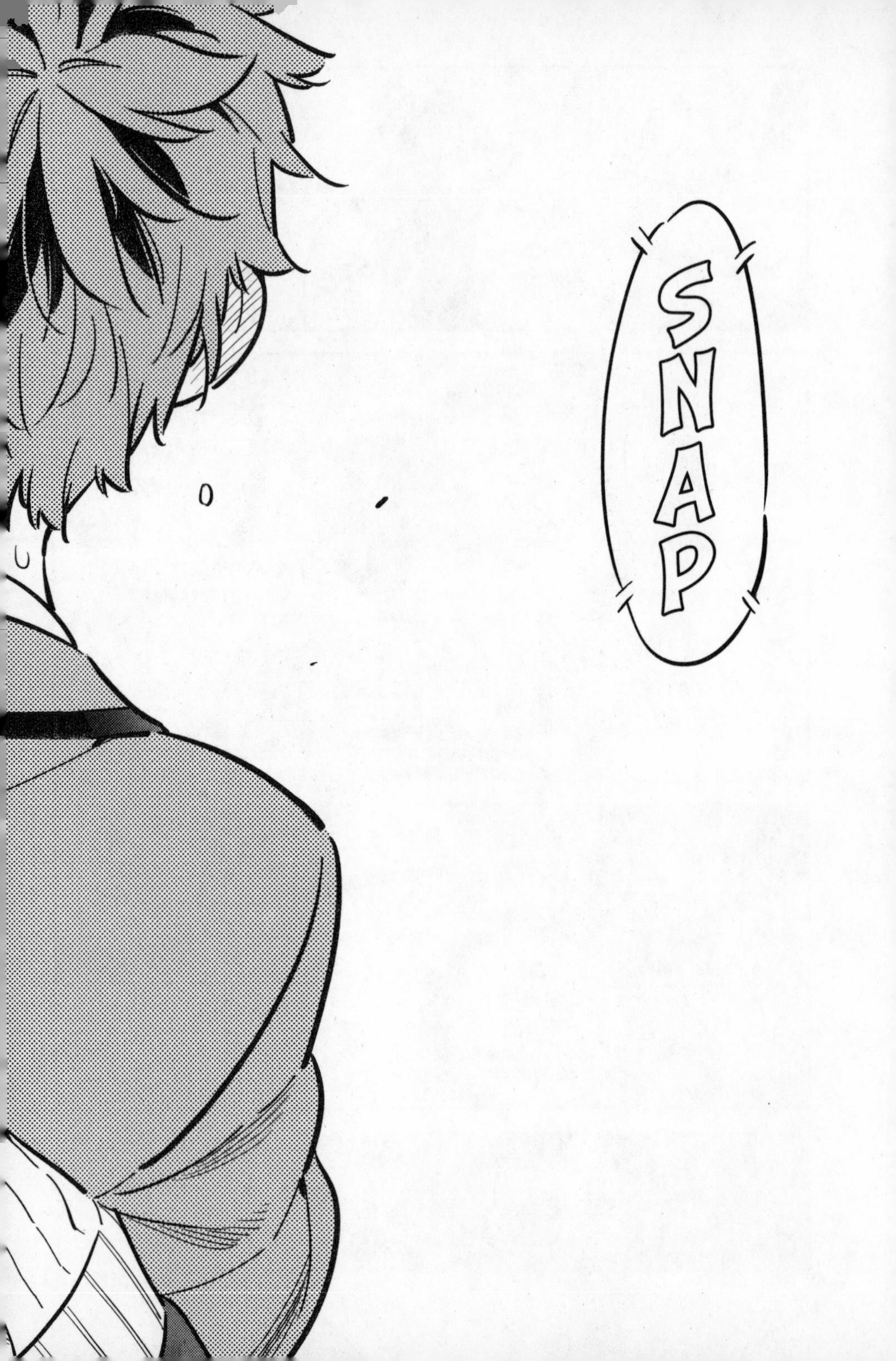
SNAP

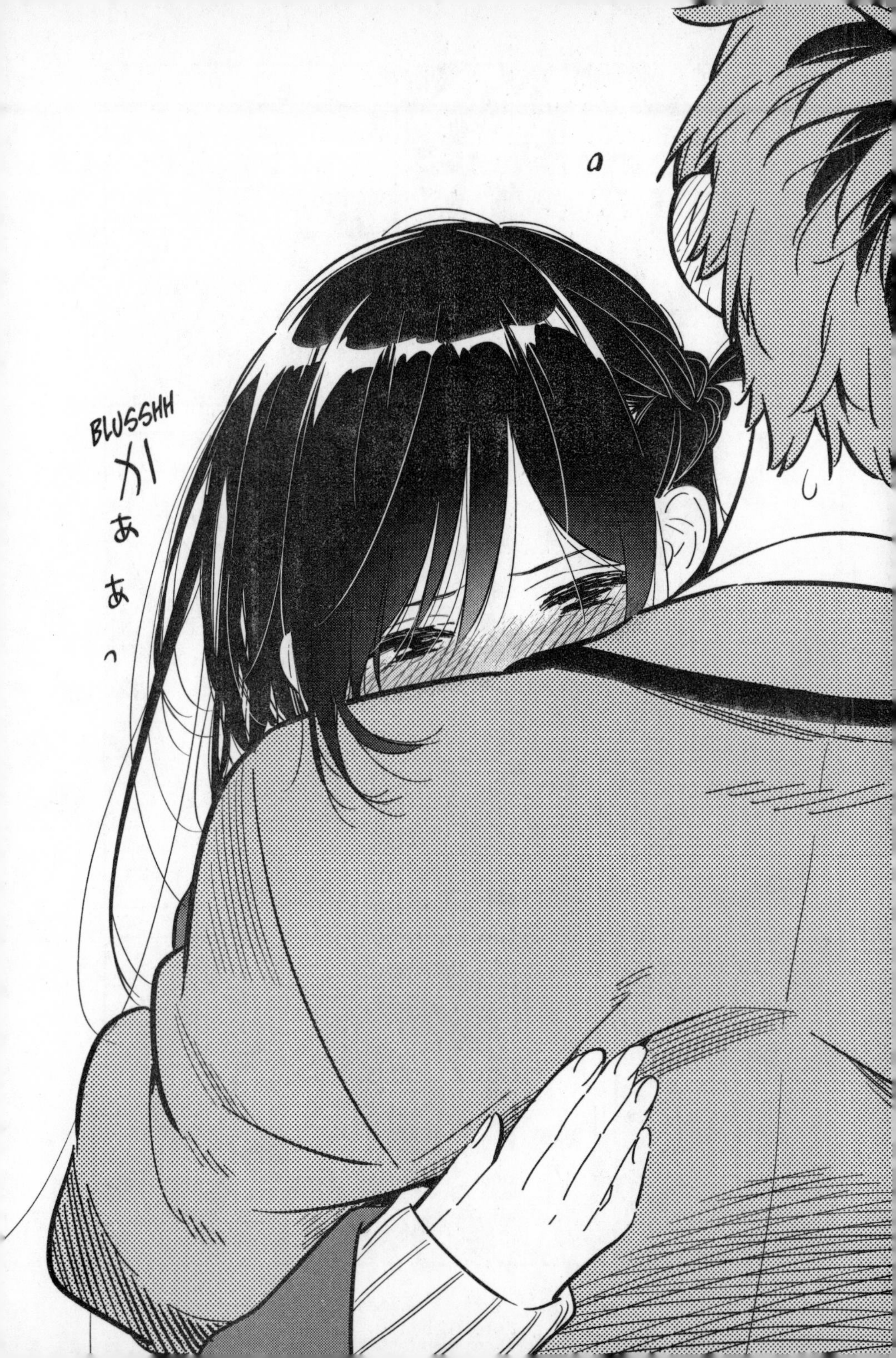
BLUSSHH
カあぁっ

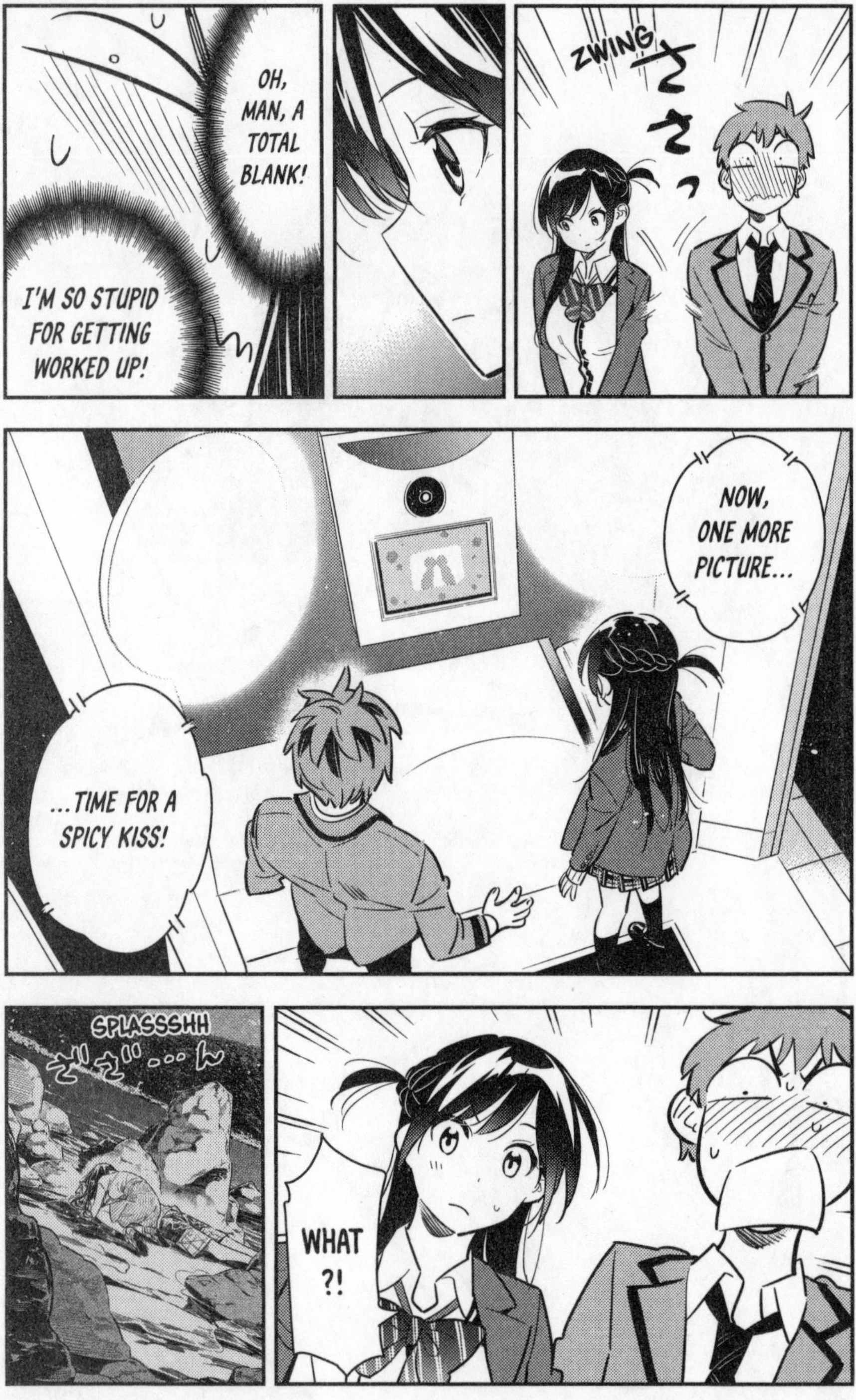
ZWING
さっ
OH, MAN, A TOTAL BLANK!
I'M SO STUPID FOR GETTING WORKED UP!
NOW, ONE MORE PICTURE...
...TIME FOR A SPICY KISS!
WHAT?!
SPLASSSHH
ざざ…ん

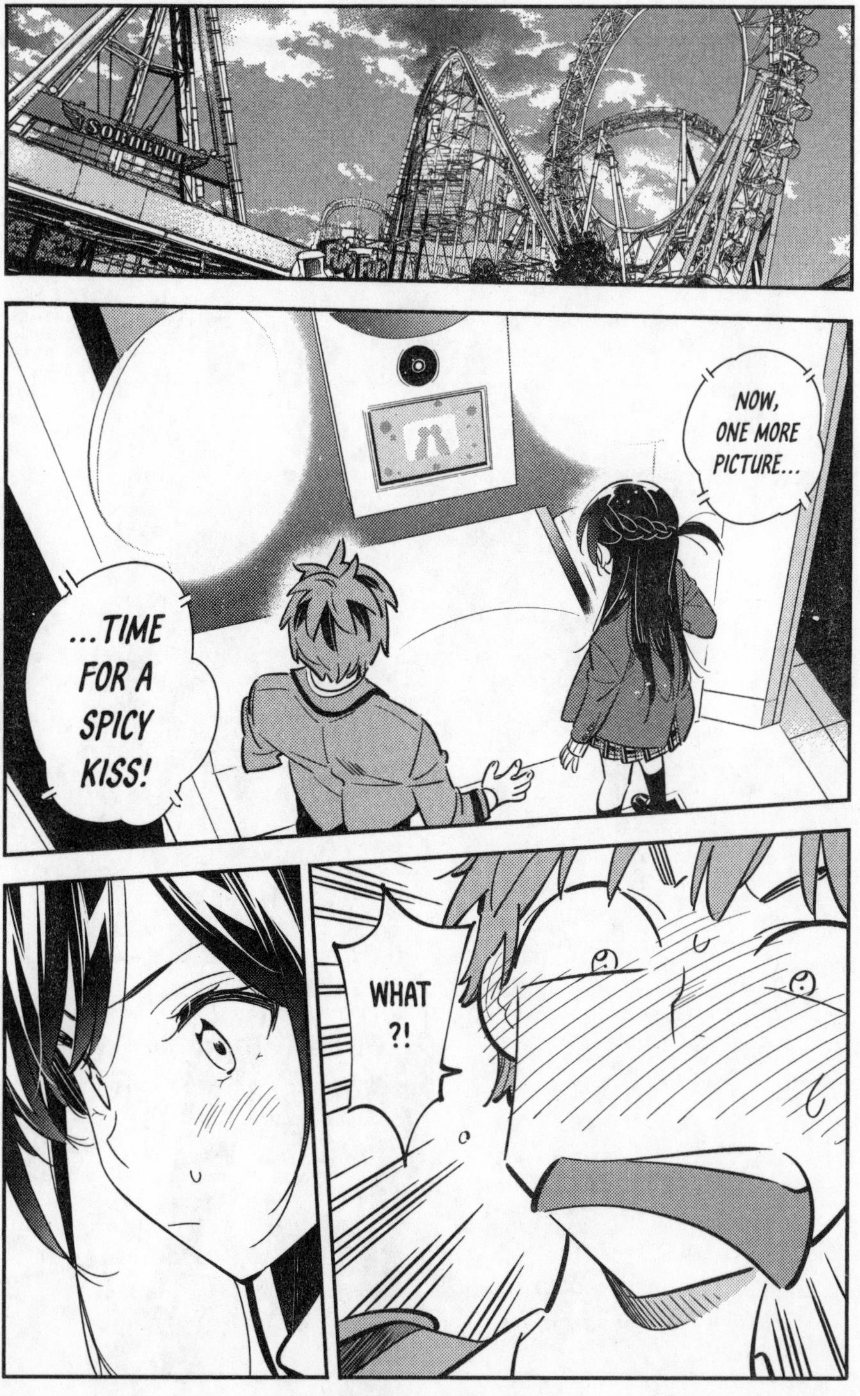
NOW, ONE MORE PICTURE...
...TIME FOR A SPICY KISS!
WHAT ?!

RATING 81 MY GIRLFRIEND AND MY DREAM DATE 4

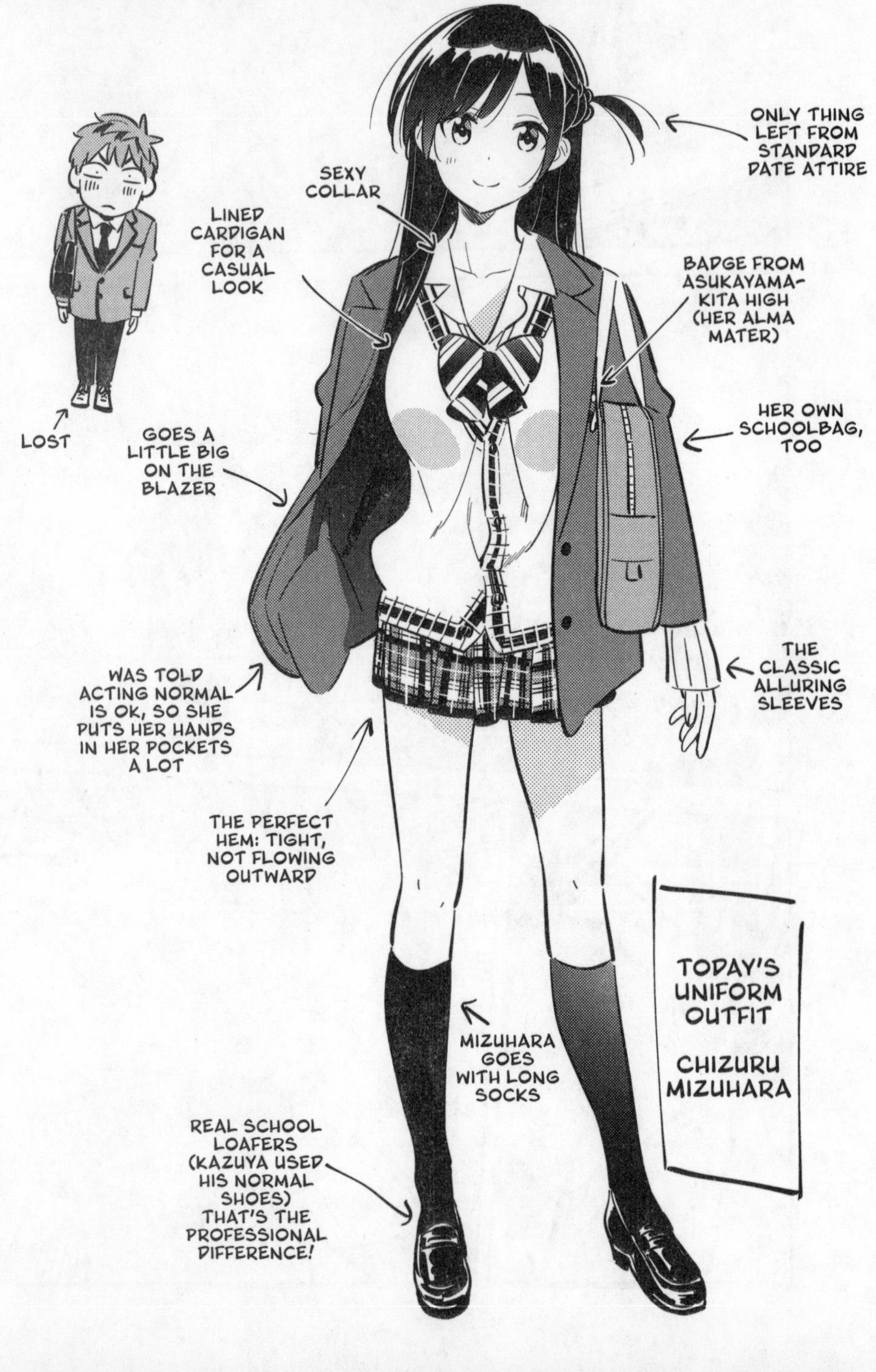

ONLY THING LEFT FROM STANDARD DATE ATTIRE
SEXY COLLAR
LINED CARDIGAN FOR A CASUAL LOOK
BADGE FROM ASUKAYAMA-KITA HIGH (HER ALMA MATER)
LOST
HER OWN SCHOOLBAG, TOO
GOES A LITTLE BIG ON THE BLAZER
THE CLASSIC ALLURING SLEEVES
WAS TOLD ACTING NORMAL IS OK, SO SHE PUTS HER HANDS IN HER POCKETS A LOT
THE PERFECT HEM: TIGHT, NOT FLOWING OUTWARD
TODAY'S UNIFORM OUTFIT
CHIZURU MIZUHARA
MIZUHARA GOES WITH LONG SOCKS
REAL SCHOOL LOAFERS (KAZUYA USED HIS NORMAL SHOES) THAT'S THE PROFESSIONAL DIFFERENCE!

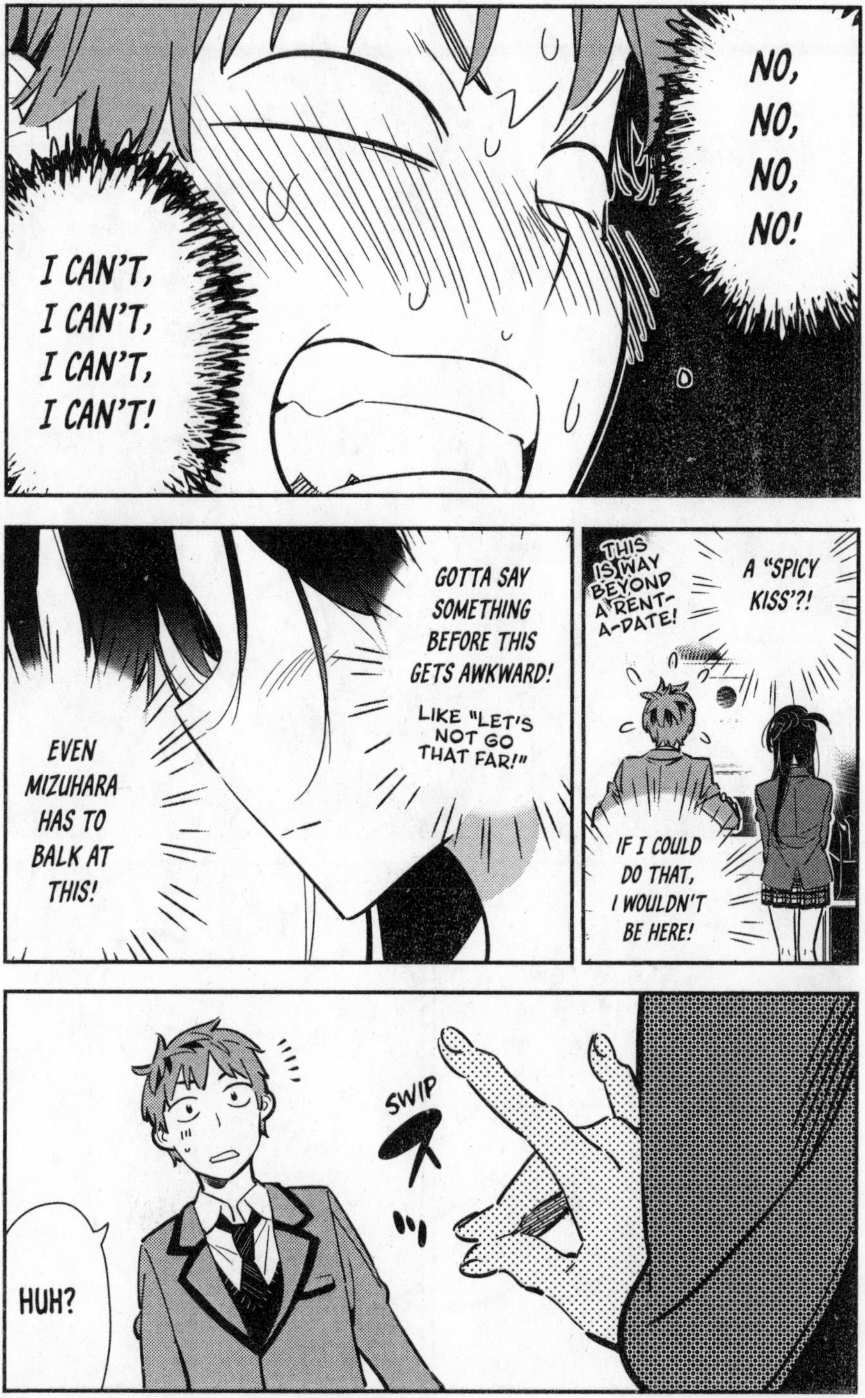
NO, NO, NO, NO!
I CAN'T, I CAN'T, I CAN'T, I CAN'T!
A "SPICY KISS"?!
THIS IS WAY BEYOND A RENT-A-DATE!
IF I COULD DO THAT, I WOULDN'T BE HERE!
GOTTA SAY SOMETHING BEFORE THIS GETS AWKWARD!
LIKE "LET'S NOT GO THAT FAR!"
EVEN MIZUHARA HAS TO BALK AT THIS!
SWIP
HUH?

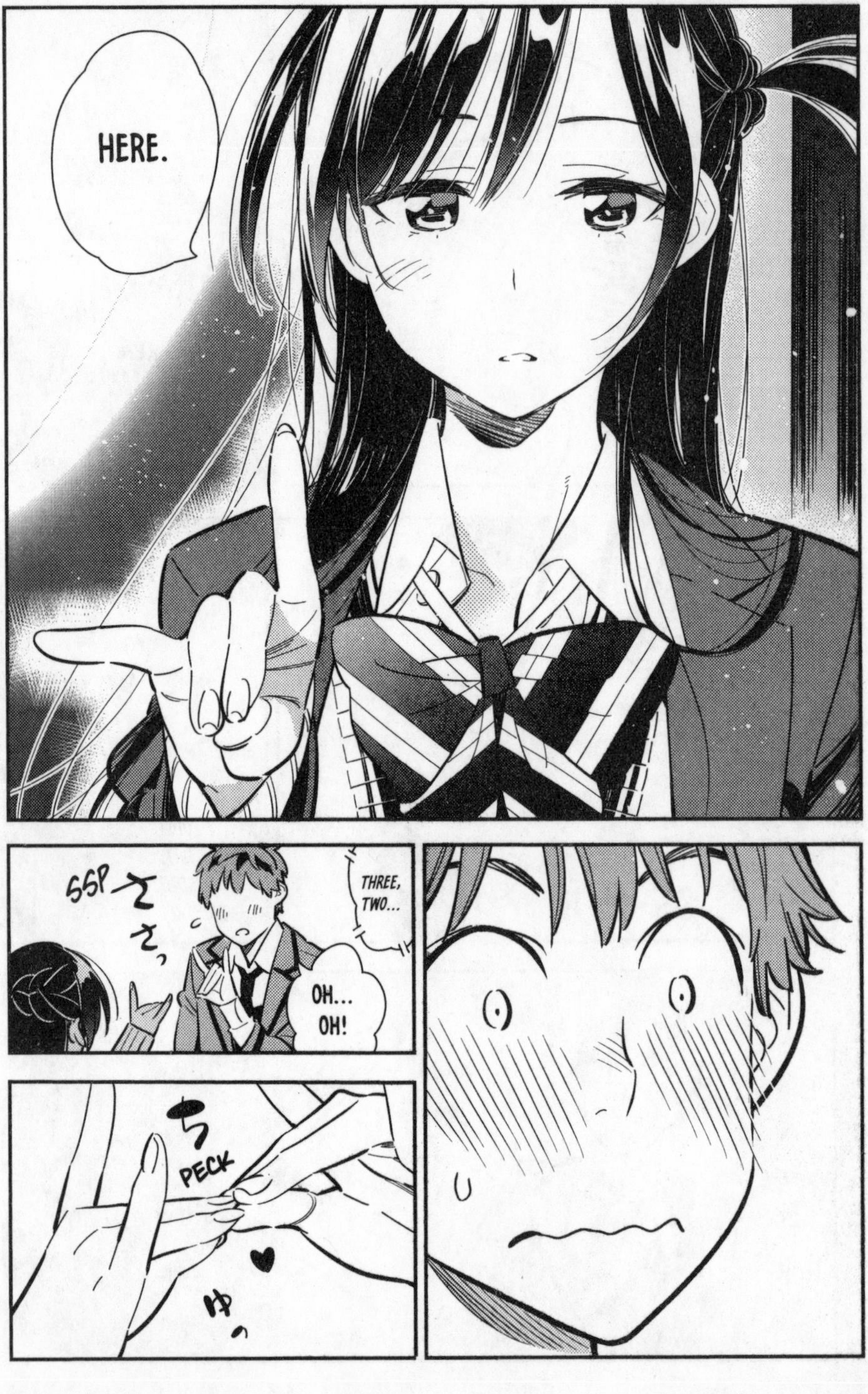
HERE.
THREE, TWO...
OH... OH!
SSP
さっ
PECK

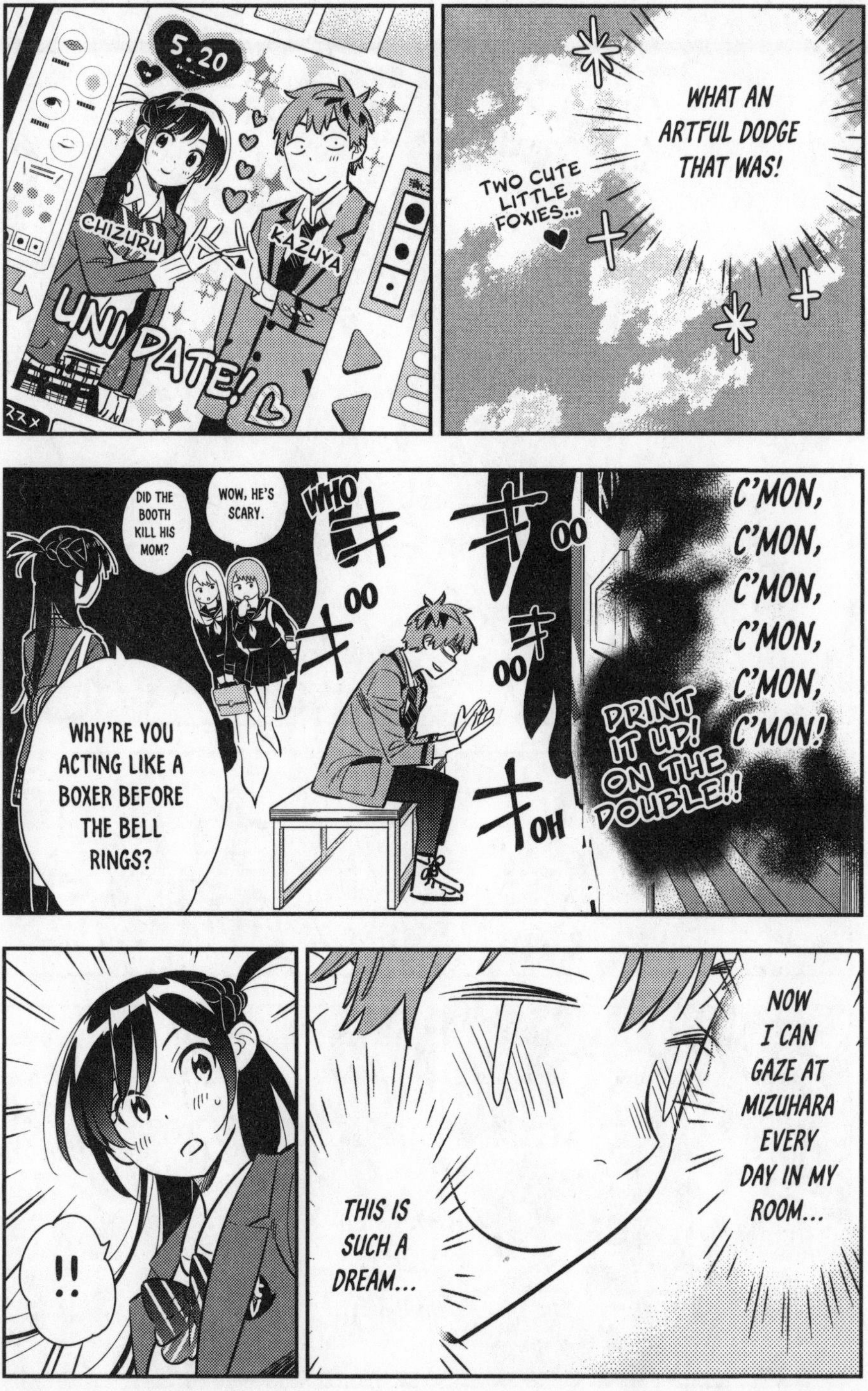
WHAT AN ARTFUL DODGE THAT WAS!
TWO CUTE LITTLE FOXIES... ♥
5.20
CHIZURU
KAZUYA
UNI DATE!
ススメ
C'MON, C'MON, C'MON, C'MON, C'MON, C'MON!
PRINT IT UP! ON THE DOUBLE!!
WHO
OO
OO
OO
OH
WOW, HE'S SCARY.
DID THE BOOTH KILL HIS MOM?
WHY'RE YOU ACTING LIKE A BOXER BEFORE THE BELL RINGS?
NOW I CAN GAZE AT MIZUHARA EVERY DAY IN MY ROOM...
THIS IS SUCH A DREAM...
!!

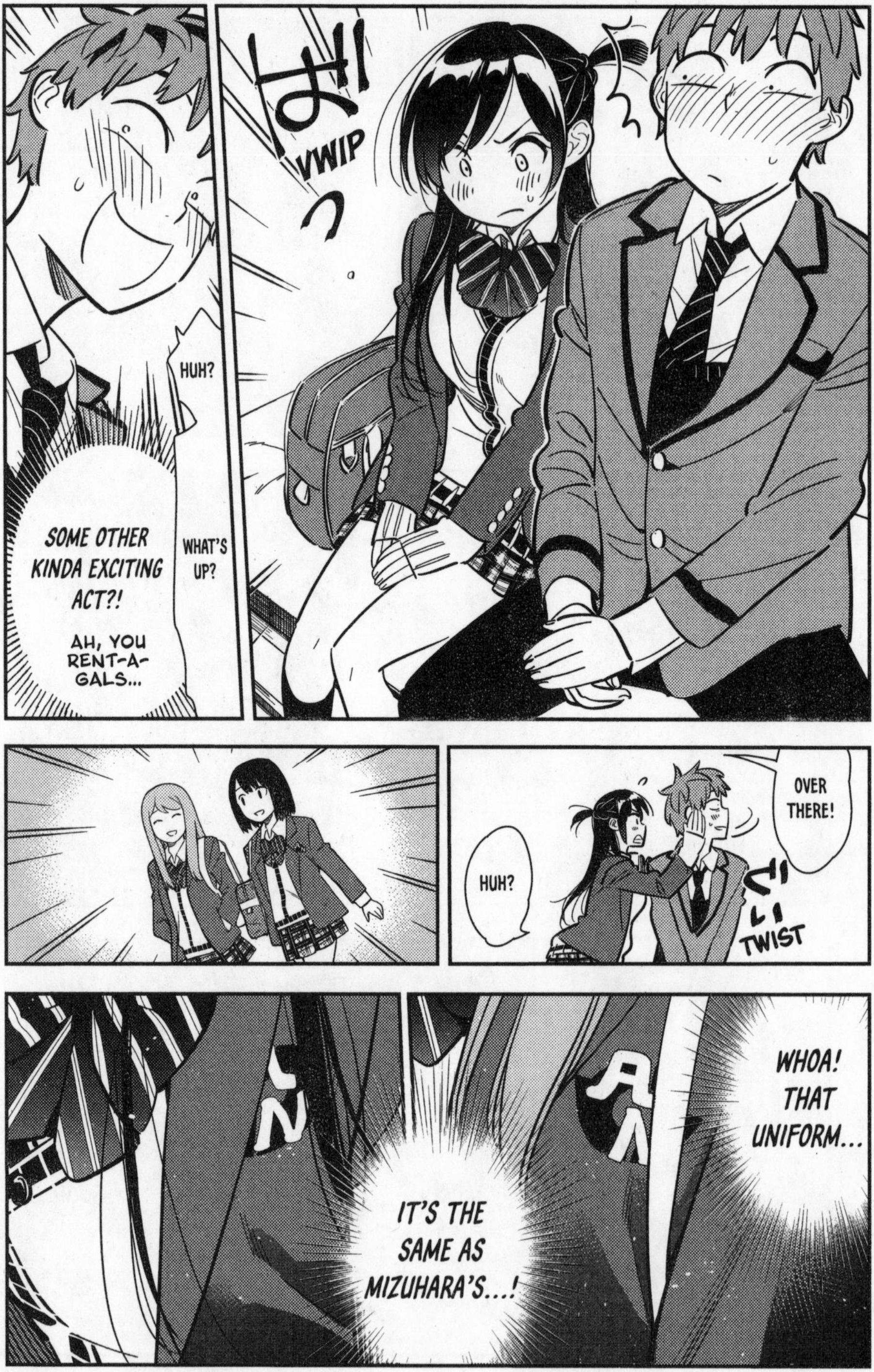
VWIP
HUH?
WHAT'S UP?
SOME OTHER KINDA EXCITING ACT?!
AH, YOU RENT-A-GALS...
OVER THERE!
HUH?
TWIST
WHOA! THAT UNIFORM...
IT'S THE SAME AS MIZUHARA'S...!

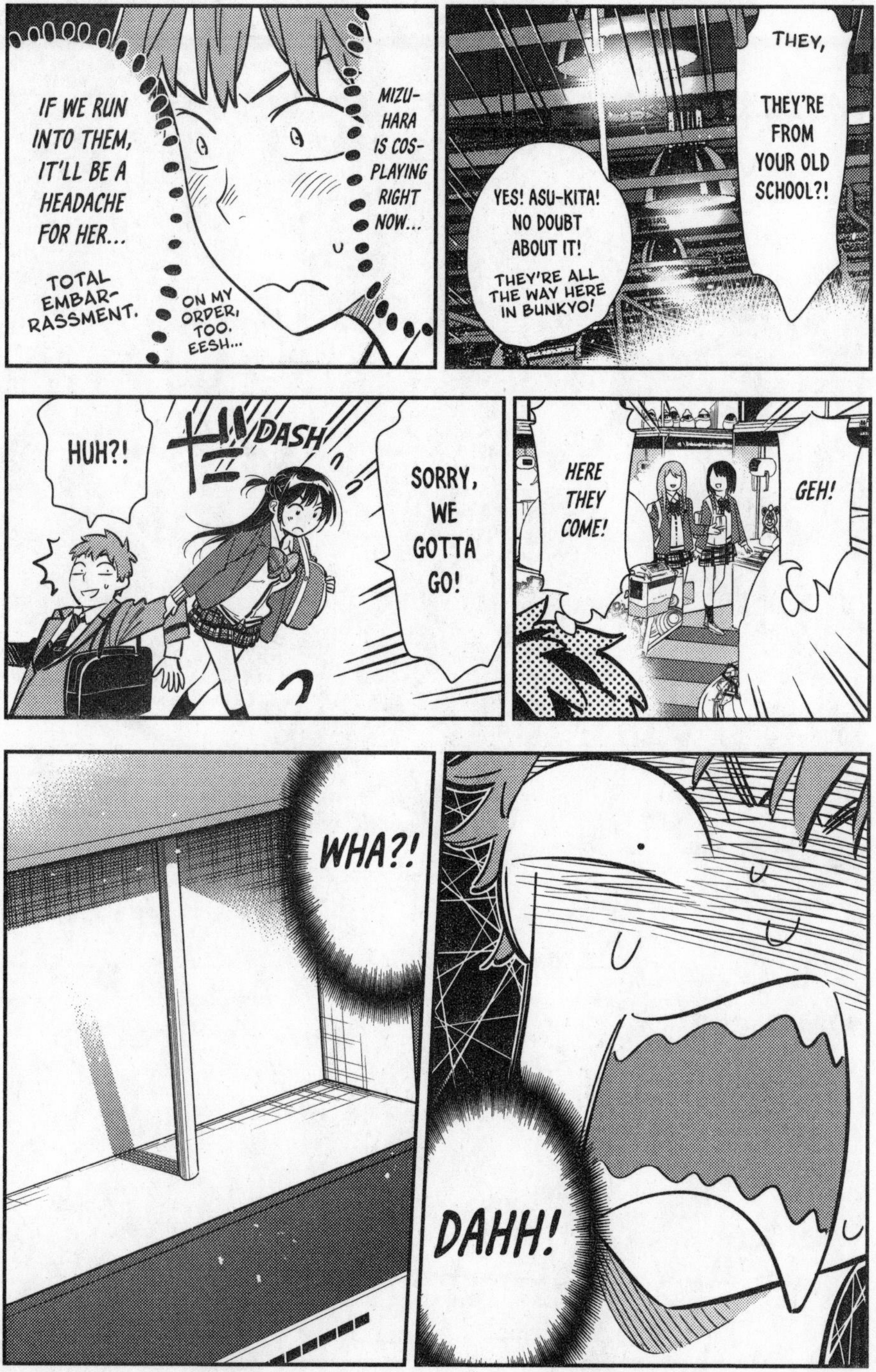
THEY,
THEY'RE FROM YOUR OLD SCHOOL?!
YES! ASU-KITA! NO DOUBT ABOUT IT!
THEY'RE ALL THE WAY HERE IN BUNKYO!
MIZU-HARA IS COS-PLAYING RIGHT NOW...
IF WE RUN INTO THEM, IT'LL BE A HEADACHE FOR HER...
TOTAL EMBAR-RASSMENT.
ON MY ORDER, TOO. EESH...
GEH!
HERE THEY COME!
SORRY, WE GOTTA GO!
DASH
HUH?!
WHA?!
DAHH!

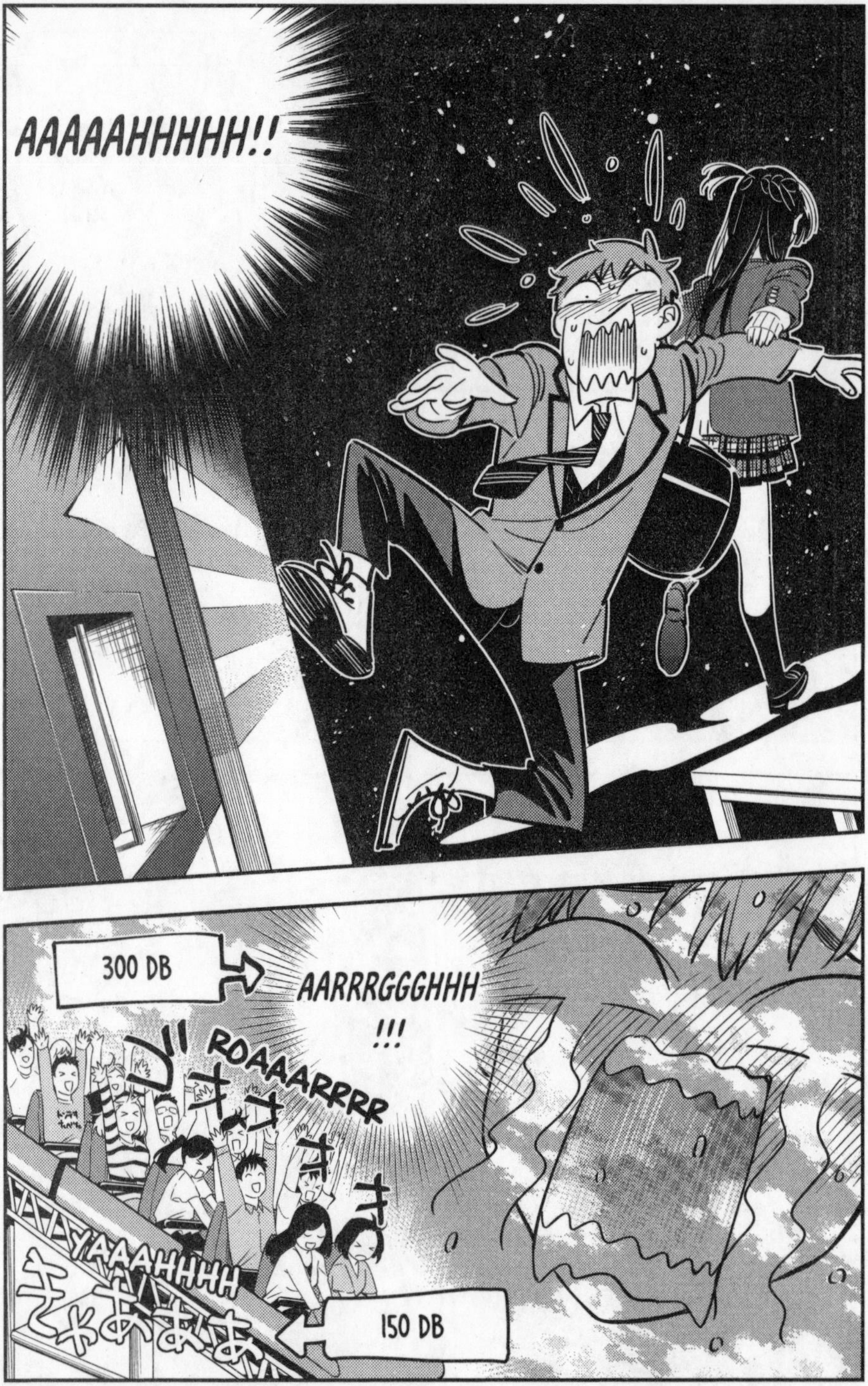
AAAAAHHHHH!!
300 DB
AARRRGGGHHH
!!!
ROAAAARRRR
YAAAHHHH
150 DB

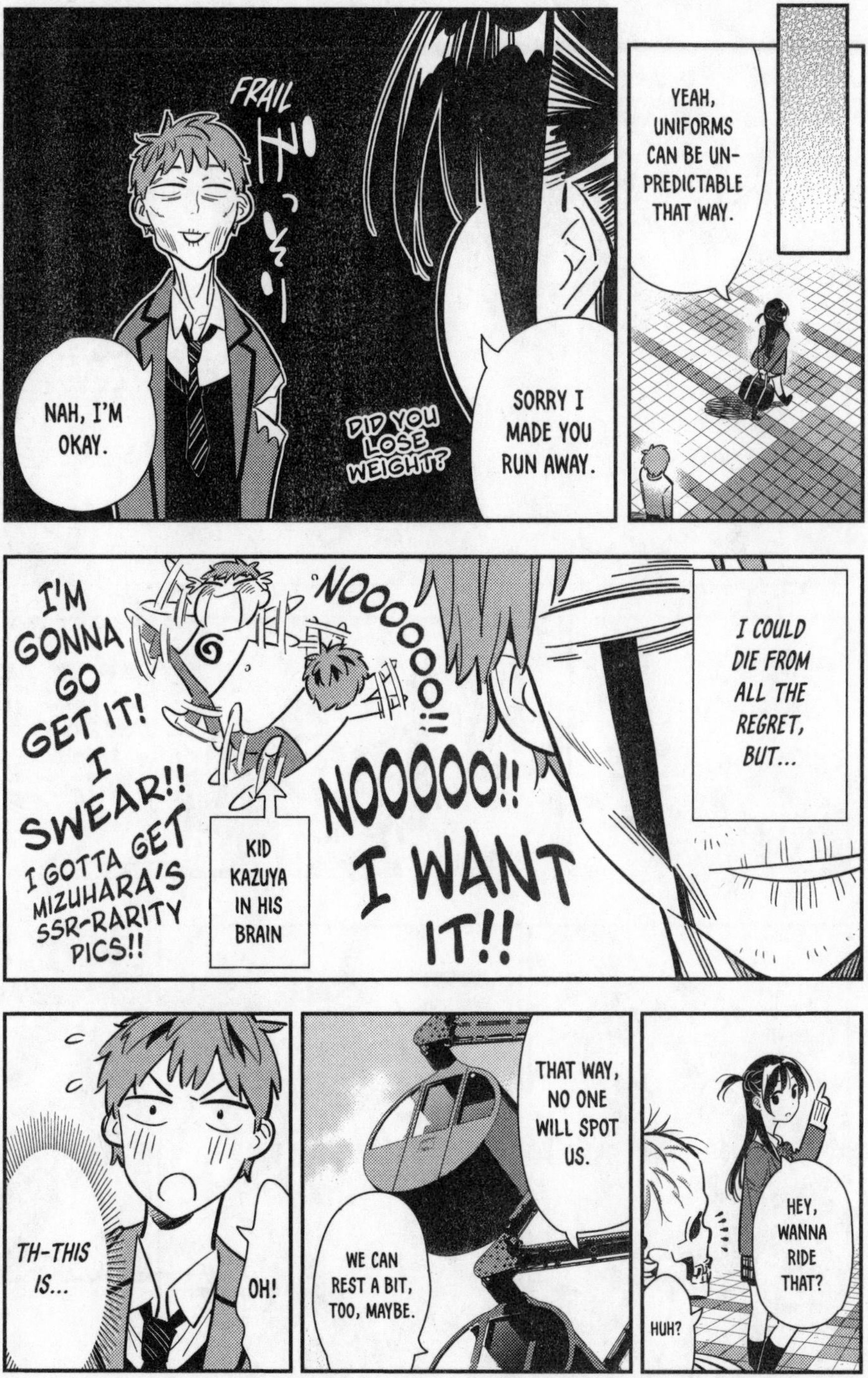
YEAH, UNIFORMS CAN BE UN-PREDICTABLE THAT WAY.
SORRY I MADE YOU RUN AWAY.
DID YOU LOSE WEIGHT?
FRAIL
NAH, I'M OKAY.
I COULD DIE FROM ALL THE REGRET, BUT...
NOOOOOOO!!
NOOOOO!! I WANT IT!!
KID KAZUYA IN HIS BRAIN
I'M GONNA GO GET IT! I SWEAR!!
I GOTTA GET MIZUHARA'S SSR-RARITY PICS!!
HEY, WANNA RIDE THAT?
HUH?
THAT WAY, NO ONE WILL SPOT US.
WE CAN REST A BIT, TOO, MAYBE.
OH!
TH-THIS IS...

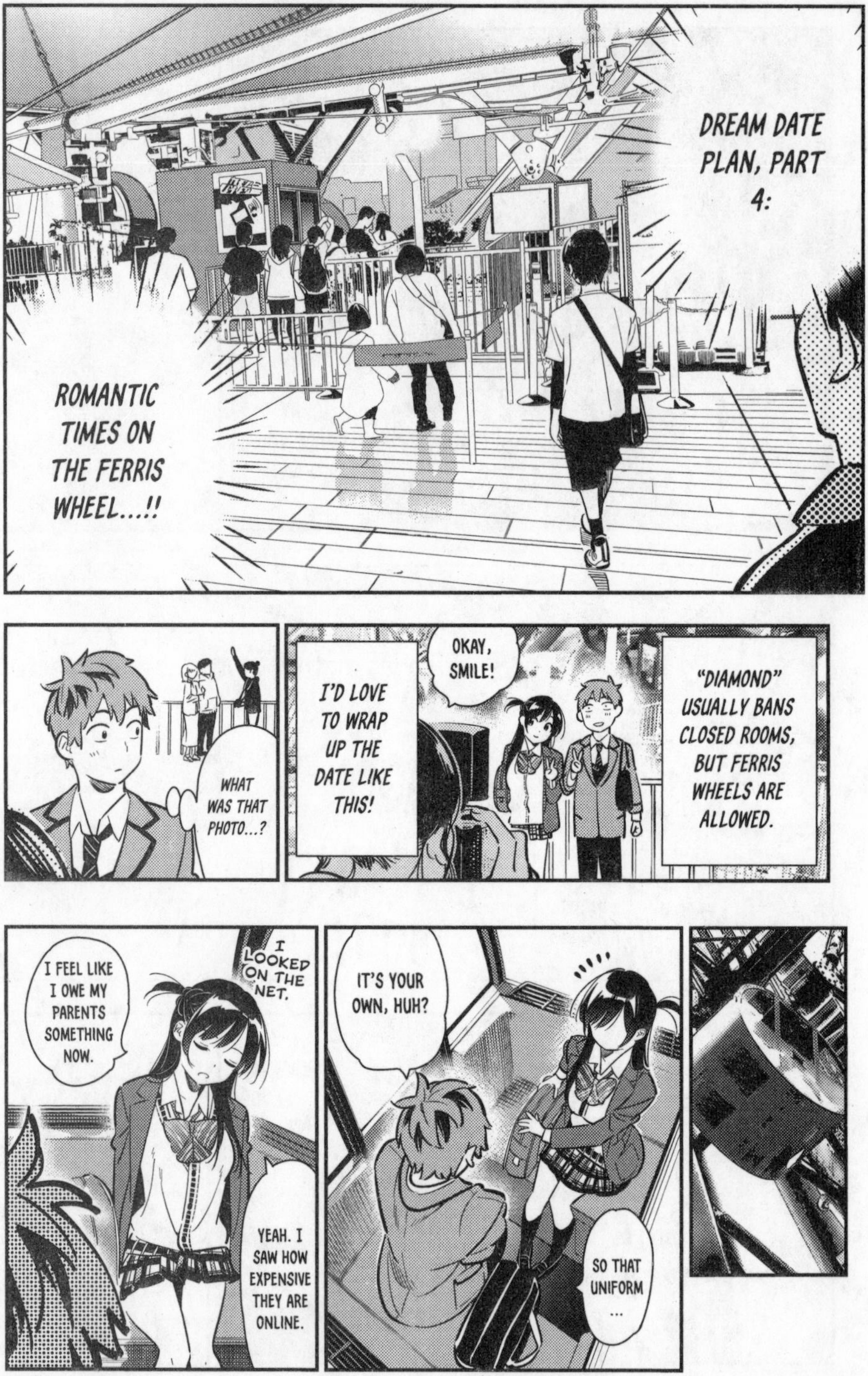
DREAM DATE PLAN, PART 4:
ROMANTIC TIMES ON THE FERRIS WHEEL...!!
“DIAMOND” USUALLY BANS CLOSED ROOMS, BUT FERRIS WHEELS ARE ALLOWED.
OKAY, SMILE!
I'D LOVE TO WRAP UP THE DATE LIKE THIS!
WHAT WAS THAT PHOTO...?
SO THAT UNIFORM ...
IT'S YOUR OWN, HUH?
I LOOKED ON THE NET.
YEAH. I SAW HOW EXPENSIVE THEY ARE ONLINE.
I FEEL LIKE I OWE MY PARENTS SOMETHING NOW.

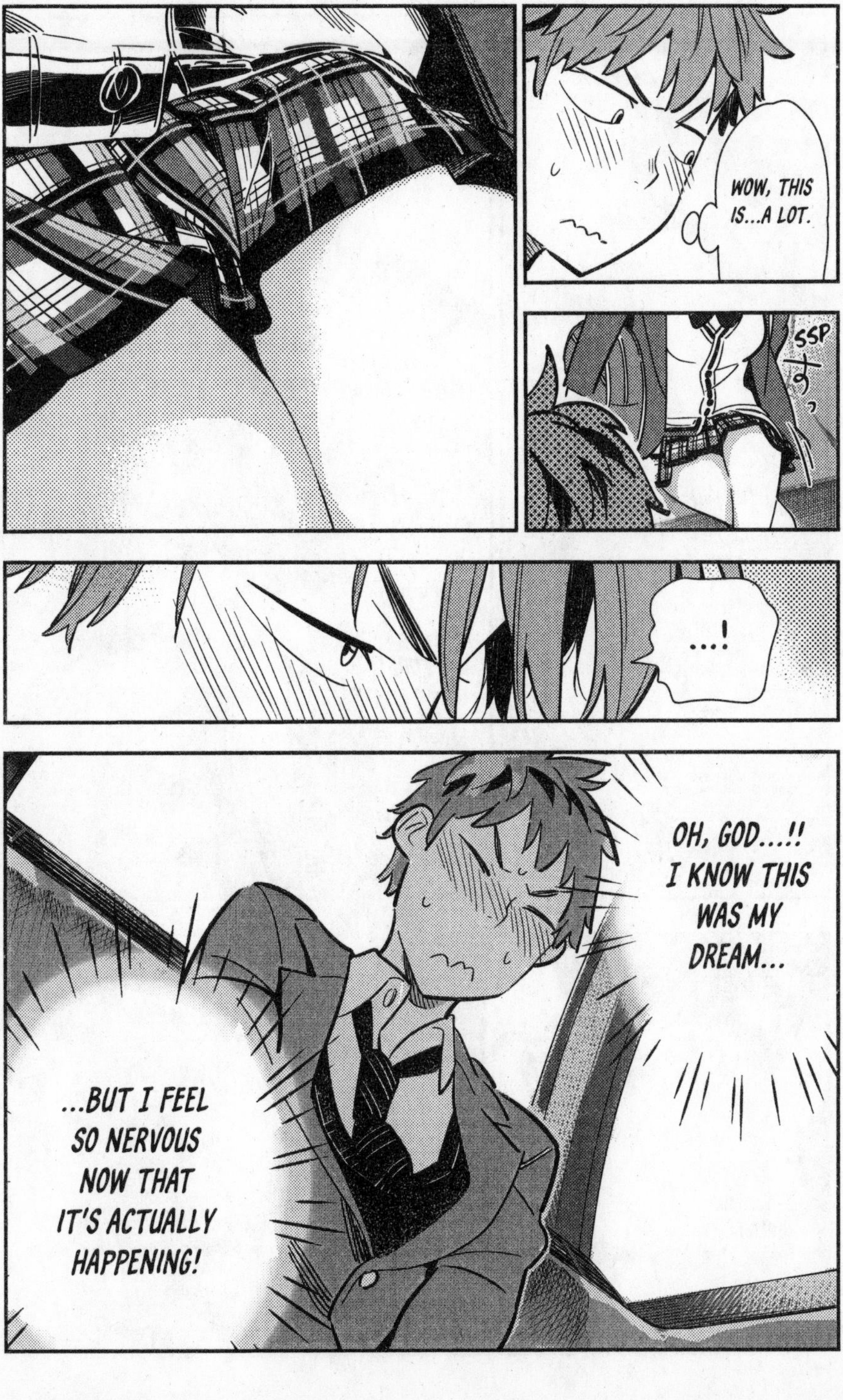
WOW, THIS IS...A LOT.
SSP
すっ
...!
OH, GOD...!! I KNOW THIS WAS MY DREAM...
...BUT I FEEL SO NERVOUS NOW THAT IT'S ACTUALLY HAPPENING!

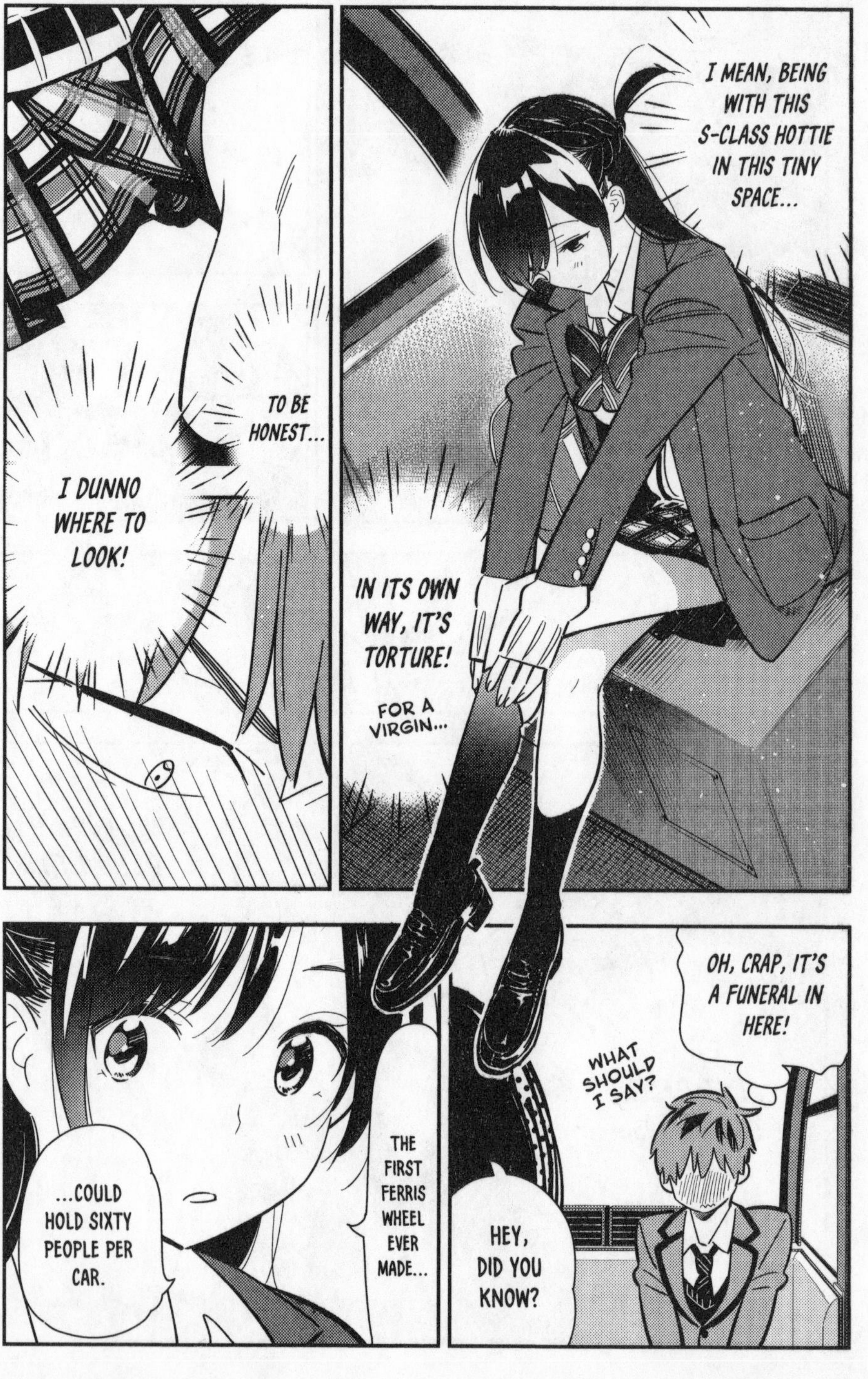
I MEAN, BEING WITH THIS S-CLASS HOTTIE IN THIS TINY SPACE...
IN ITS OWN WAY, IT'S TORTURE!
FOR A VIRGIN...
TO BE HONEST...
I DUNNO WHERE TO LOOK!
OH, CRAP, IT'S A FUNERAL IN HERE!
WHAT SHOULD I SAY?
HEY, DID YOU KNOW?
THE FIRST FERRIS WHEEL EVER MADE...
...COULD HOLD SIXTY PEOPLE PER CAR.

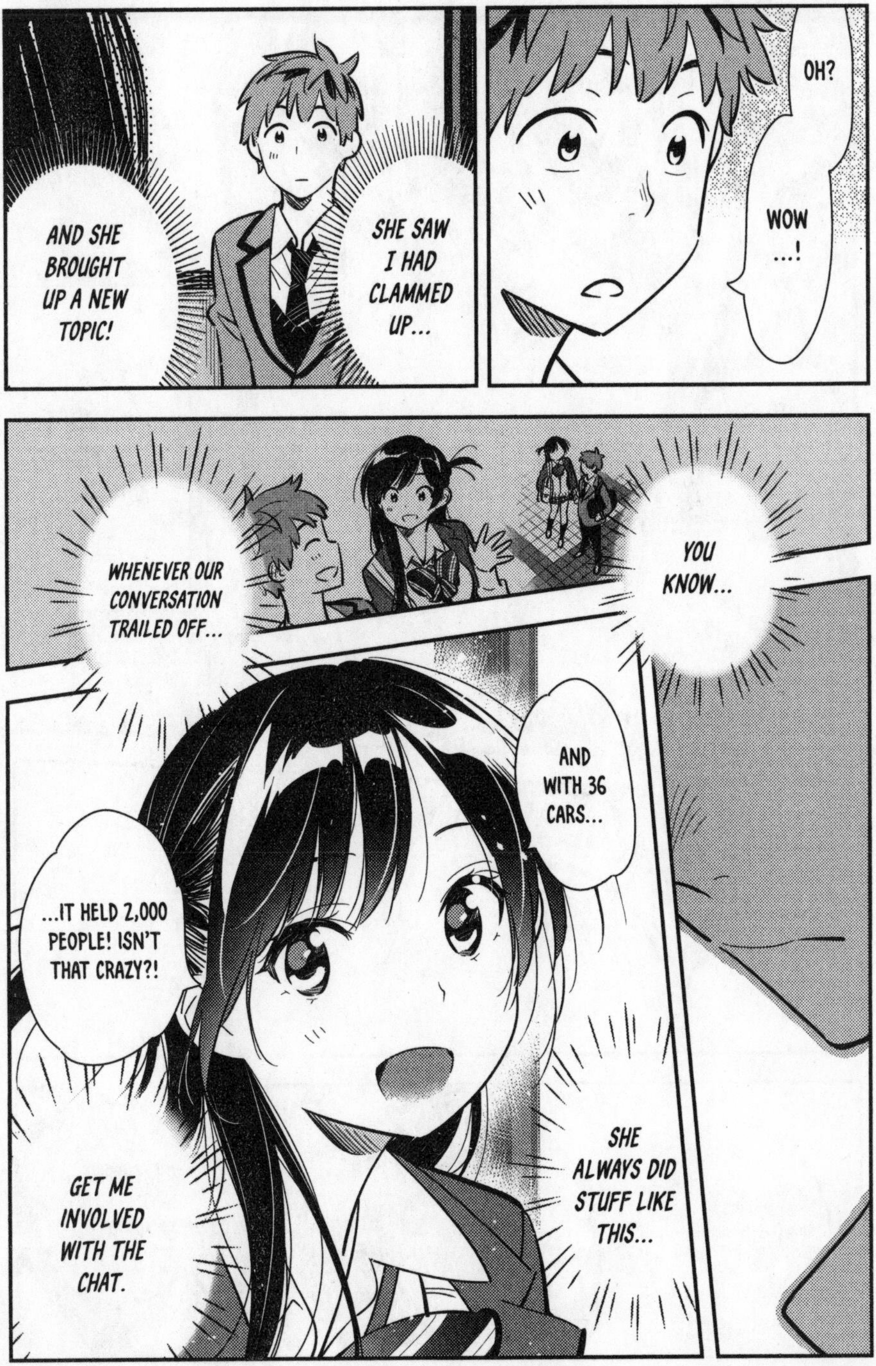
OH?
WOW ...!
SHE SAW I HAD CLAMMED UP...
AND SHE BROUGHT UP A NEW TOPIC!
YOU KNOW...
WHENEVER OUR CONVERSATION TRAILED OFF...
AND WITH 36 CARS...
...IT HELD 2,000 PEOPLE! ISN'T THAT CRAZY?!
SHE ALWAYS DID STUFF LIKE THIS...
GET ME INVOLVED WITH THE CHAT.

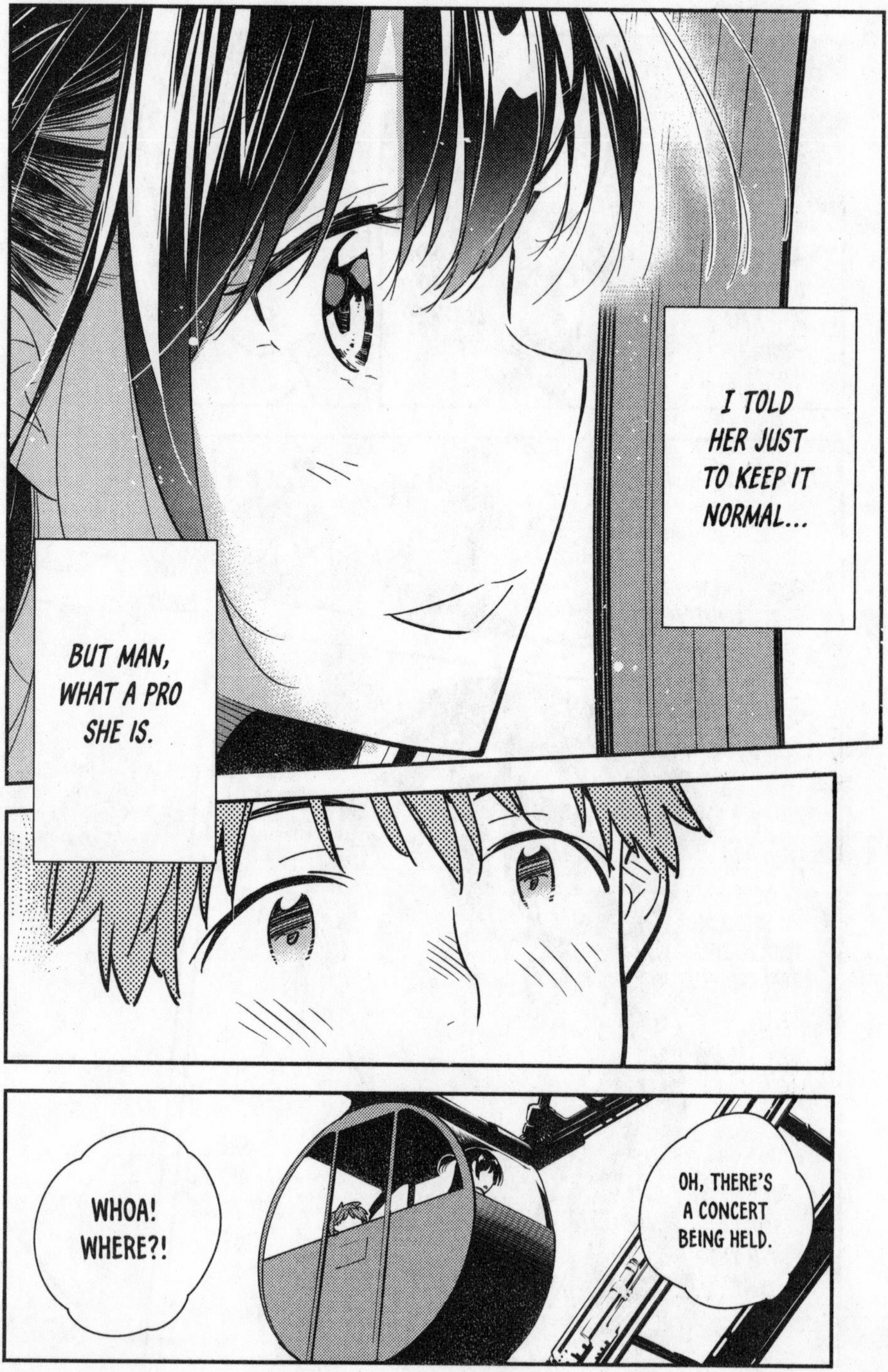
I TOLD HER JUST TO KEEP IT NORMAL...
BUT MAN, WHAT A PRO SHE IS.
OH, THERE'S A CONCERT BEING HELD.
WHOA! WHERE?!

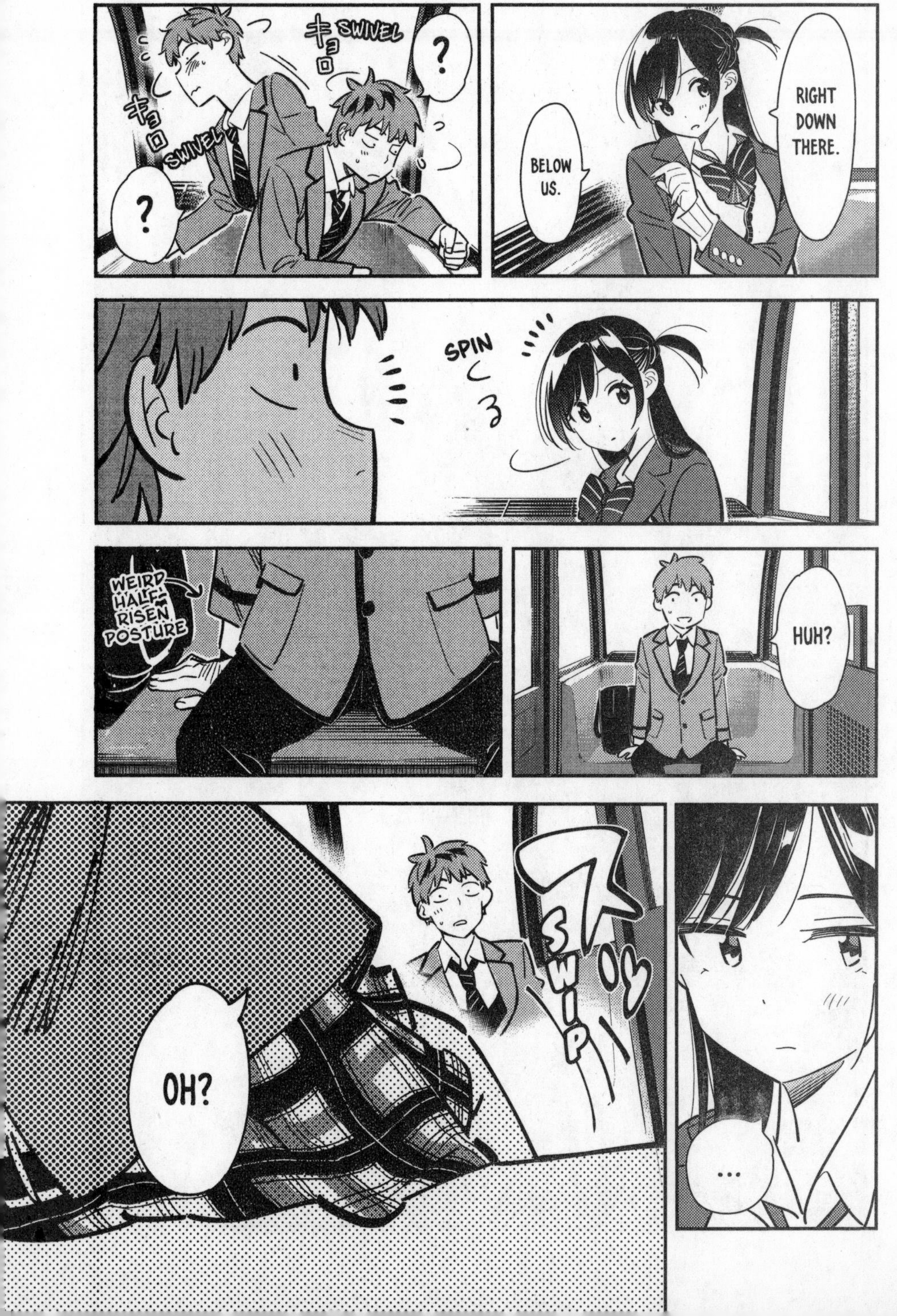
RIGHT DOWN THERE.
BELOW US.
?
キョロ SWIVEL
キョロ SWIVEL
?
SPIN
HUH?
WEIRD HALF-RISEN POSTURE
...
SWIP
OH?

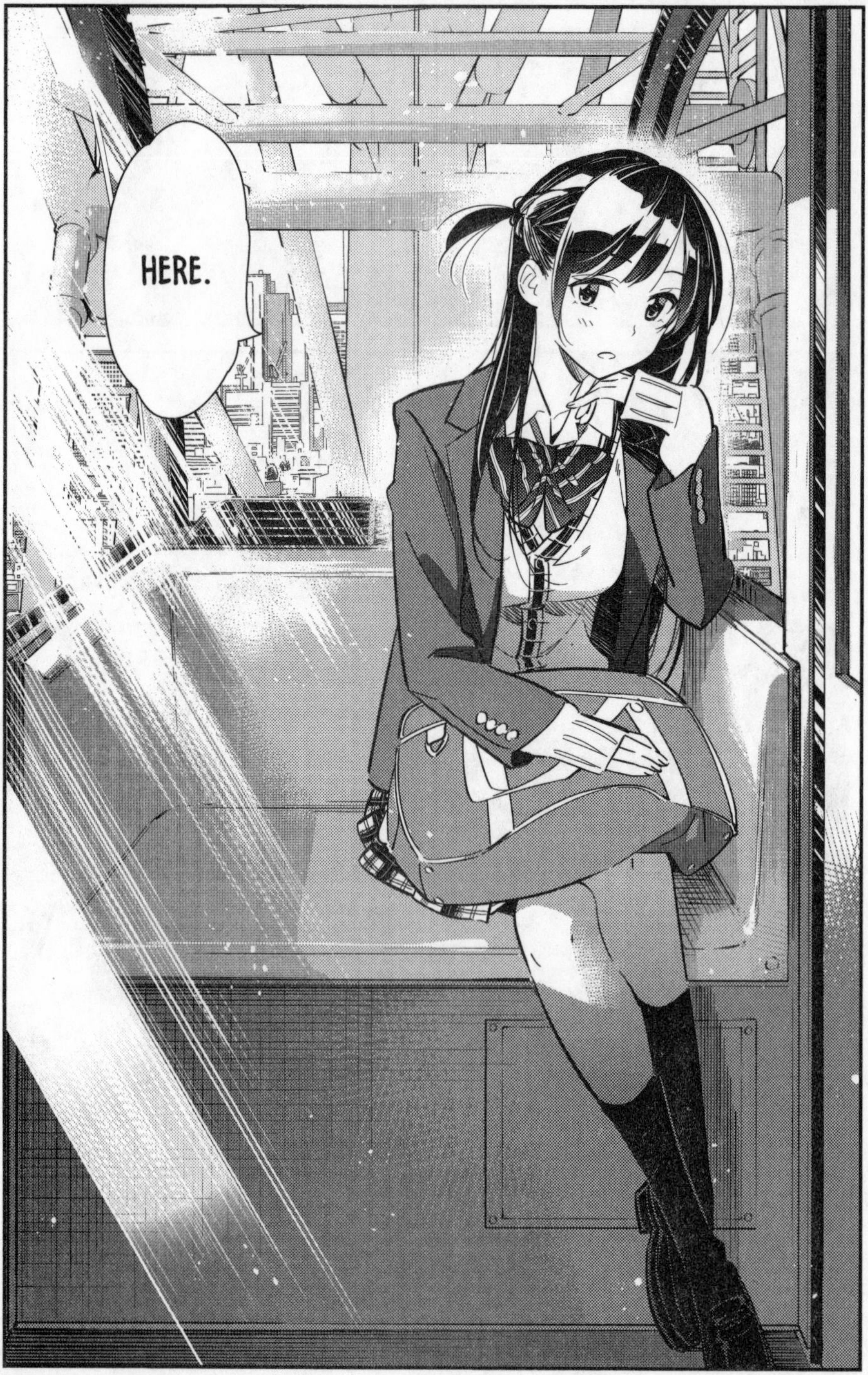
HERE.

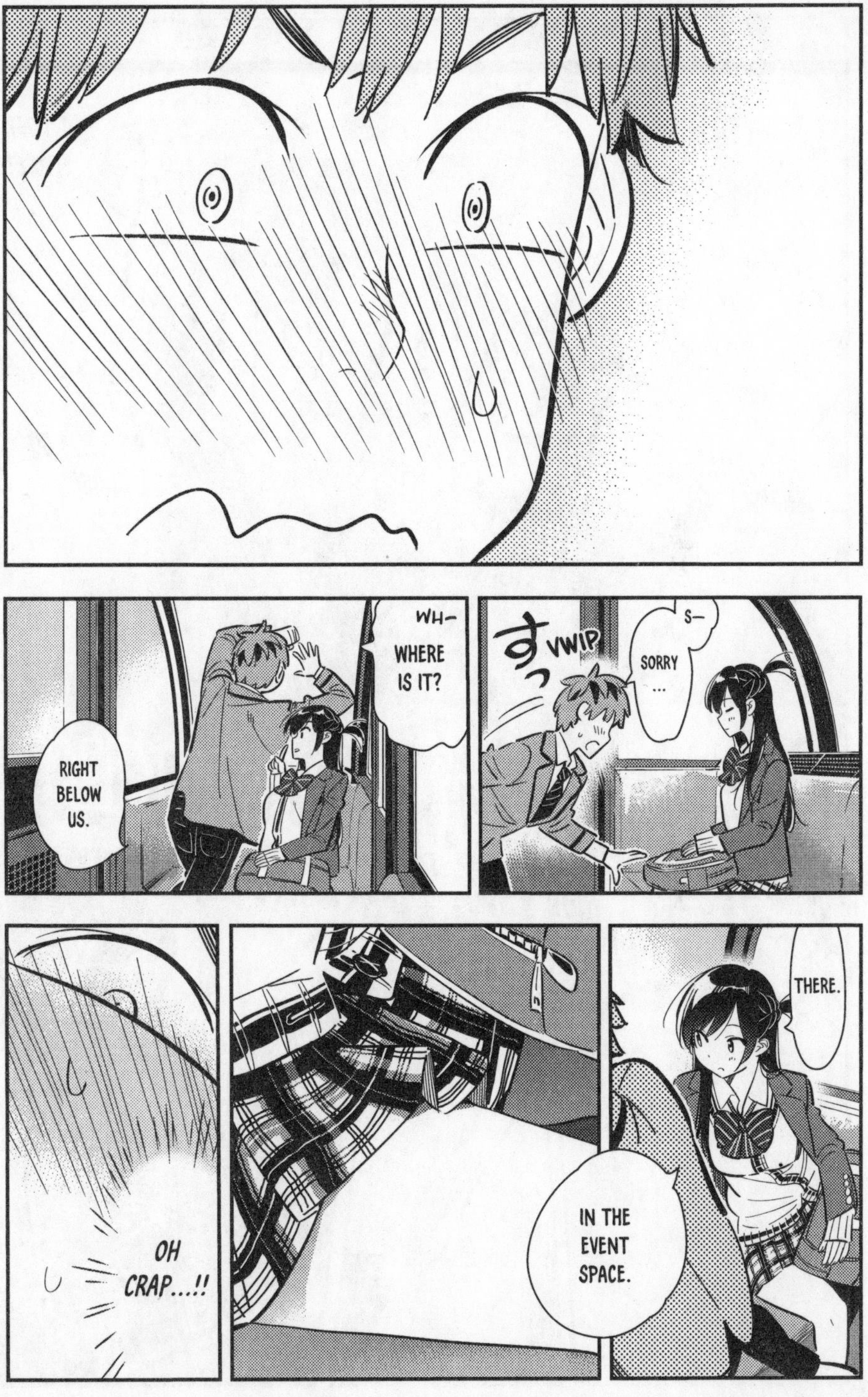
すっ VWIP
S— SORRY ...
WH— WHERE IS IT?
RIGHT BELOW US.
THERE.
IN THE EVENT SPACE.
OH CRAP...!!

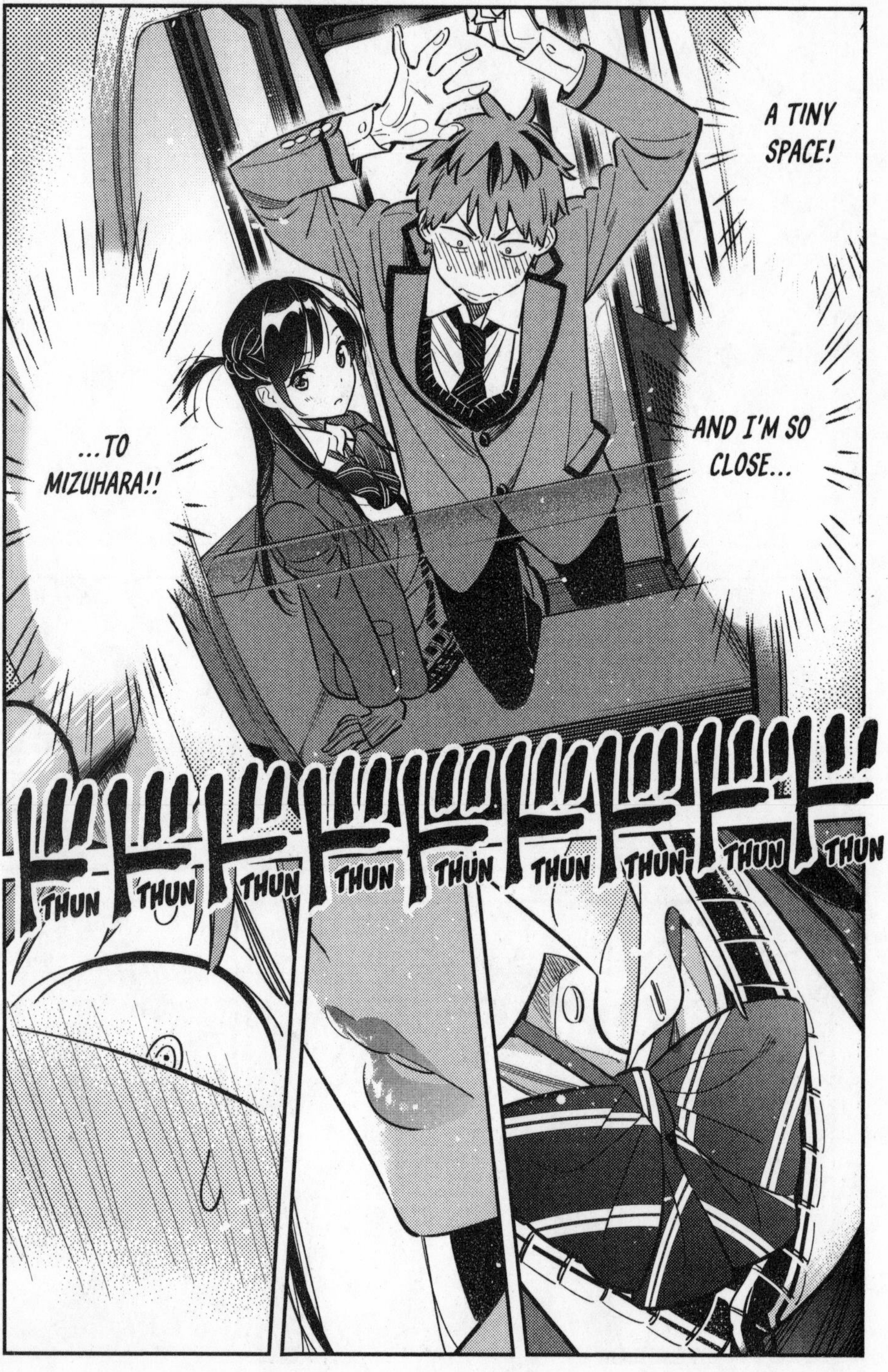
A TINY SPACE!
AND I'M SO CLOSE...
...TO MIZUHARA!!
THUN THUN THUN THUN THUN THUN THUN THUN THUN

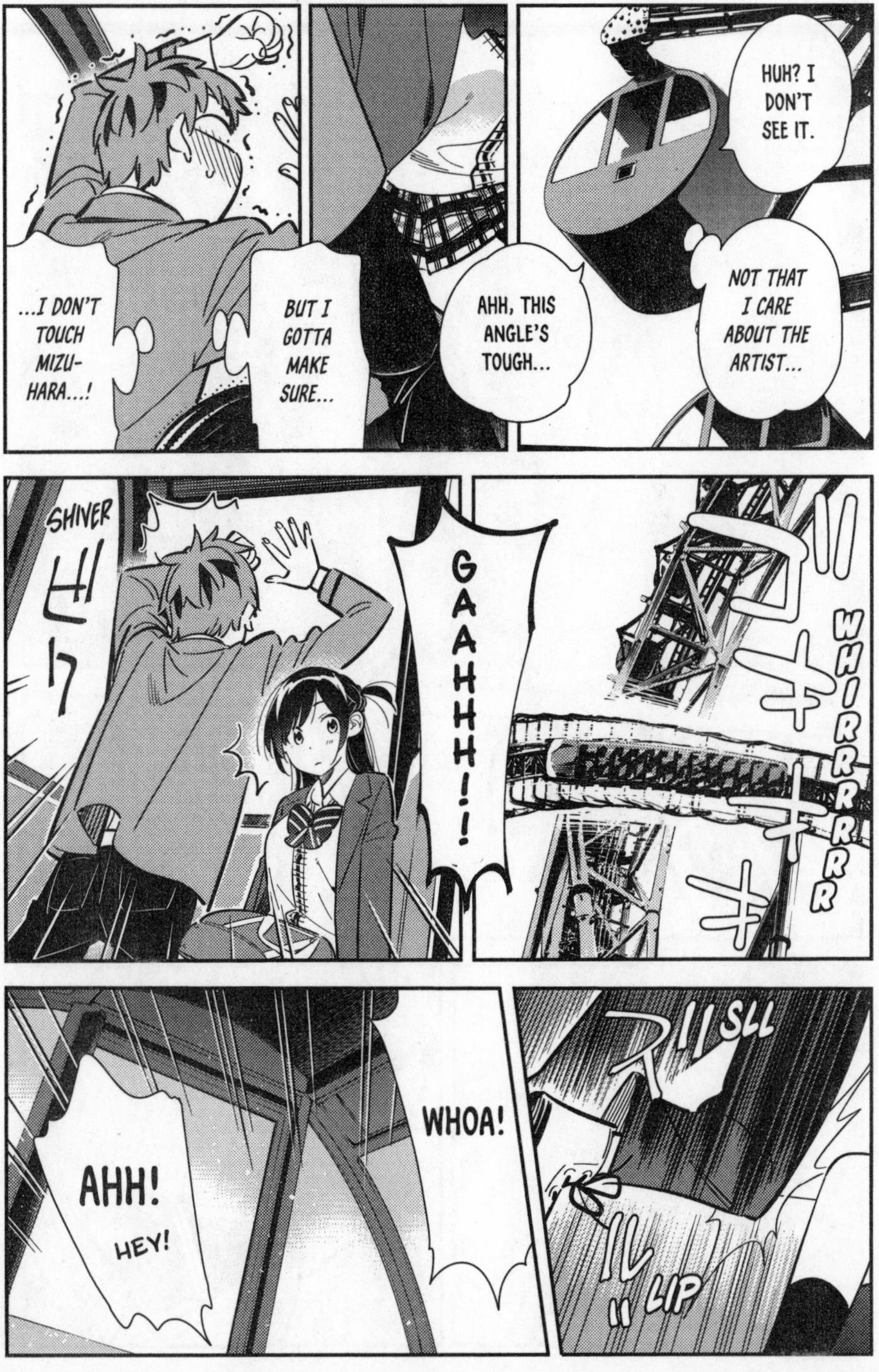
HUH? I DON'T SEE IT.
NOT THAT I CARE ABOUT THE ARTIST...
AHH, THIS ANGLE'S TOUGH...
BUT I GOTTA MAKE SURE...
...I DON'T TOUCH MIZU-HARA...!
WHIRRRRRRR
GAAHHH!!
SHIVER
SLL
LIP
WHOA!
AHH!
HEY!

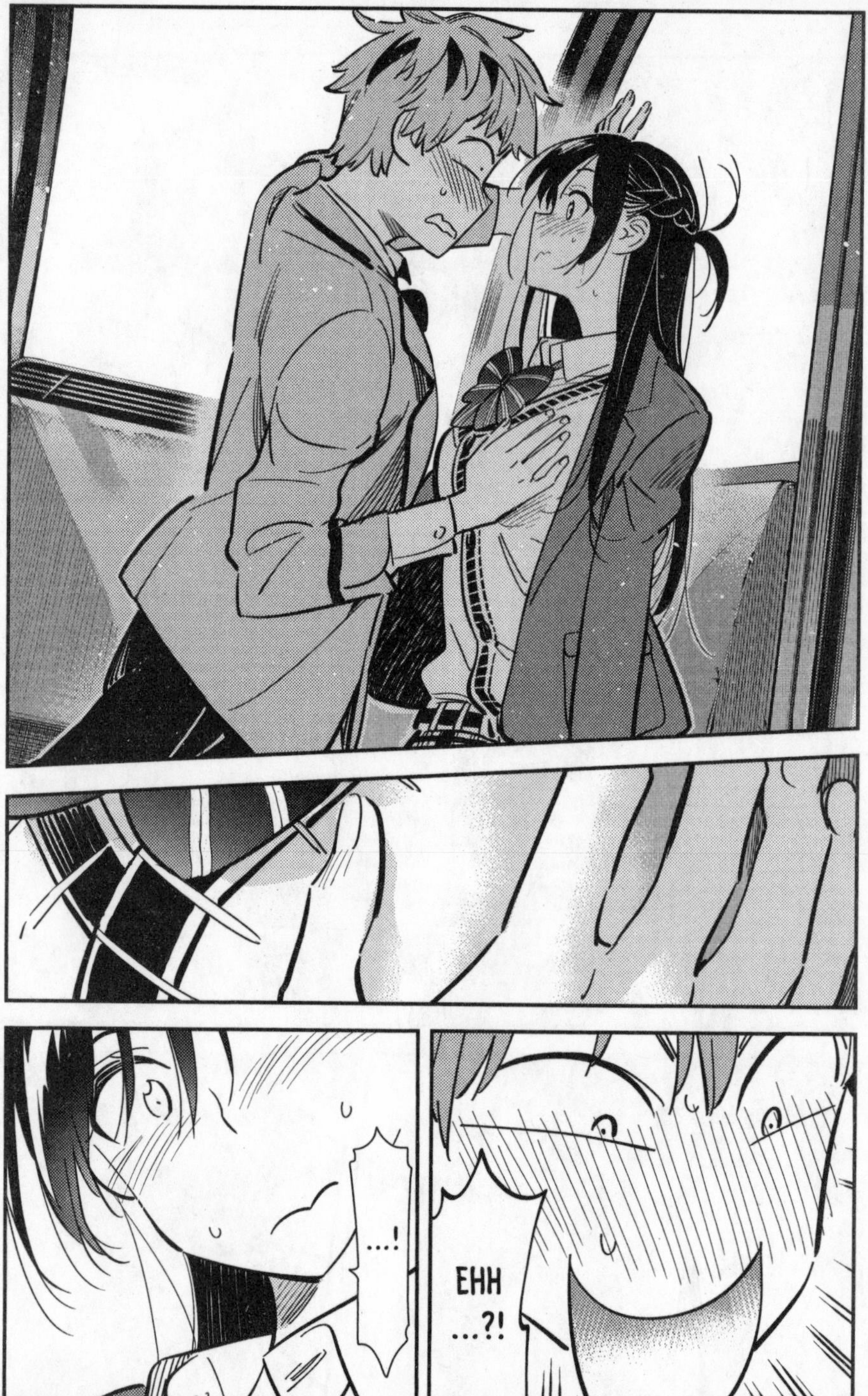
EHH
...?!
...!

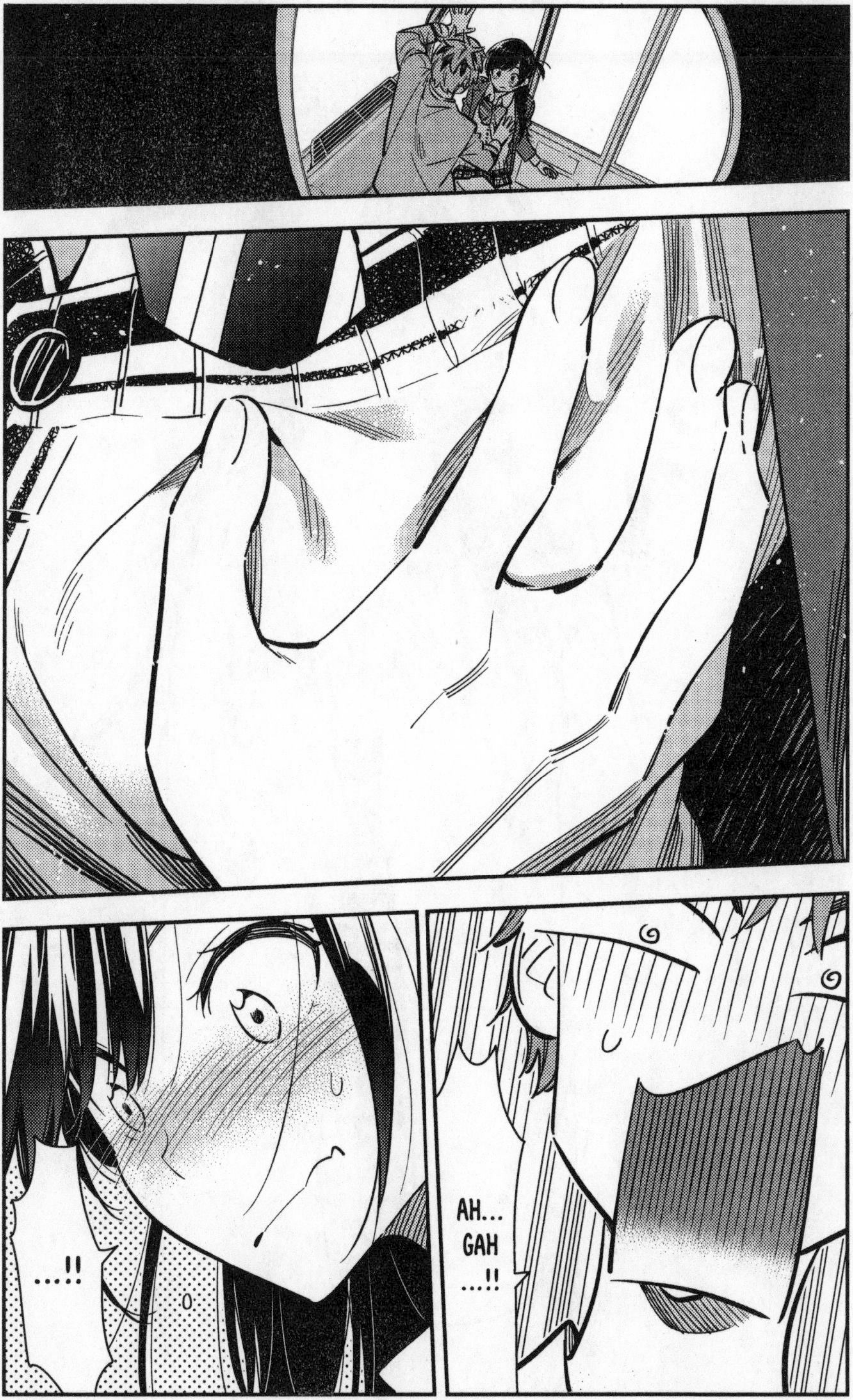
AH... GAH ...!!
...!!

RATING 82 MY GIRLFRIEND AND MY DREAM DATE 5

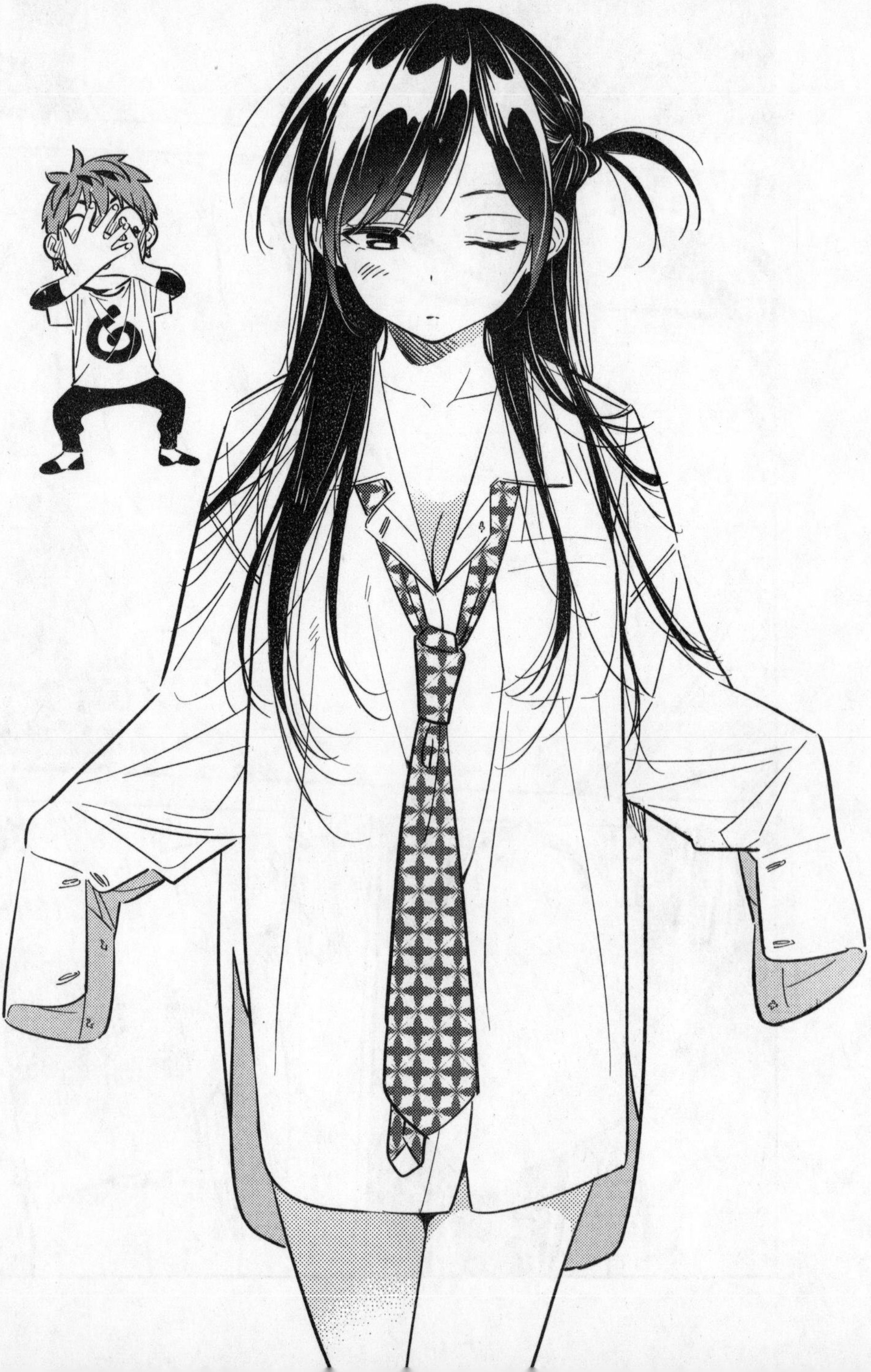

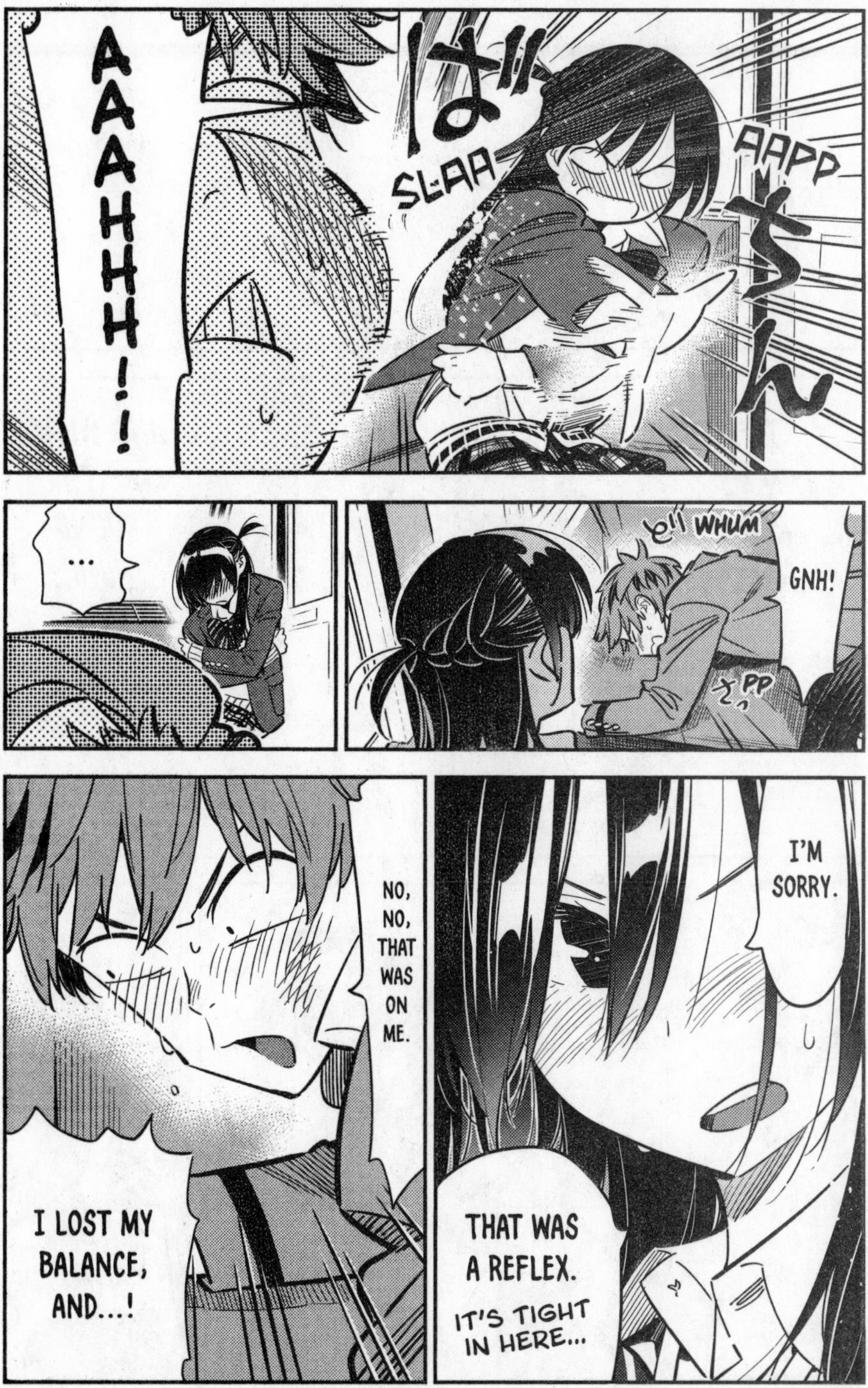
SLAA
AAPP
AAAHHH!!
WHUM
GNH!
PP
...
I'M SORRY.
THAT WAS A REFLEX.
IT'S TIGHT IN HERE...
NO, NO, THAT WAS ON ME.
I LOST MY BALANCE, AND...!

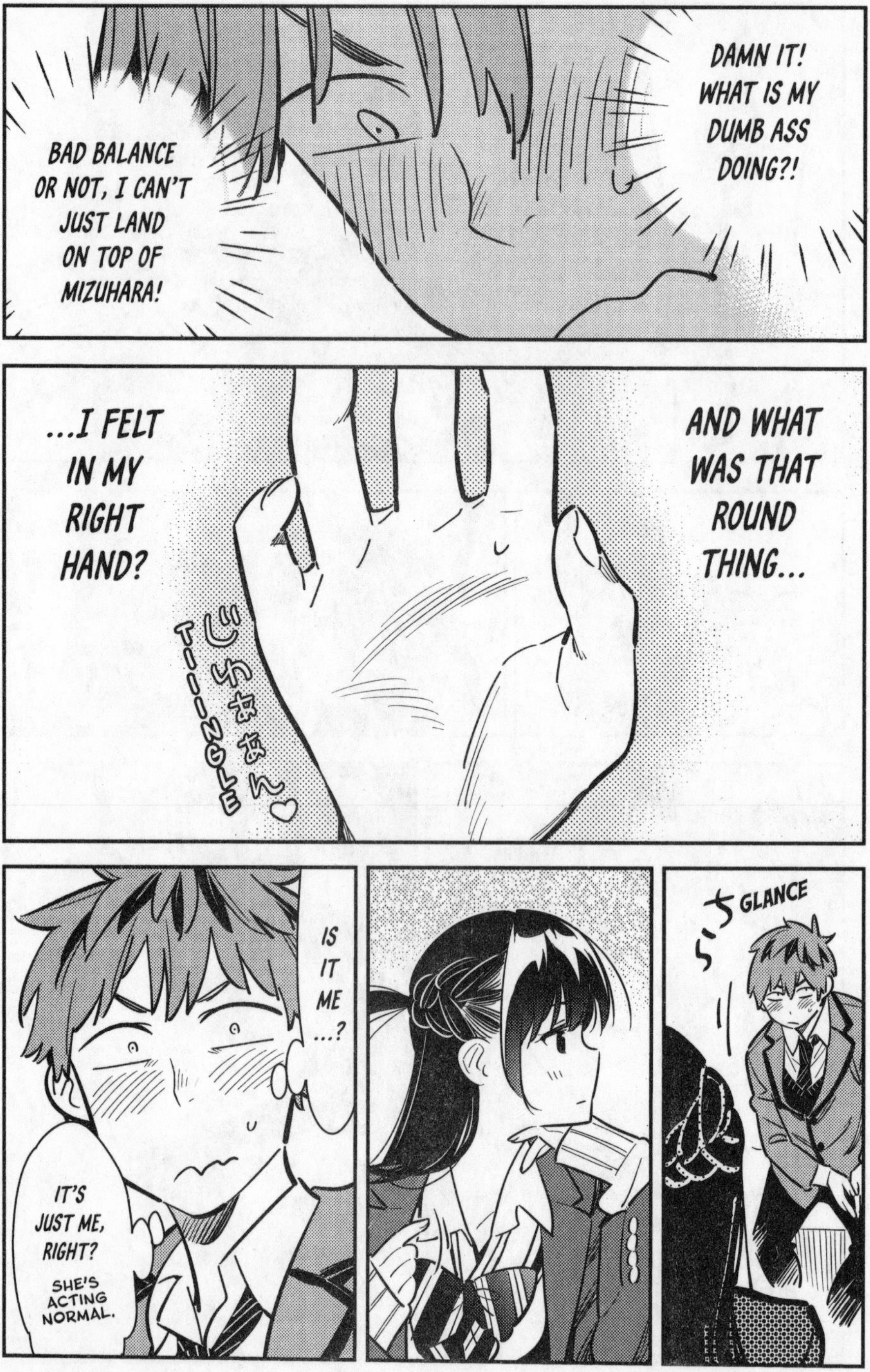
DAMN IT! WHAT IS MY DUMB ASS DOING?!
BAD BALANCE OR NOT, I CAN'T JUST LAND ON TOP OF MIZUHARA!
AND WHAT WAS THAT ROUND THING...
...I FELT IN MY RIGHT HAND?
じわあん♡
TIIINGLE
ち
GLANCE
IS IT ME ...?
IT'S JUST ME, RIGHT?
SHE'S ACTING NORMAL.

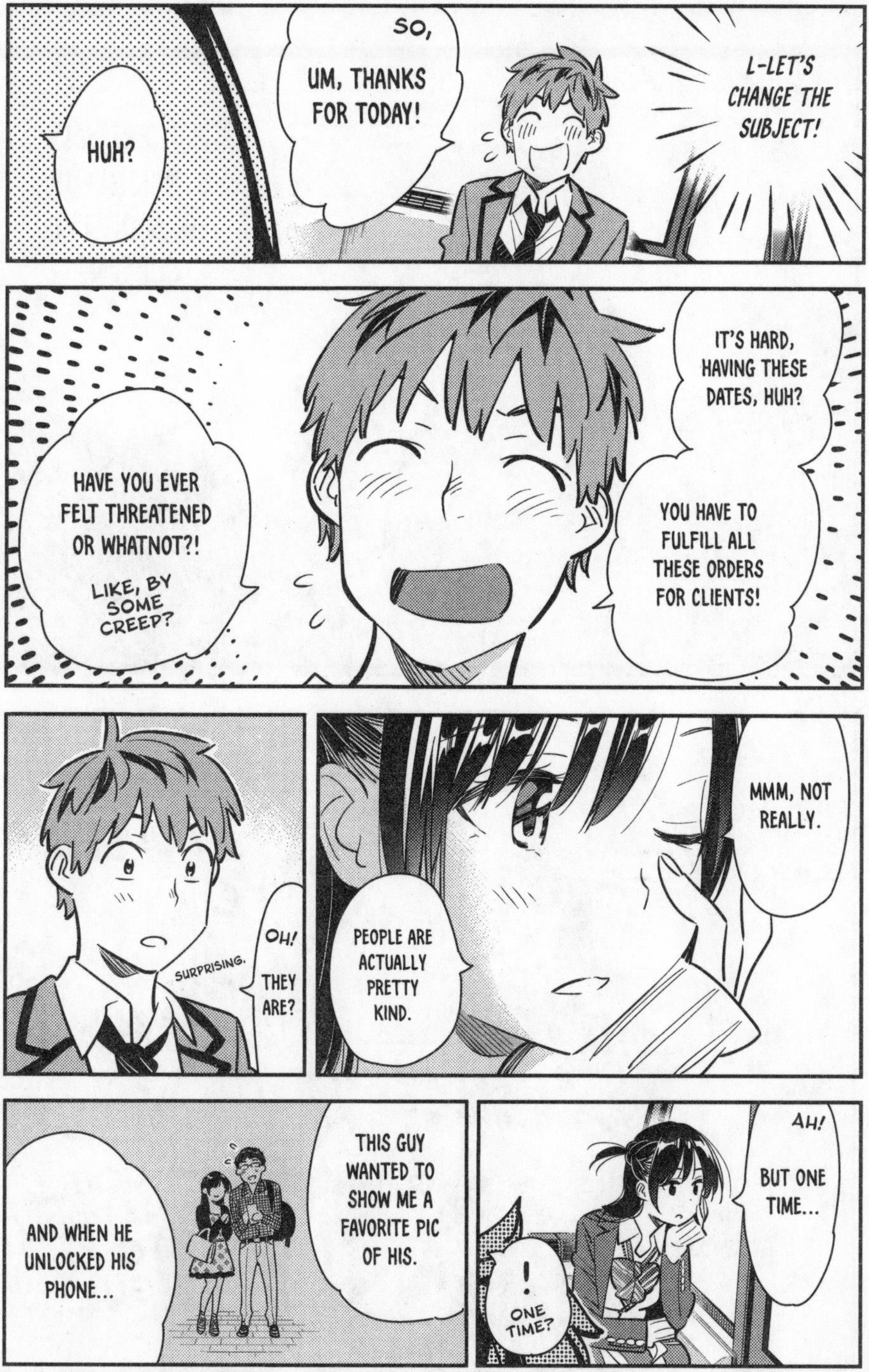
L-LET'S CHANGE THE SUBJECT!
SO, UM, THANKS FOR TODAY!
HUH?
IT'S HARD, HAVING THESE DATES, HUH?
YOU HAVE TO FULFILL ALL THESE ORDERS FOR CLIENTS!
HAVE YOU EVER FELT THREATENED OR WHATNOT?!
LIKE, BY SOME CREEP?
MMM, NOT REALLY.
PEOPLE ARE ACTUALLY PRETTY KIND.
OH!
THEY ARE?
SURPRISING.
AH!
BUT ONE TIME...
!
ONE TIME?
THIS GUY WANTED TO SHOW ME A FAVORITE PIC OF HIS.
AND WHEN HE UNLOCKED HIS PHONE...

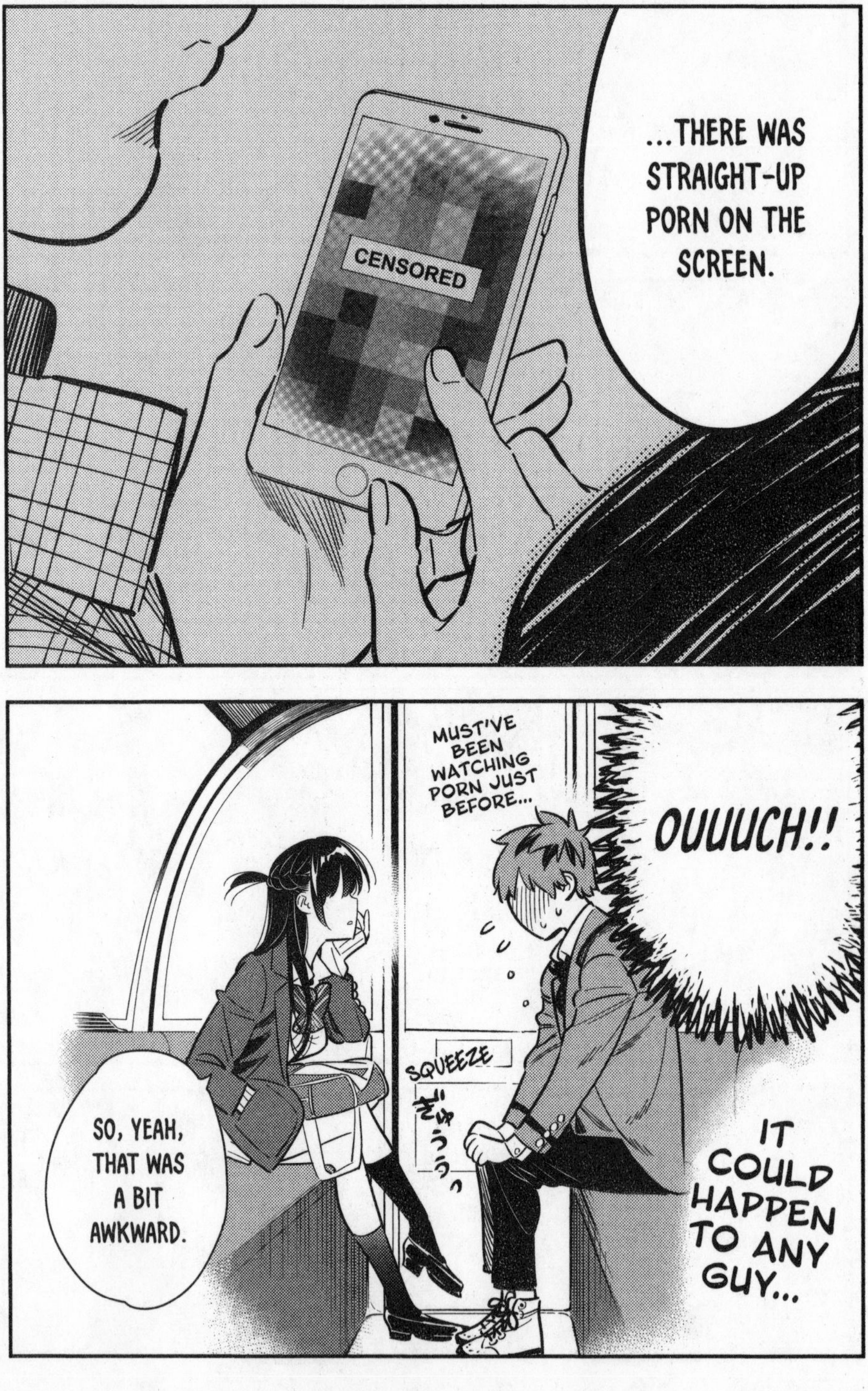
...THERE WAS STRAIGHT-UP PORN ON THE SCREEN.
CENSORED
OUUUCH!!
MUST'VE BEEN WATCHING PORN JUST BEFORE...
IT COULD HAPPEN TO ANY GUY...
SQUEEZE
ぎゅううっ
SO, YEAH, THAT WAS A BIT AWKWARD.

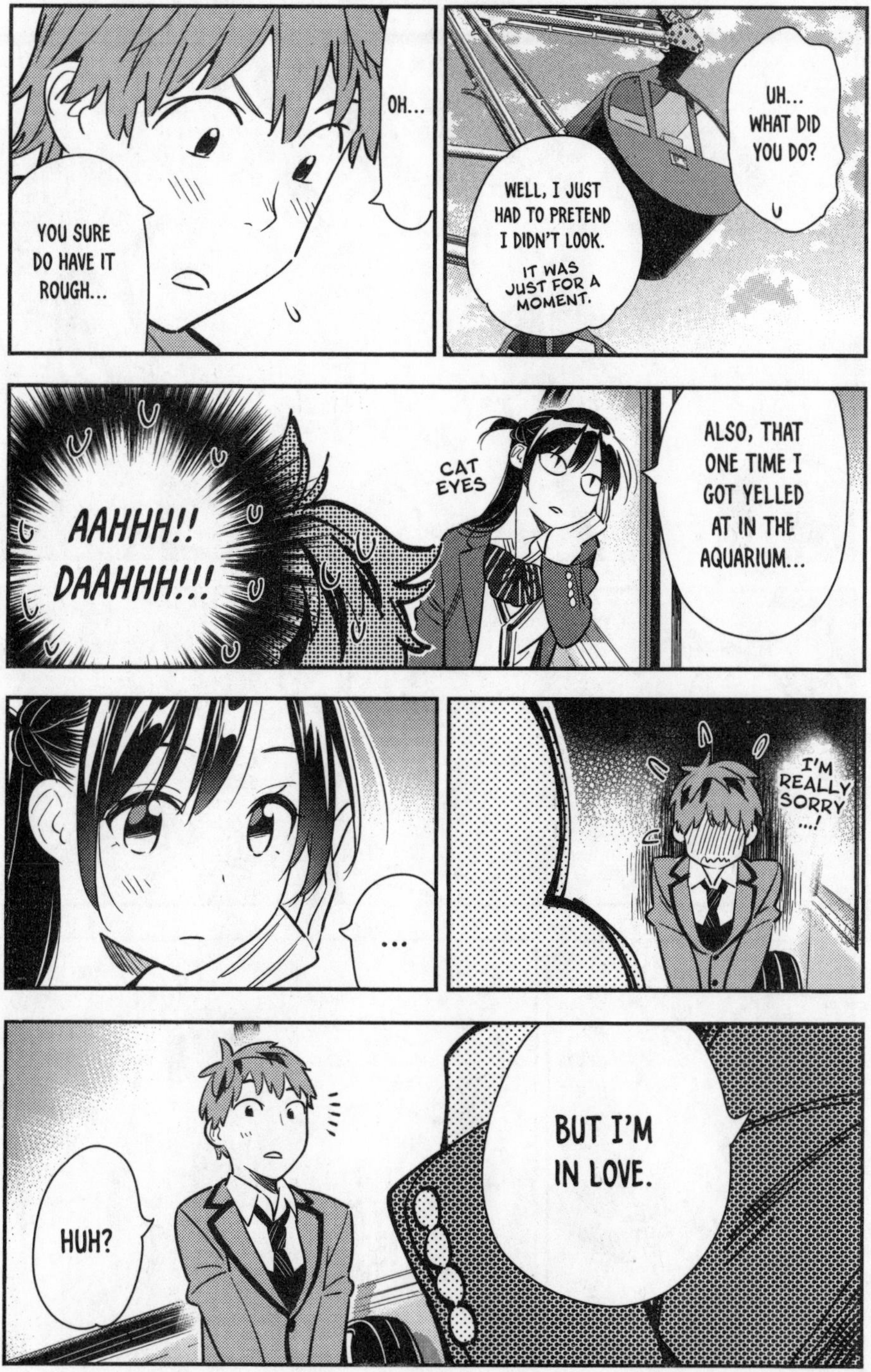
UH... WHAT DID YOU DO?
WELL, I JUST HAD TO PRETEND I DIDN'T LOOK.
IT WAS JUST FOR A MOMENT.
OH...
YOU SURE DO HAVE IT ROUGH...
ALSO, THAT ONE TIME I GOT YELLED AT IN THE AQUARIUM...
CAT EYES
AAHHH!! DAAHHH!!!
I'M REALLY SORRY ...!
...
BUT I'M IN LOVE.
HUH?

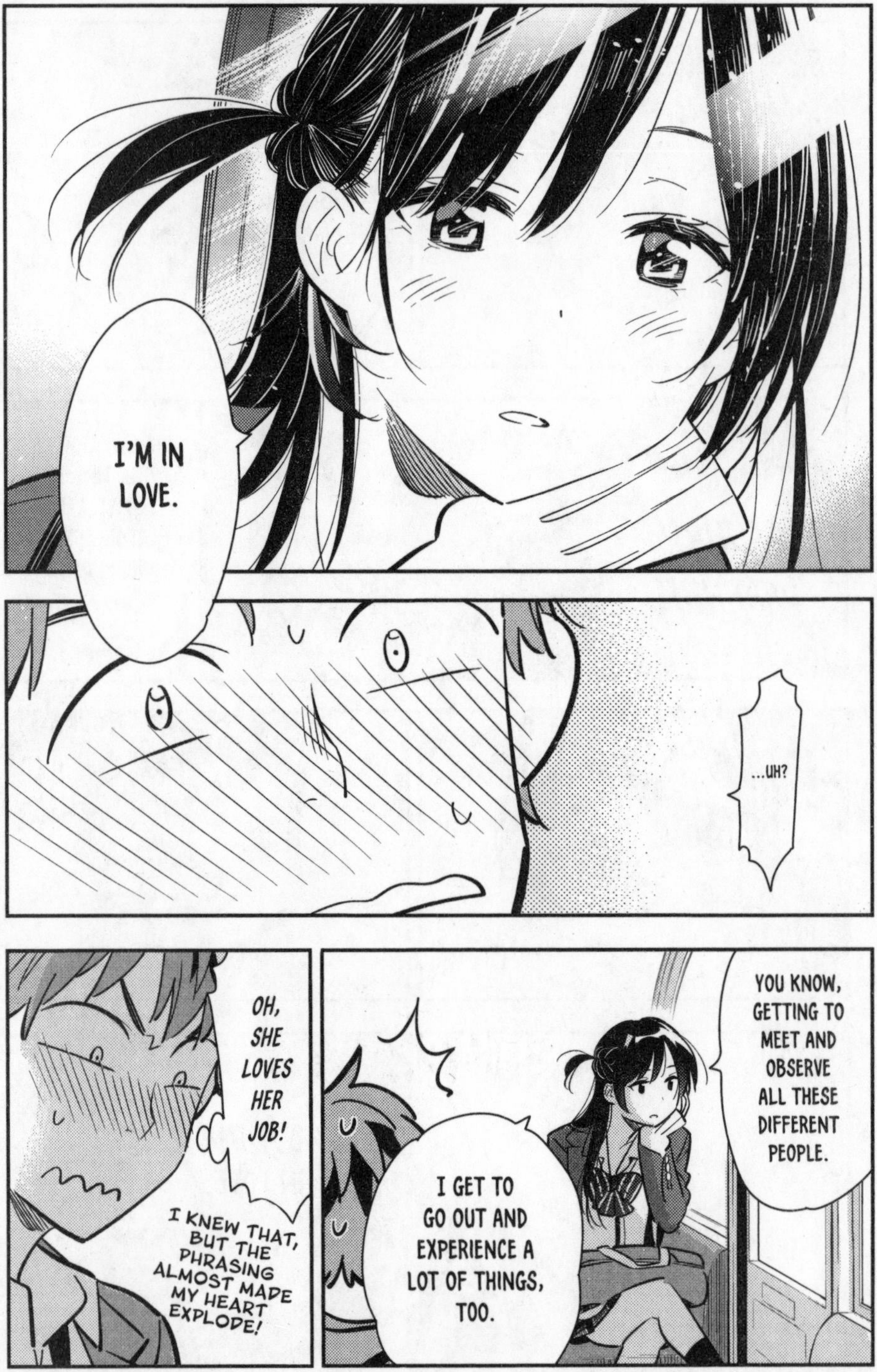
I'M IN LOVE.
...UH?
YOU KNOW, GETTING TO MEET AND OBSERVE ALL THESE DIFFERENT PEOPLE.
I GET TO GO OUT AND EXPERIENCE A LOT OF THINGS, TOO.
OH, SHE LOVES HER JOB!
I KNEW THAT, BUT THE PHRASING ALMOST MADE MY HEART EXPLODE!

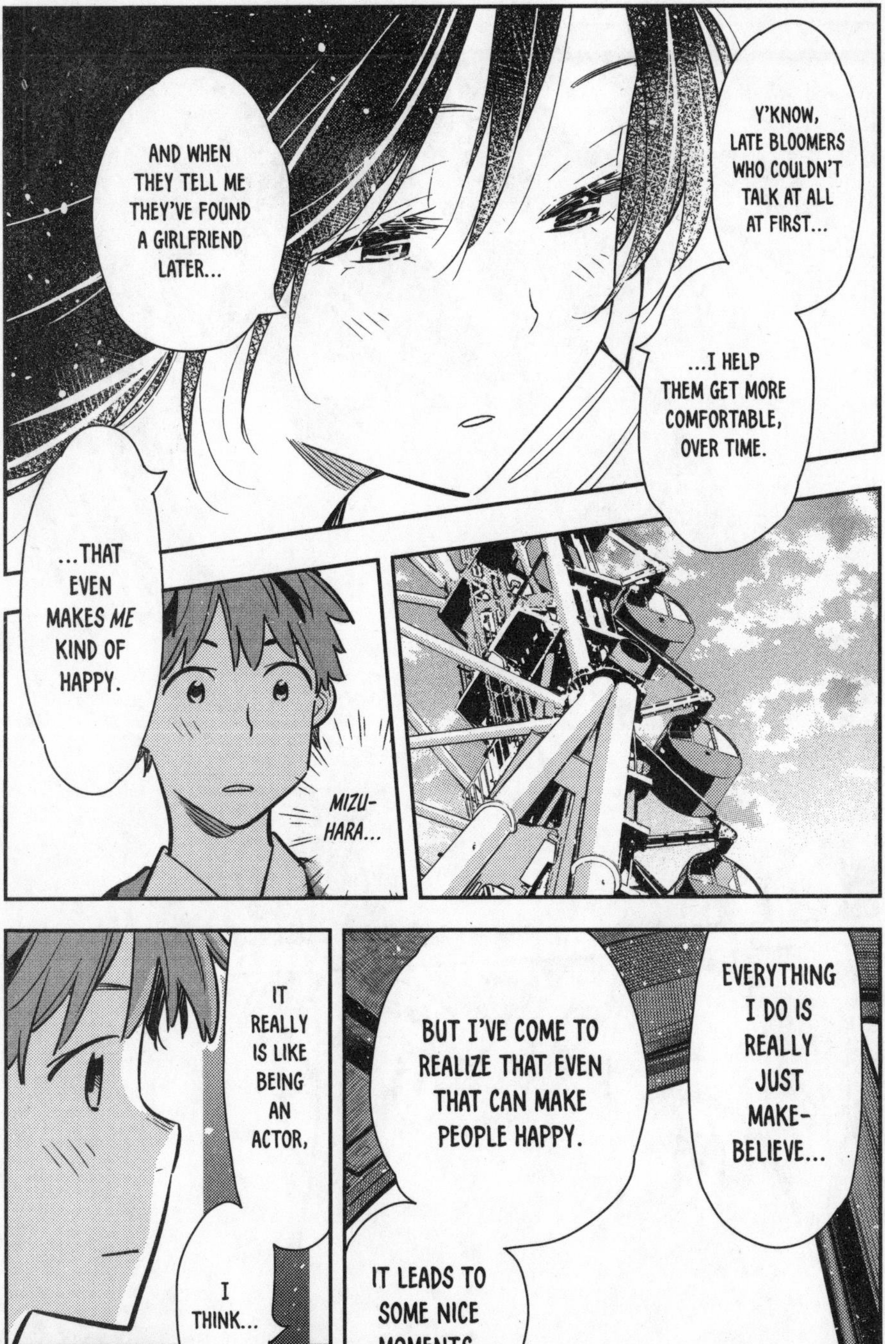
Y'KNOW, LATE BLOOMERS WHO COULDN'T TALK AT ALL AT FIRST...
...I HELP THEM GET MORE COMFORTABLE, OVER TIME.
AND WHEN THEY TELL ME THEY'VE FOUND A GIRLFRIEND LATER...
...THAT EVEN MAKES *ME* KIND OF HAPPY.
MIZU-HARA...
EVERYTHING I DO IS REALLY JUST MAKE-BELIEVE...
BUT I'VE COME TO REALIZE THAT EVEN THAT CAN MAKE PEOPLE HAPPY.
IT LEADS TO SOME NICE MOMENTS.
IT REALLY IS LIKE BEING AN ACTOR,
I THINK...

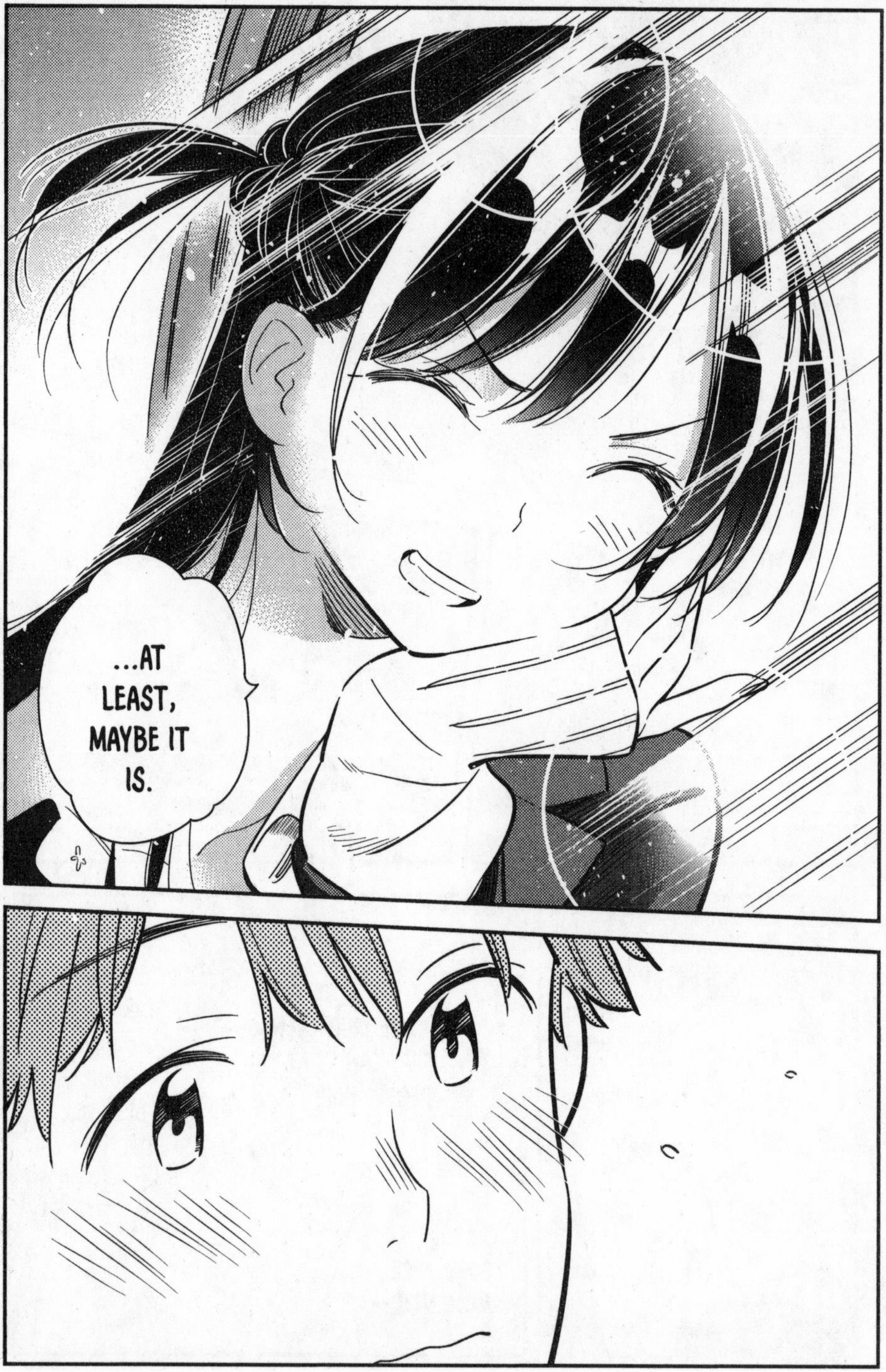
...AT LEAST, MAYBE IT IS.

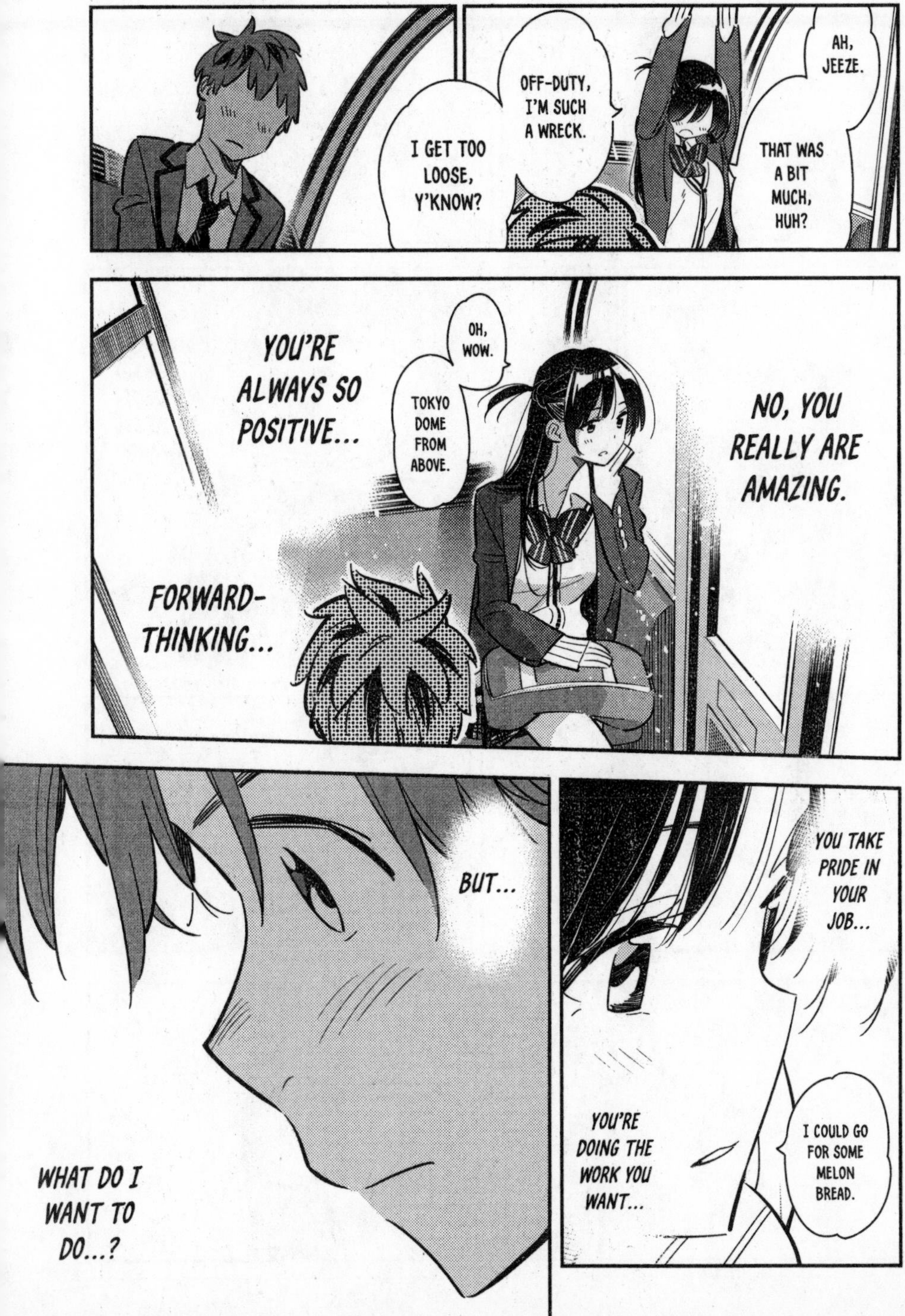
AH, JEEZE.
THAT WAS A BIT MUCH, HUH?
OFF-DUTY, I'M SUCH A WRECK.
I GET TOO LOOSE, Y'KNOW?
NO, YOU REALLY ARE AMAZING.
OH, WOW.
TOKYO DOME FROM ABOVE.
YOU'RE ALWAYS SO POSITIVE...
FORWARD-THINKING...
YOU TAKE PRIDE IN YOUR JOB...
I COULD GO FOR SOME MELON BREAD.
YOU'RE DOING THE WORK YOU WANT...
BUT...
WHAT DO I WANT TO DO...?

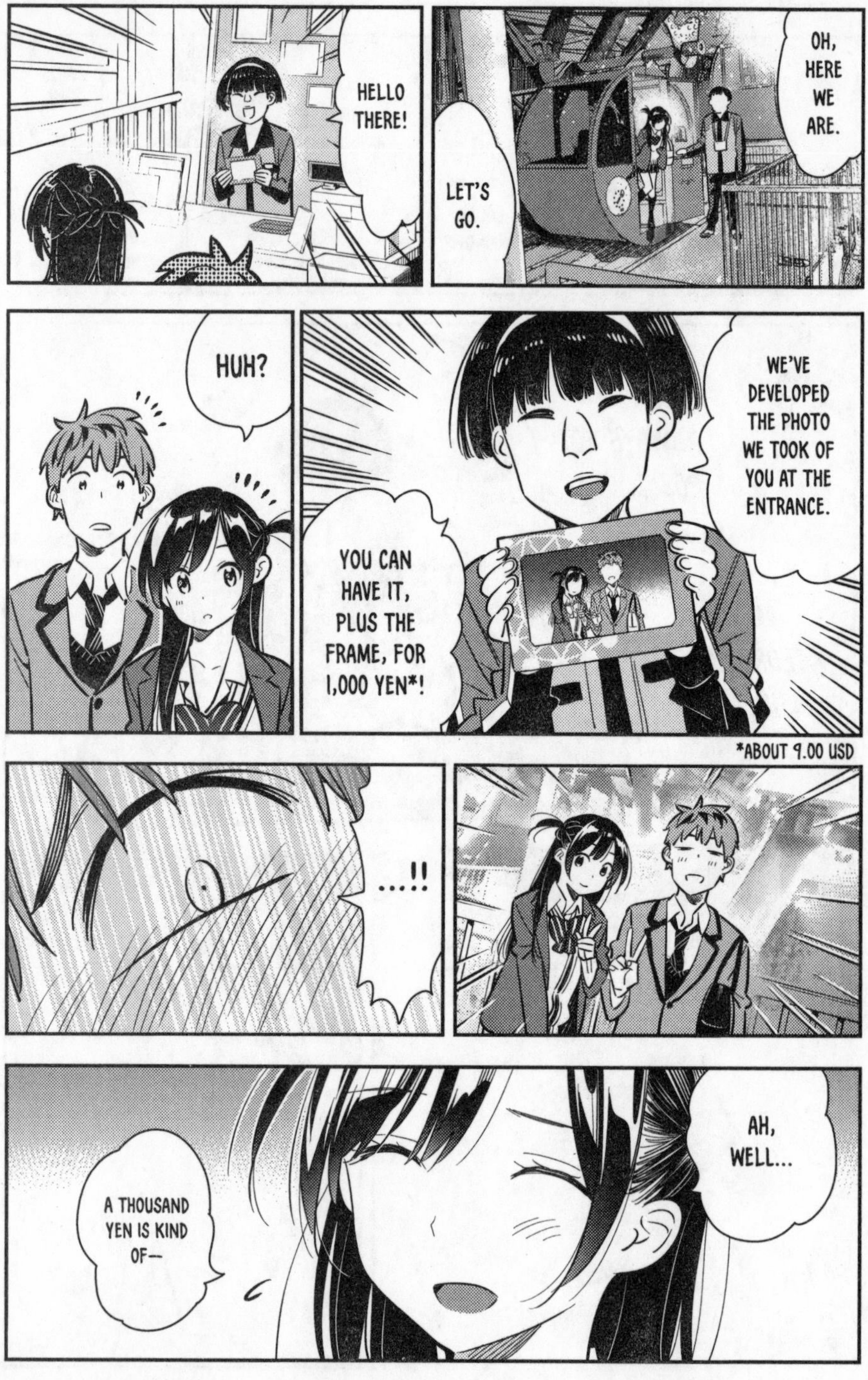
OH, HERE WE ARE.
LET'S GO.
HELLO THERE!
WE'VE DEVELOPED THE PHOTO WE TOOK OF YOU AT THE ENTRANCE.
YOU CAN HAVE IT, PLUS THE FRAME, FOR 1,000 YEN*!
HUH?
...!!
AH, WELL...
A THOUSAND YEN IS KIND OF—

*ABOUT 9.00 USD

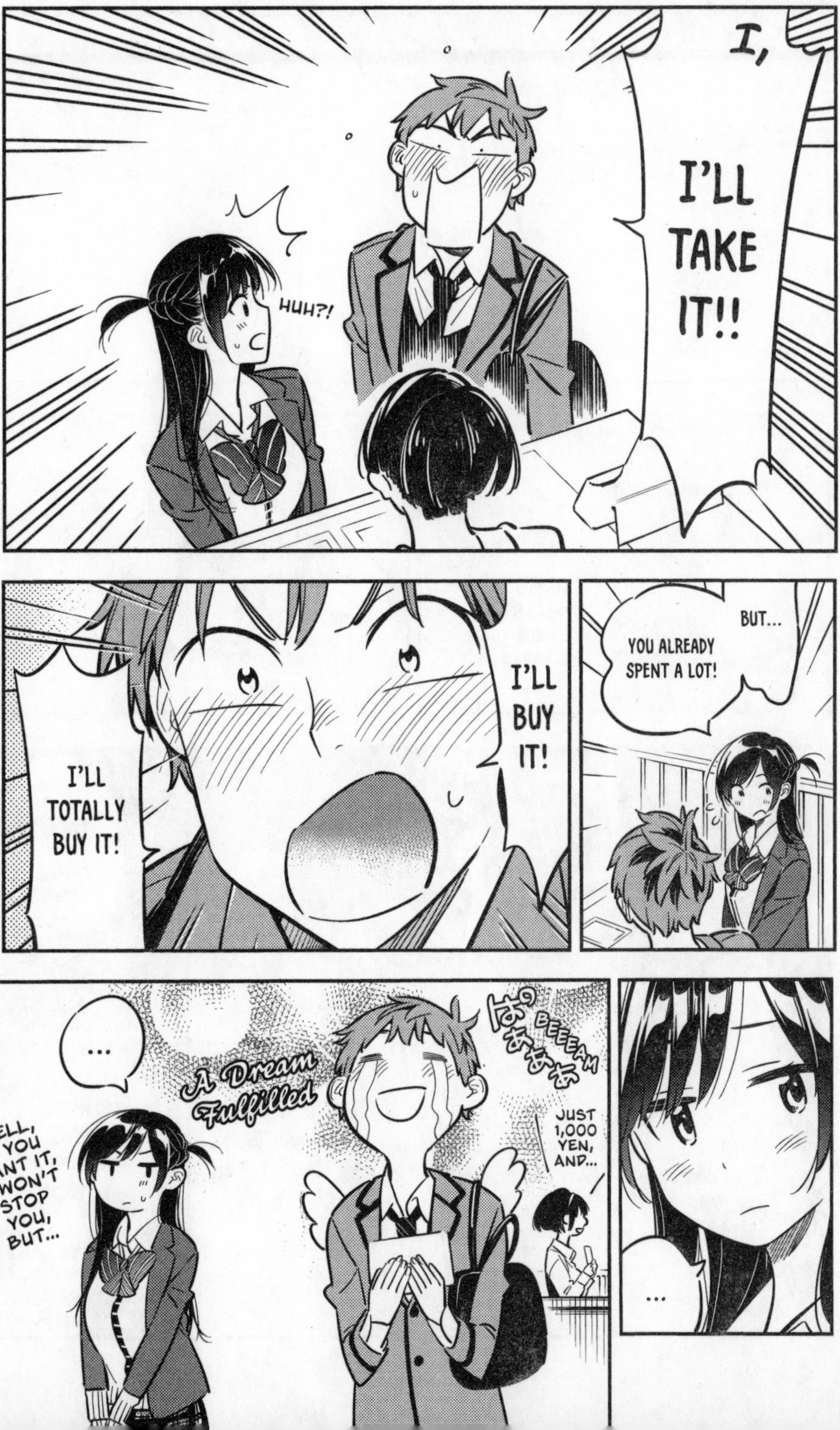
I,
I'LL TAKE IT!!
HUH?!
BUT...
YOU ALREADY SPENT A LOT!
I'LL BUY IT!
I'LL TOTALLY BUY IT!
...
ぱあああ
BEEEEAM
A Dream Fulfilled
...
JUST 1,000 YEN, AND...
WELL, IF YOU WANT IT, I WON'T STOP YOU, BUT...

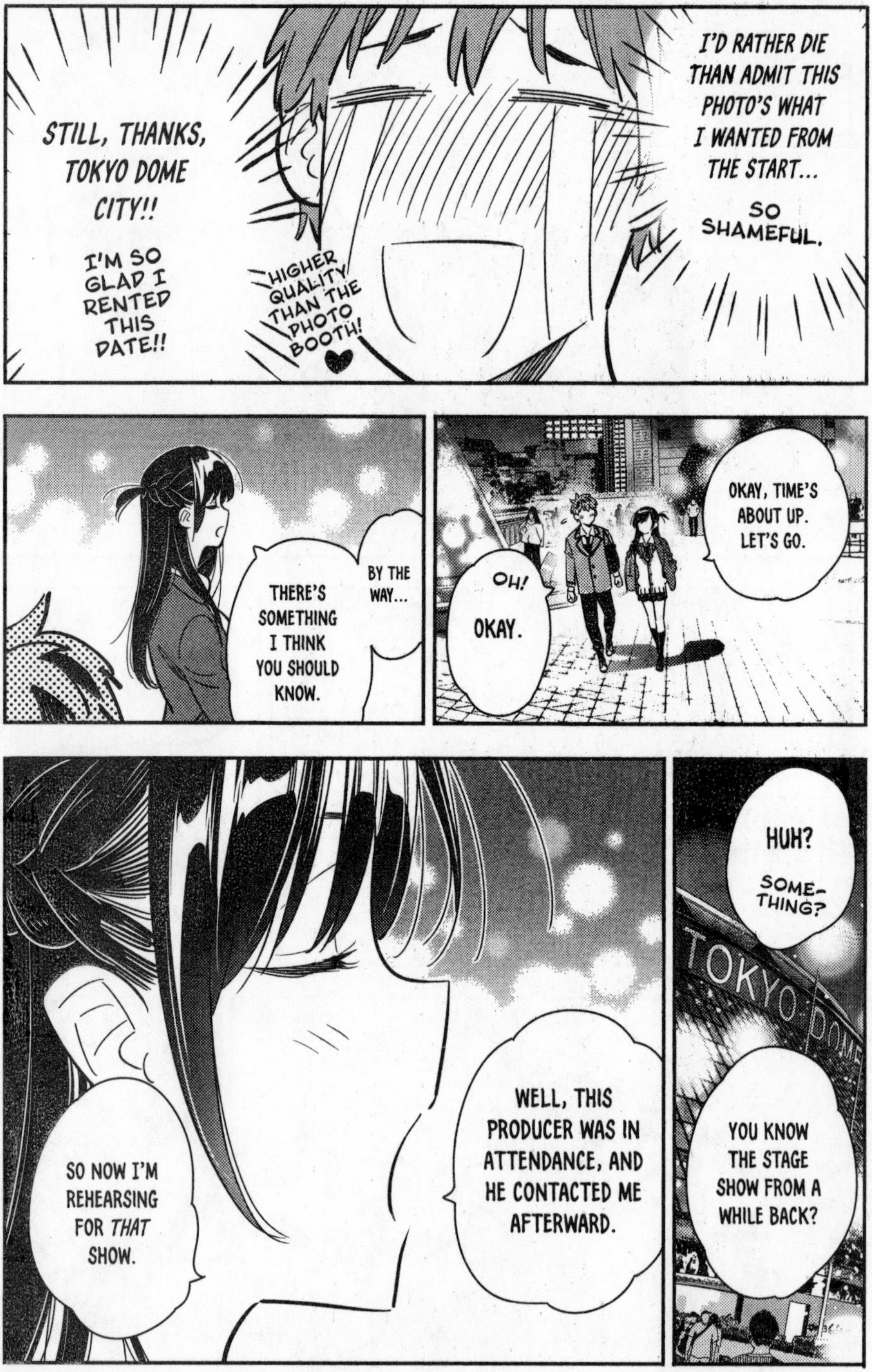
I'D RATHER DIE THAN ADMIT THIS PHOTO'S WHAT I WANTED FROM THE START...
SO SHAMEFUL.
HIGHER QUALITY THAN THE PHOTO BOOTH!
STILL, THANKS, TOKYO DOME CITY!!
I'M SO GLAD I RENTED THIS DATE!!
OKAY, TIME'S ABOUT UP. LET'S GO.
OH!
OKAY.
BY THE WAY...
THERE'S SOMETHING I THINK YOU SHOULD KNOW.
HUH?
SOME-THING?
TOKYO DOME
YOU KNOW THE STAGE SHOW FROM A WHILE BACK?
WELL, THIS PRODUCER WAS IN ATTENDANCE, AND HE CONTACTED ME AFTERWARD.
SO NOW I'M REHEARSING FOR *THAT* SHOW.

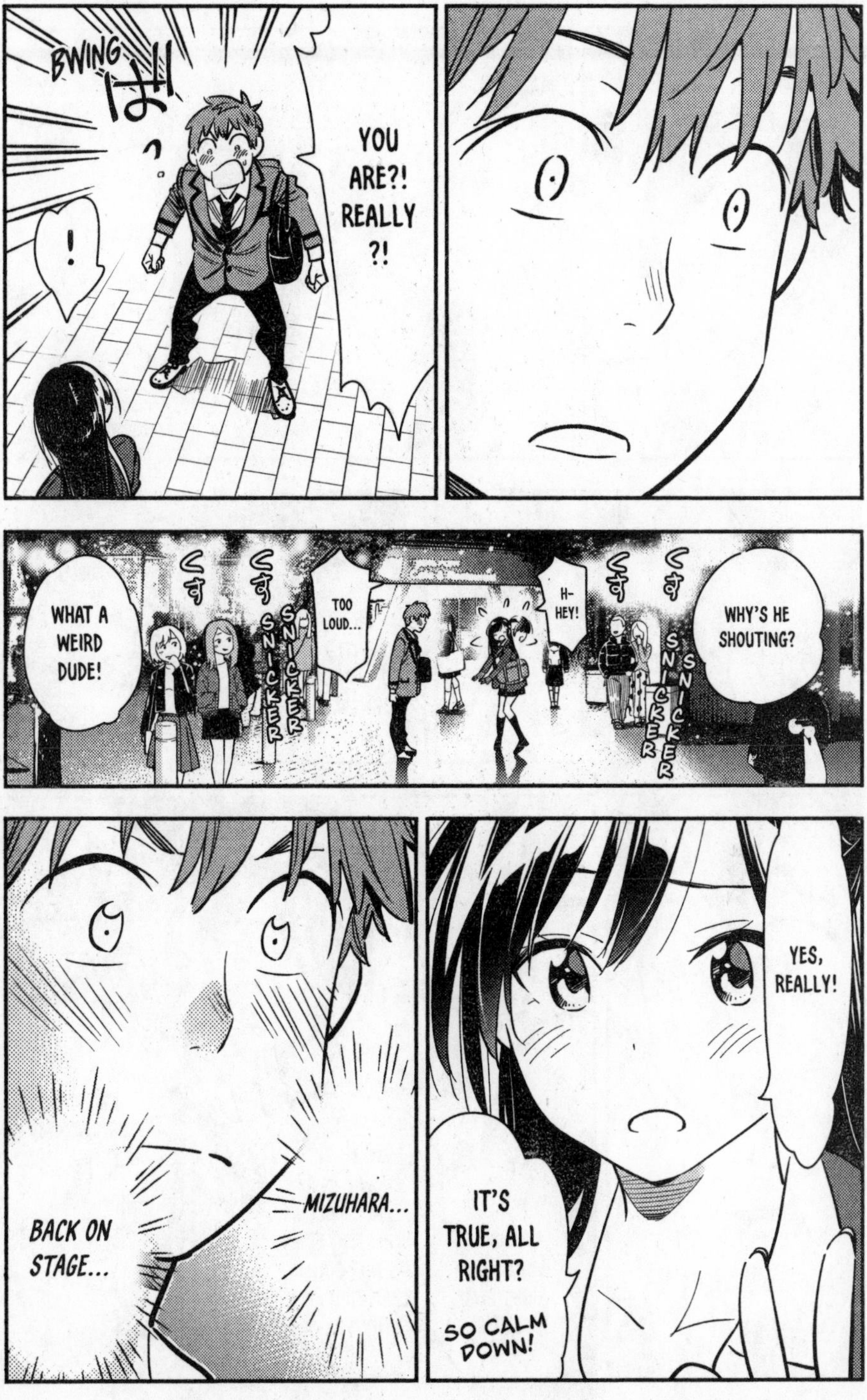
YOU ARE?! REALLY?!
BWING
は!!
!
WHY'S HE SHOUTING?
くす くす
SNICKER SNICKER
H-HEY!
TOO LOUD...
くす くす
SNICKER SNICKER
WHAT A WEIRD DUDE!
YES, REALLY!
IT'S TRUE, ALL RIGHT?
SO CALM DOWN!
MIZUHARA...
BACK ON STAGE...

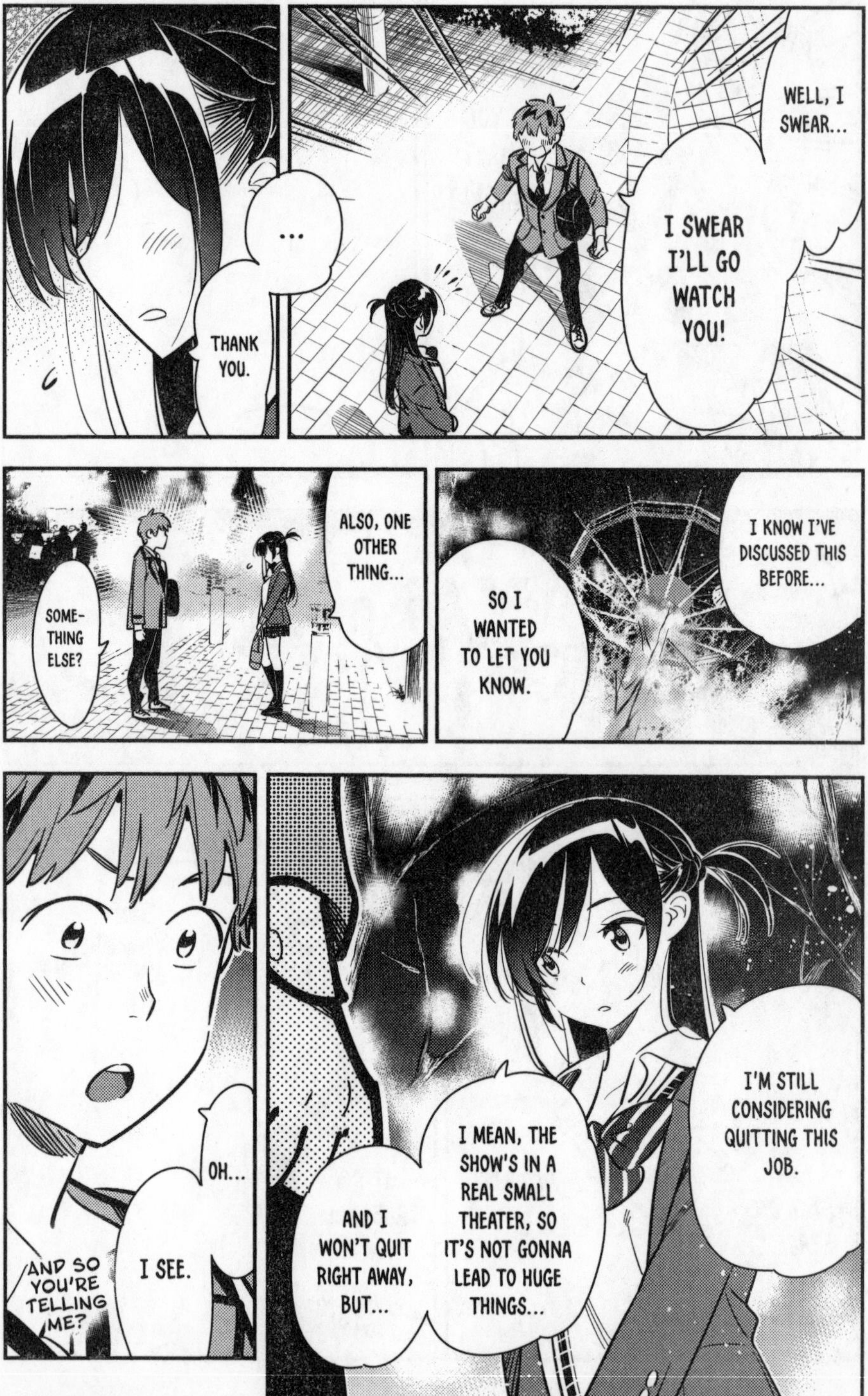
WELL, I SWEAR...
I SWEAR I'LL GO WATCH YOU!
...
THANK YOU.
I KNOW I'VE DISCUSSED THIS BEFORE...
SO I WANTED TO LET YOU KNOW.
ALSO, ONE OTHER THING...
SOME-THING ELSE?
I'M STILL CONSIDERING QUITTING THIS JOB.
I MEAN, THE SHOW'S IN A REAL SMALL THEATER, SO IT'S NOT GONNA LEAD TO HUGE THINGS...
AND I WON'T QUIT RIGHT AWAY, BUT...
OH...
I SEE.
AND SO YOU'RE TELLING ME?

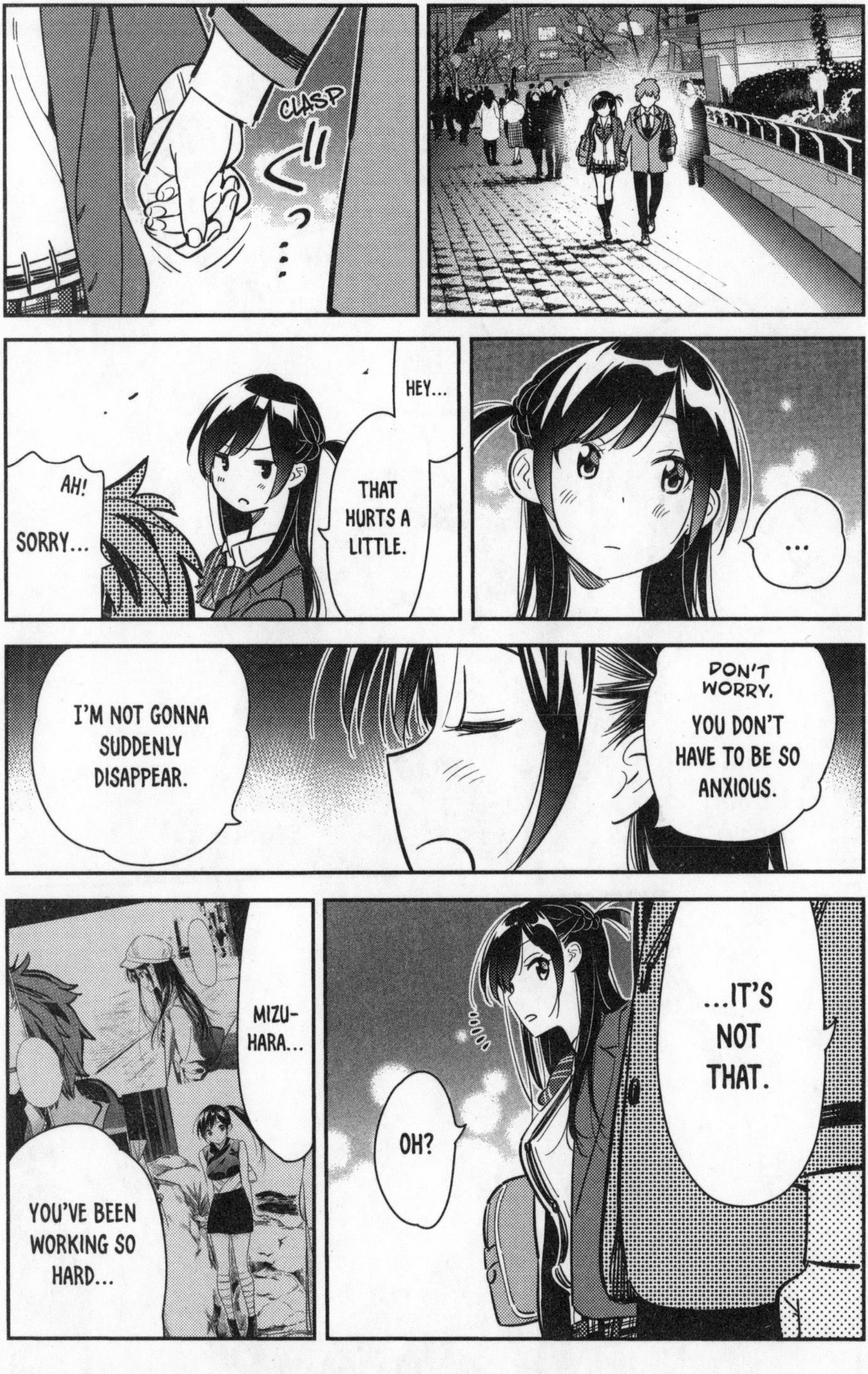
CLASP
ぐっ…
...
HEY...
THAT HURTS A LITTLE.
AH!
SORRY...
DON'T WORRY.
YOU DON'T HAVE TO BE SO ANXIOUS.
I'M NOT GONNA SUDDENLY DISAPPEAR.
...IT'S NOT THAT.
OH?
MIZU-HARA...
YOU'VE BEEN WORKING SO HARD...

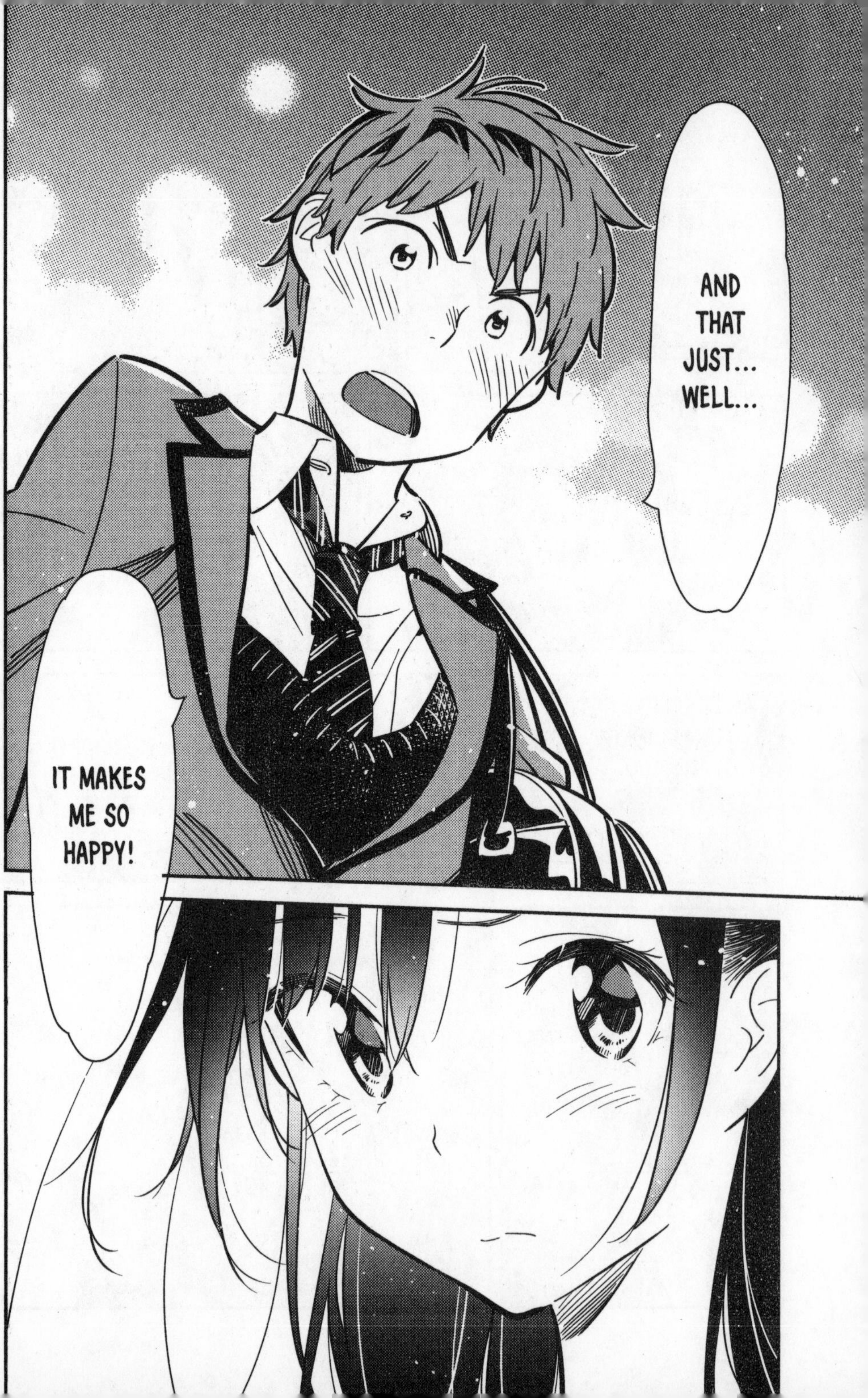
AND THAT JUST... WELL...
IT MAKES ME SO HAPPY!

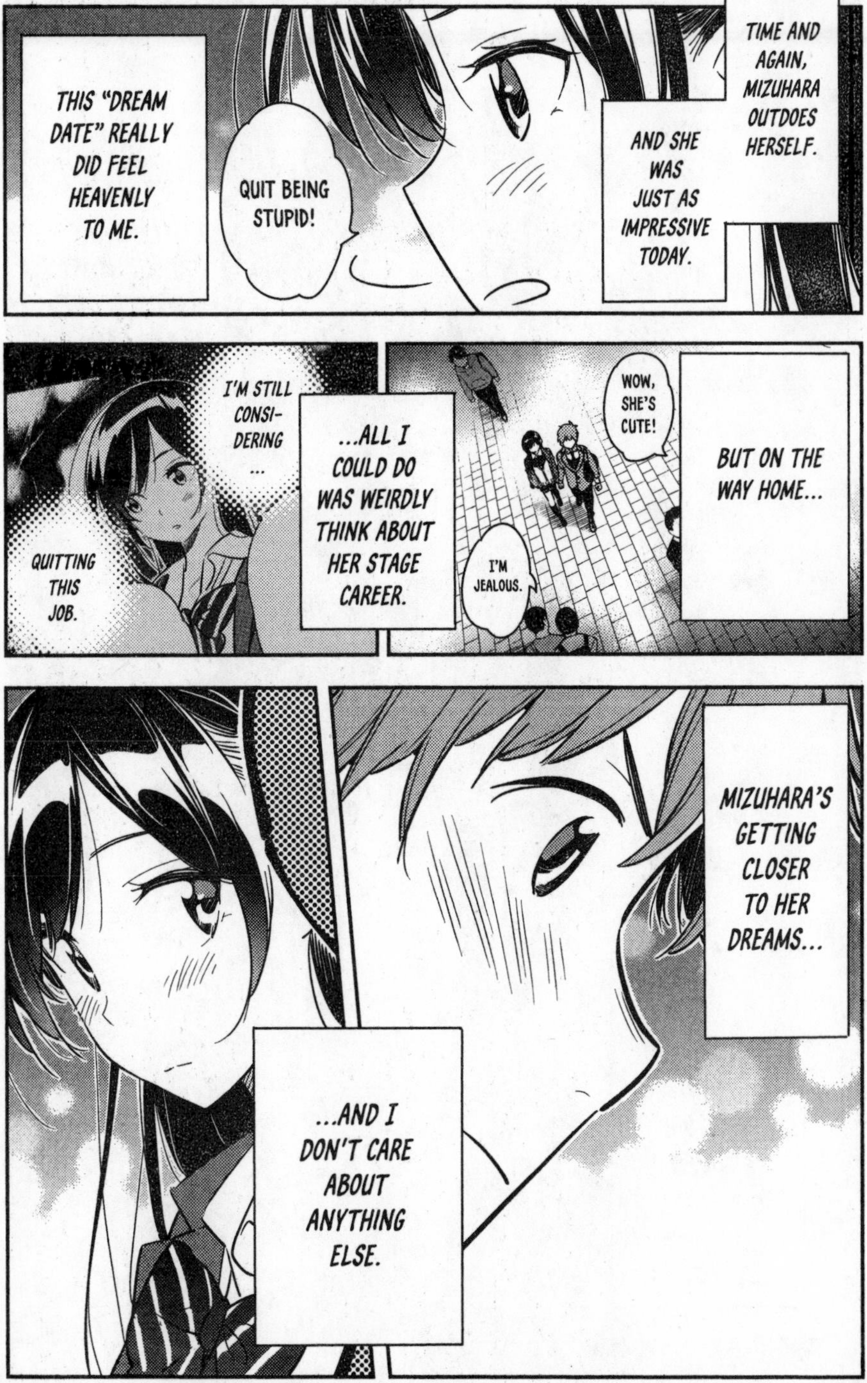
TIME AND AGAIN, MIZUHARA OUTDOES HERSELF.
AND SHE WAS JUST AS IMPRESSIVE TODAY.
QUIT BEING STUPID!
THIS "DREAM DATE" REALLY DID FEEL HEAVENLY TO ME.
BUT ON THE WAY HOME...
WOW, SHE'S CUTE!
I'M JEALOUS.
...ALL I COULD DO WAS WEIRDLY THINK ABOUT HER STAGE CAREER.
I'M STILL CONSIDERING...
QUITTING THIS JOB.
MIZUHARA'S GETTING CLOSER TO HER DREAMS...
...AND I DON'T CARE ABOUT ANYTHING ELSE.

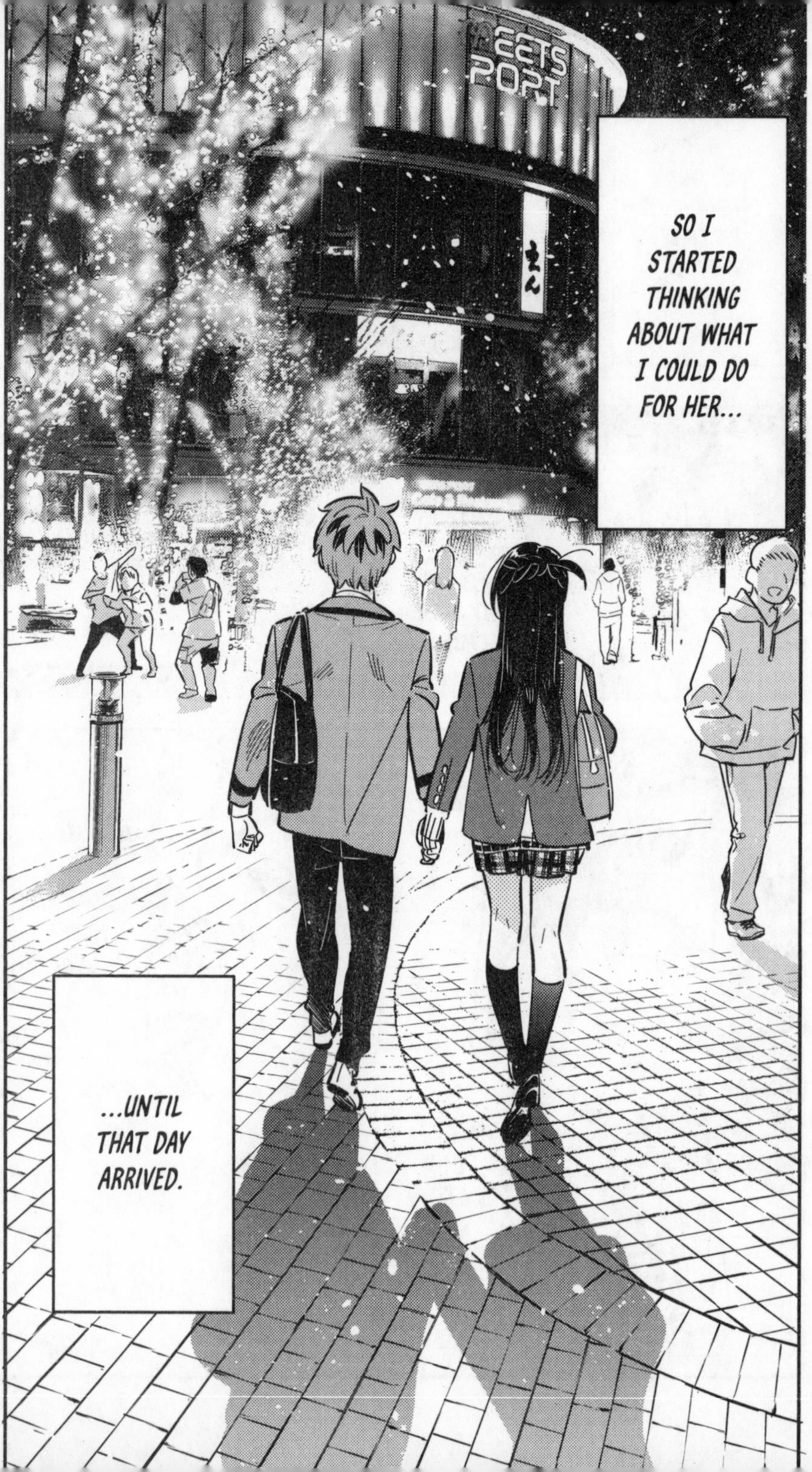
SO I STARTED THINKING ABOUT WHAT I COULD DO FOR HER...
...UNTIL THAT DAY ARRIVED.

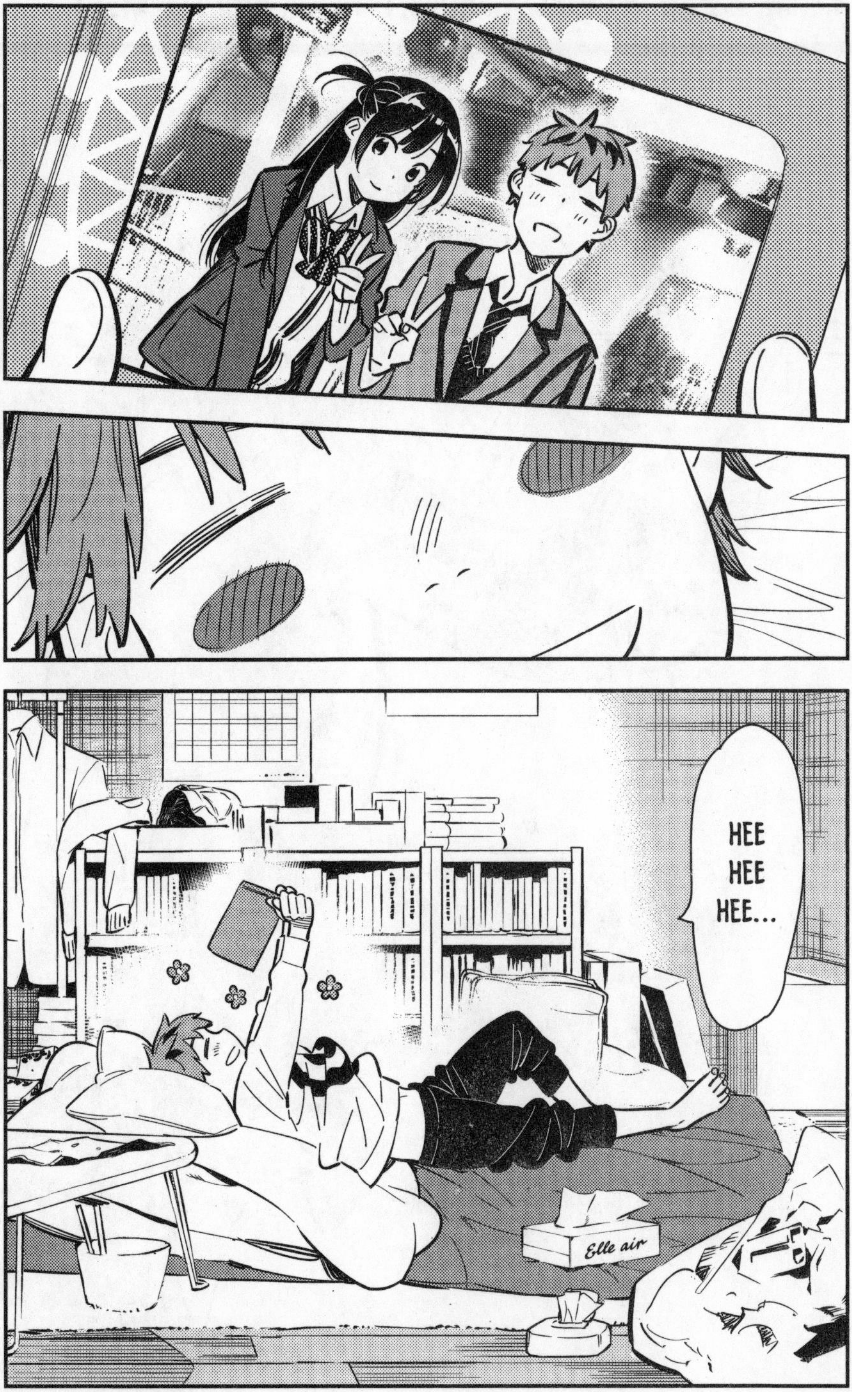
HEE
HEE
HEE...
Elle air

RATING 83 MY GIRLFRIEND, MY HOUSE, AND THE KISS 1

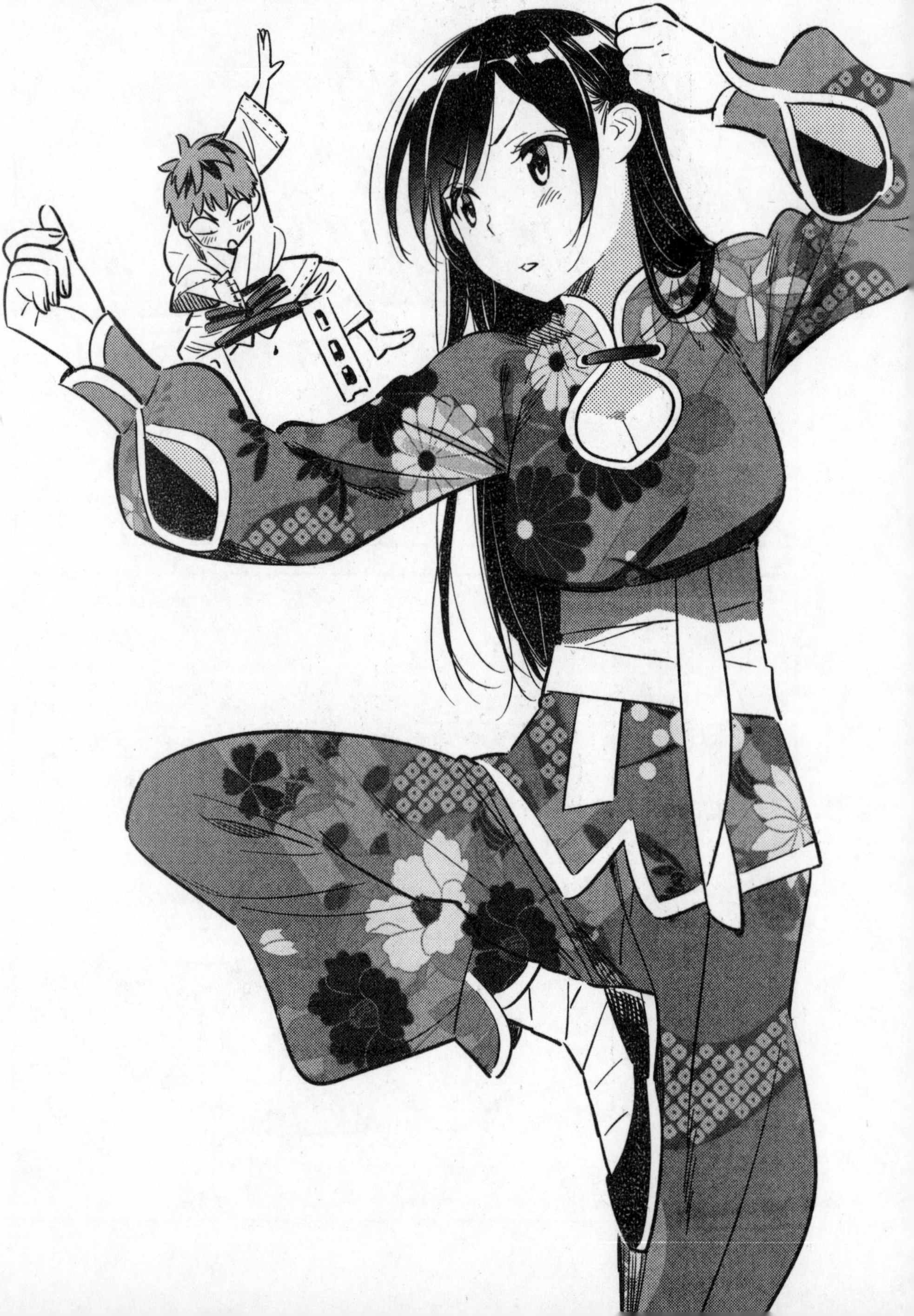

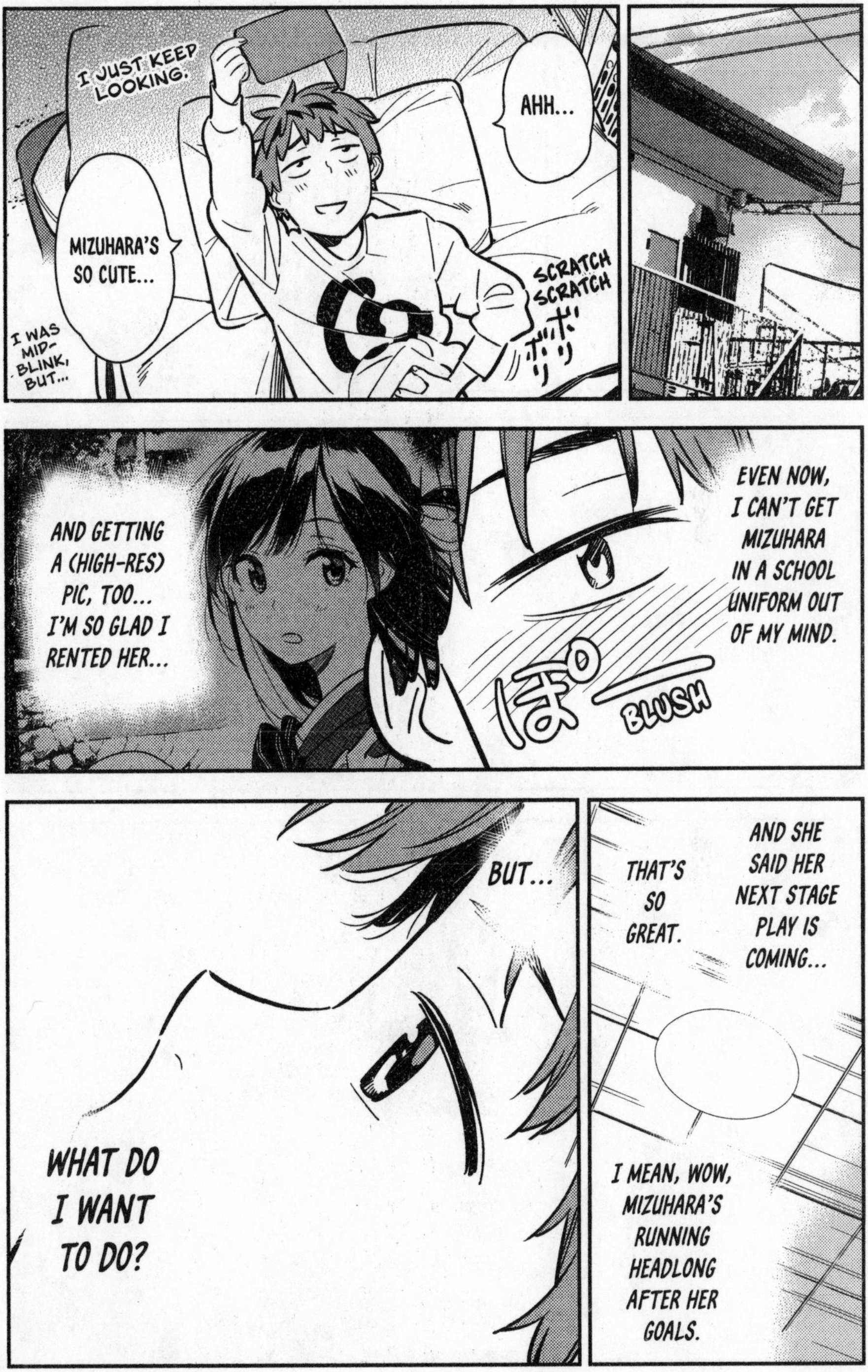
AHH...
I JUST KEEP LOOKING.
SCRATCH SCRATCH
ボリボリ
MIZUHARA'S SO CUTE...
I WAS MID-BLINK, BUT...
EVEN NOW, I CAN'T GET MIZUHARA IN A SCHOOL UNIFORM OUT OF MY MIND.
ぽー
BLUSH
AND GETTING A (HIGH-RES) PIC, TOO... I'M SO GLAD I RENTED HER...
AND SHE SAID HER NEXT STAGE PLAY IS COMING...
THAT'S SO GREAT.
I MEAN, WOW, MIZUHARA'S RUNNING HEADLONG AFTER HER GOALS.
BUT...
WHAT DO I WANT TO DO?

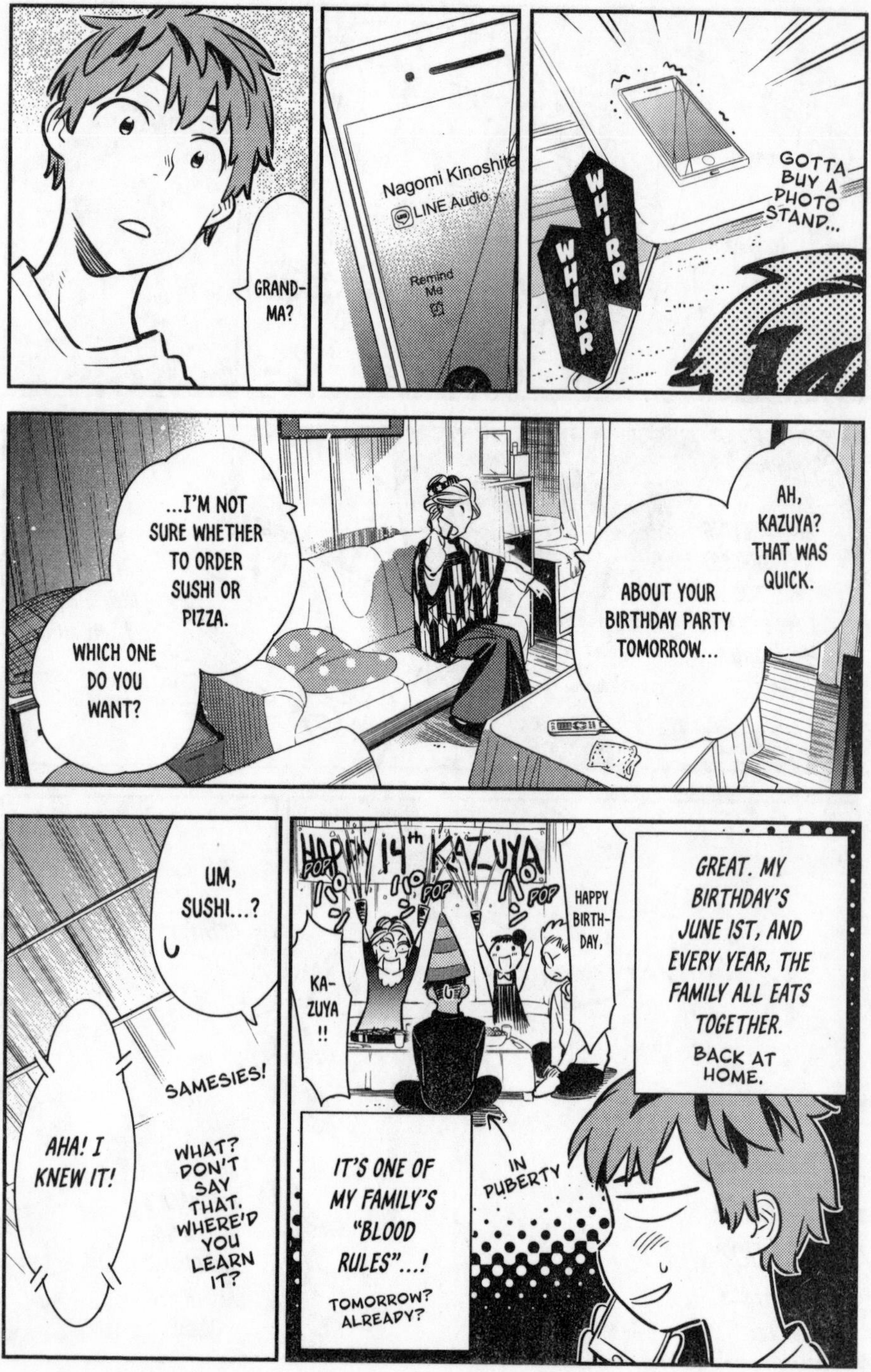
WHIRR
WHIRR
GOTTA BUY A PHOTO STAND...
Nagomi Kinoshita
LINE Audio
Remind Me
GRAND-MA?
AH, KAZUYA? THAT WAS QUICK.
ABOUT YOUR BIRTHDAY PARTY TOMORROW...
...I'M NOT SURE WHETHER TO ORDER SUSHI OR PIZZA.
WHICH ONE DO YOU WANT?
GREAT. MY BIRTHDAY'S JUNE 1ST, AND EVERY YEAR, THE FAMILY ALL EATS TOGETHER.
BACK AT HOME.
HAPPY BIRTHDAY,
HAPPY 14th KAZUYA
POP
POP
POP
POP
KAZUYA!!
IN PUBERTY
IT'S ONE OF MY FAMILY'S "BLOOD RULES"...!
TOMORROW? ALREADY?
UM, SUSHI...?
SAMESIES!
AHA! I KNEW IT!
WHAT? DON'T SAY THAT. WHERE'D YOU LEARN IT?

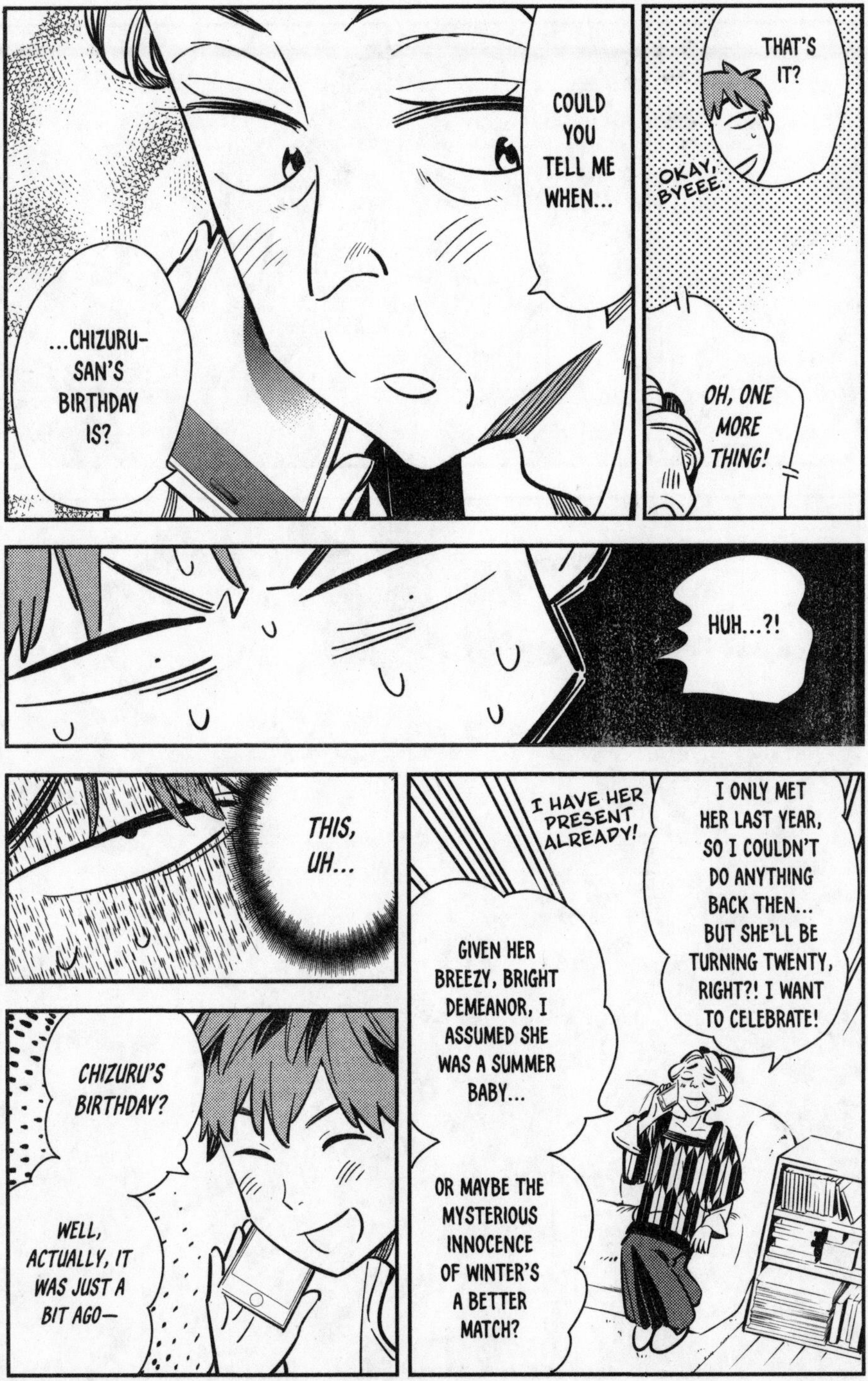
THAT'S IT?
OKAY, BYEEE.
OH, ONE MORE THING!
COULD YOU TELL ME WHEN...
...CHIZURU-SAN'S BIRTHDAY IS?
HUH...?!
I ONLY MET HER LAST YEAR, SO I COULDN'T DO ANYTHING BACK THEN... BUT SHE'LL BE TURNING TWENTY, RIGHT?! I WANT TO CELEBRATE!
I HAVE HER PRESENT ALREADY!
GIVEN HER BREEZY, BRIGHT DEMEANOR, I ASSUMED SHE WAS A SUMMER BABY...
OR MAYBE THE MYSTERIOUS INNOCENCE OF WINTER'S A BETTER MATCH?
THIS, UH...
CHIZURU'S BIRTHDAY?
WELL, ACTUALLY, IT WAS JUST A BIT AGO—

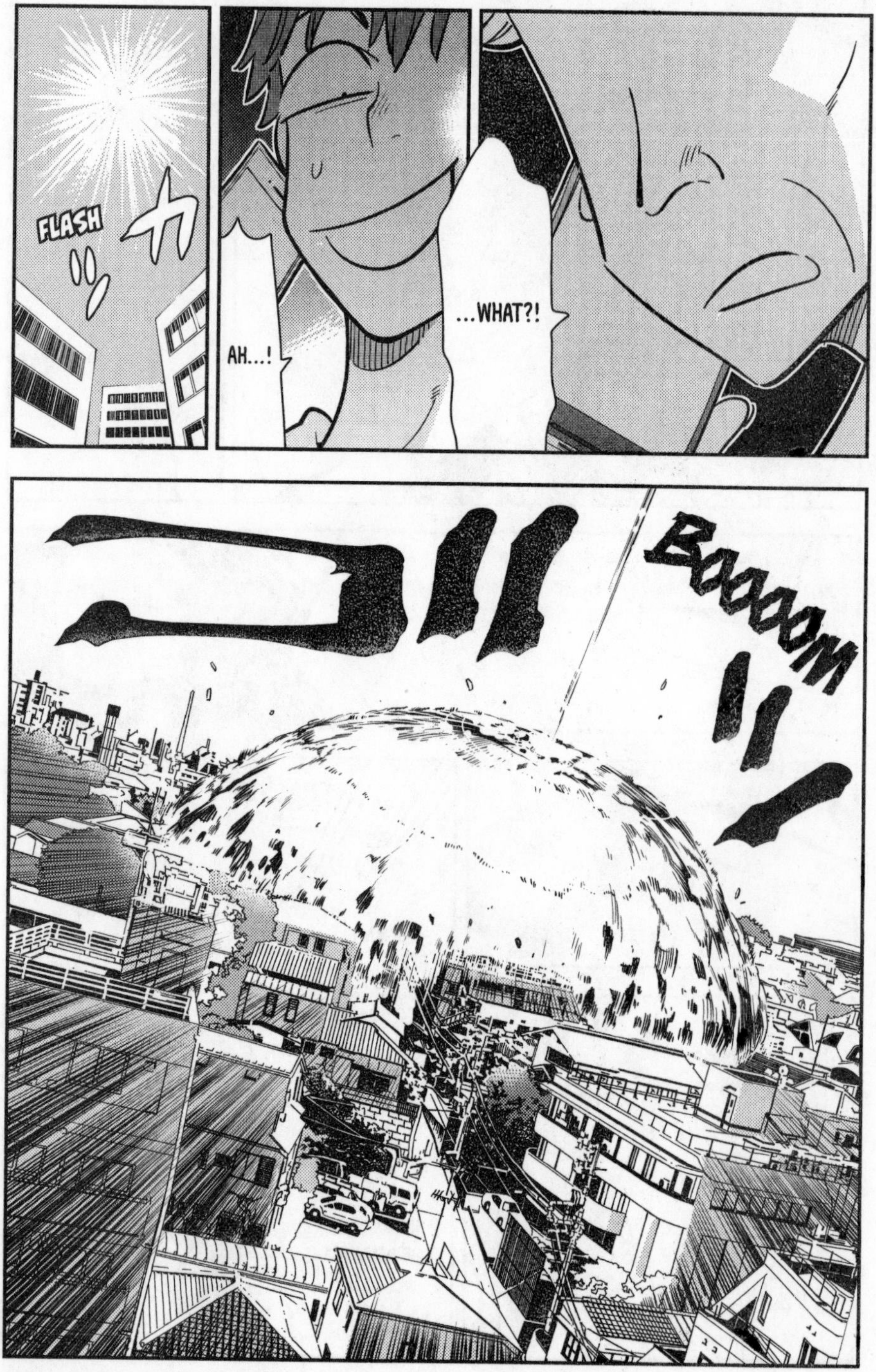
...WHAT?!
AH...!
FLASH
Boooom

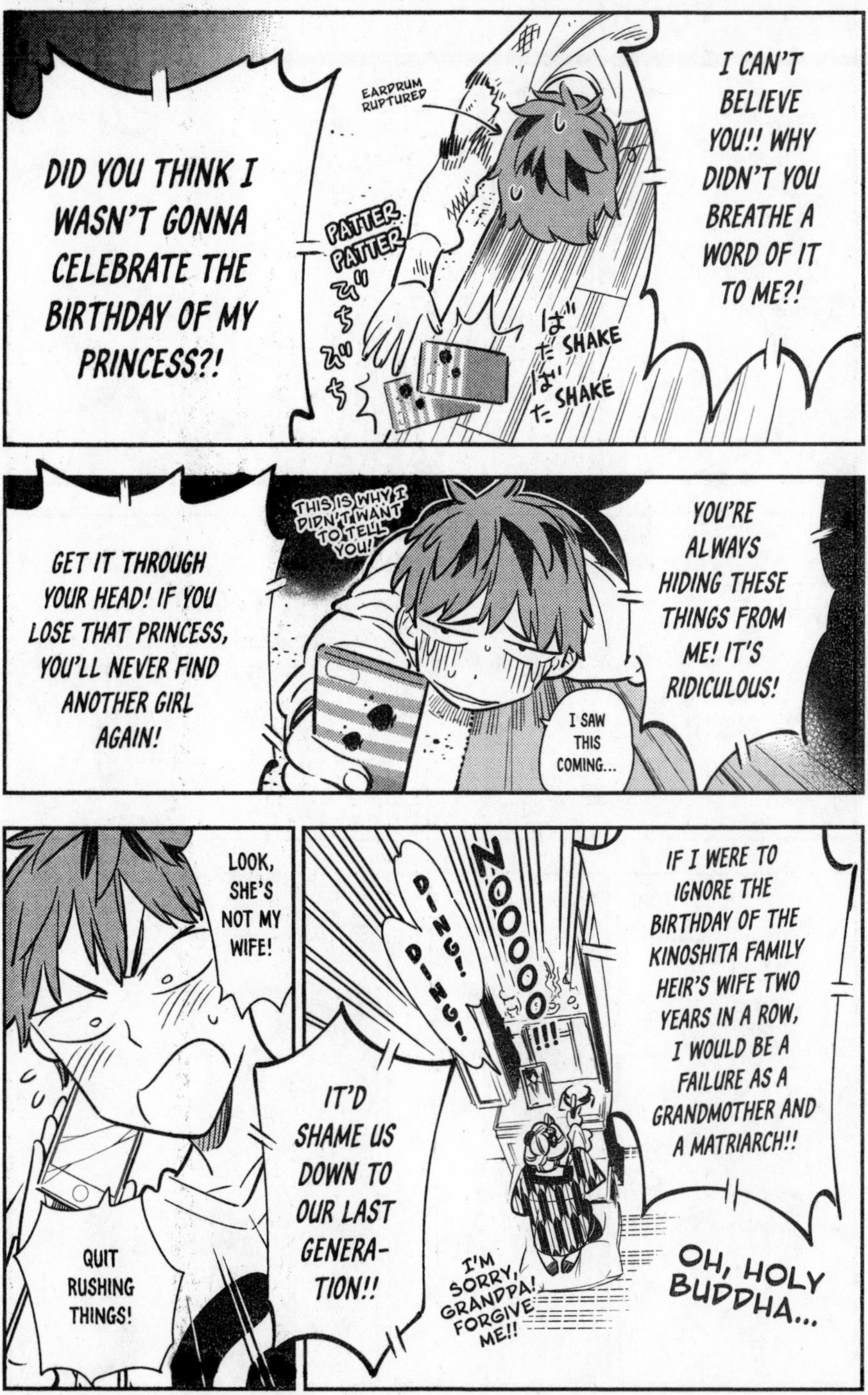
I CAN'T BELIEVE YOU!! WHY DIDN'T YOU BREATHE A WORD OF IT TO ME?!
EARDRUM RUPTURED
ばたばた SHAKE SHAKE
PATTER PATTER びちびち
DID YOU THINK I WASN'T GONNA CELEBRATE THE BIRTHDAY OF MY PRINCESS?!
YOU'RE ALWAYS HIDING THESE THINGS FROM ME! IT'S RIDICULOUS!
THIS IS WHY I DIDN'T WANT TO TELL YOU!!
I SAW THIS COMING...
GET IT THROUGH YOUR HEAD! IF YOU LOSE THAT PRINCESS, YOU'LL NEVER FIND ANOTHER GIRL AGAIN!
IF I WERE TO IGNORE THE BIRTHDAY OF THE KINOSHITA FAMILY HEIR'S WIFE TWO YEARS IN A ROW, I WOULD BE A FAILURE AS A GRANDMOTHER AND A MATRIARCH!!
NOOOOOO!!!
DING! DING! DING!
OH, HOLY BUDDHA...
I'M SORRY, GRANDPA! FORGIVE ME!!
IT'D SHAME US DOWN TO OUR LAST GENERA-TION!!
LOOK, SHE'S NOT MY WIFE!
QUIT RUSHING THINGS!

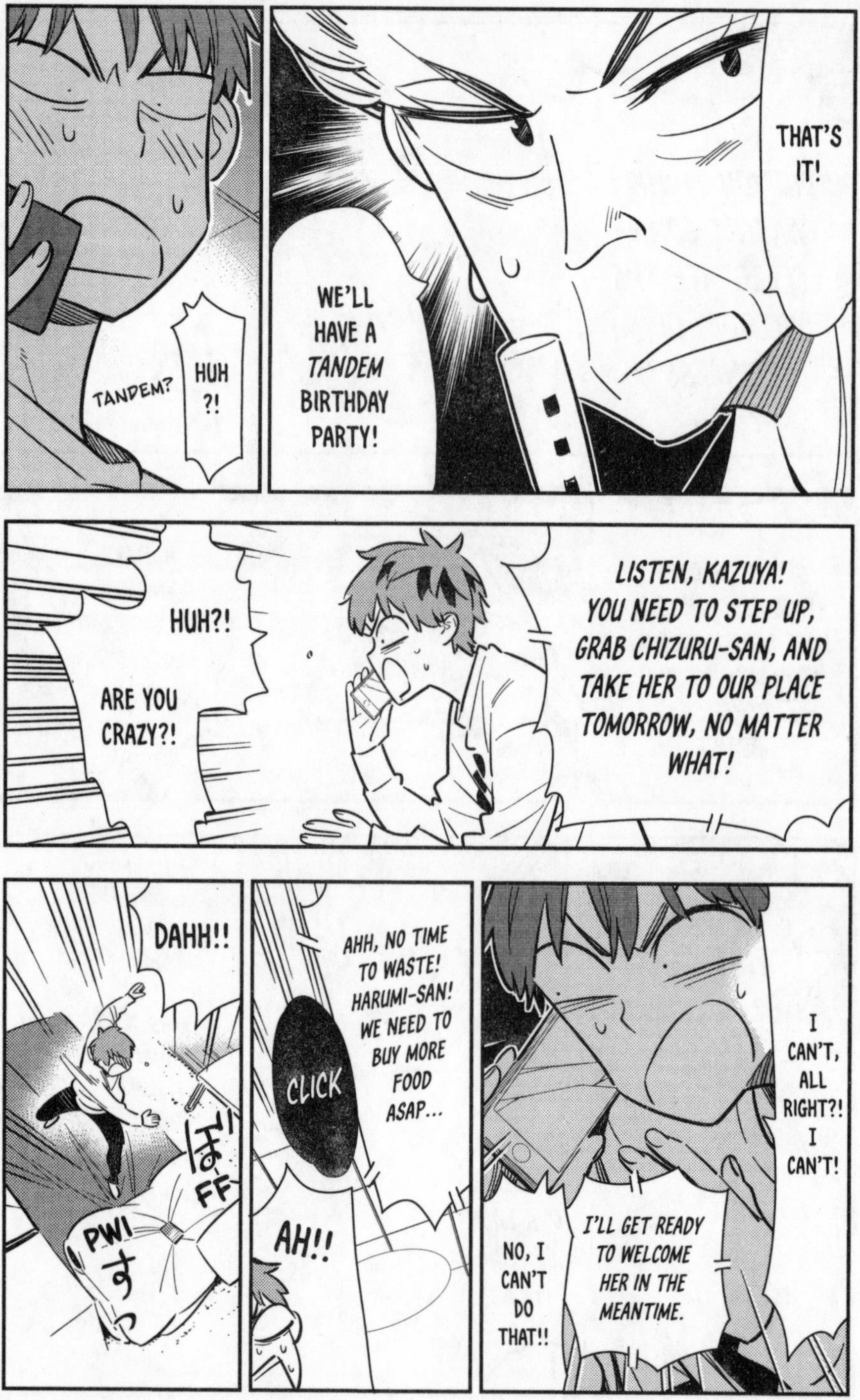
THAT'S IT!
WE'LL HAVE A *TANDEM* BIRTHDAY PARTY!
HUH?!
TANDEM?
LISTEN, KAZUYA! YOU NEED TO STEP UP, GRAB CHIZURU-SAN, AND TAKE HER TO OUR PLACE TOMORROW, NO MATTER WHAT!
HUH?!
ARE YOU CRAZY?!
I CAN'T, ALL RIGHT?! I CAN'T!
I'LL GET READY TO WELCOME HER IN THE MEANTIME.
NO, I CAN'T DO THAT!!
AHH, NO TIME TO WASTE! HARUMI-SAN! WE NEED TO BUY MORE FOOD ASAP...
CLICK
AH!!
DAHH!!
FF
PWI

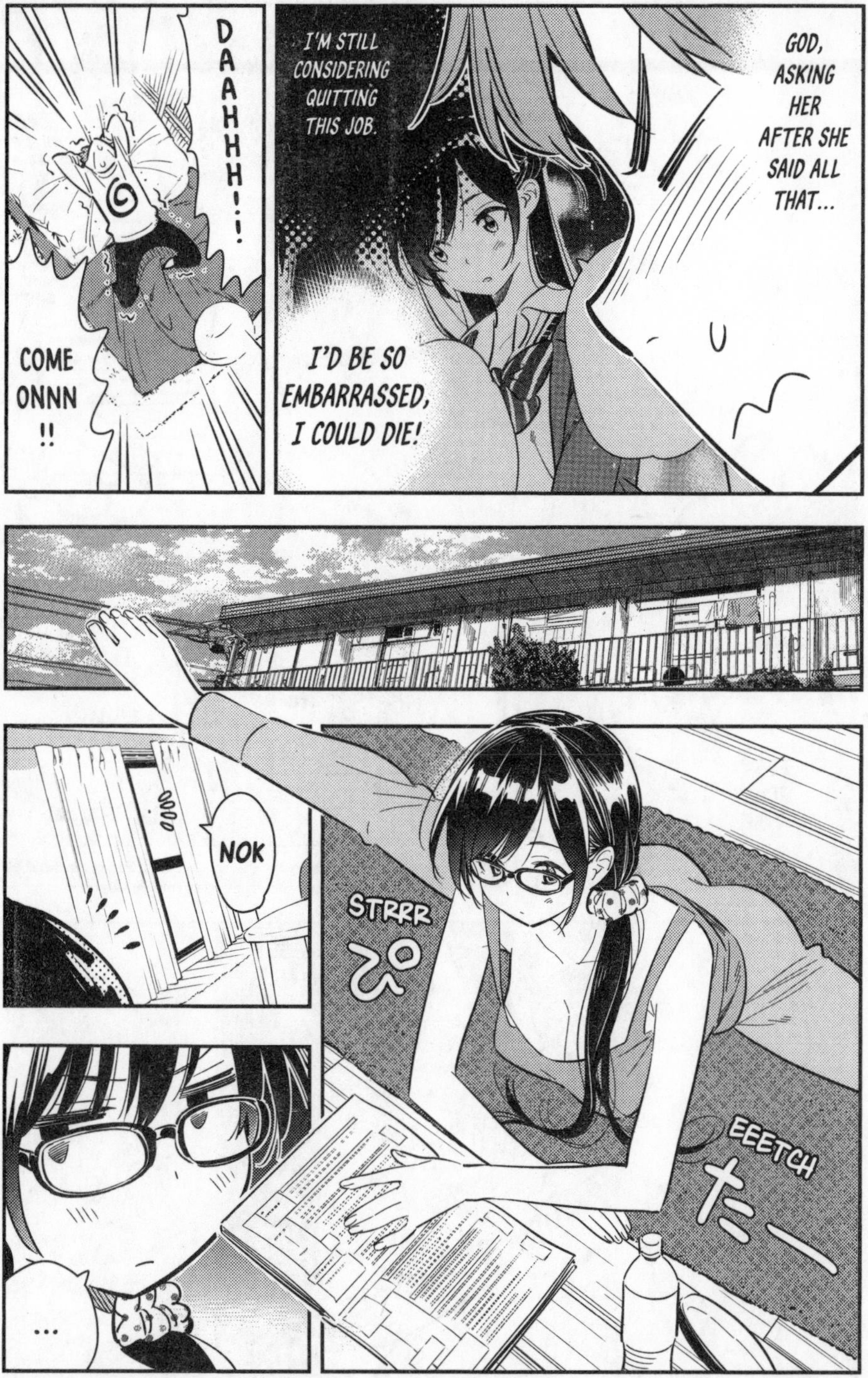
GOD, ASKING HER AFTER SHE SAID ALL THAT...
I'M STILL CONSIDERING QUITTING THIS JOB.
I'D BE SO EMBARRASSED, I COULD DIE!
DAAHHH!!
COME ONNN!!
STRRR
ぴ
EEETCH
たー
NOK
...

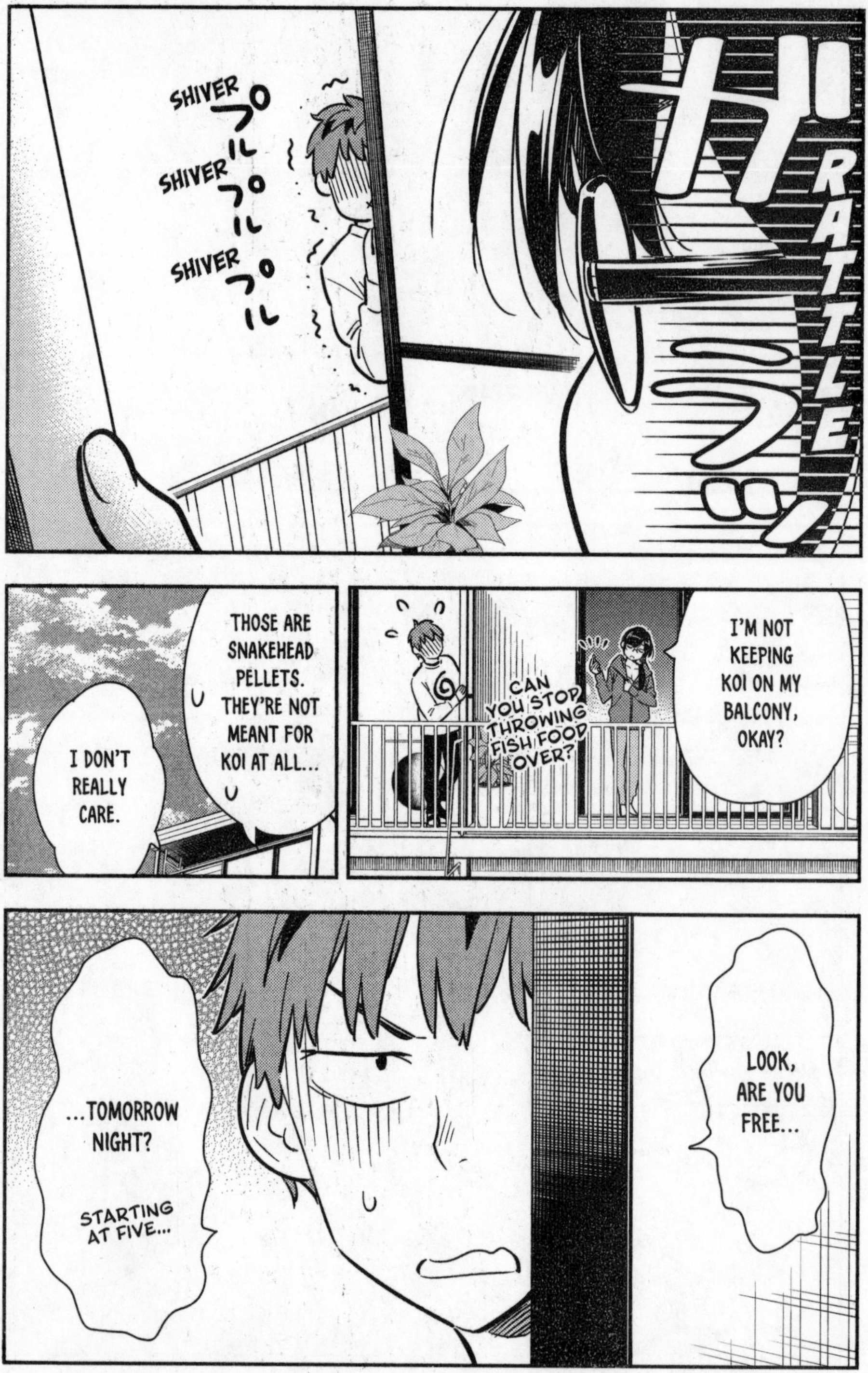
ガラッ
RATTLE
SHIVER プル
SHIVER プル
SHIVER プル
I'M NOT KEEPING KOI ON MY BALCONY, OKAY?
CAN YOU STOP THROWING FISH FOOD OVER?
THOSE ARE SNAKEHEAD PELLETS. THEY'RE NOT MEANT FOR KOI AT ALL...
I DON'T REALLY CARE.
LOOK, ARE YOU FREE...
...TOMORROW NIGHT?
STARTING AT FIVE...

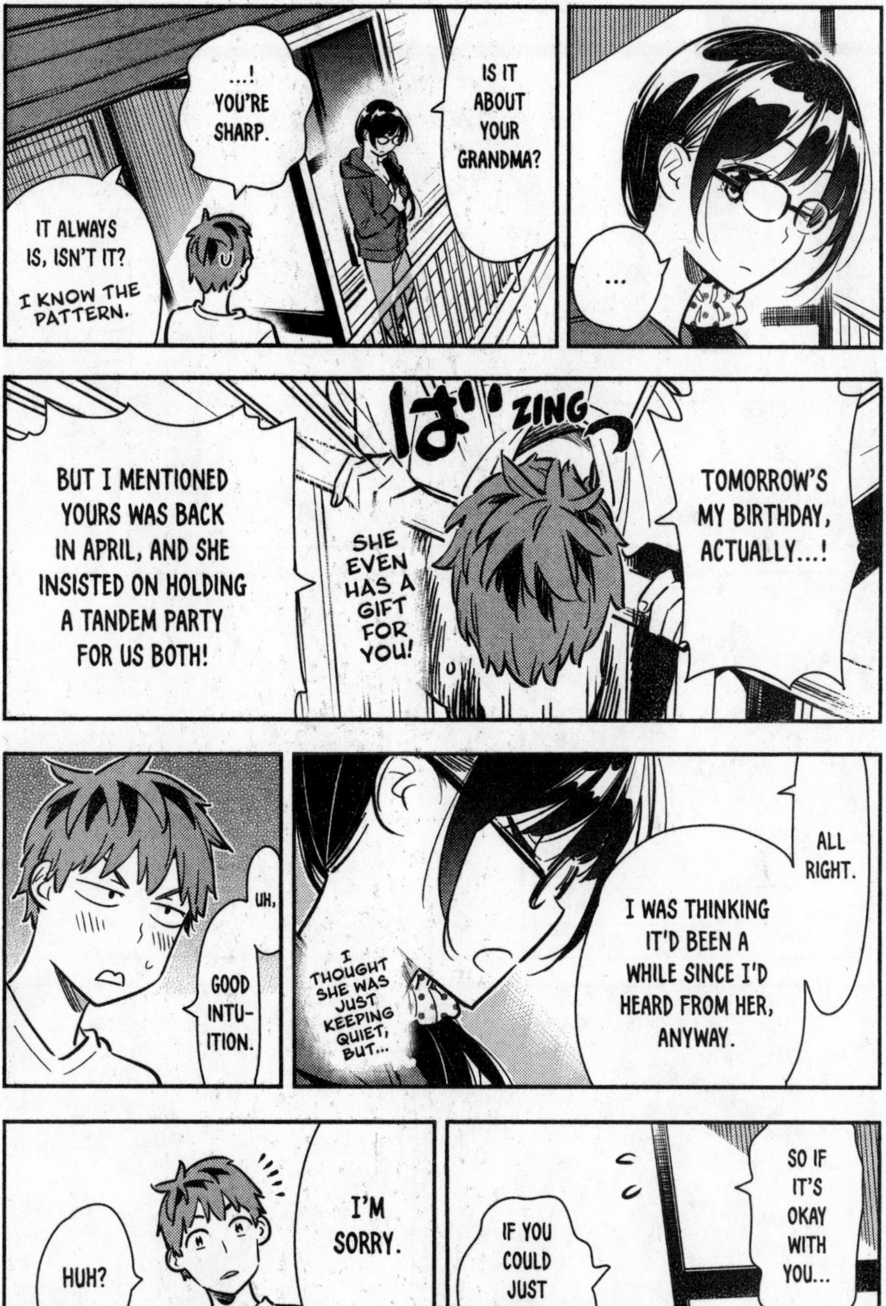
...
IS IT ABOUT YOUR GRANDMA?
...! YOU'RE SHARP.
IT ALWAYS IS, ISN'T IT?
I KNOW THE PATTERN.
TOMORROW'S MY BIRTHDAY, ACTUALLY...!
ばっ ZING
SHE EVEN HAS A GIFT FOR YOU!
BUT I MENTIONED YOURS WAS BACK IN APRIL, AND SHE INSISTED ON HOLDING A TANDEM PARTY FOR US BOTH!
ALL RIGHT.
I WAS THINKING IT'D BEEN A WHILE SINCE I'D HEARD FROM HER, ANYWAY.
I THOUGHT SHE WAS JUST KEEPING QUIET, BUT...
UH,
GOOD INTU-ITION.
SO IF IT'S OKAY WITH YOU...
IF YOU COULD JUST SWING BY FOR A BIT...
I'M SORRY.
HUH?

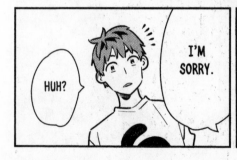

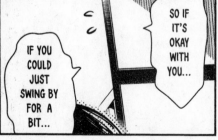

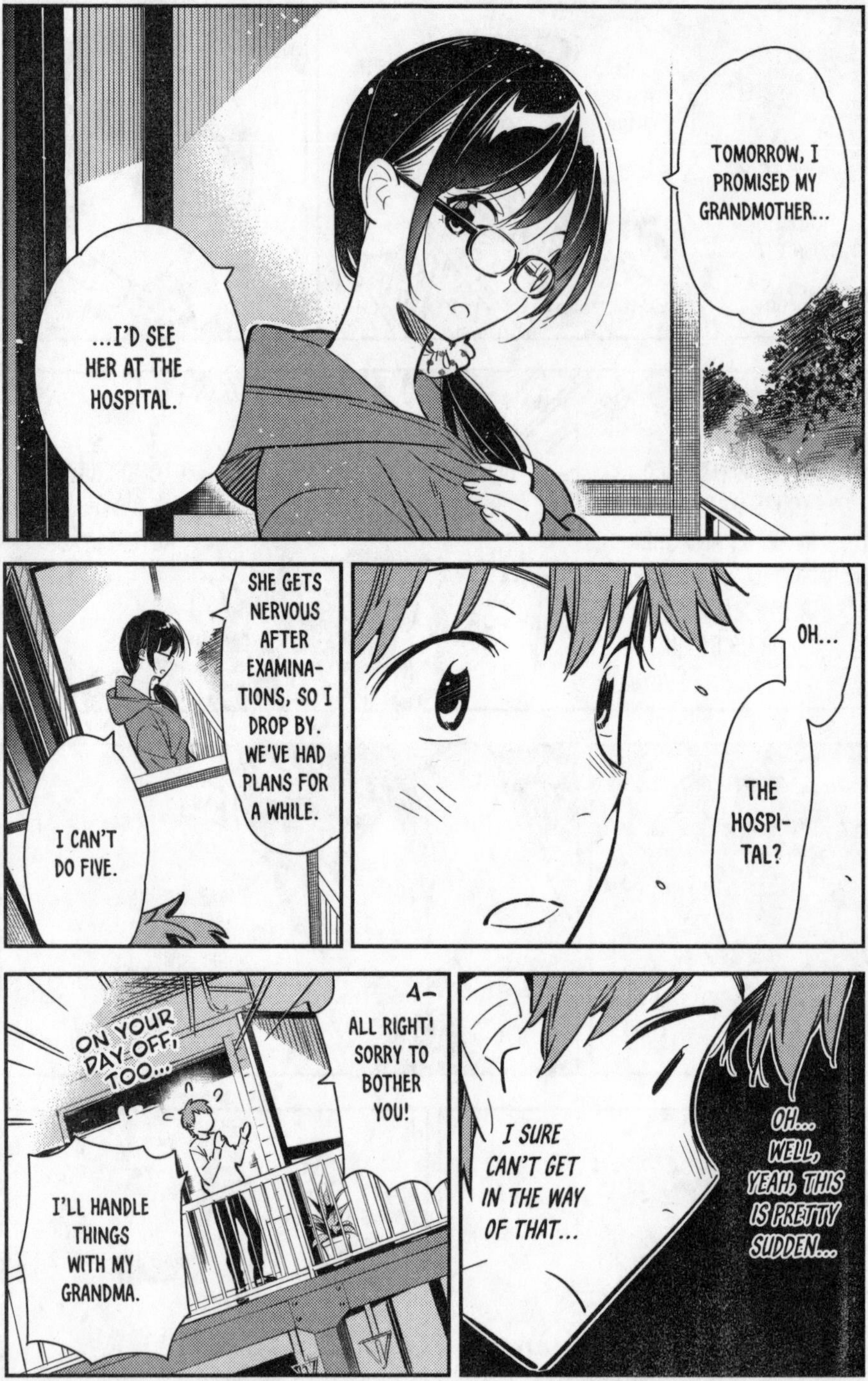
TOMORROW, I PROMISED MY GRANDMOTHER...
...I'D SEE HER AT THE HOSPITAL.
OH...
THE HOSPITAL?
SHE GETS NERVOUS AFTER EXAMINATIONS, SO I DROP BY. WE'VE HAD PLANS FOR A WHILE.
I CAN'T DO FIVE.
OH... WELL, YEAH, THIS IS PRETTY SUDDEN...
I SURE CAN'T GET IN THE WAY OF THAT...
A— ALL RIGHT! SORRY TO BOTHER YOU!
ON YOUR DAY OFF, TOO...
I'LL HANDLE THINGS WITH MY GRANDMA.

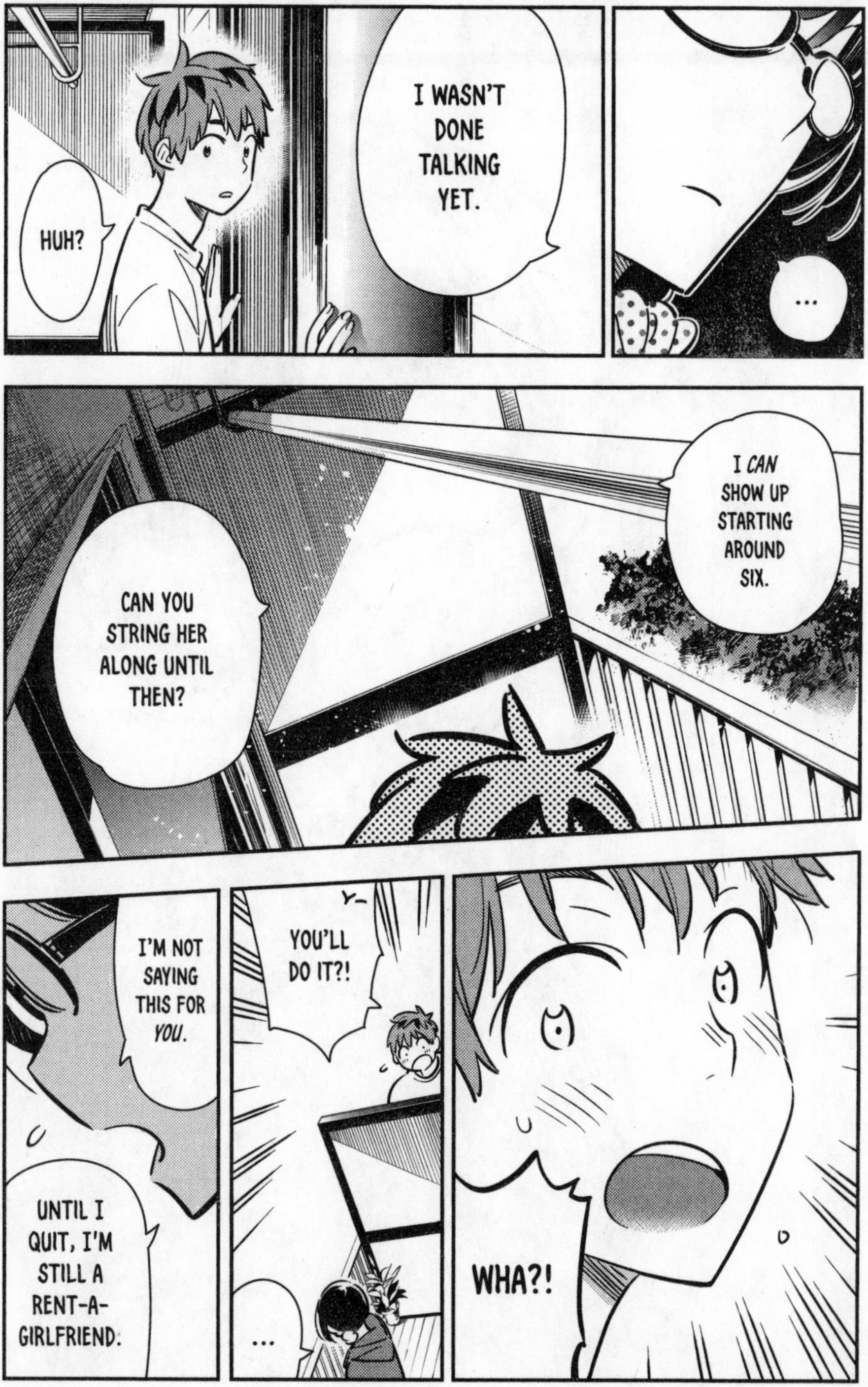
...
I WASN'T DONE TALKING YET.
HUH?
I *CAN* SHOW UP STARTING AROUND SIX.
CAN YOU STRING HER ALONG UNTIL THEN?
WHA?!
YOU'LL DO IT?!
...
I'M NOT SAYING THIS FOR *YOU*.
UNTIL I QUIT, I'M STILL A RENT-A-GIRLFRIEND.

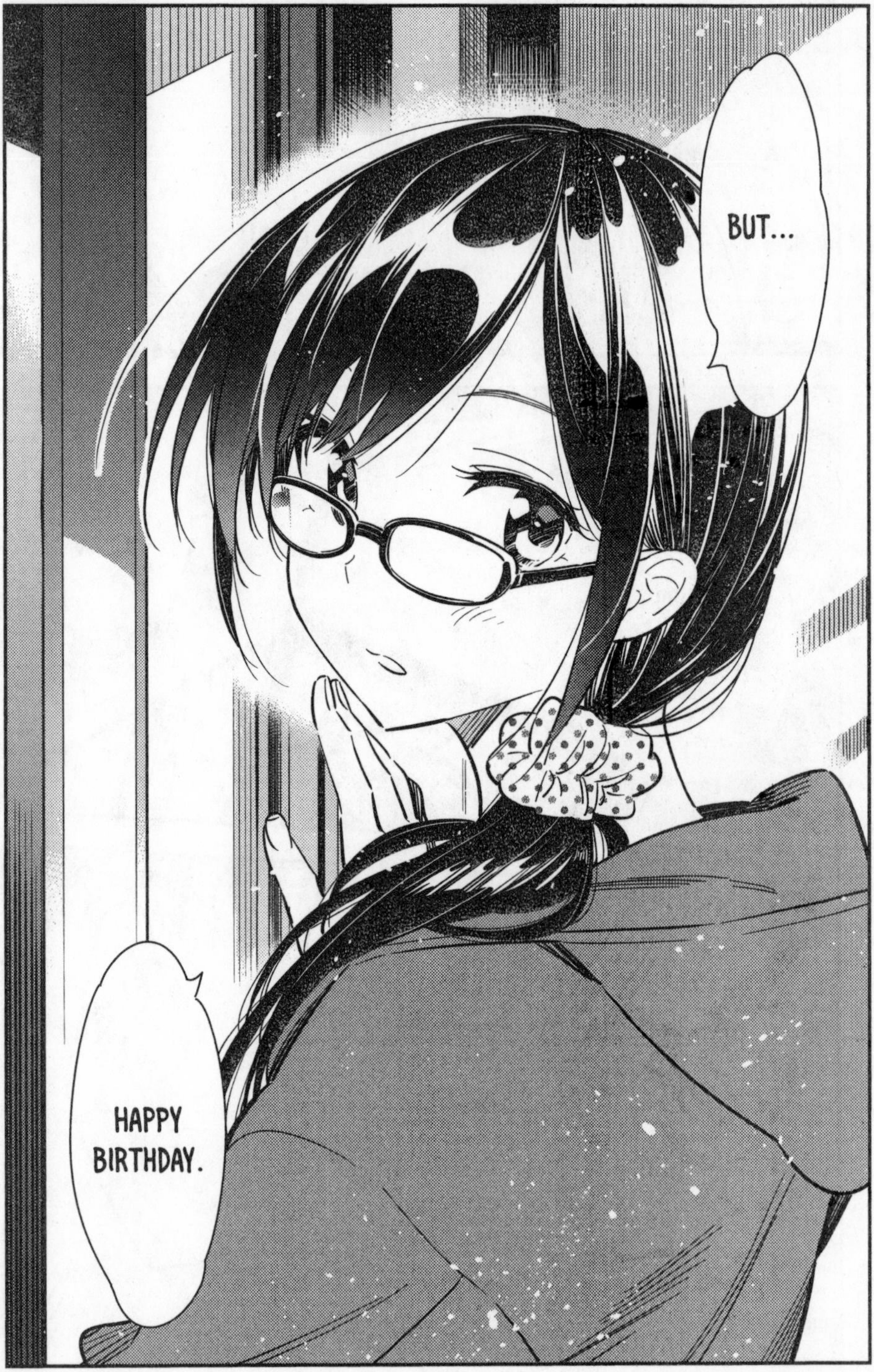
BUT...
HAPPY BIRTHDAY.

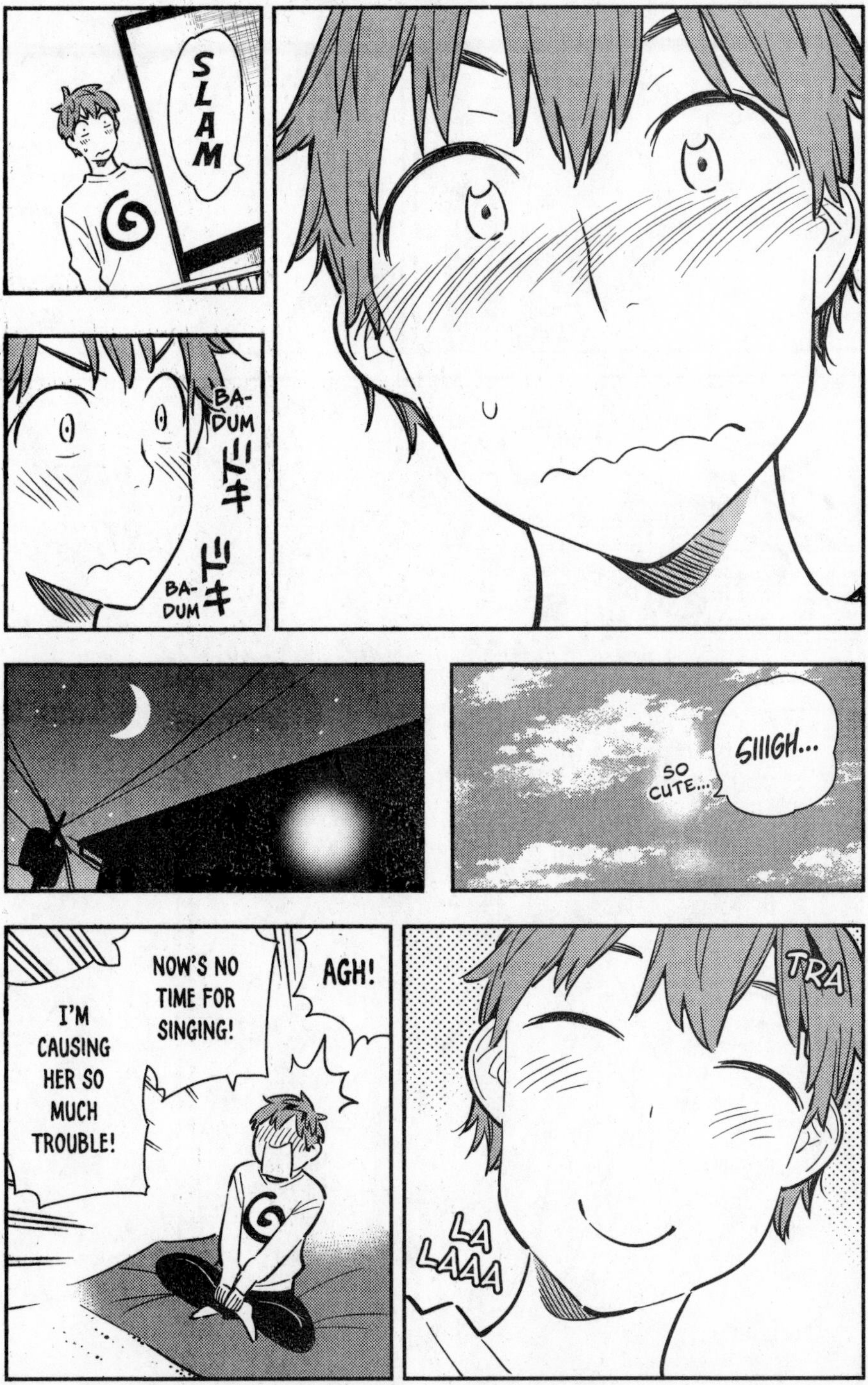
SLAM
BA-DUM
ドキ
ドキ
BA-DUM
SIIIGH...
SO CUTE...
TRA
LA LAAA
AGH!
NOW'S NO TIME FOR SINGING!
I'M CAUSING HER SO MUCH TROUBLE!

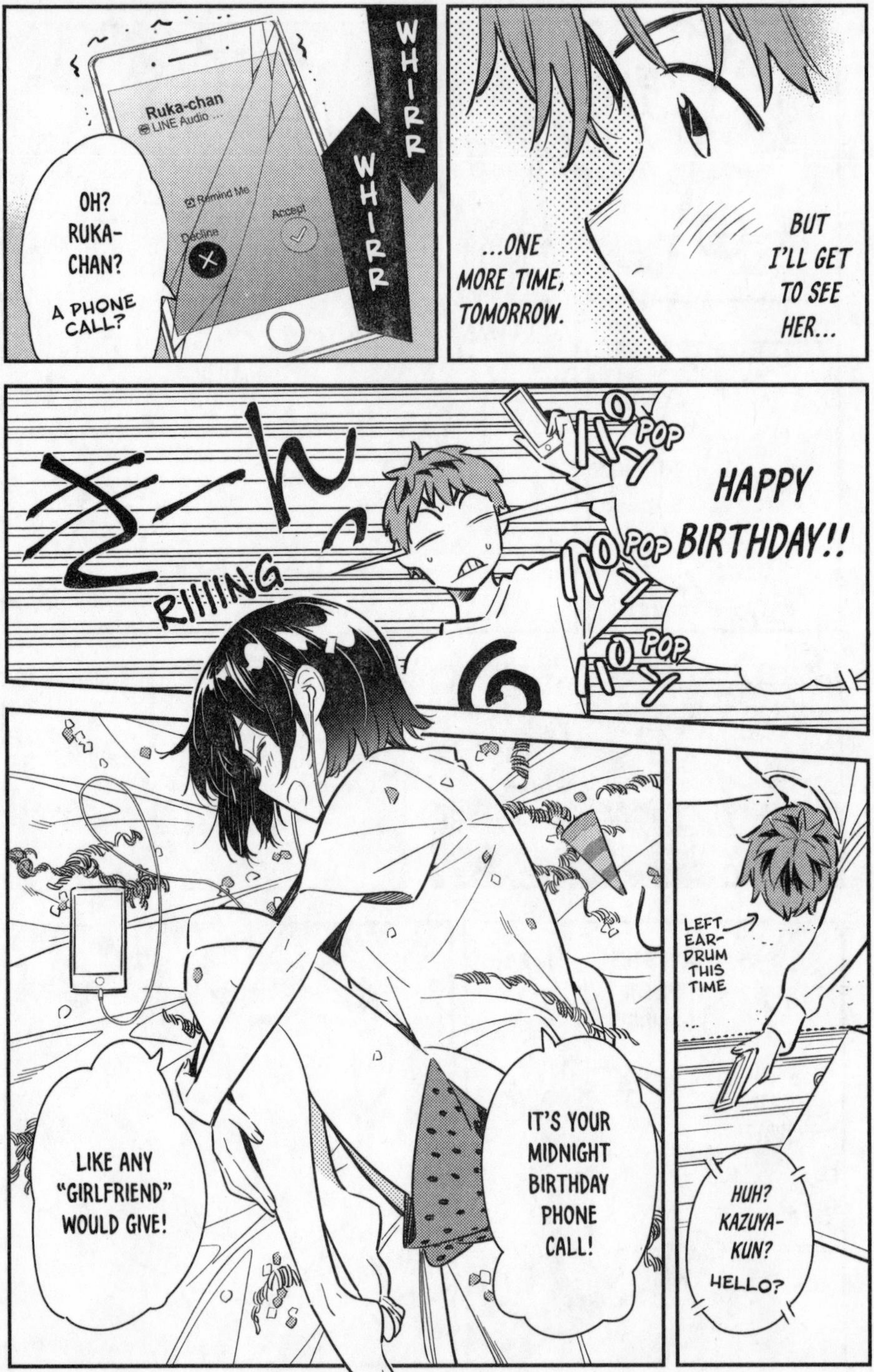
BUT I'LL GET TO SEE HER...
...ONE MORE TIME, TOMORROW.
Ruka-chan
LINE Audio ...
Remind Me
Accept
Decline
WHIRR
WHIRR
OH? RUKA-CHAN?
A PHONE CALL?
HAPPY BIRTHDAY!!
POP
POP
POP
RIIIING
HUH? KAZUYA-KUN?
HELLO?
LEFT EAR-DRUM THIS TIME
IT'S YOUR MIDNIGHT BIRTHDAY PHONE CALL!
LIKE ANY "GIRLFRIEND" WOULD GIVE!

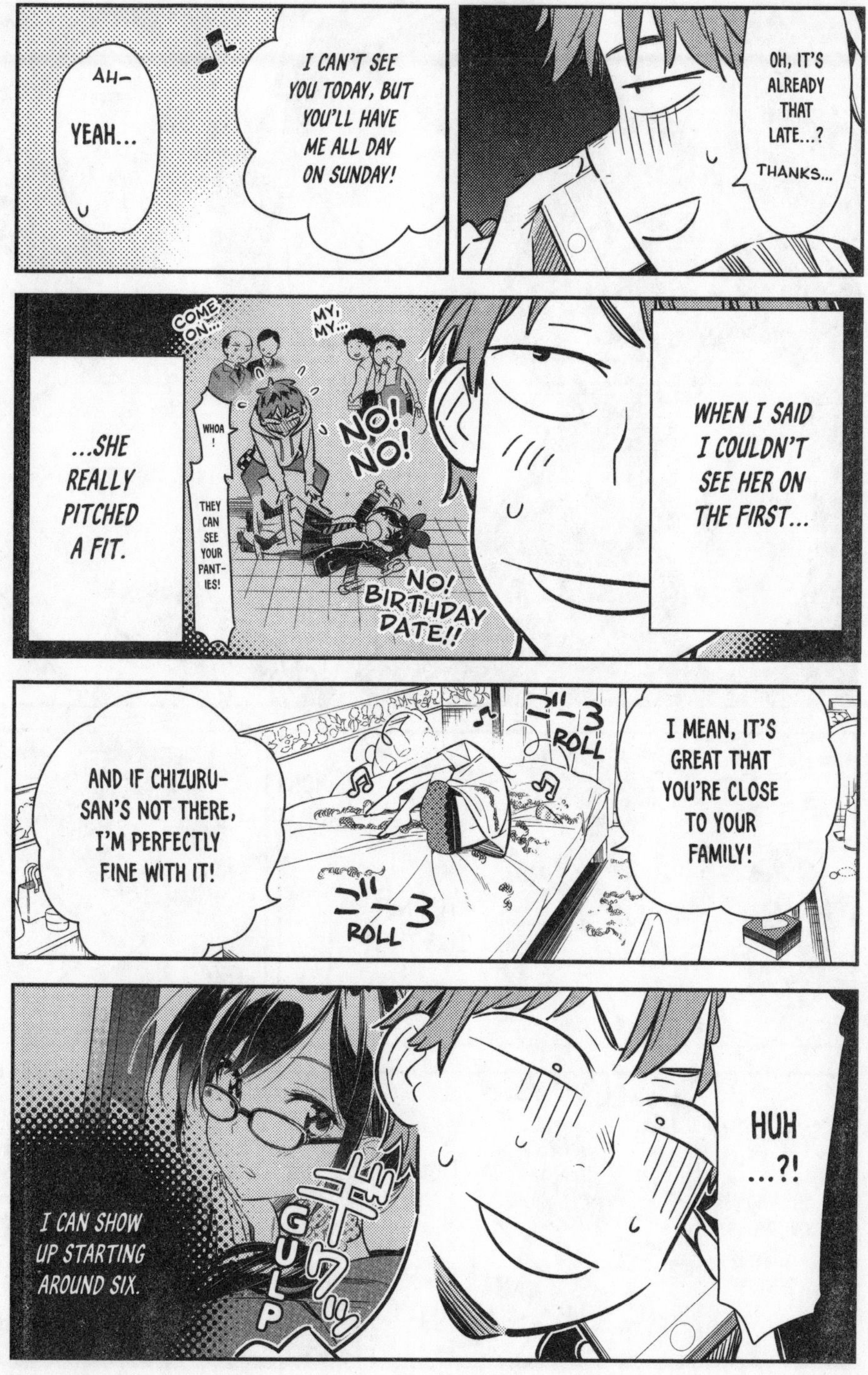
OH, IT'S ALREADY THAT LATE...? THANKS...
I CAN'T SEE YOU TODAY, BUT YOU'LL HAVE ME ALL DAY ON SUNDAY!
AH- YEAH...
WHEN I SAID I COULDN'T SEE HER ON THE FIRST...
MY, MY...
COME ON...
NO! NO!
WHOA!
THEY CAN SEE YOUR PANTIES!
NO! BIRTHDAY DATE!!
...SHE REALLY PITCHED A FIT.
I MEAN, IT'S GREAT THAT YOU'RE CLOSE TO YOUR FAMILY!
ROLL
AND IF CHIZURU-SAN'S NOT THERE, I'M PERFECTLY FINE WITH IT!
ROLL
HUH ...?!
GULP
I CAN SHOW UP STARTING AROUND SIX.

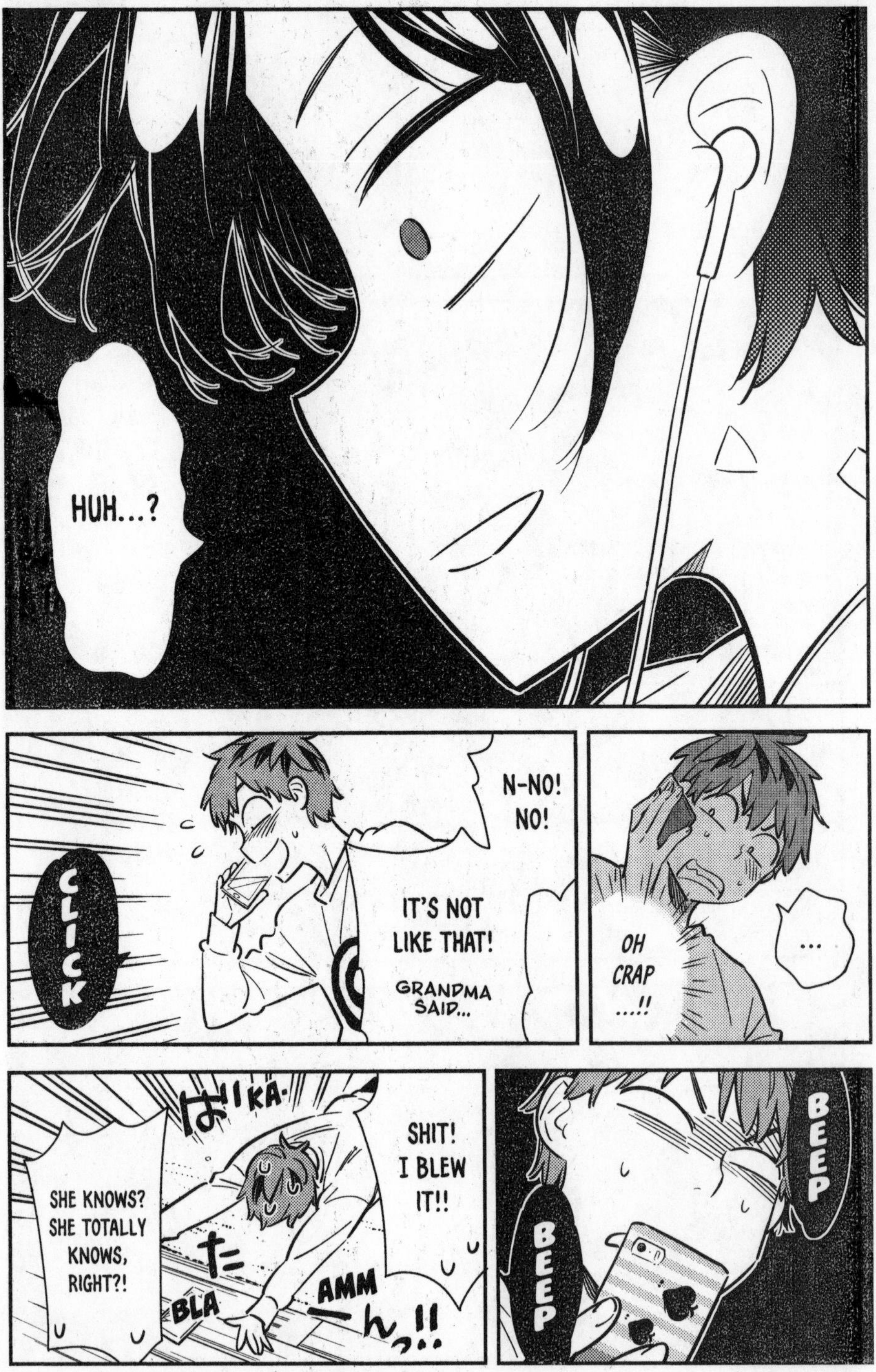
HUH...?
...
OH CRAP ....!!
N-NO! NO!
IT'S NOT LIKE THAT!
GRANDMA SAID...
CLICK
BEEP
BEEP BEEP
SHIT! I BLEW IT!!
ぱIKA-
SHE KNOWS? SHE TOTALLY KNOWS, RIGHT?!
たBLA
AMM ーんっ!!

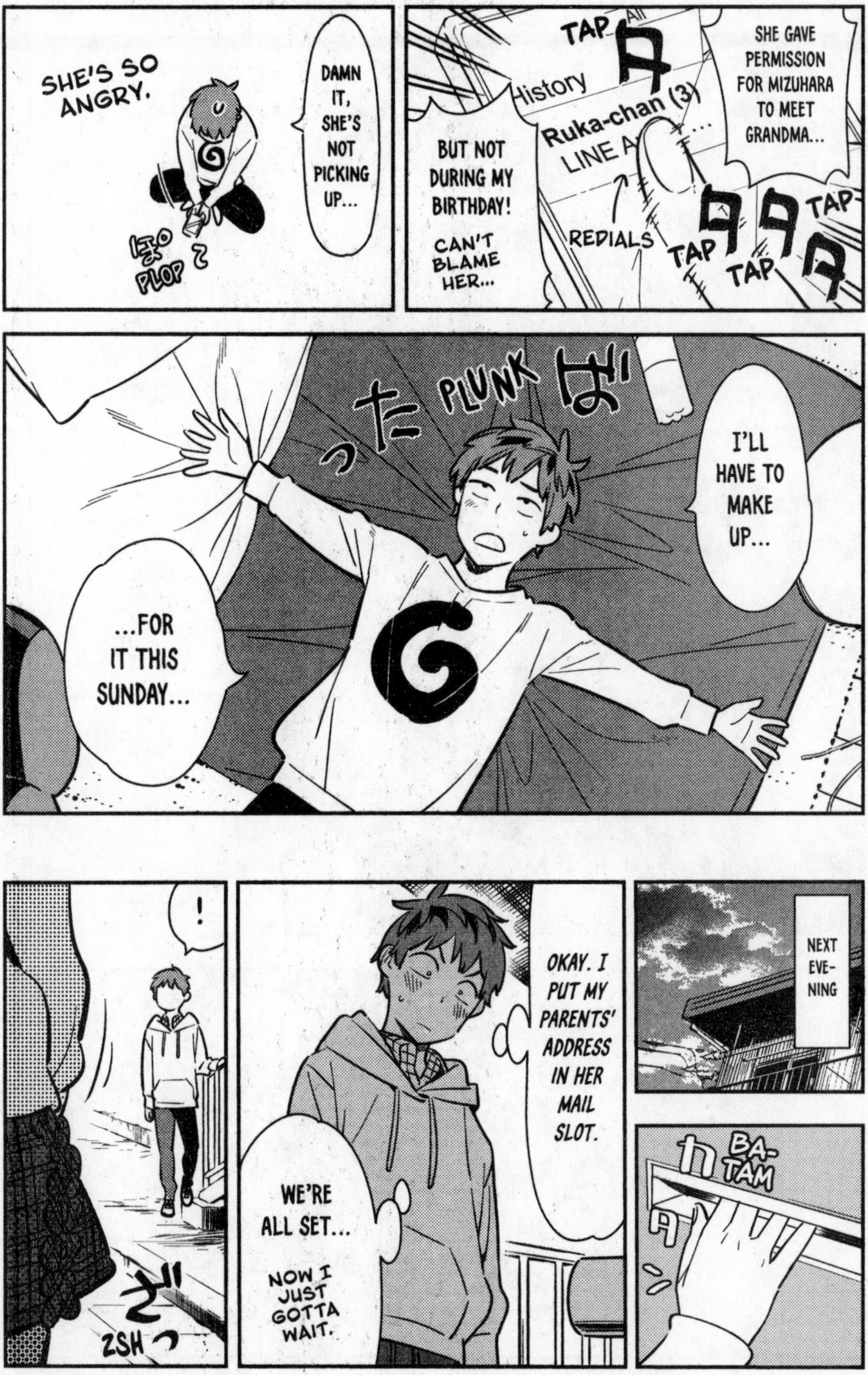
SHE GAVE PERMISSION FOR MIZUHARA TO MEET GRANDMA...
TAP
History
Ruka-chan (3)
LINE A...
REDIALS
TAP TAP TAP
BUT NOT DURING MY BIRTHDAY!
CAN'T BLAME HER...
DAMN IT, SHE'S NOT PICKING UP...
SHE'S SO ANGRY.
PLOP
PLUNK
I'LL HAVE TO MAKE UP...
...FOR IT THIS SUNDAY...
NEXT EVE-NING
BA-TAM
OKAY. I PUT MY PARENTS' ADDRESS IN HER MAIL SLOT.
WE'RE ALL SET...
NOW I JUST GOTTA WAIT.
!
ZSH

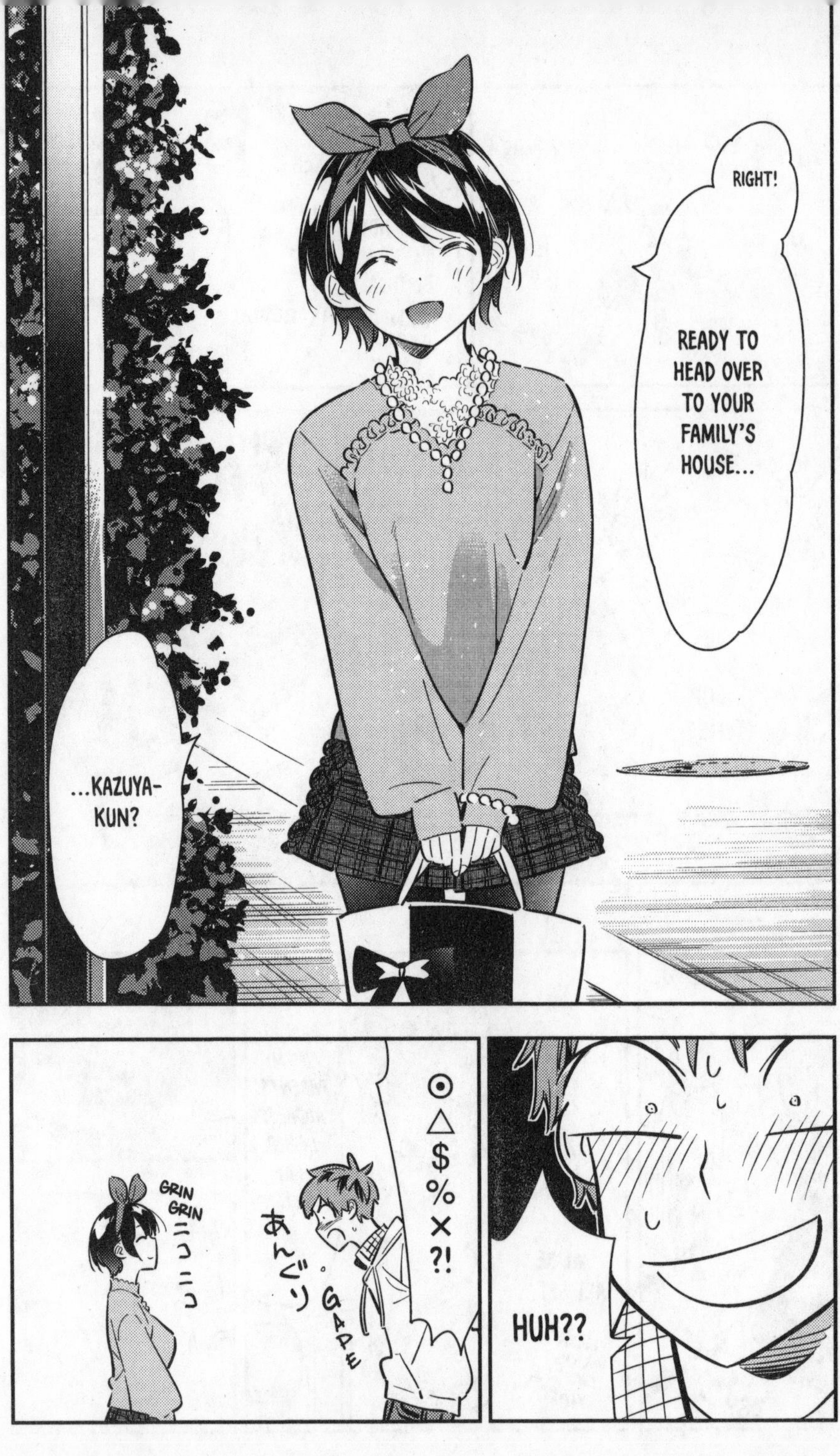
RIGHT!
READY TO HEAD OVER TO YOUR FAMILY'S HOUSE...
...KAZUYA-KUN?
HUH??
⊙△$%×?!
あんぐり
GAPE
GRIN GRIN
ニコニコ

RATING 84 MY GIRLFRIEND, MY HOUSE, AND THE KISS 2

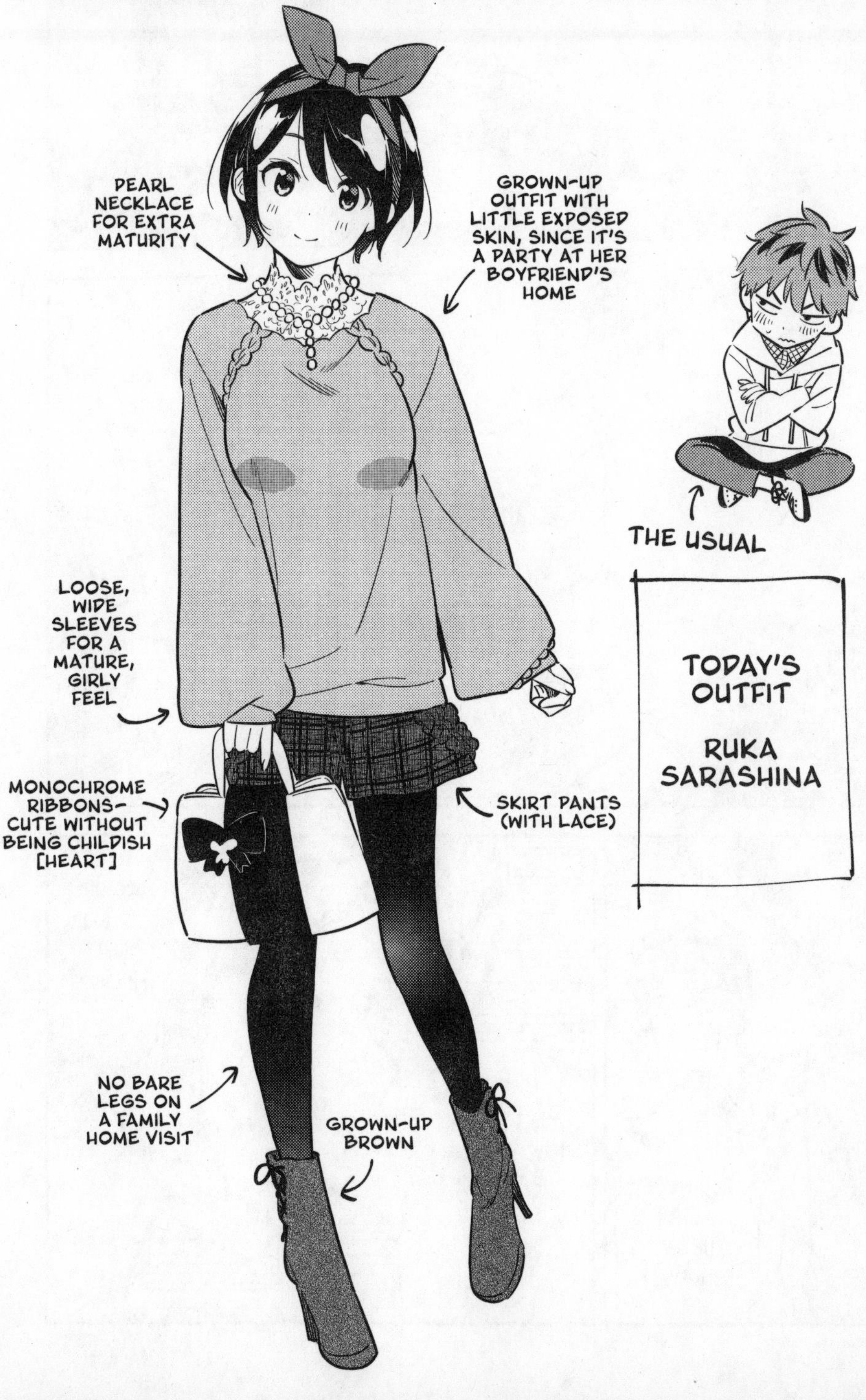
TODAY'S OUTFIT
RUKA SARASHINA
THE USUAL
GROWN-UP OUTFIT WITH LITTLE EXPOSED SKIN, SINCE IT'S A PARTY AT HER BOYFRIEND'S HOME
PEARL NECKLACE FOR EXTRA MATURITY
SKIRT PANTS (WITH LACE)
LOOSE, WIDE SLEEVES FOR A MATURE, GIRLY FEEL
MONOCHROME RIBBONS-CUTE WITHOUT BEING CHILDISH [HEART]
GROWN-UP BROWN
NO BARE LEGS ON A FAMILY HOME VISIT

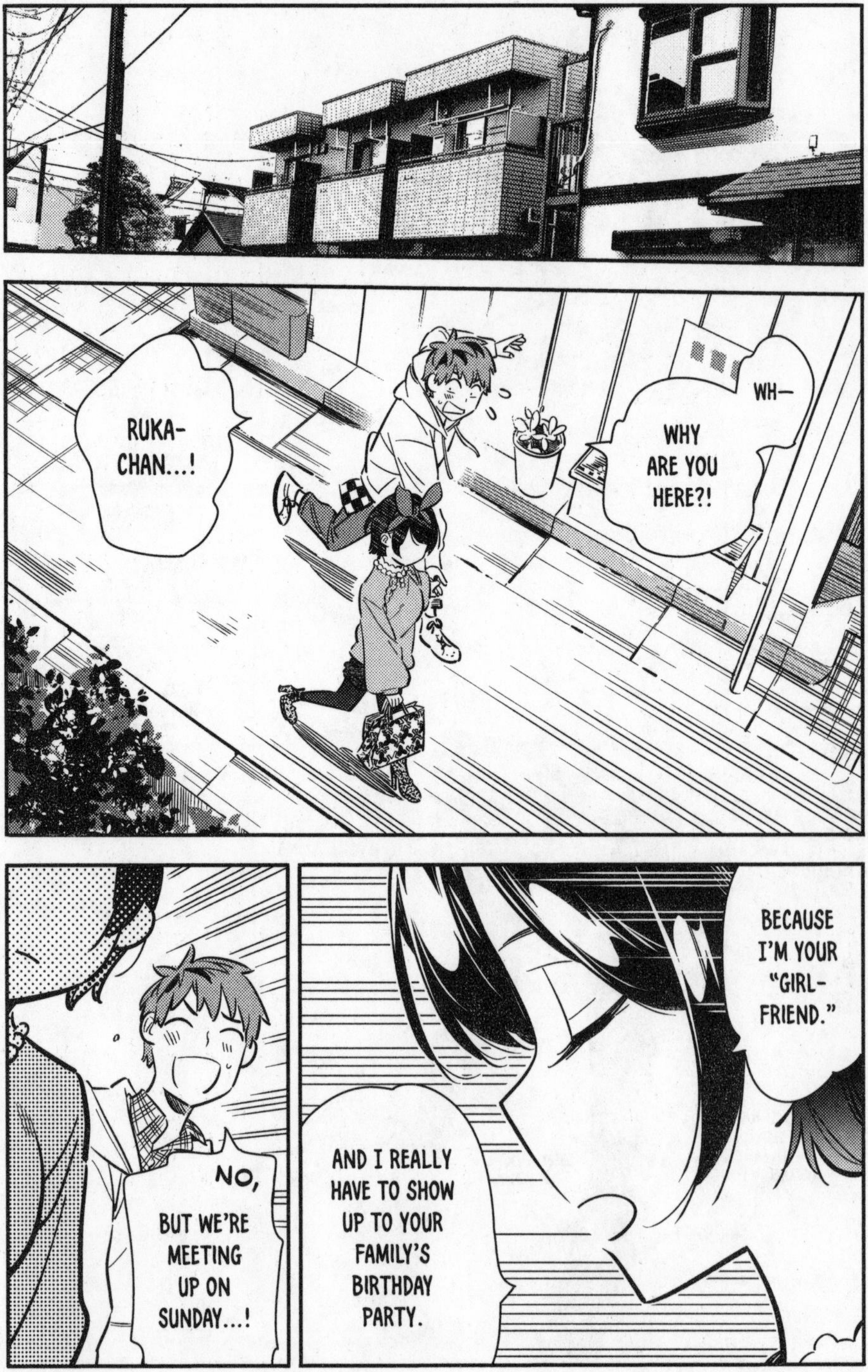
WH—
WHY ARE YOU HERE?!
RUKA-CHAN...!
BECAUSE I'M YOUR "GIRL-FRIEND."
AND I REALLY HAVE TO SHOW UP TO YOUR FAMILY'S BIRTHDAY PARTY.
NO,
BUT WE'RE MEETING UP ON SUNDAY...!

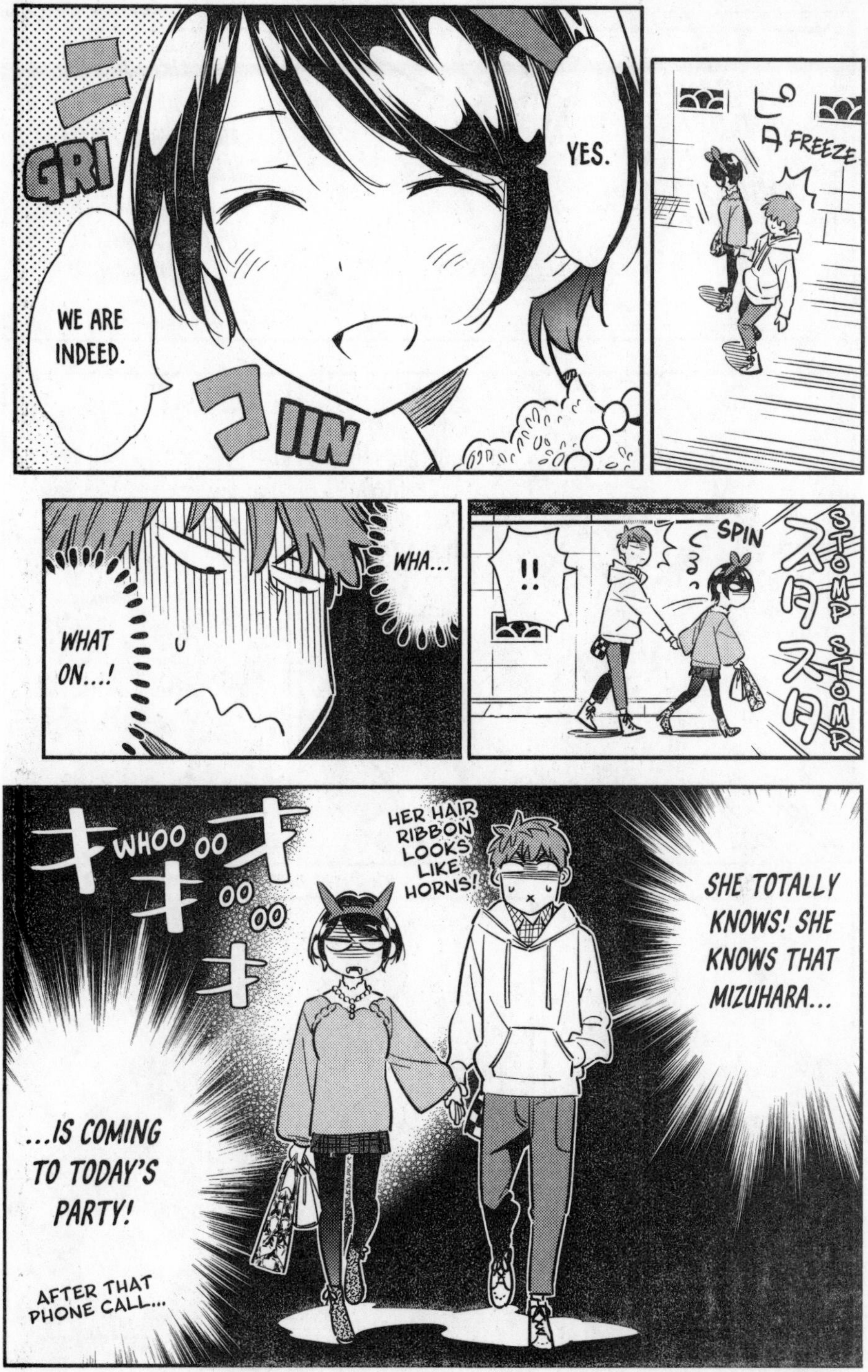
ピタ FREEZE
YES.
GRI
WE ARE INDEED.
IIN
!!
SPIN
STOMP STOMP
WHA...
WHAT ON...!
WHOO OO OO OO
HER HAIR RIBBON LOOKS LIKE HORNS!
SHE TOTALLY KNOWS! SHE KNOWS THAT MIZUHARA...
...IS COMING TO TODAY'S PARTY!
AFTER THAT PHONE CALL...

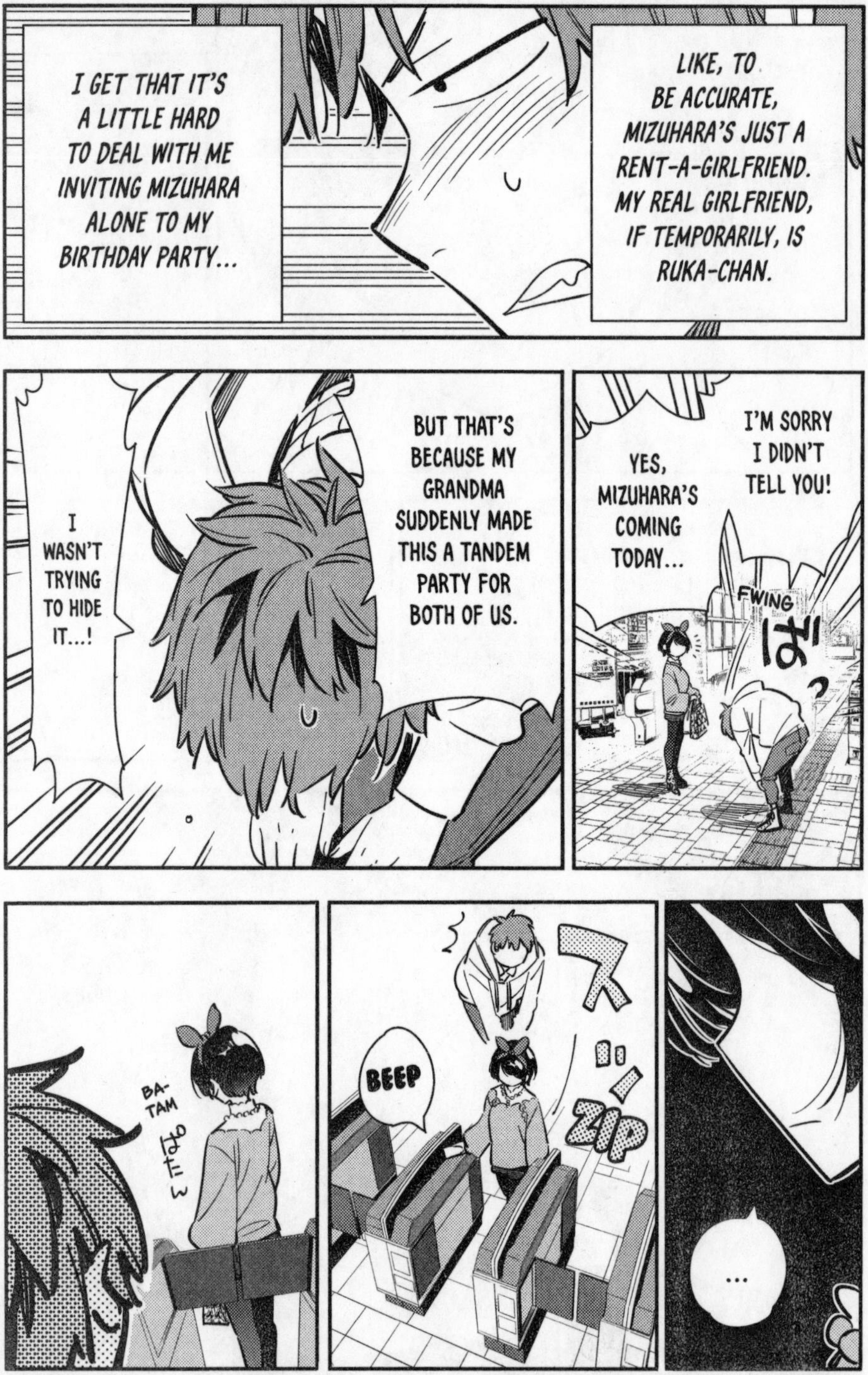
LIKE, TO BE ACCURATE, MIZUHARA'S JUST A RENT-A-GIRLFRIEND. MY REAL GIRLFRIEND, IF TEMPORARILY, IS RUKA-CHAN.
I GET THAT IT'S A LITTLE HARD TO DEAL WITH ME INVITING MIZUHARA ALONE TO MY BIRTHDAY PARTY...
I'M SORRY I DIDN'T TELL YOU!
YES, MIZUHARA'S COMING TODAY...
FWING
ばっ
BUT THAT'S BECAUSE MY GRANDMA SUDDENLY MADE THIS A TANDEM PARTY FOR BOTH OF US.
I WASN'T TRYING TO HIDE IT...!
...
ス
ZIP
BEEP
BA-TAM
ぱたん

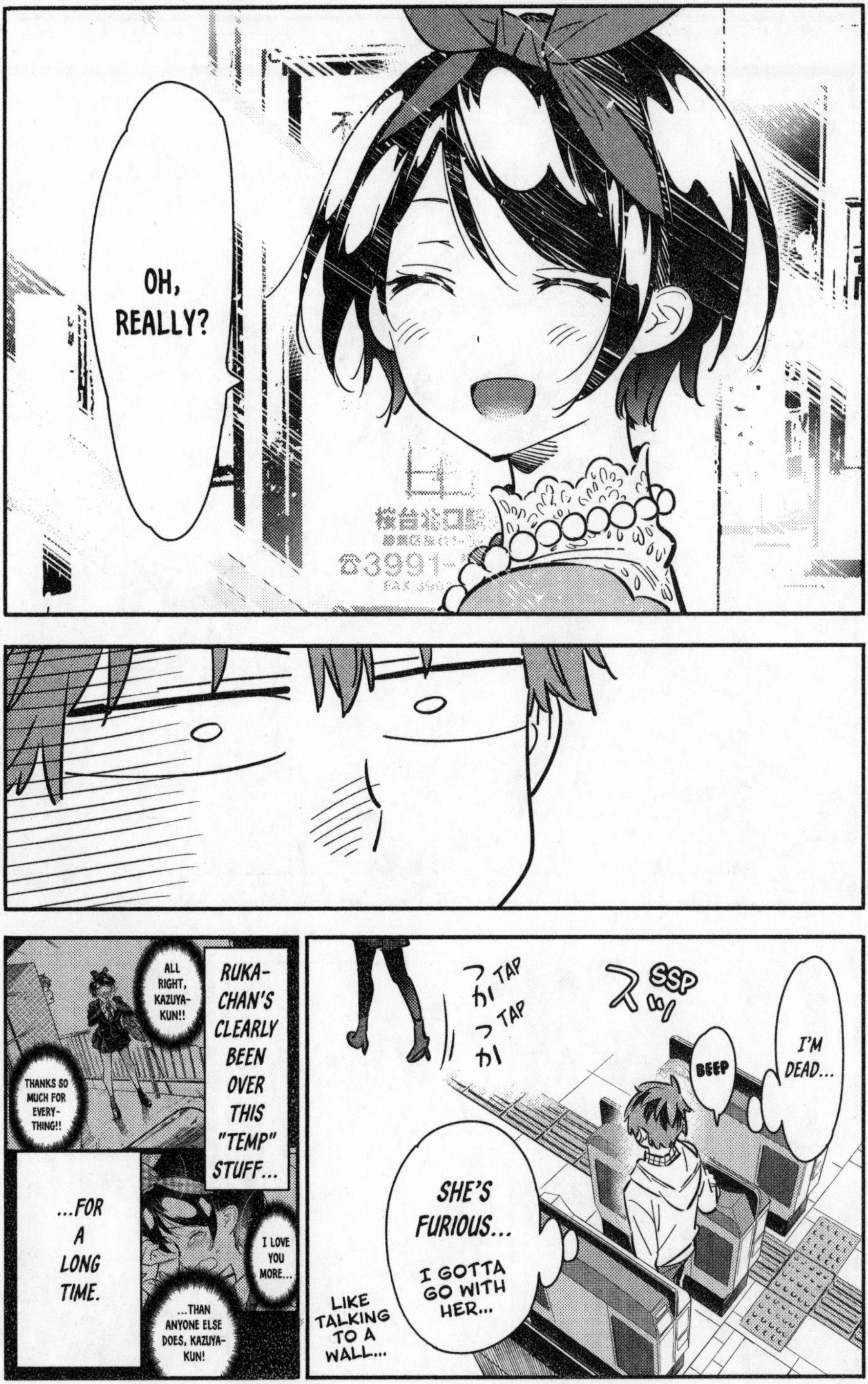
OH, REALLY?
I'M DEAD...
BEEP
スッ SSP
つかつか TAP TAP
SHE'S FURIOUS...
I GOTTA GO WITH HER...
LIKE TALKING TO A WALL...
RUKA-CHAN'S CLEARLY BEEN OVER THIS "TEMP" STUFF...
ALL RIGHT, KAZUYA-KUN!!
THANKS SO MUCH FOR EVERY-THING!!
I LOVE YOU MORE...
...FOR A LONG TIME.
...THAN ANYONE ELSE DOES, KAZUYA-KUN!

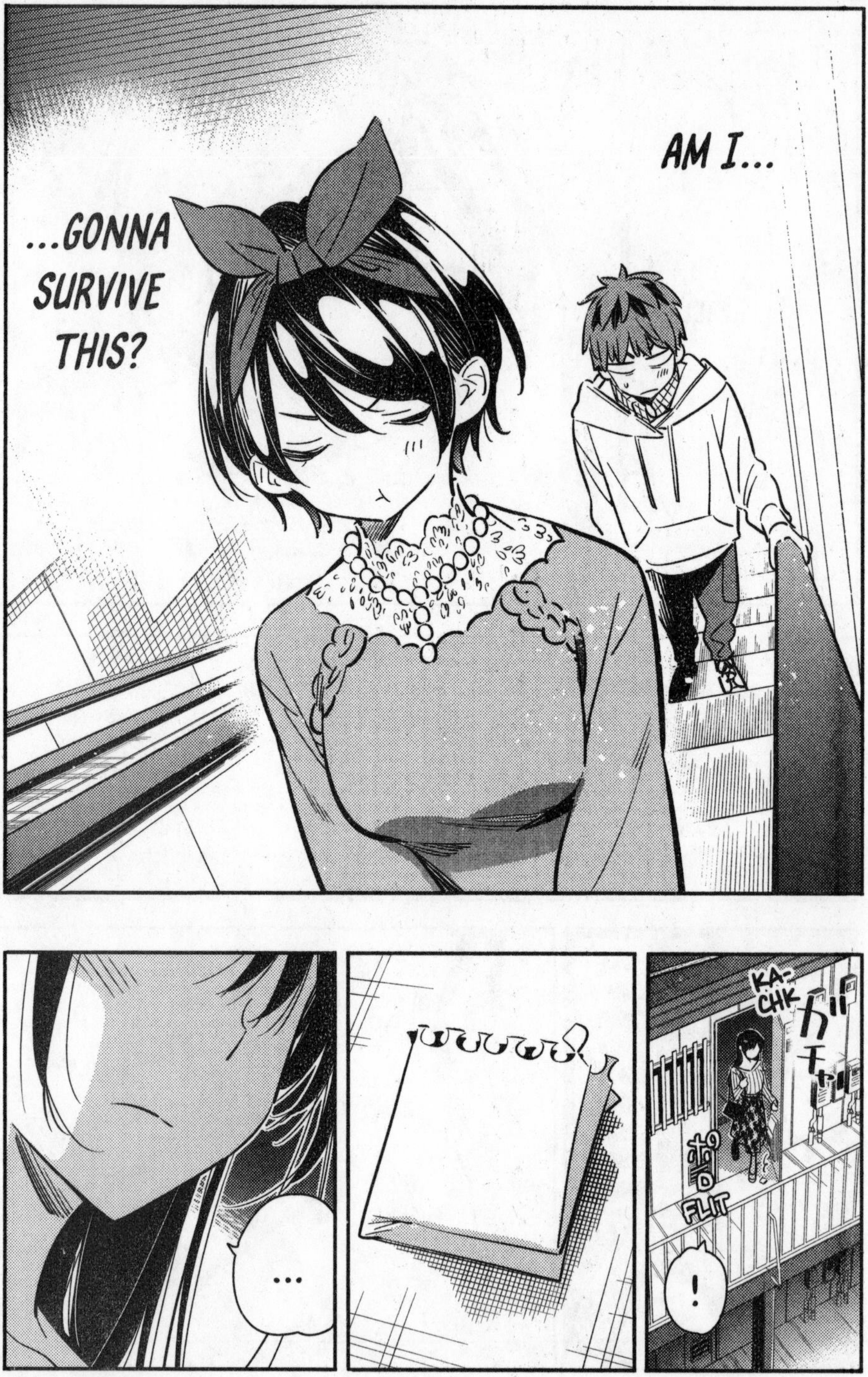
AM I...
...GONNA SURVIVE THIS?
KA-CHK
ガチャ
FLIT
!
...

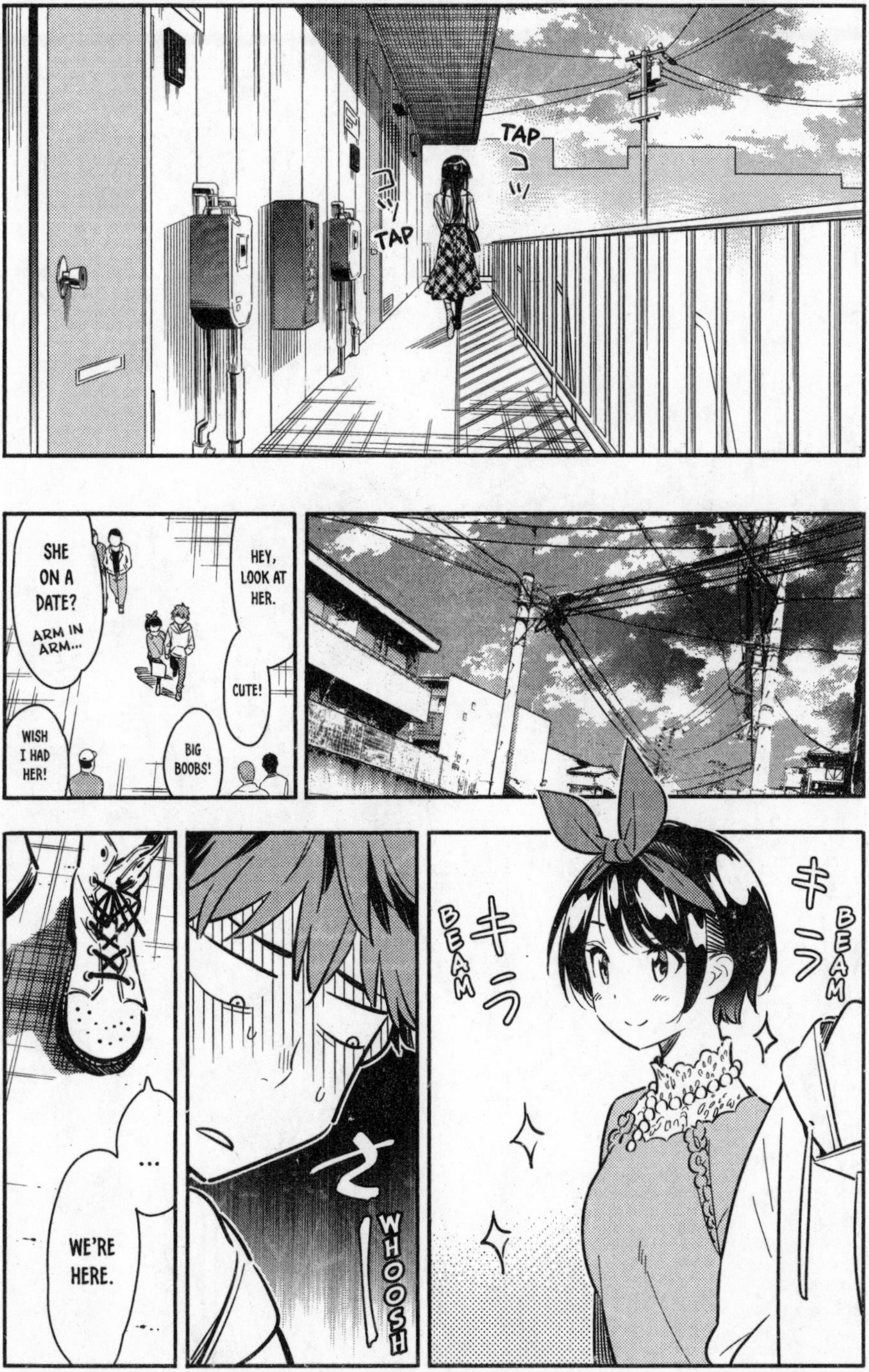
TAP
コツ
コツ
TAP
HEY, LOOK AT HER.
CUTE!
SHE ON A DATE?
ARM IN ARM...
BIG BOOBS!
WISH I HAD HER!
キラ
BEAM
キラ
BEAM
さっ
WHOOSH
...
WE'RE HERE.

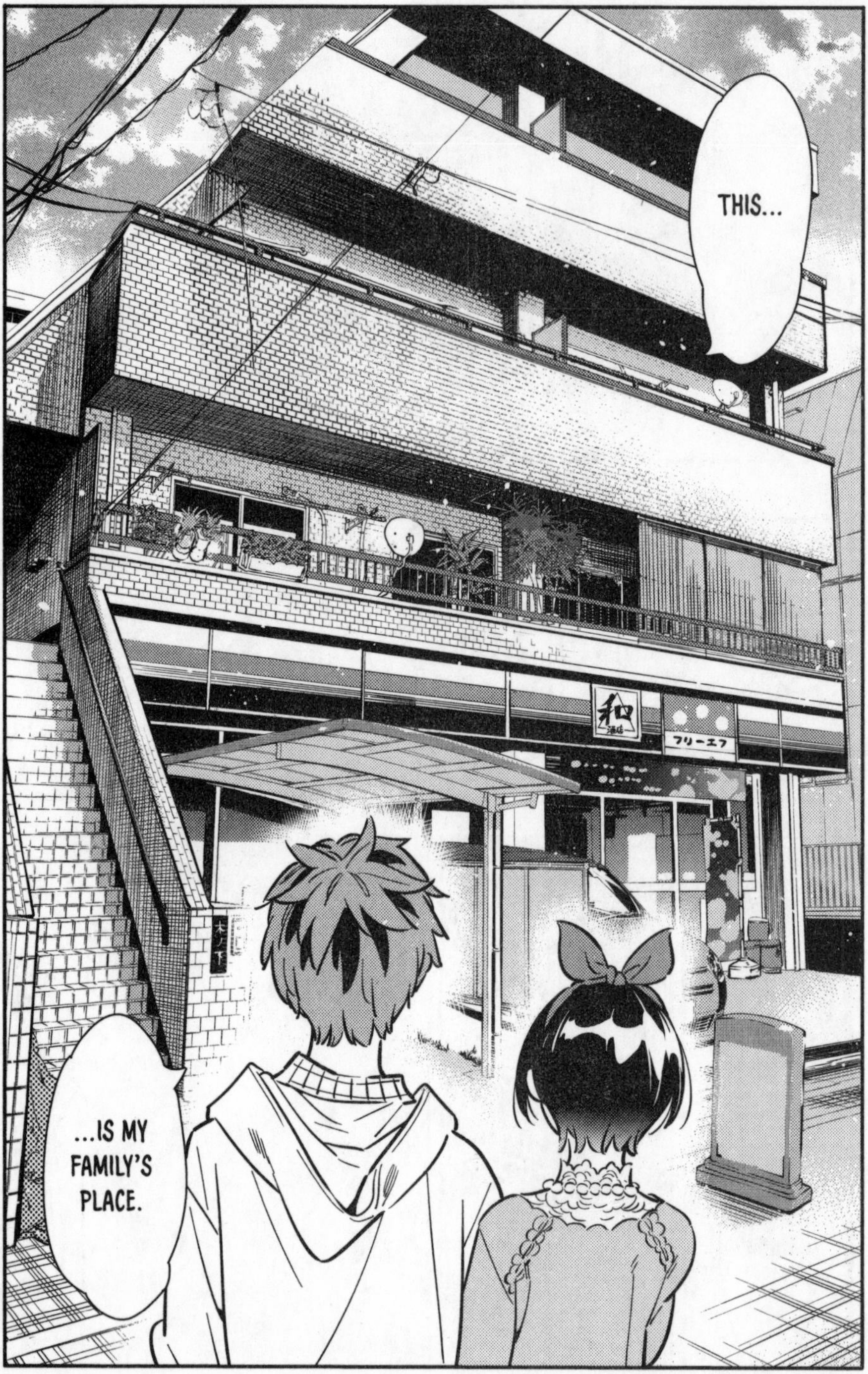
THIS...
和
フリーエフ
...IS MY FAMILY'S PLACE.

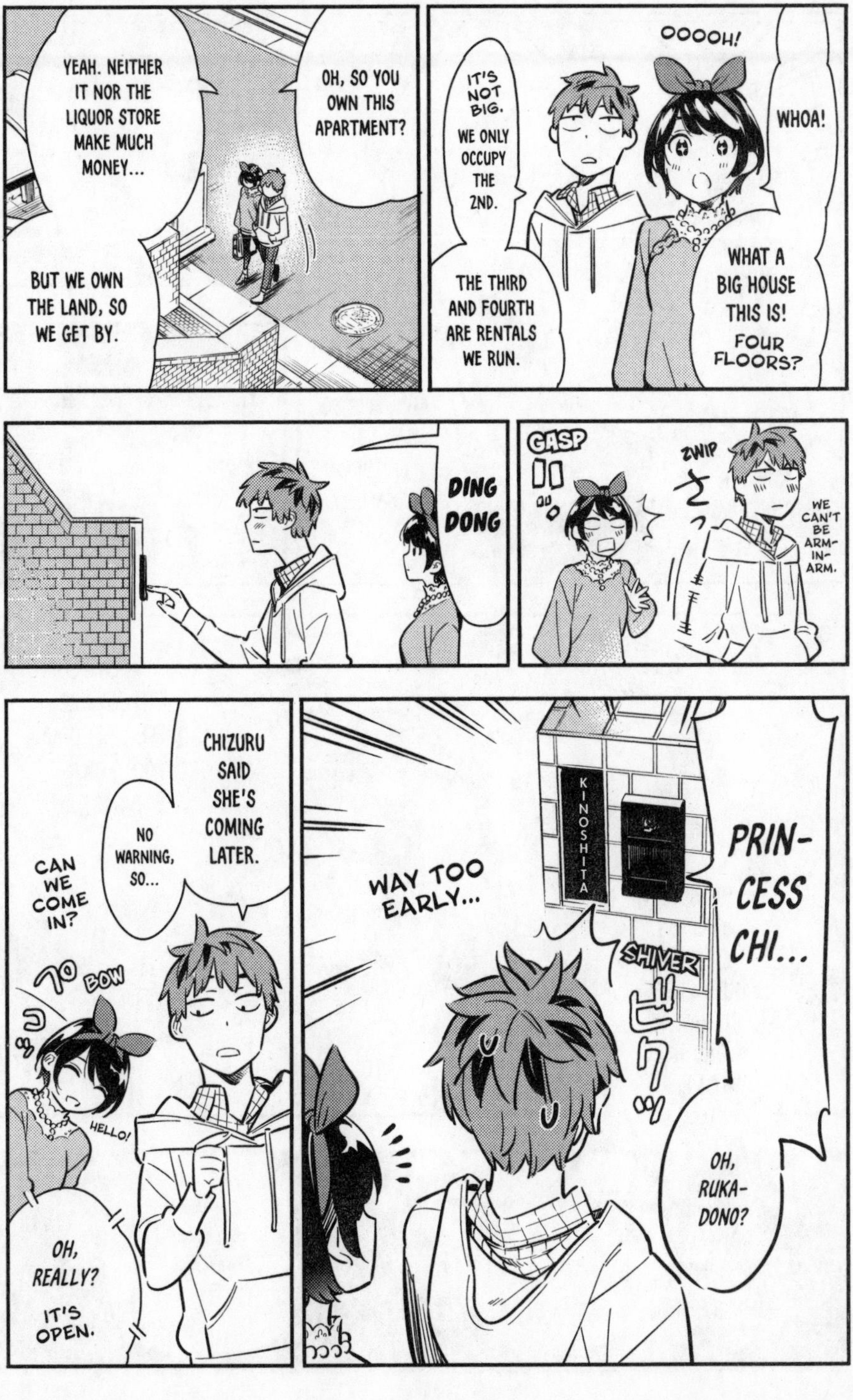
OOOOH!
WHOA!
WHAT A BIG HOUSE THIS IS!
FOUR FLOORS?
IT'S NOT BIG.
WE ONLY OCCUPY THE 2ND.
THE THIRD AND FOURTH ARE RENTALS WE RUN.
OH, SO YOU OWN THIS APARTMENT?
YEAH. NEITHER IT NOR THE LIQUOR STORE MAKE MUCH MONEY...
BUT WE OWN THE LAND, SO WE GET BY.
GASP
ZWIP
WE CAN'T BE ARM-IN-ARM.
DING DONG
PRIN-CESS CHI...
SHIVER
KINOSHITA
WAY TOO EARLY...
OH, RUKA-DONO?
CHIZURU SAID SHE'S COMING LATER.
NO WARNING, SO...
CAN WE COME IN?
BOW
HELLO!
OH, REALLY?
IT'S OPEN.

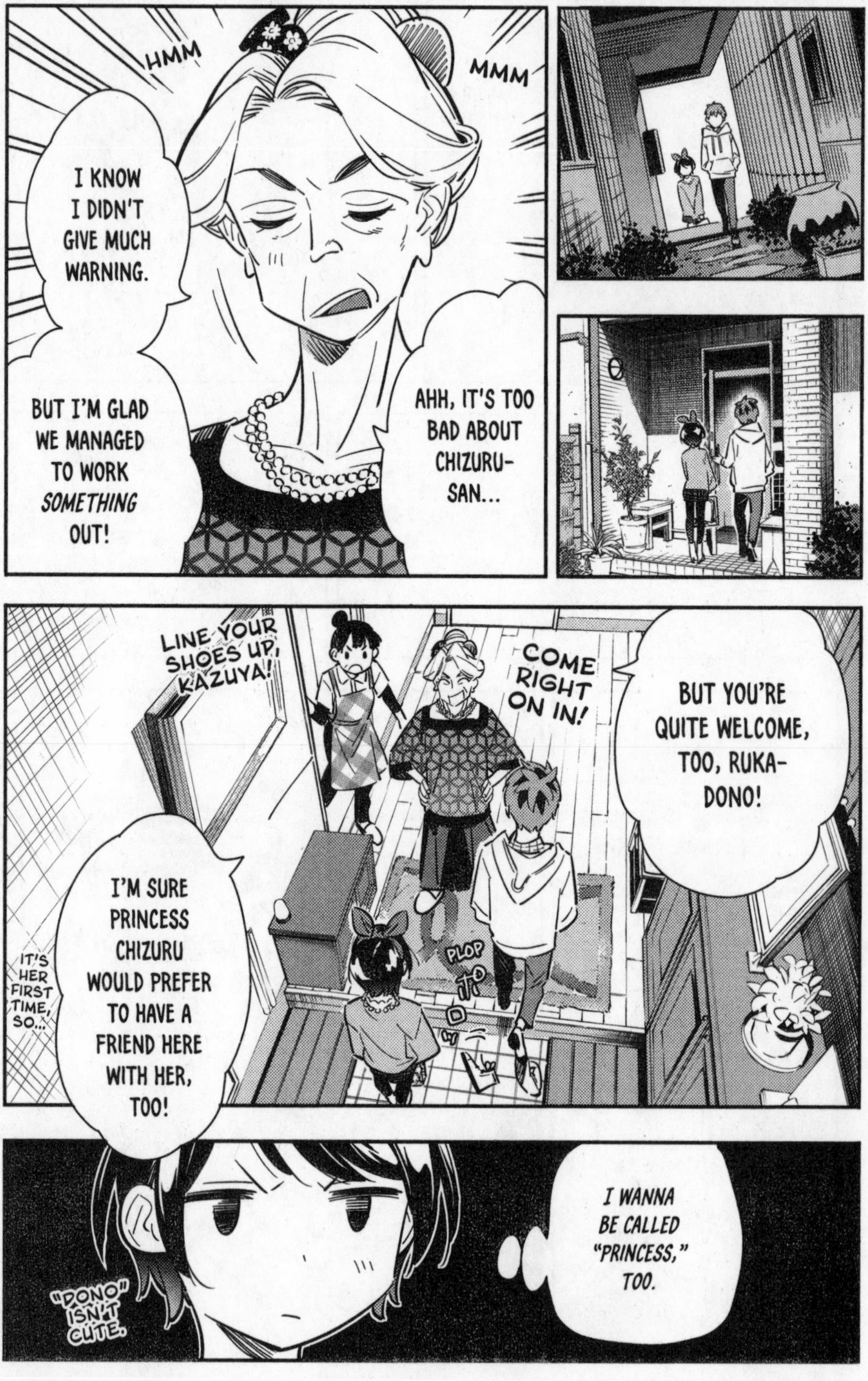
MMM
HMM
AHH, IT'S TOO BAD ABOUT CHIZURU-SAN...
I KNOW I DIDN'T GIVE MUCH WARNING.
BUT I'M GLAD WE MANAGED TO WORK *SOMETHING* OUT!
BUT YOU'RE QUITE WELCOME, TOO, RUKA-DONO!
COME RIGHT ON IN!
LINE YOUR SHOES UP, KAZUYA!
PLOP
I'M SURE PRINCESS CHIZURU WOULD PREFER TO HAVE A FRIEND HERE WITH HER, TOO!
IT'S HER FIRST TIME, SO...
I WANNA BE CALLED "PRINCESS," TOO.
"DONO" ISN'T CUTE.

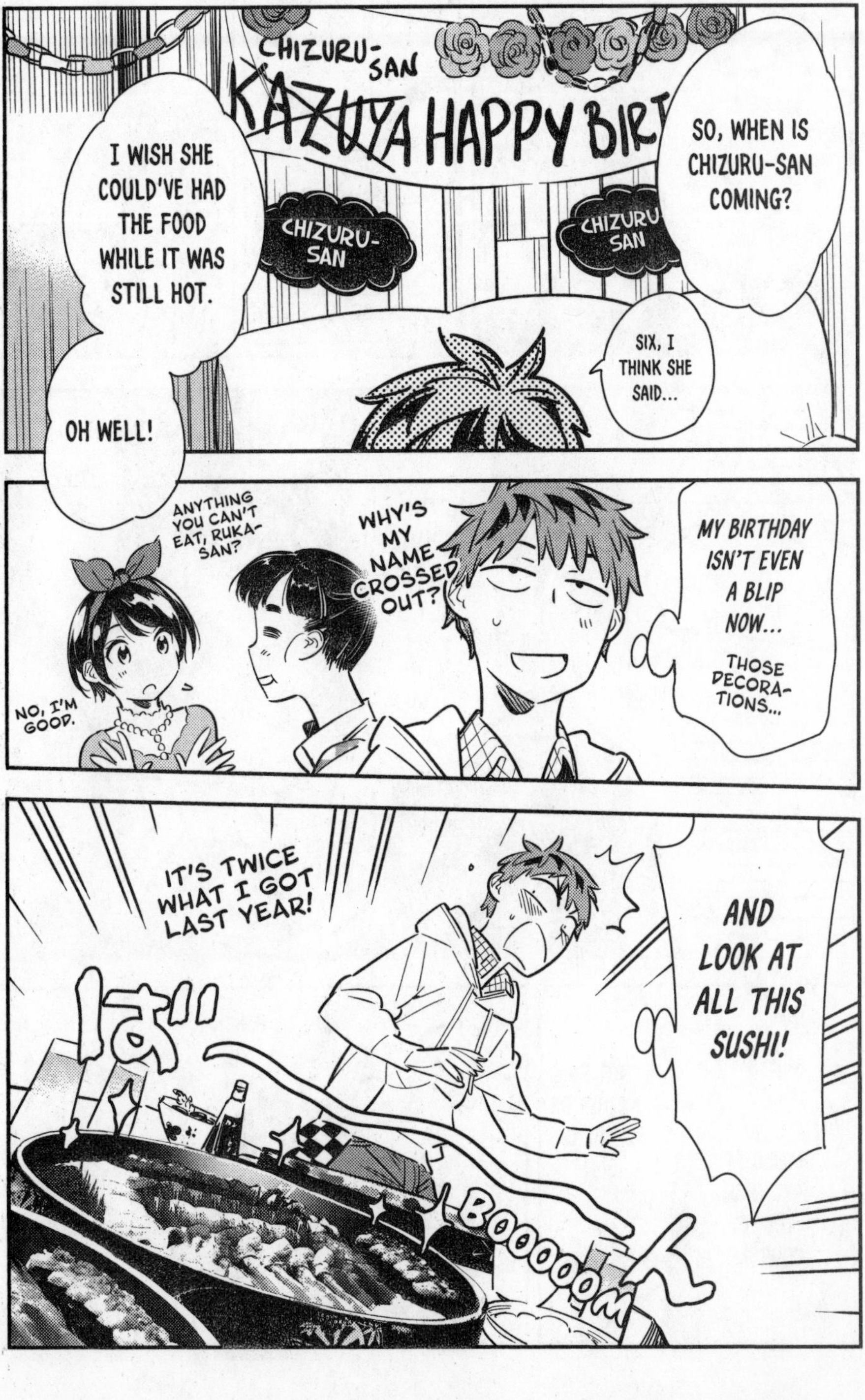

SO, WHEN IS CHIZURU-SAN COMING?
SIX, I THINK SHE SAID...
CHIZURU-SAN
KAZUYA HAPPY BIRT
CHIZURU-SAN
CHIZURU-SAN
I WISH SHE COULD'VE HAD THE FOOD WHILE IT WAS STILL HOT.
OH WELL!
MY BIRTHDAY ISN'T EVEN A BLIP NOW...
THOSE DECORATIONS...
WHY'S MY NAME CROSSED OUT?
ANYTHING YOU CAN'T EAT, RUKA-SAN?
NO, I'M GOOD.
AND LOOK AT ALL THIS SUSHI!
IT'S TWICE WHAT I GOT LAST YEAR!
BOOOOOM

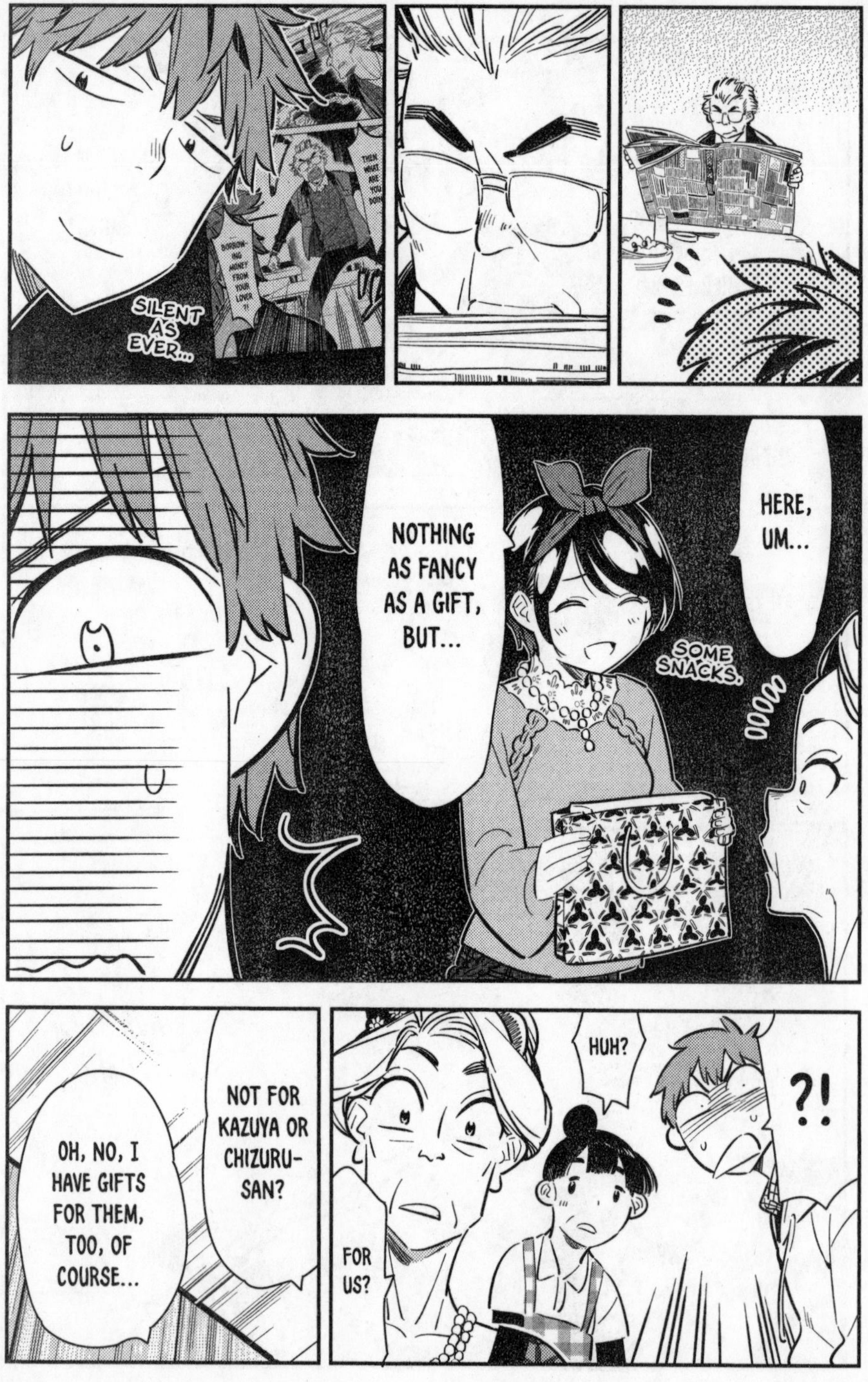
THEN WHAT ARE YOU DOIN
BORROWING MONEY FROM YOUR LOVER ?!
SILENT AS EVER...
HERE, UM...
SOME SNACKS.
NOTHING AS FANCY AS A GIFT, BUT...
?!
HUH?
FOR US?
NOT FOR KAZUYA OR CHIZURU-SAN?
OH, NO, I HAVE GIFTS FOR THEM, TOO, OF COURSE...

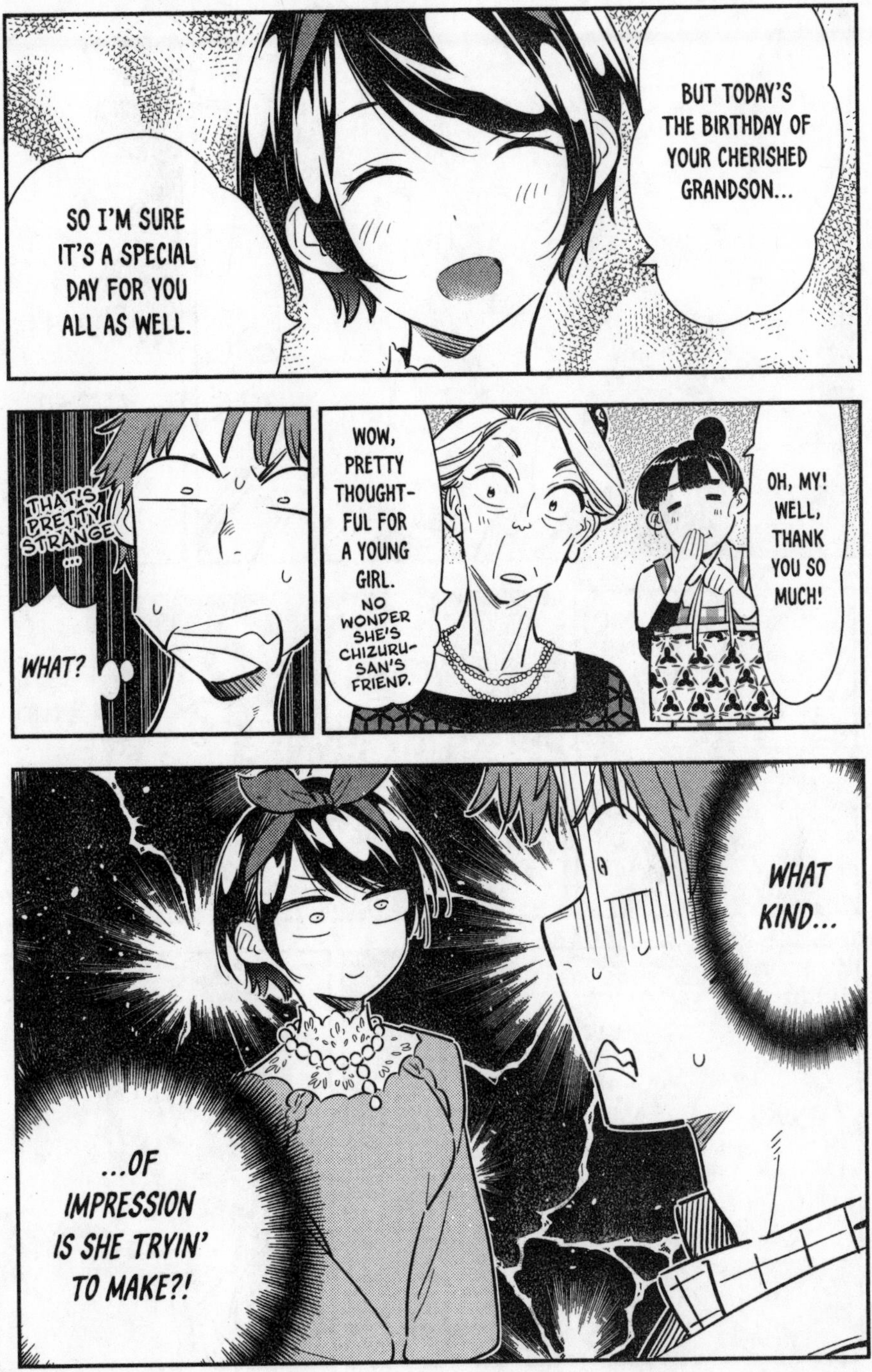
BUT TODAY'S THE BIRTHDAY OF YOUR CHERISHED GRANDSON...
SO I'M SURE IT'S A SPECIAL DAY FOR YOU ALL AS WELL.
OH, MY! WELL, THANK YOU SO MUCH!
WOW, PRETTY THOUGHT-FUL FOR A YOUNG GIRL.
NO WONDER SHE'S CHIZURU-SAN'S FRIEND.
THAT'S PRETTY STRANGE...
WHAT?
WHAT KIND...
...OF IMPRESSION IS SHE TRYIN' TO MAKE?!

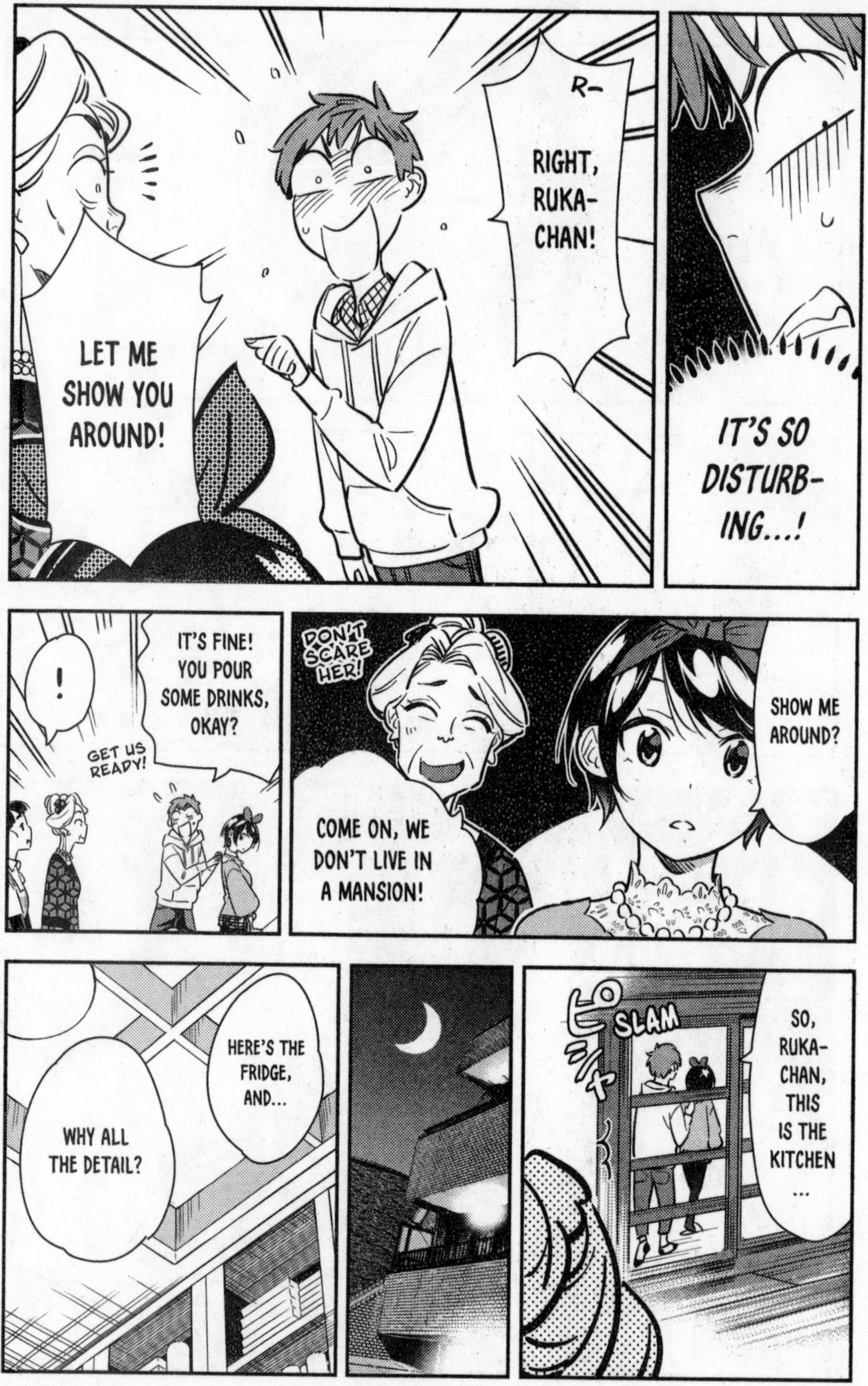
IT'S SO DISTURB-ING...!
R- RIGHT, RUKA-CHAN!
LET ME SHOW YOU AROUND!
SHOW ME AROUND?
DON'T SCARE HER!
COME ON, WE DON'T LIVE IN A MANSION!
IT'S FINE! YOU POUR SOME DRINKS, OKAY?
!
GET US READY!
SO, RUKA-CHAN, THIS IS THE KITCHEN...
ピシャ
SLAM
HERE'S THE FRIDGE, AND...
WHY ALL THE DETAIL?

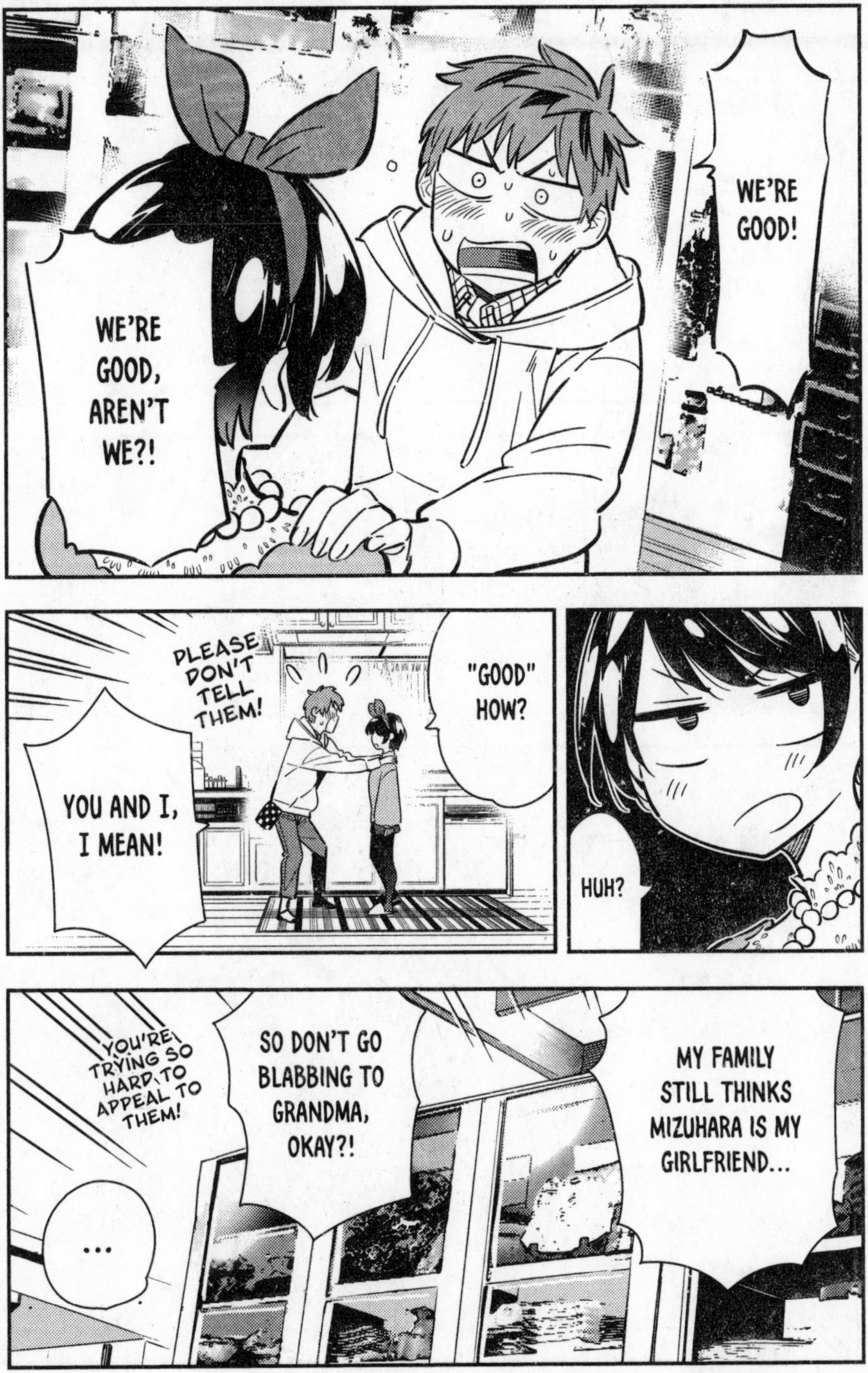
WE'RE GOOD!
WE'RE GOOD, AREN'T WE?!
HUH?
"GOOD" HOW?
PLEASE DON'T TELL THEM!
YOU AND I, I MEAN!
MY FAMILY STILL THINKS MIZUHARA IS MY GIRLFRIEND...
SO DON'T GO BLABBING TO GRANDMA, OKAY?!
YOU'RE TRYING SO HARD TO APPEAL TO THEM!
...

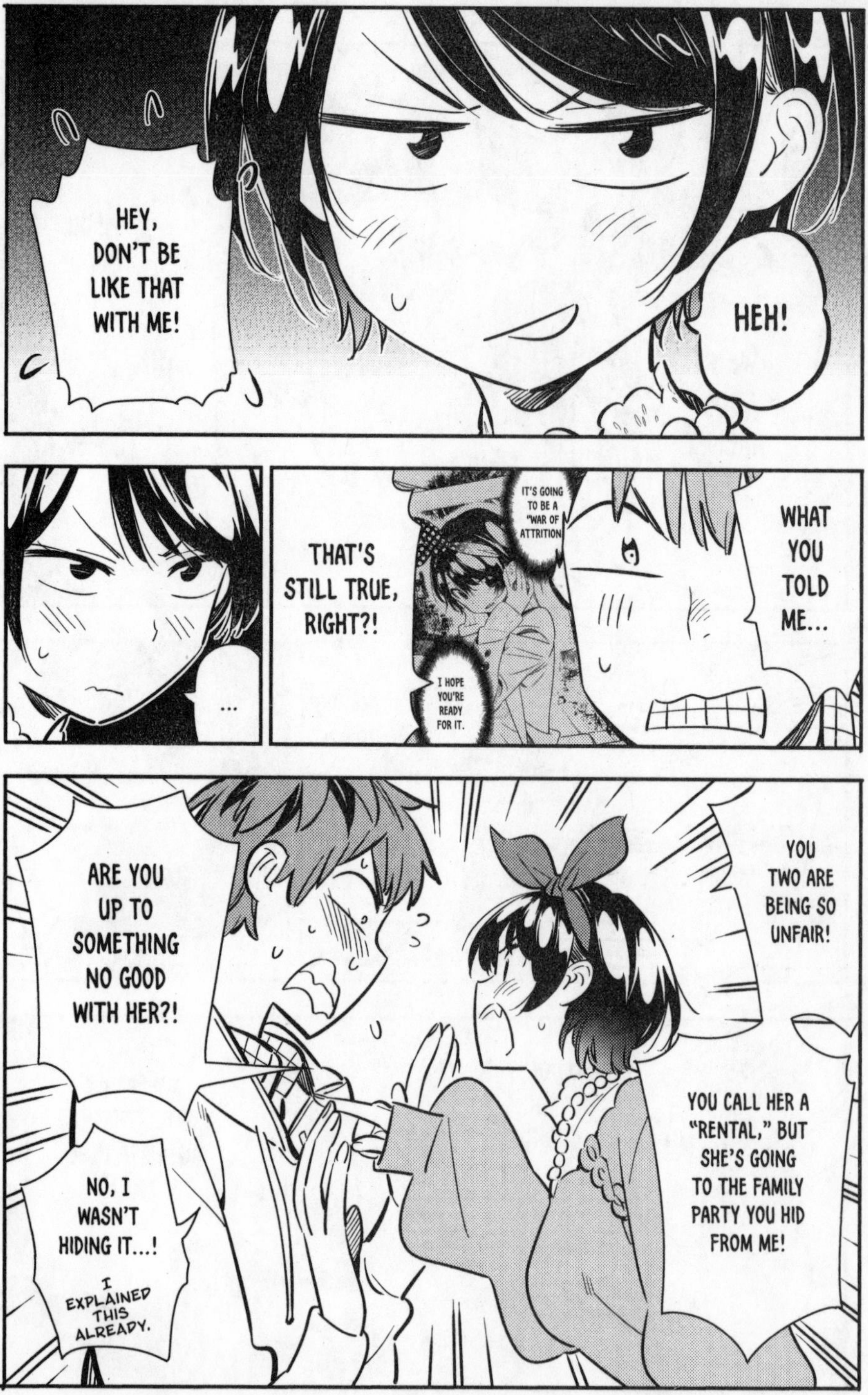
HEH!
HEY, DON'T BE LIKE THAT WITH ME!
WHAT YOU TOLD ME...
IT'S GOING TO BE A "WAR OF ATTRITION
THAT'S STILL TRUE, RIGHT?!
I HOPE YOU'RE READY FOR IT.
...
YOU TWO ARE BEING SO UNFAIR!
ARE YOU UP TO SOMETHING NO GOOD WITH HER?!
YOU CALL HER A "RENTAL," BUT SHE'S GOING TO THE FAMILY PARTY YOU HID FROM ME!
NO, I WASN'T HIDING IT...!
I EXPLAINED THIS ALREADY.

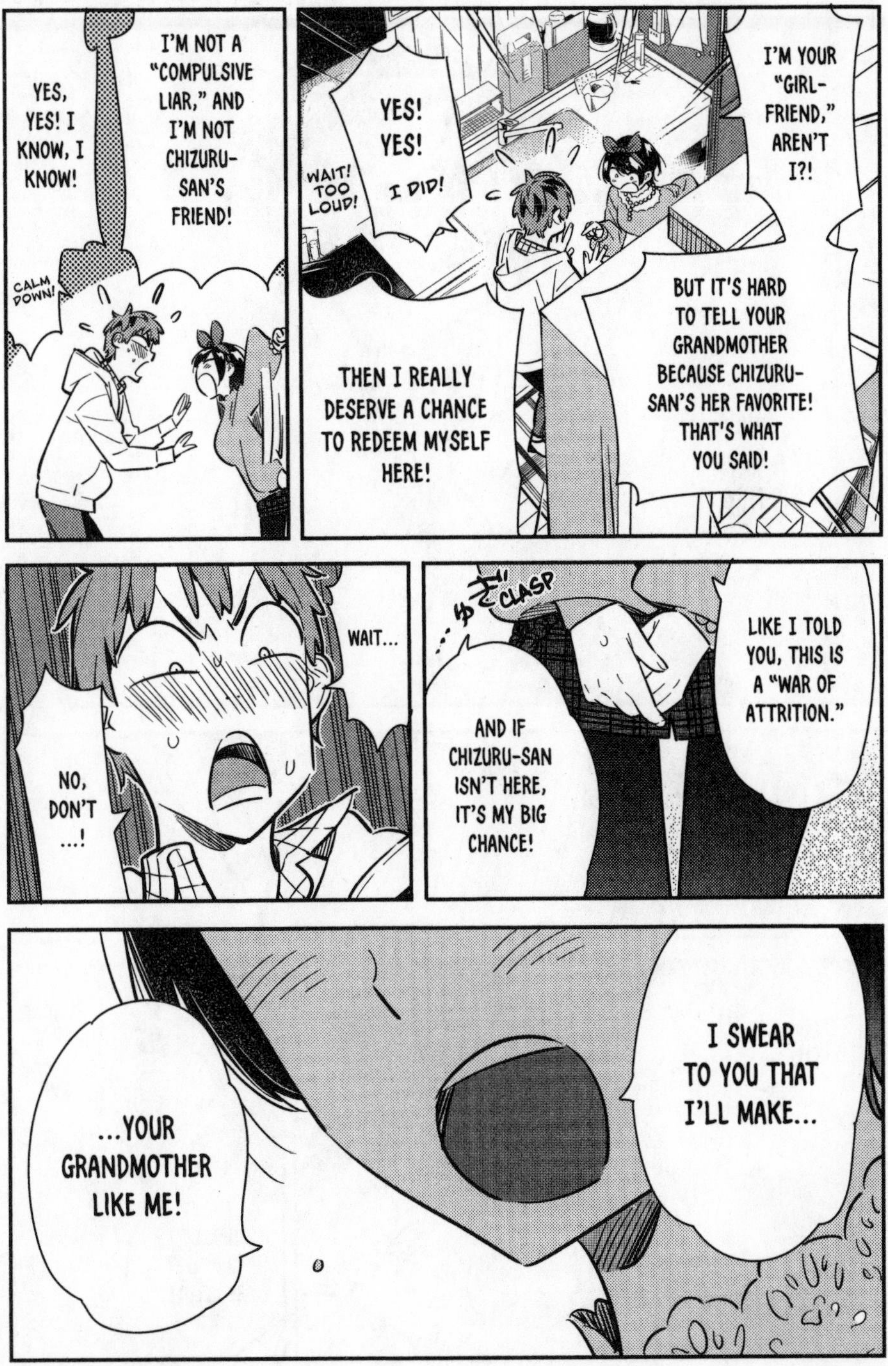
I'M YOUR "GIRL-FRIEND," AREN'T I?!
YES! YES!
I DID!
WAIT! TOO LOUD!
BUT IT'S HARD TO TELL YOUR GRANDMOTHER BECAUSE CHIZURU-SAN'S HER FAVORITE! THAT'S WHAT YOU SAID!
THEN I REALLY DESERVE A CHANCE TO REDEEM MYSELF HERE!
I'M NOT A "COMPULSIVE LIAR," AND I'M NOT CHIZURU-SAN'S FRIEND!
YES, YES! I KNOW, I KNOW!
CALM DOWN!
CLASP
LIKE I TOLD YOU, THIS IS A "WAR OF ATTRITION."
AND IF CHIZURU-SAN ISN'T HERE, IT'S MY BIG CHANCE!
WAIT...
NO, DON'T ...!
I SWEAR TO YOU THAT I'LL MAKE...
...YOUR GRANDMOTHER LIKE ME!

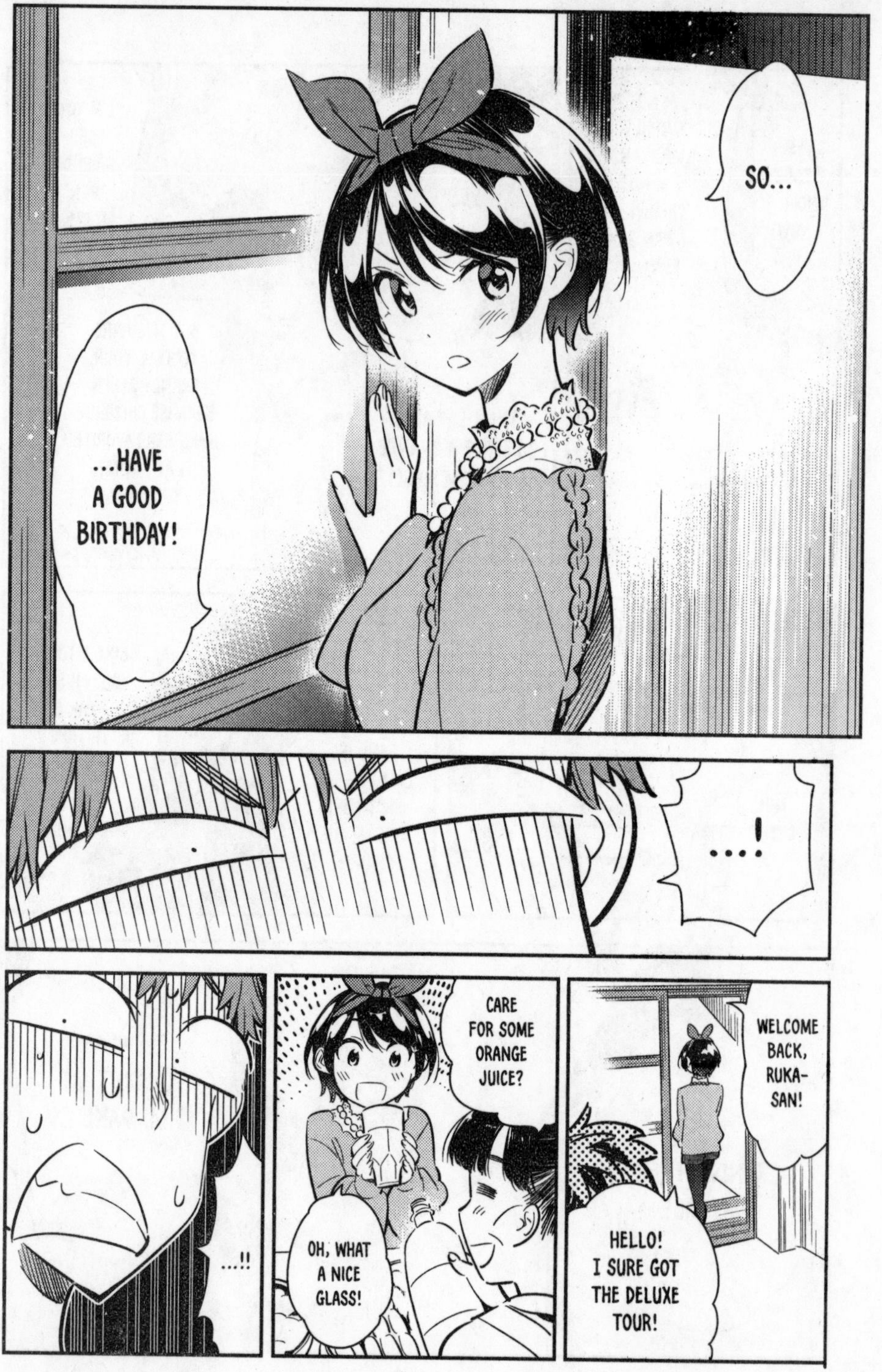
SO...
...HAVE A GOOD BIRTHDAY!
...!
WELCOME BACK, RUKA-SAN!
HELLO! I SURE GOT THE DELUXE TOUR!
CARE FOR SOME ORANGE JUICE?
OH, WHAT A NICE GLASS!
...!!

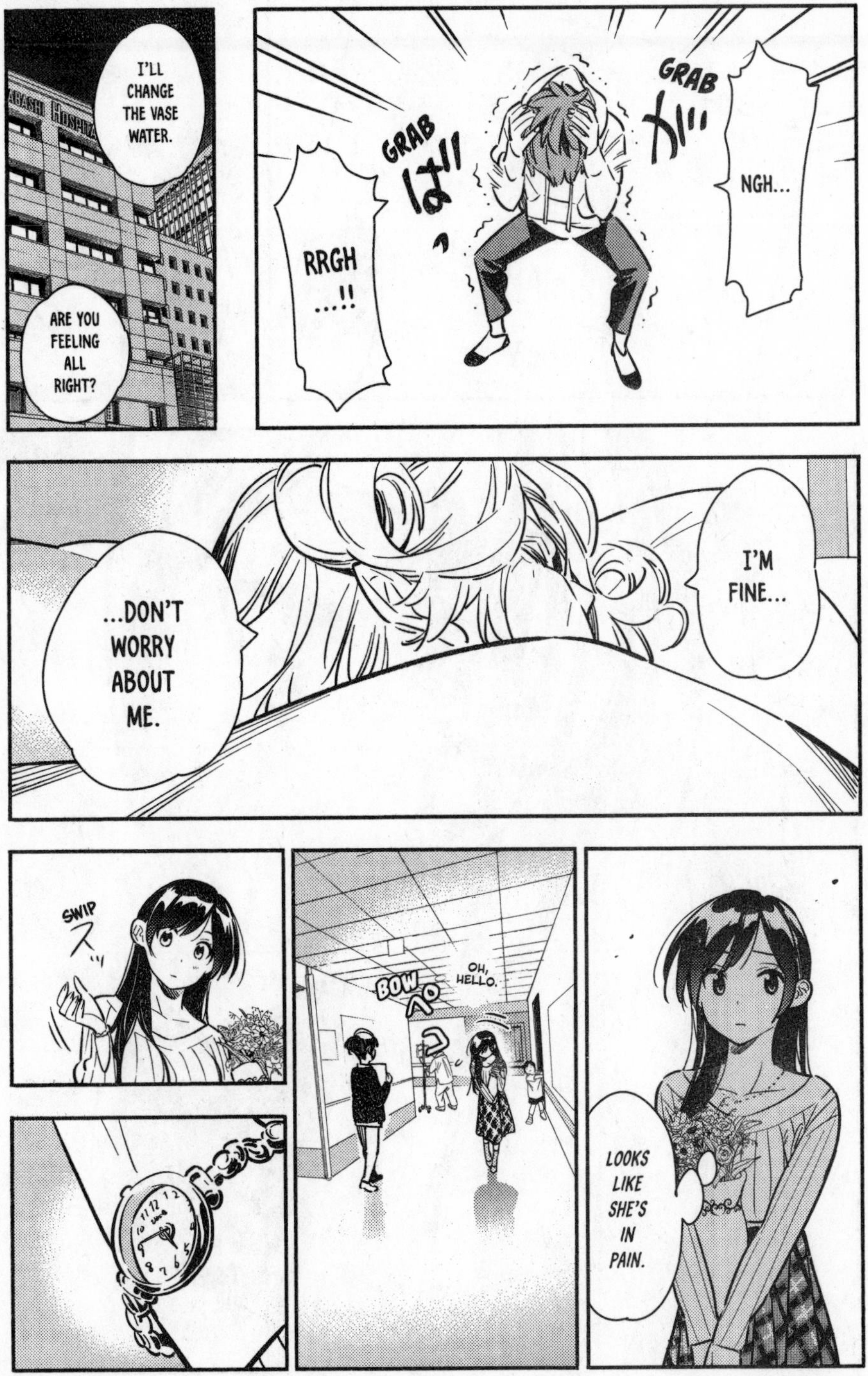
GRAB
NGH...
GRAB
RRGH ...!!
I'LL CHANGE THE VASE WATER.
ARE YOU FEELING ALL RIGHT?
I'M FINE...
...DON'T WORRY ABOUT ME.
LOOKS LIKE SHE'S IN PAIN.
OH, HELLO.
BOW
SWIP

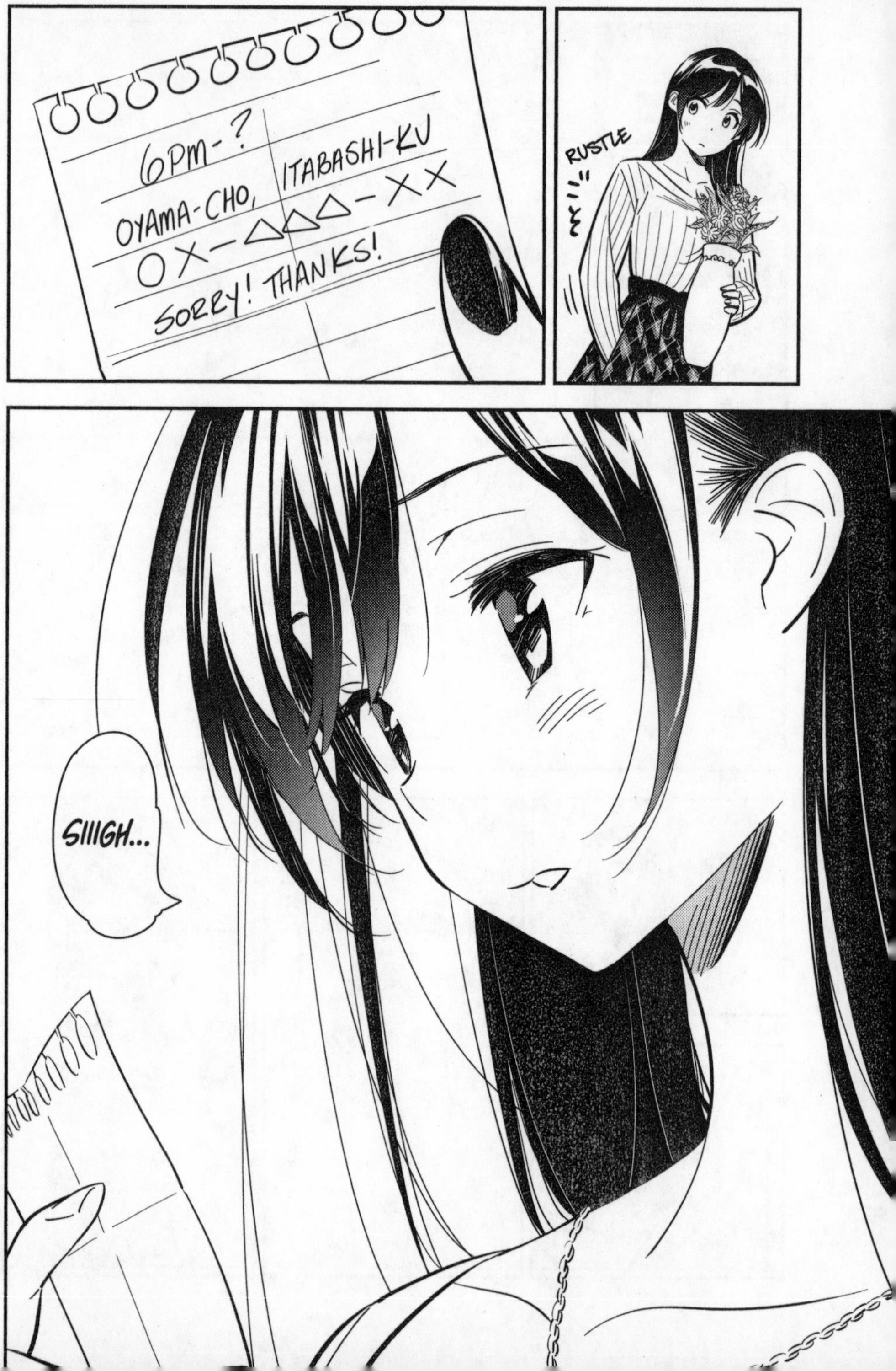
RUSTLE
6PM-?
OYAMA-CHO, ITABASHI-KU
○×-△△△-××
SORRY! THANKS!
SIIIGH...

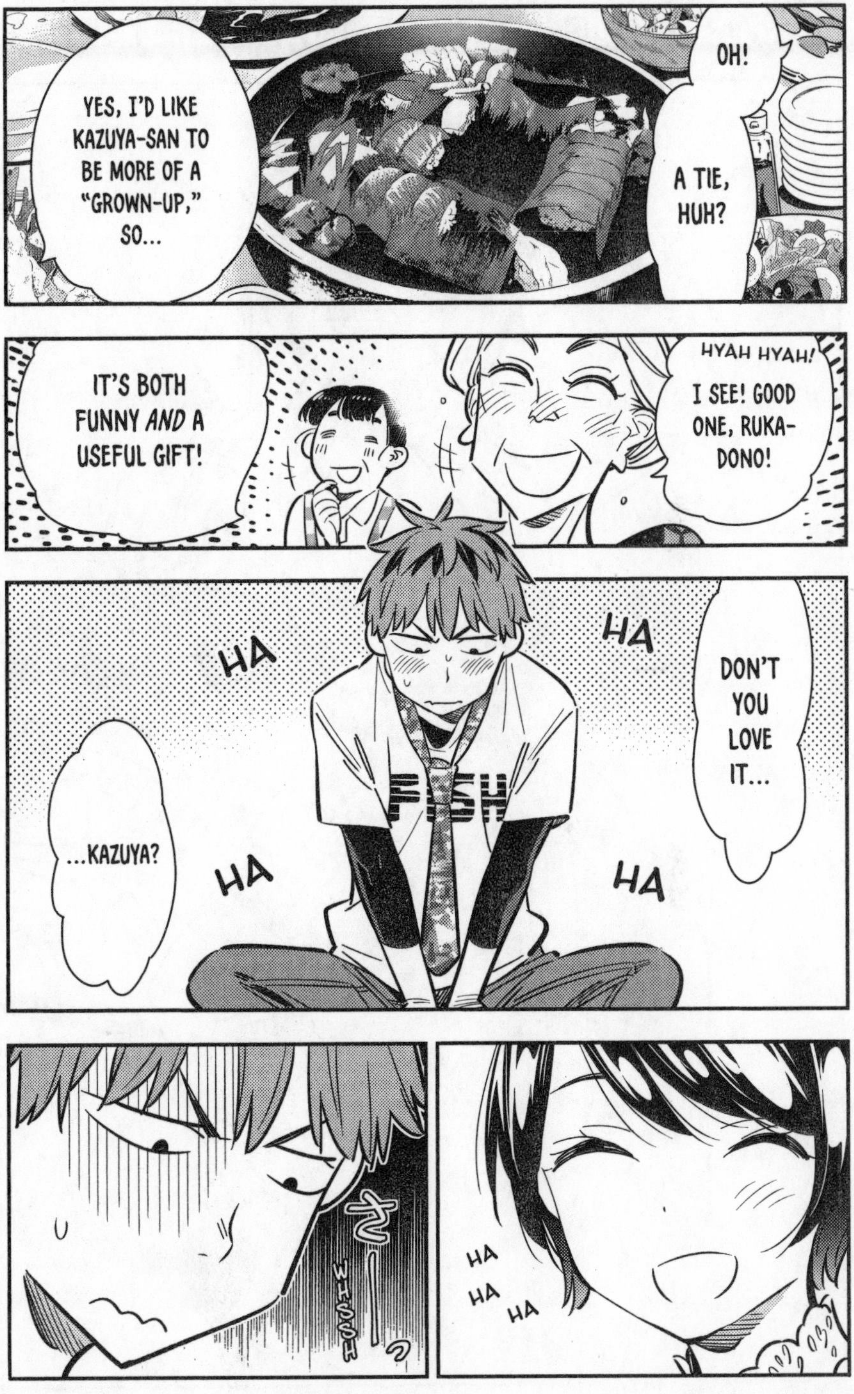
OH!
A TIE, HUH?
YES, I'D LIKE KAZUYA-SAN TO BE MORE OF A "GROWN-UP," SO...
HYAH HYAH!
I SEE! GOOD ONE, RUKA-DONO!
IT'S BOTH FUNNY *AND* A USEFUL GIFT!
DON'T YOU LOVE IT...
HA
HA
HA
HA
...KAZUYA?
FISH
HA HA HA
WHSSH

RATING 85 MY GIRLFRIEND, MY HOUSE, AND THE KISS 3

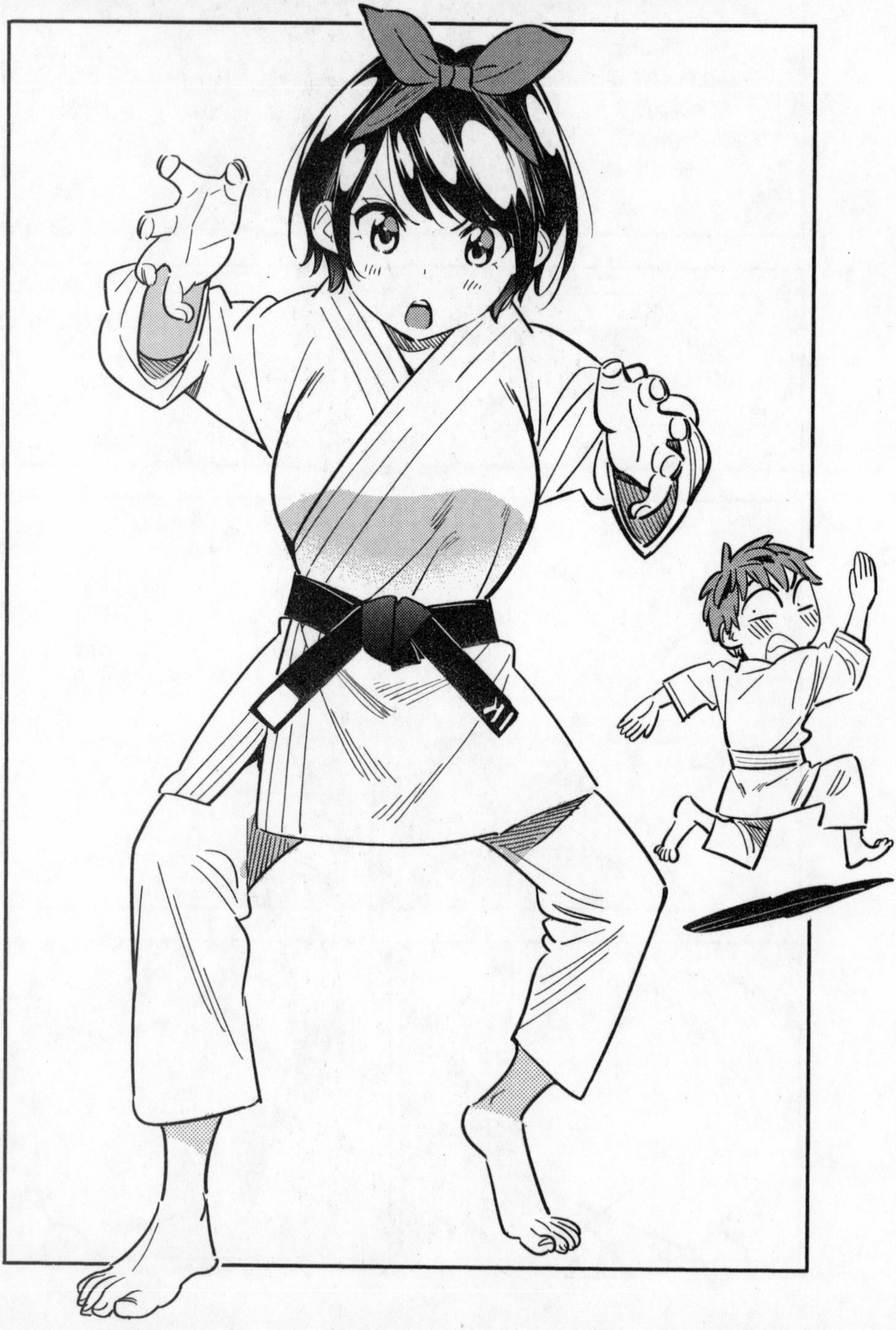

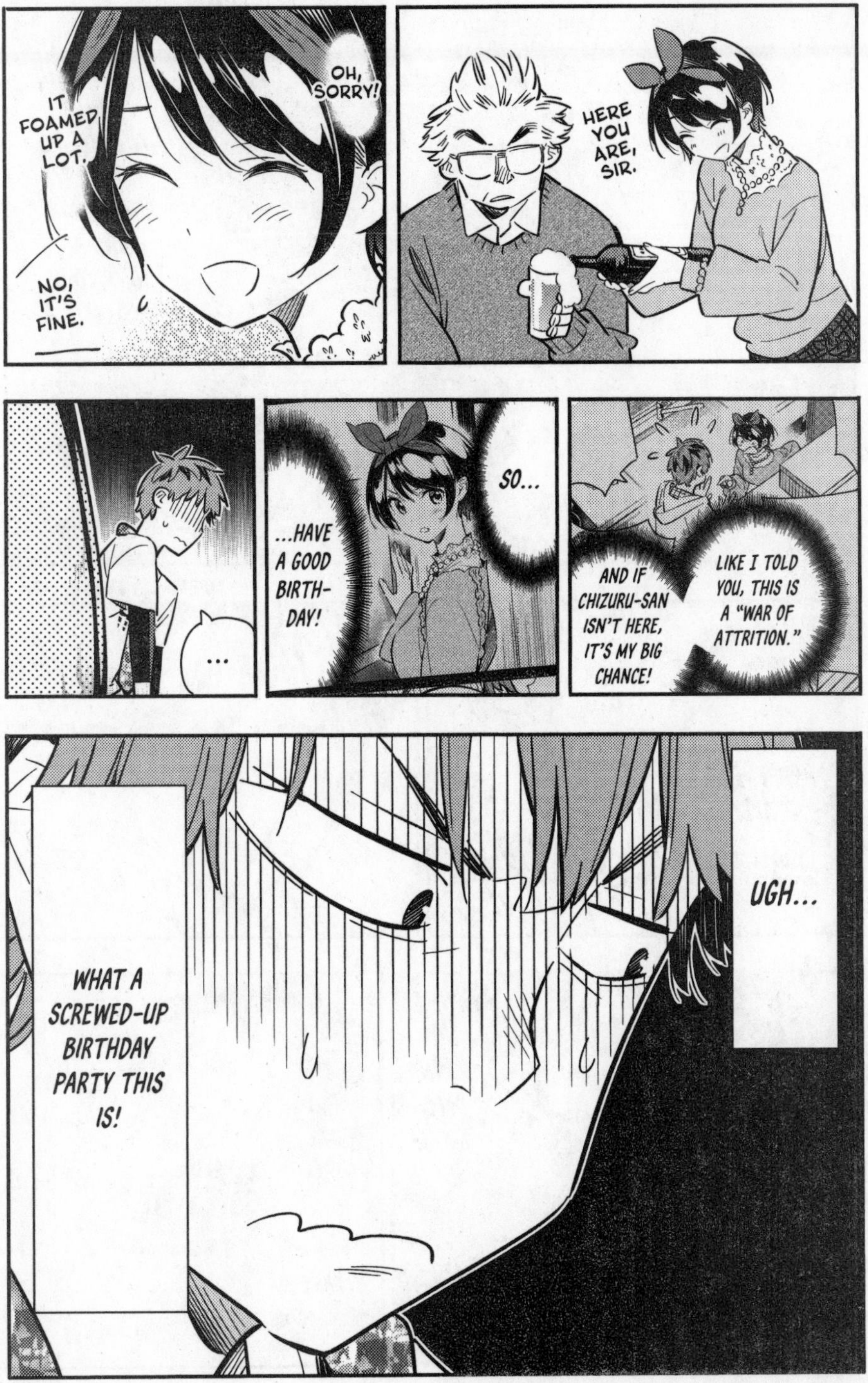
HERE YOU ARE, SIR.
OH, SORRY!
IT FOAMED UP A LOT.
NO, IT'S FINE.
LIKE I TOLD YOU, THIS IS A "WAR OF ATTRITION."
AND IF CHIZURU-SAN ISN'T HERE, IT'S MY BIG CHANCE!
SO...
...HAVE A GOOD BIRTH-DAY!
...
UGH...
WHAT A SCREWED-UP BIRTHDAY PARTY THIS IS!

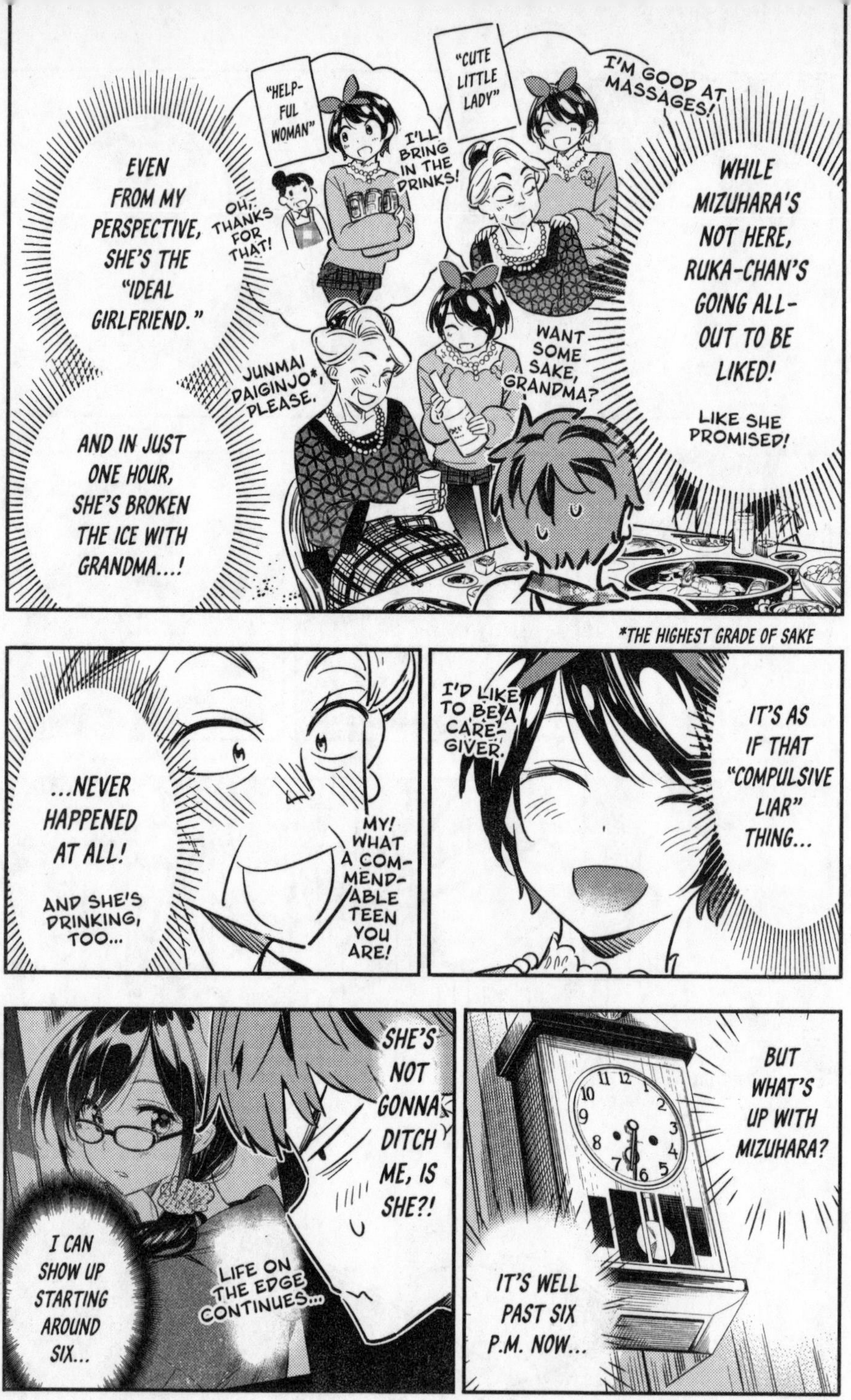
WHILE MIZUHARA'S NOT HERE, RUKA-CHAN'S GOING ALL-OUT TO BE LIKED!
LIKE SHE PROMISED!
I'M GOOD AT MASSAGES!
"CUTE LITTLE LADY"
I'LL BRING IN THE DRINKS!
"HELPFUL WOMAN"
OH, THANKS FOR THAT!
EVEN FROM MY PERSPECTIVE, SHE'S THE "IDEAL GIRLFRIEND."
WANT SOME SAKE, GRANDMA?
JUNMAI DAIGINJO*, PLEASE.
AND IN JUST ONE HOUR, SHE'S BROKEN THE ICE WITH GRANDMA...!
*THE HIGHEST GRADE OF SAKE
IT'S AS IF THAT "COMPULSIVE LIAR" THING...
I'D LIKE TO BE A CAREGIVER.
MY! WHAT A COMMENDABLE TEEN YOU ARE!
...NEVER HAPPENED AT ALL!
AND SHE'S DRINKING, TOO...
BUT WHAT'S UP WITH MIZUHARA?
IT'S WELL PAST SIX P.M. NOW...
SHE'S NOT GONNA DITCH ME, IS SHE?!
LIFE ON THE EDGE CONTINUES...
I CAN SHOW UP STARTING AROUND SIX...

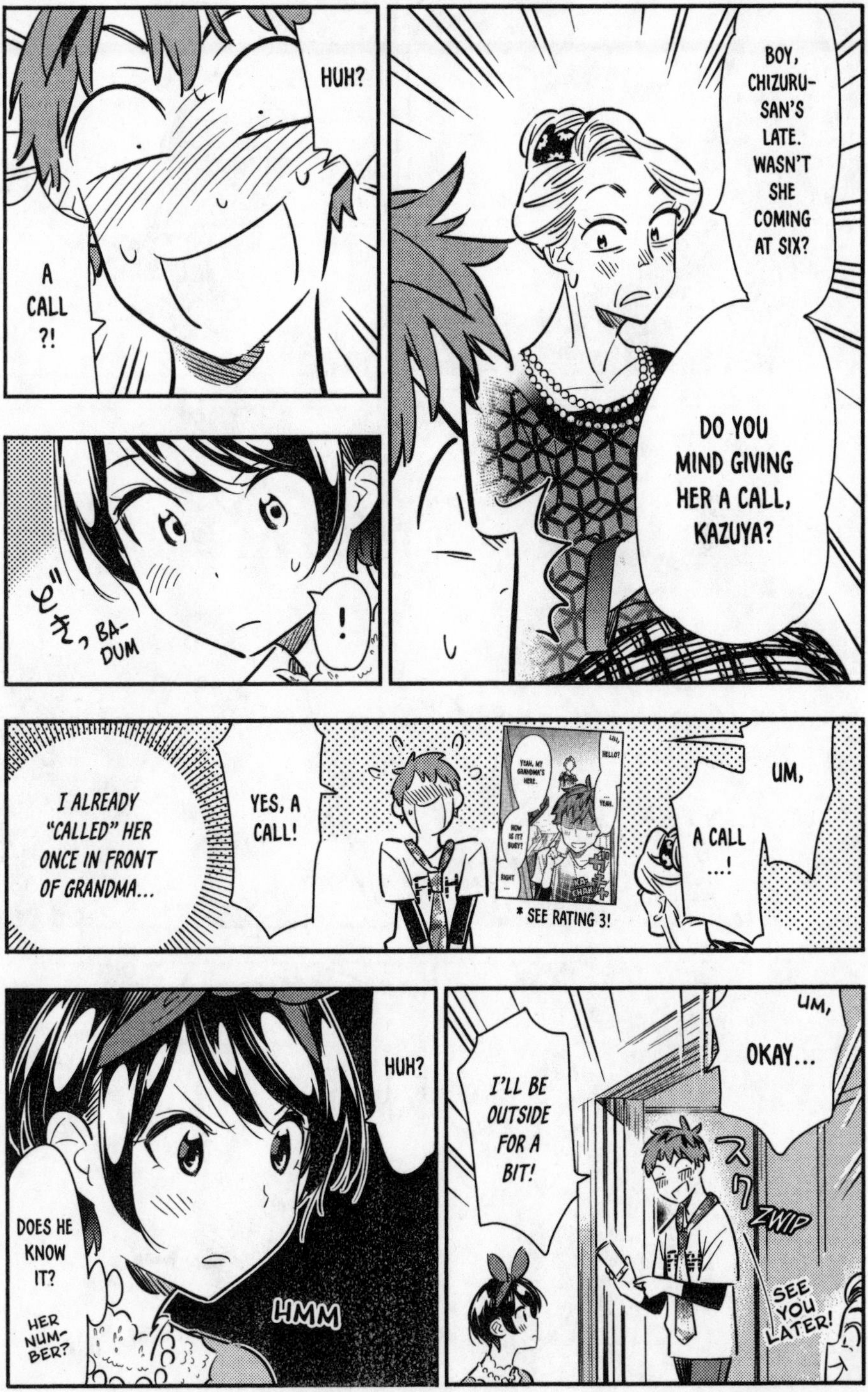
BOY, CHIZURU-SAN'S LATE. WASN'T SHE COMING AT SIX?
DO YOU MIND GIVING HER A CALL, KAZUYA?
HUH?
A CALL ?!
!
どきっ BA-DUM
UM,
A CALL ...!
UH, HELLO?
YEAH, MY GRANDMA'S HERE...
...YEAH.
HOW IS IT? BUSY?
RIGHT ...
KA-CHAK
* SEE RATING 3!
YES, A CALL!
I ALREADY "CALLED" HER ONCE IN FRONT OF GRANDMA...
UM,
OKAY...
I'LL BE OUTSIDE FOR A BIT!
スク ZWIP
SEE YOU LATER!
HUH?
DOES HE KNOW IT?
HER NUMBER?
HMM

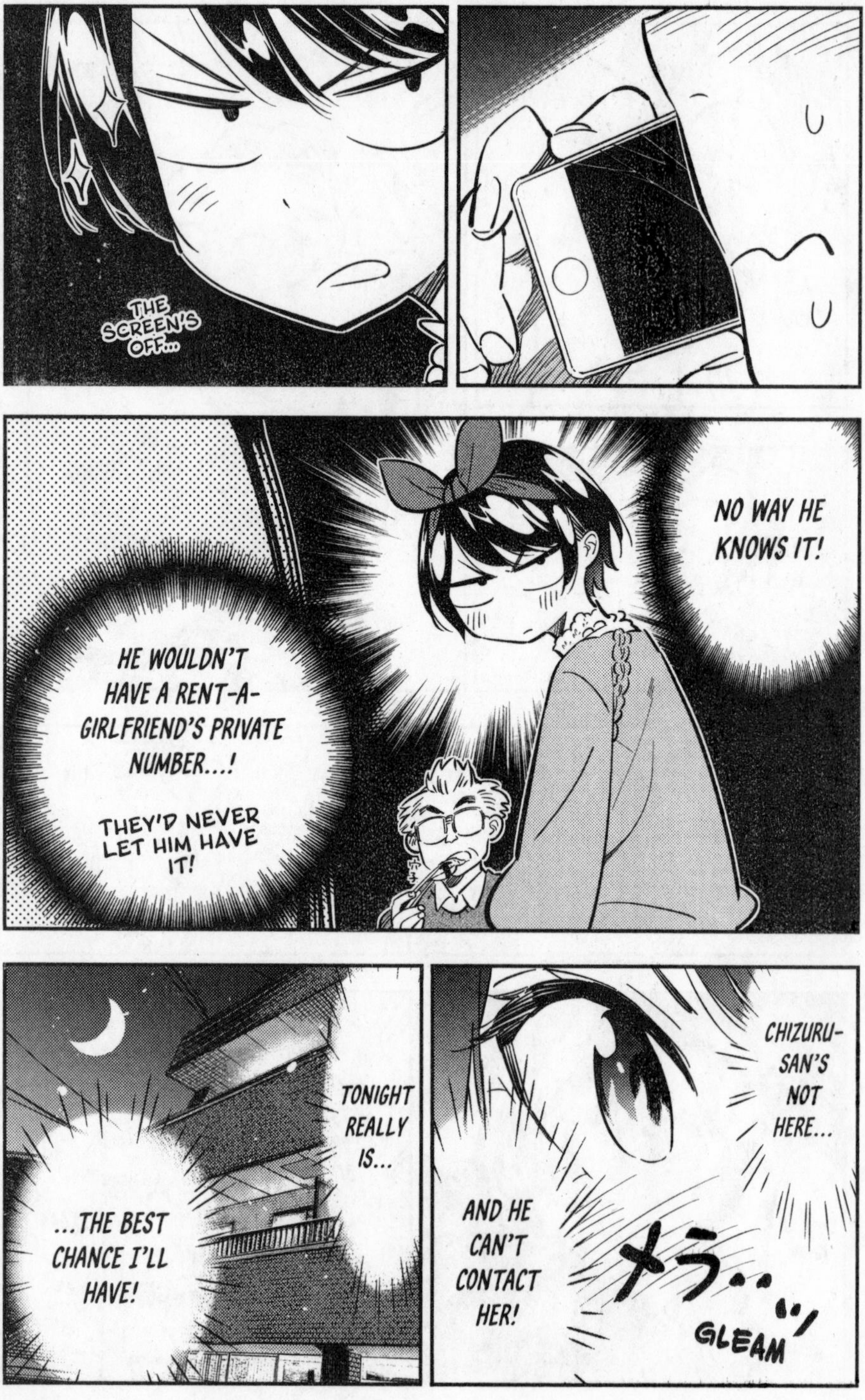
THE SCREEN'S OFF...
NO WAY HE KNOWS IT!
HE WOULDN'T HAVE A RENT-A-GIRLFRIEND'S PRIVATE NUMBER...!
THEY'D NEVER LET HIM HAVE IT!
CHIZURU-SAN'S NOT HERE...
AND HE CAN'T CONTACT HER!
メラ…
GLEAM
TONIGHT REALLY IS...
...THE BEST CHANCE I'LL HAVE!

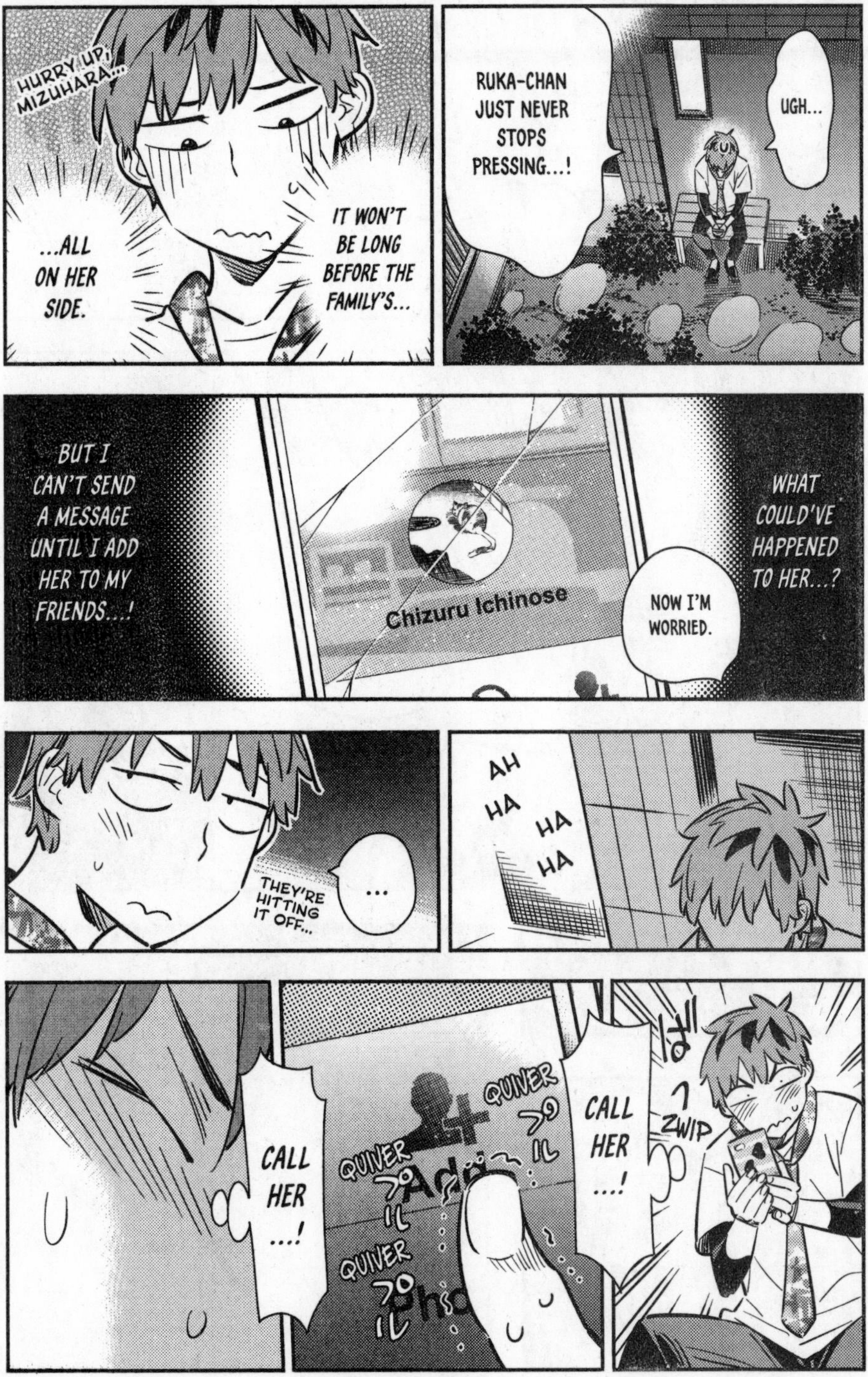
UGH...
RUKA-CHAN JUST NEVER STOPS PRESSING...!
IT WON'T BE LONG BEFORE THE FAMILY'S...
...ALL ON HER SIDE.
HURRY UP, MIZUHARA...
WHAT COULD'VE HAPPENED TO HER...?
NOW I'M WORRIED.
Chizuru Ichinose
BUT I CAN'T SEND A MESSAGE UNTIL I ADD HER TO MY FRIENDS...!
AH HA HA HA
...
THEY'RE HITTING IT OFF...
ばっ
ZWIP
CALL HER...!
QUIVER プル
QUIVER プル
QUIVER プル
CALL HER...!

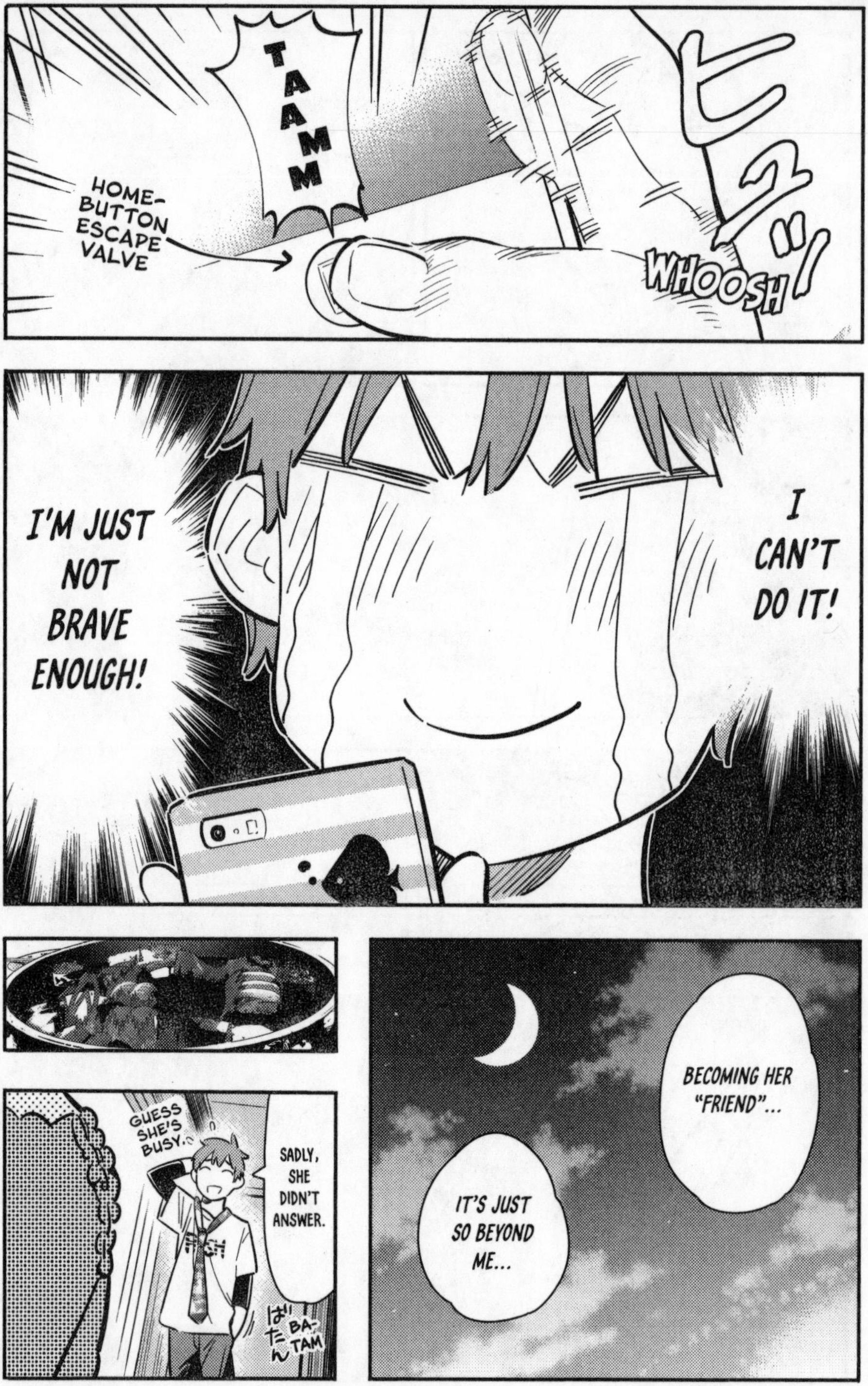
ヒュッ
WHOOSH
TAMM
HOME-BUTTON ESCAPE VALVE
I CAN'T DO IT!
I'M JUST NOT BRAVE ENOUGH!
BECOMING HER "FRIEND"...
IT'S JUST SO BEYOND ME...
SADLY, SHE DIDN'T ANSWER.
GUESS SHE'S BUSY.
ばたん
BA-TAM

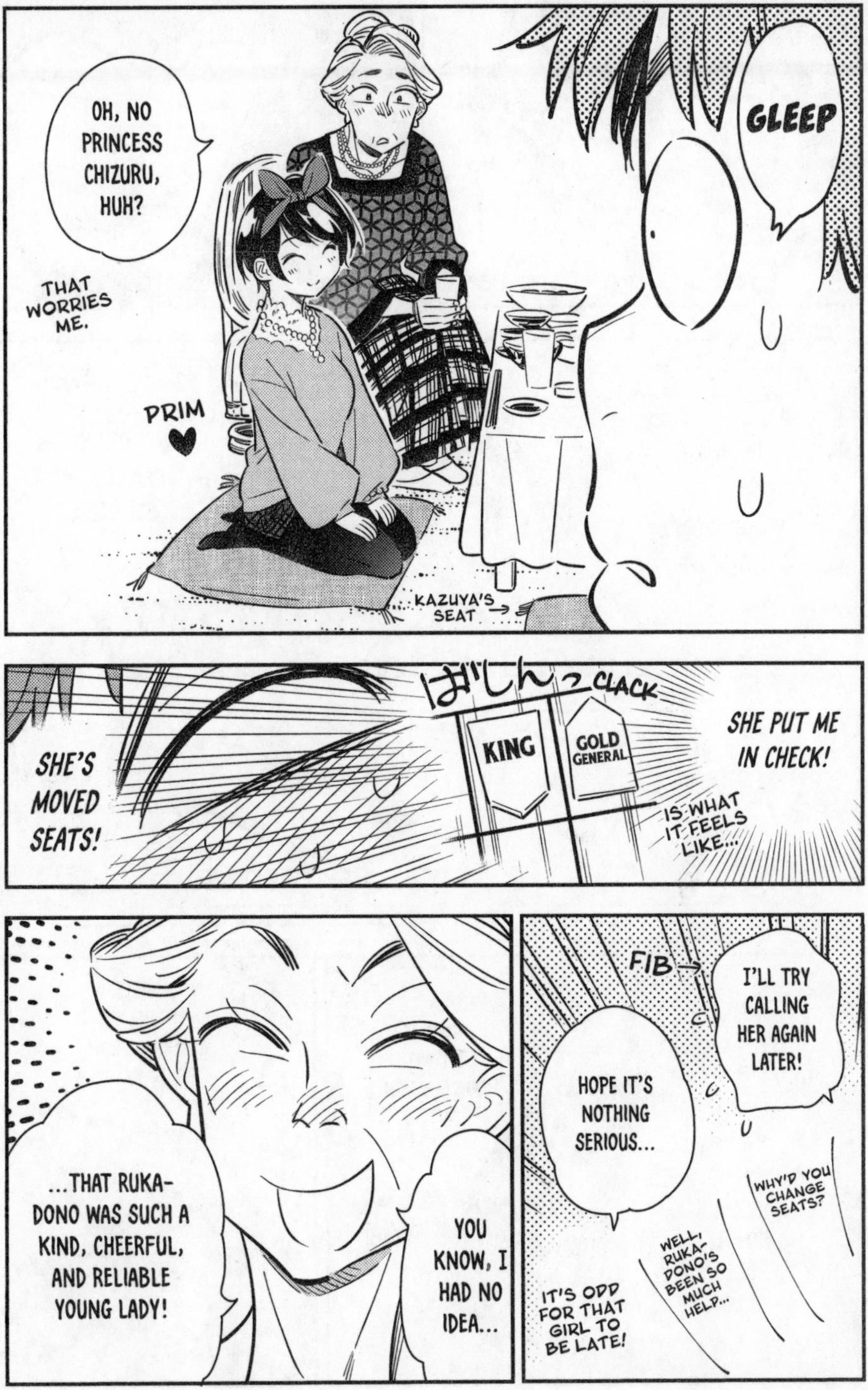
GLEEP
OH, NO PRINCESS CHIZURU, HUH?
THAT WORRIES ME.
PRIM
KAZUYA'S SEAT
SHE PUT ME IN CHECK!
IS WHAT IT FEELS LIKE...
ばしんっ CLACK
GOLD GENERAL
KING
SHE'S MOVED SEATS!
I'LL TRY CALLING HER AGAIN LATER!
FIB
HOPE IT'S NOTHING SERIOUS...
WHY'D YOU CHANGE SEATS?
WELL, RUKA-DONO'S BEEN SO MUCH HELP...
IT'S ODD FOR THAT GIRL TO BE LATE!
YOU KNOW, I HAD NO IDEA...
...THAT RUKA-DONO WAS SUCH A KIND, CHEERFUL, AND RELIABLE YOUNG LADY!

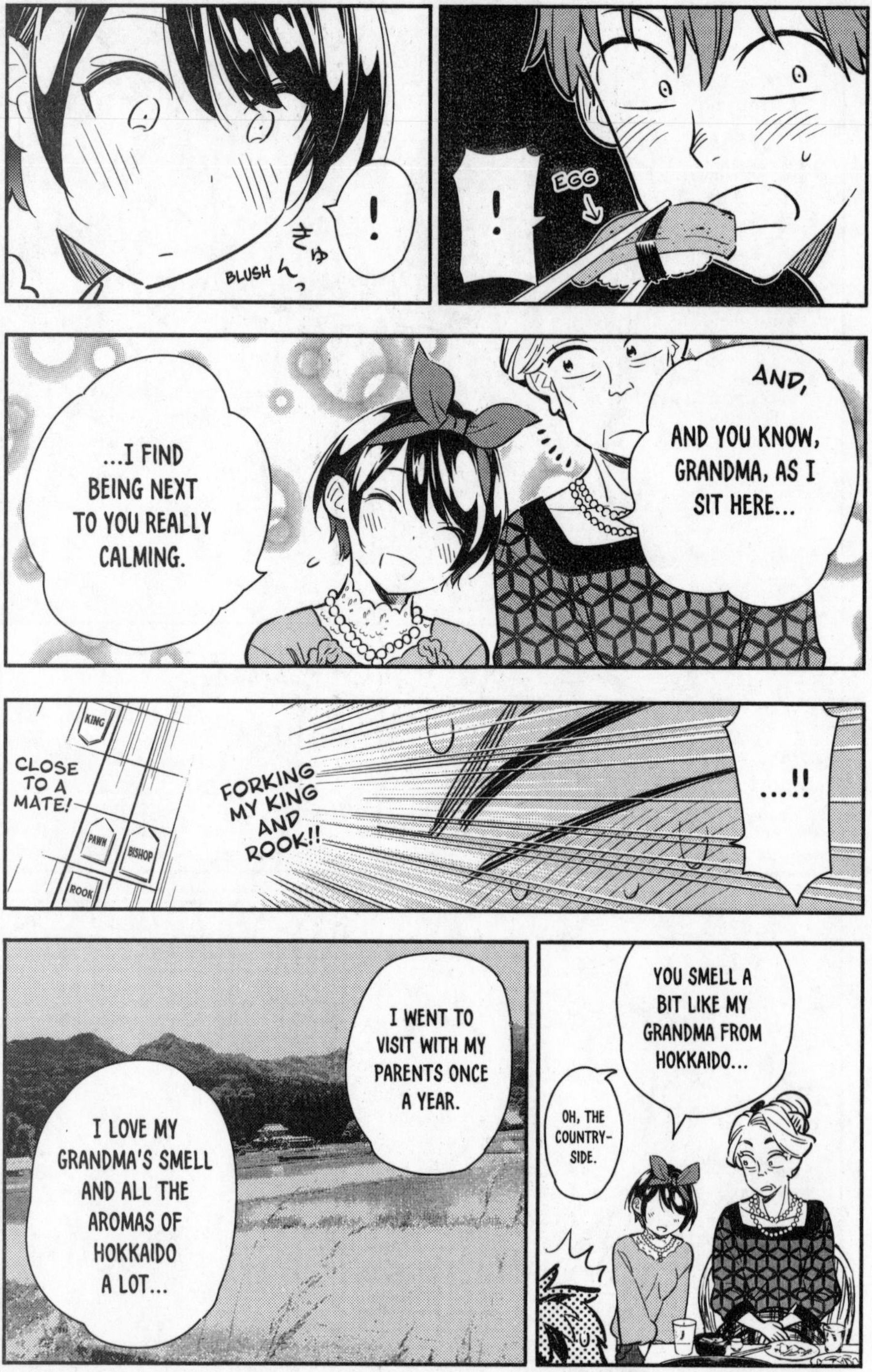
EGG
!
!
BLUSH
きゅんっ
AND,
AND YOU KNOW, GRANDMA, AS I SIT HERE...
...I FIND BEING NEXT TO YOU REALLY CALMING.
...!!
FORKING MY KING AND ROOK!!
KING
CLOSE TO A MATE!
PAWN
BISHOP
ROOK
YOU SMELL A BIT LIKE MY GRANDMA FROM HOKKAIDO...
OH, THE COUNTRY-SIDE.
I WENT TO VISIT WITH MY PARENTS ONCE A YEAR.
I LOVE MY GRANDMA'S SMELL AND ALL THE AROMAS OF HOKKAIDO A LOT...

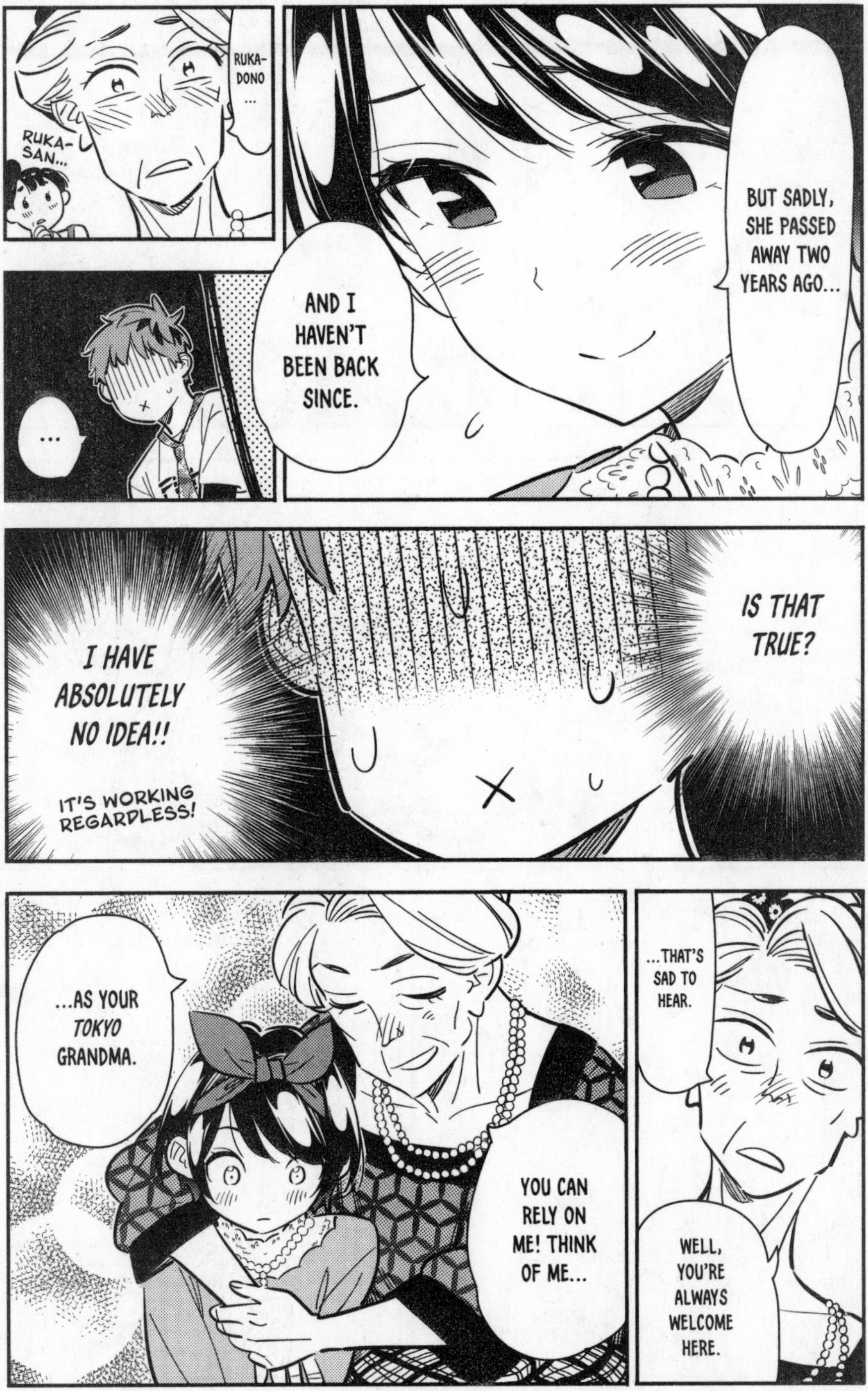

BUT SADLY, SHE PASSED AWAY TWO YEARS AGO...
AND I HAVEN'T BEEN BACK SINCE.
RUKA-DONO...
RUKA-SAN...
...
IS THAT TRUE?
I HAVE ABSOLUTELY NO IDEA!!
IT'S WORKING REGARDLESS!
...THAT'S SAD TO HEAR.
WELL, YOU'RE ALWAYS WELCOME HERE.
YOU CAN RELY ON ME! THINK OF ME...
...AS YOUR *TOKYO* GRANDMA.

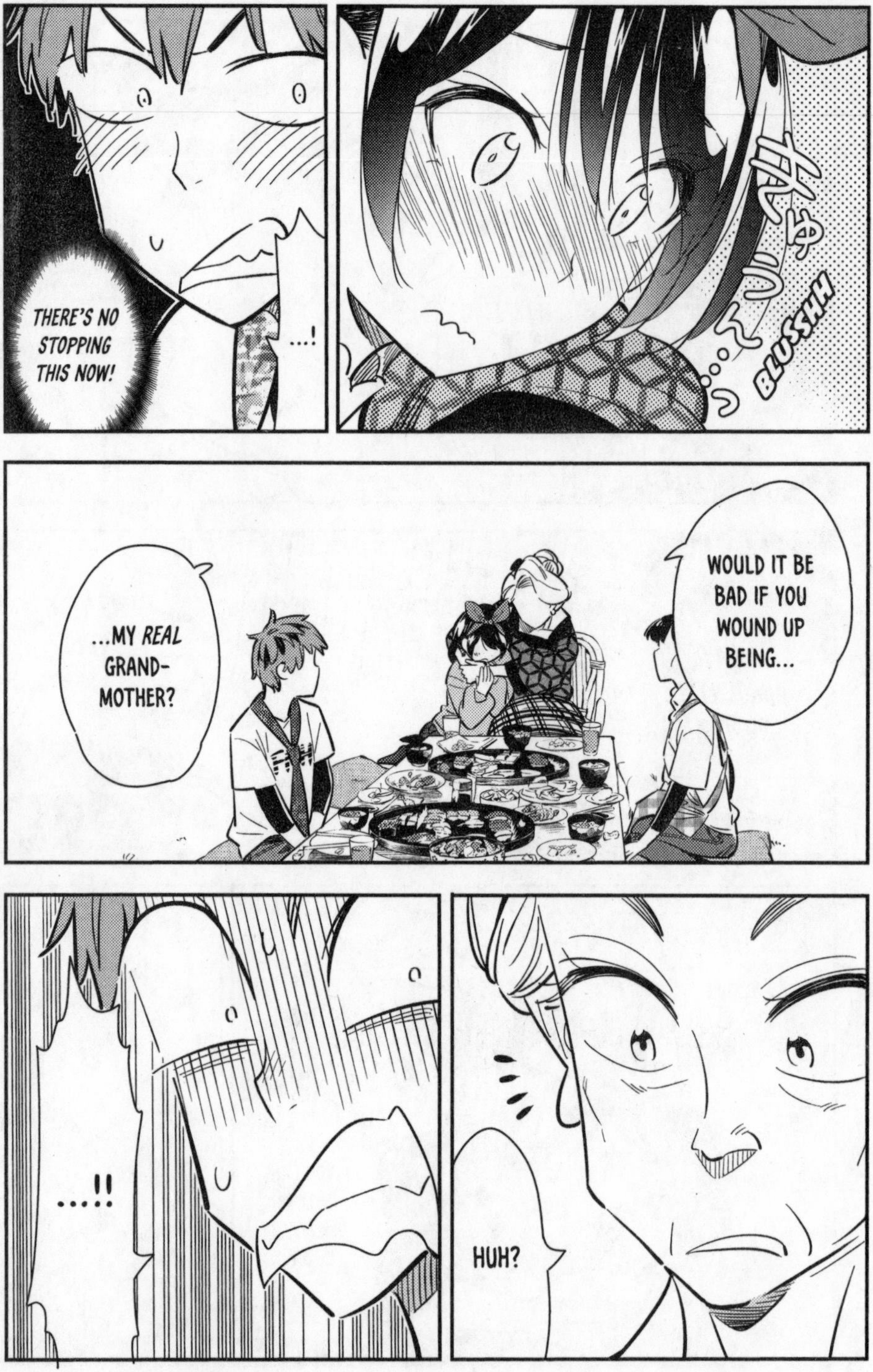
BLUSSHH
...!
THERE'S NO STOPPING THIS NOW!
WOULD IT BE BAD IF YOU WOUND UP BEING...
...MY *REAL* GRAND-MOTHER?
HUH?
...!!

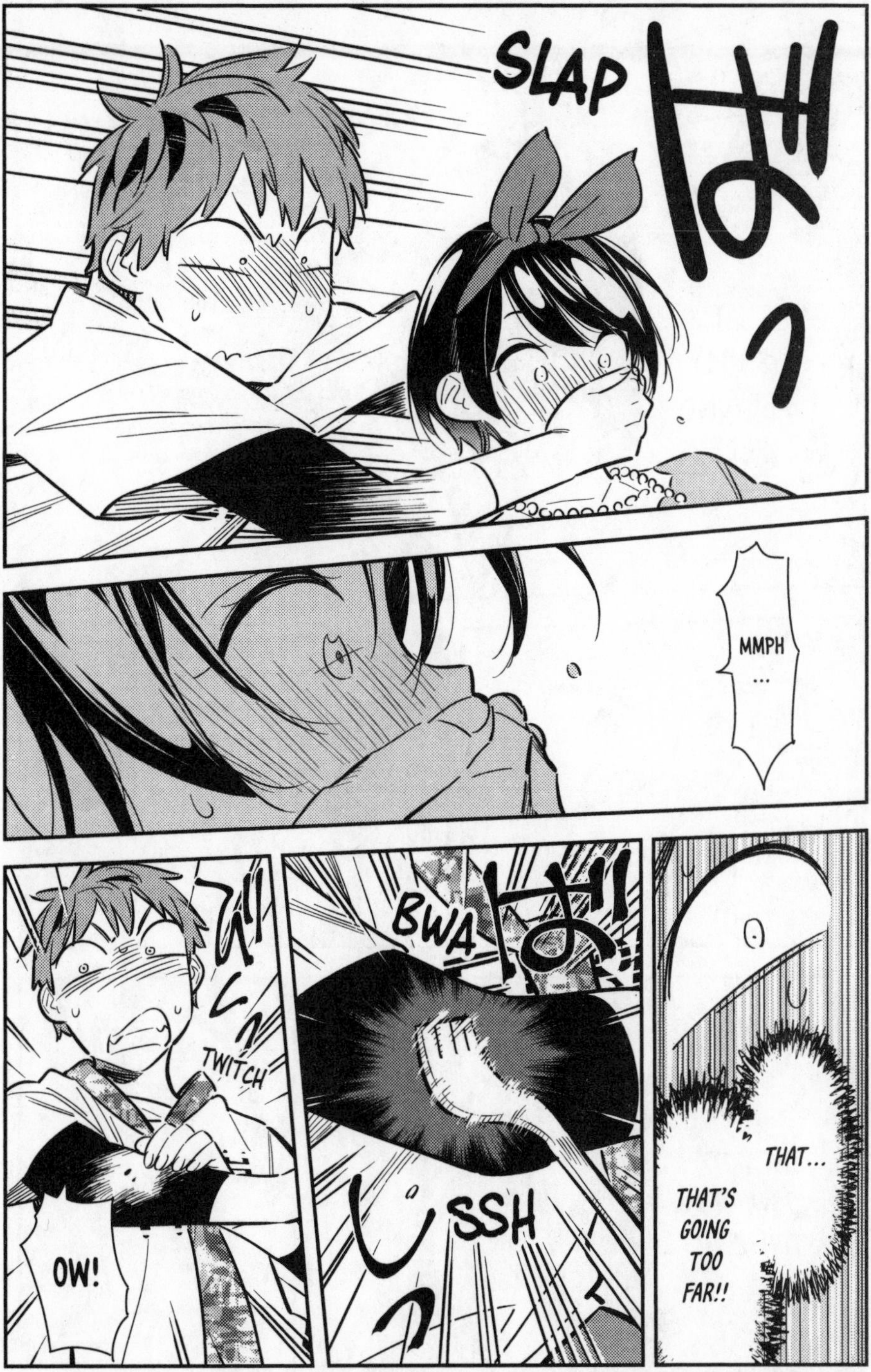
SLAP
MMPH ...
THAT...
THAT'S GOING TOO FAR!!
BWA
SSH
TWITCH
OW!

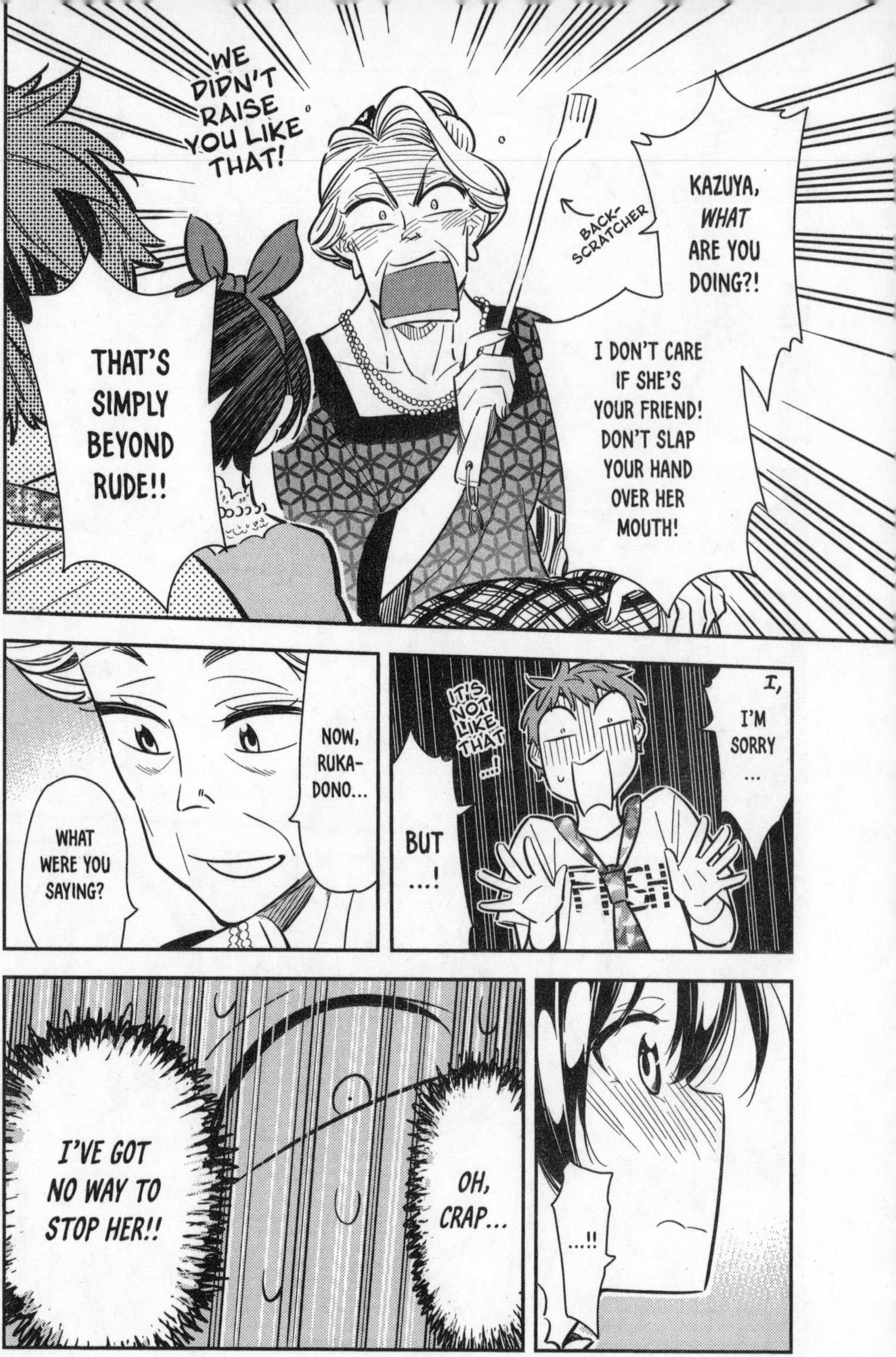
KAZUYA, WHAT ARE YOU DOING?!
I DON'T CARE IF SHE'S YOUR FRIEND! DON'T SLAP YOUR HAND OVER HER MOUTH!
BACK-SCRATCHER
WE DIDN'T RAISE YOU LIKE THAT!
THAT'S SIMPLY BEYOND RUDE!!
I, I'M SORRY ...
IT'S NOT LIKE THAT ...!
BUT ...!
NOW, RUKA-DONO...
WHAT WERE YOU SAYING?
...!!
OH, CRAP...
I'VE GOT NO WAY TO STOP HER!!

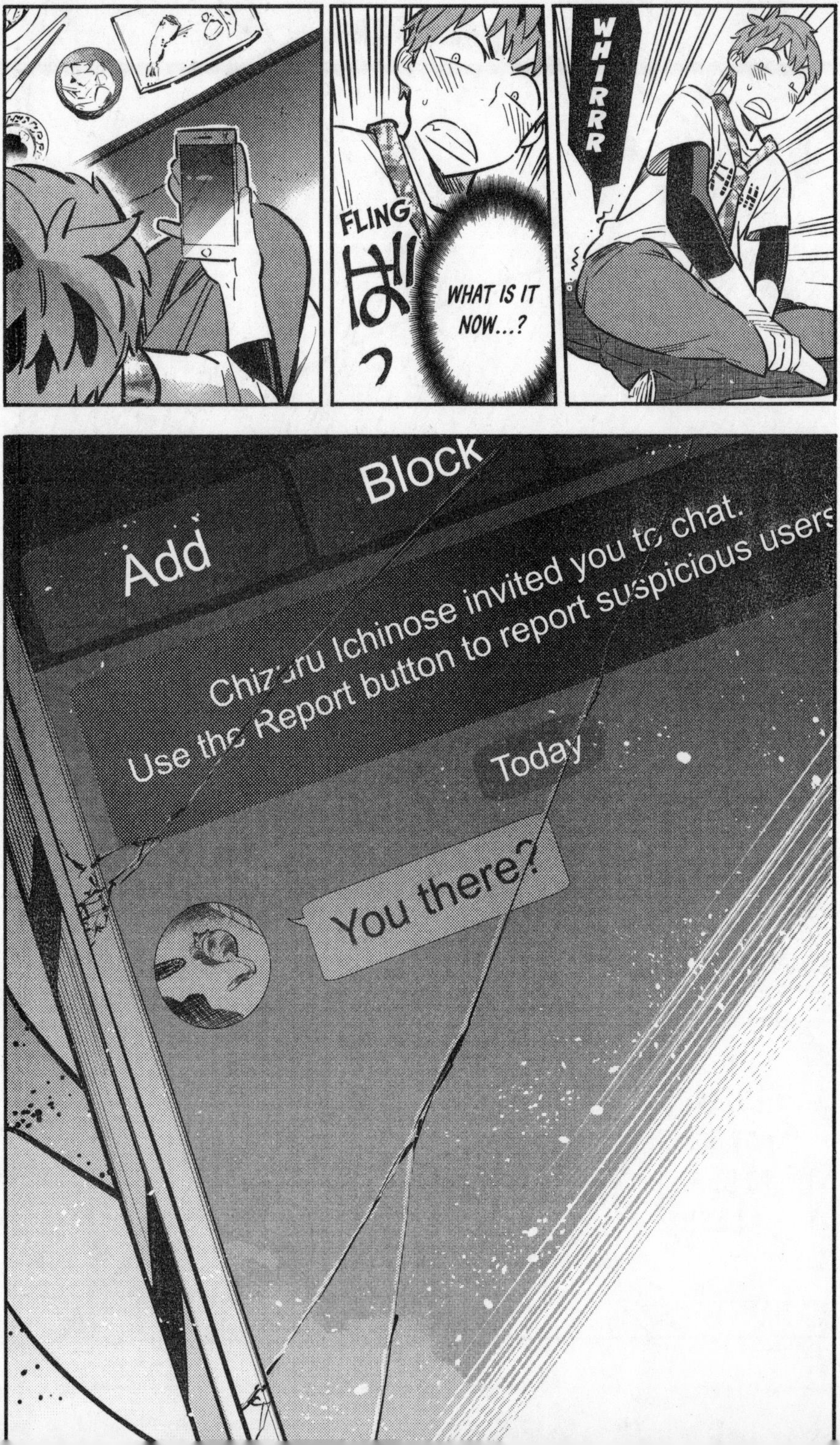
WHIRRR
FLING
WHAT IS IT NOW...?
Block
Add
Chizuru Ichinose invited you to chat.
Use the Report button to report suspicious users
Today
You there?

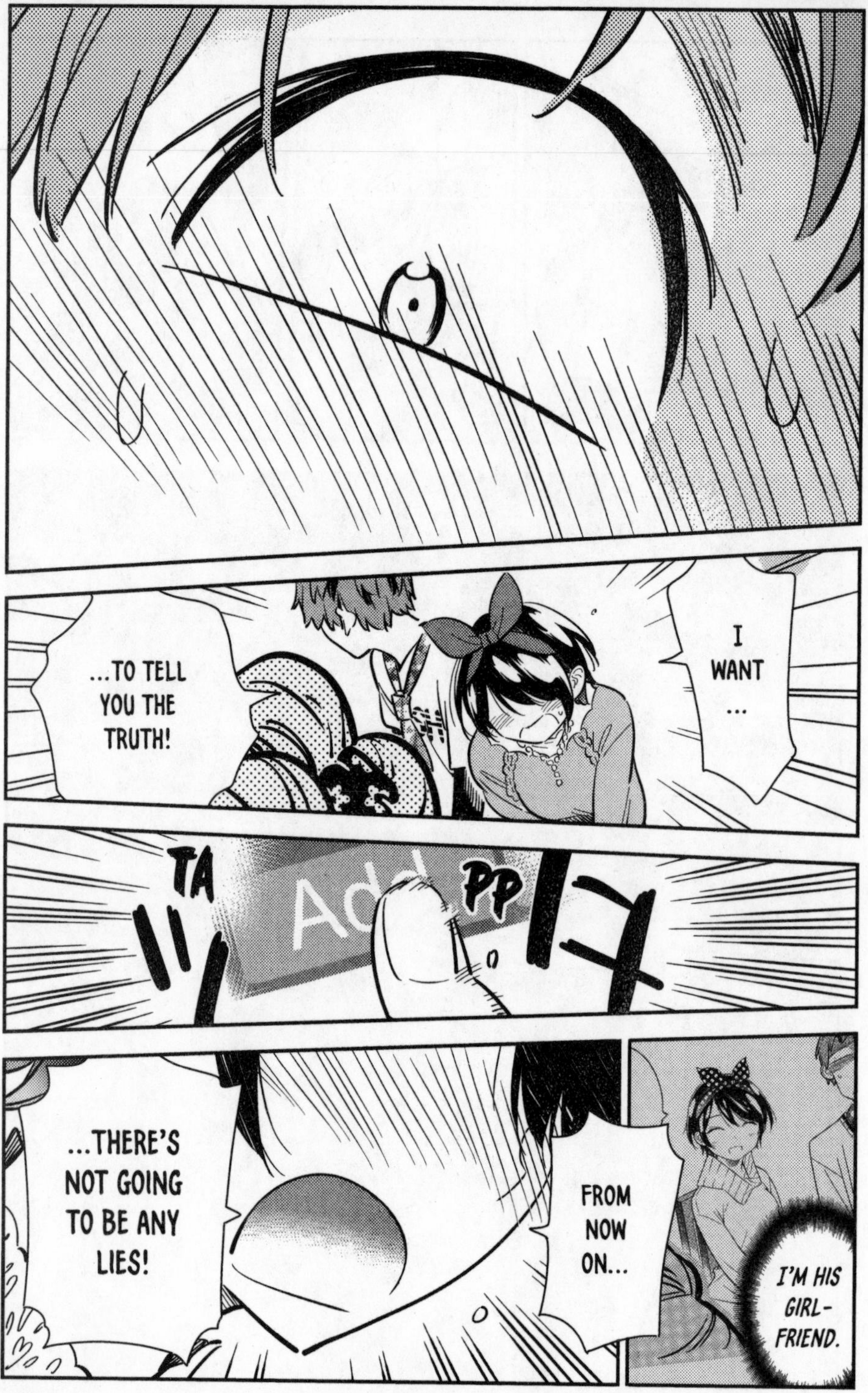
I WANT ...
...TO TELL YOU THE TRUTH!
Add
TA
PP
I'M HIS GIRL-FRIEND.
FROM NOW ON...
...THERE'S NOT GOING TO BE ANY LIES!

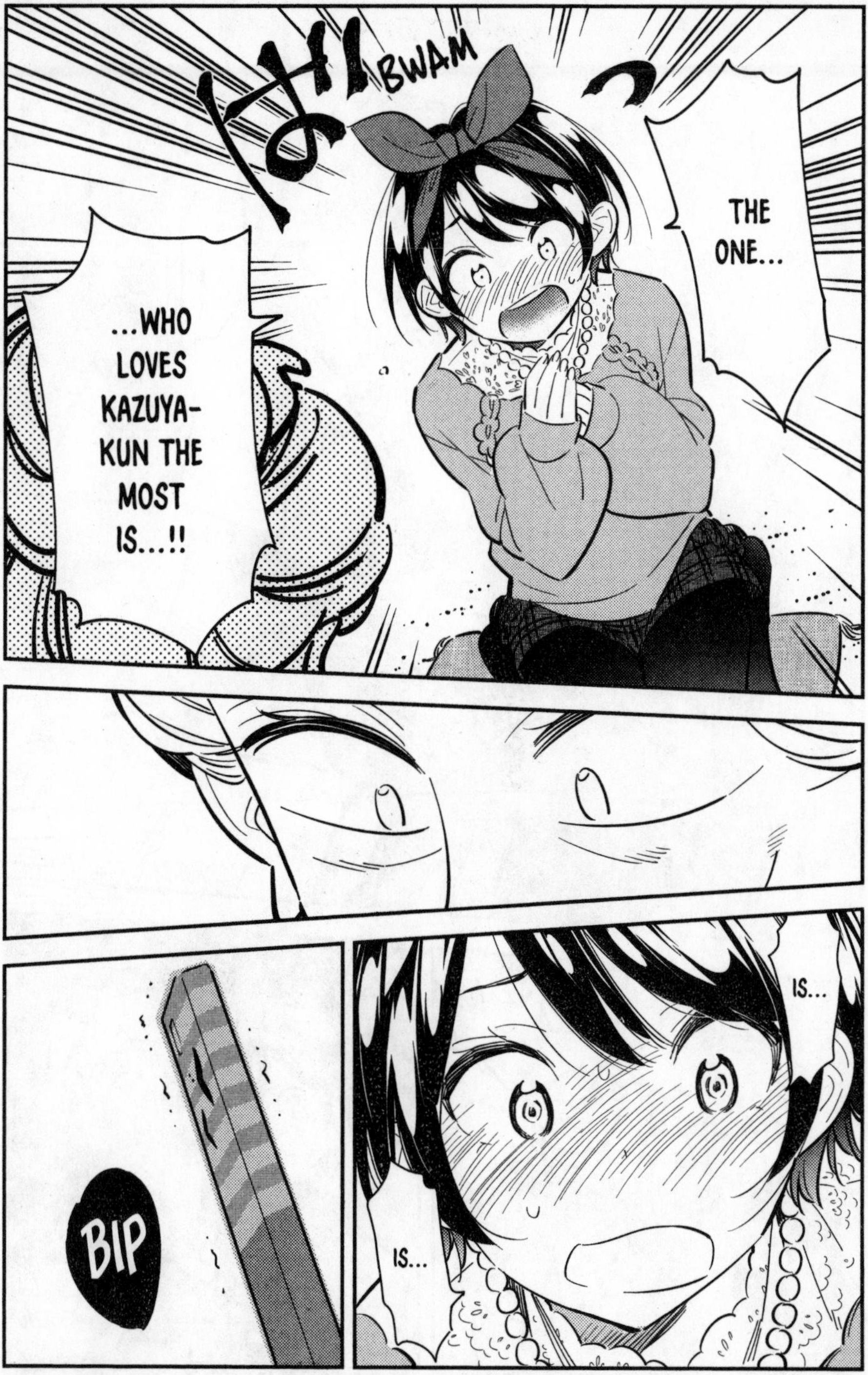
THE ONE...
BWAM
...WHO LOVES KAZUYA-KUN THE MOST IS...!!
IS...
IS...
BIP

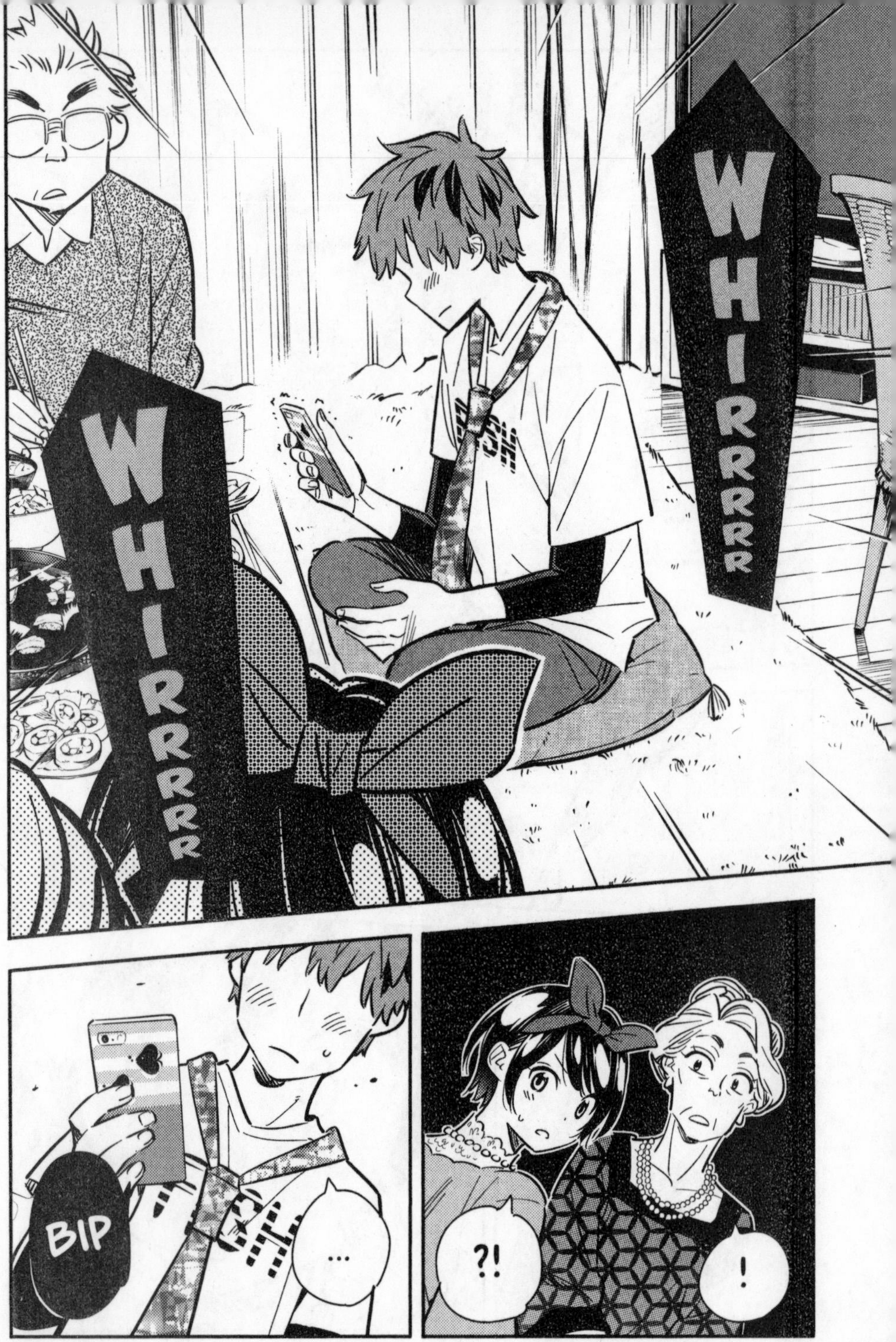
WHIRRRR
WHIRRRR
!
?!
...
BIP

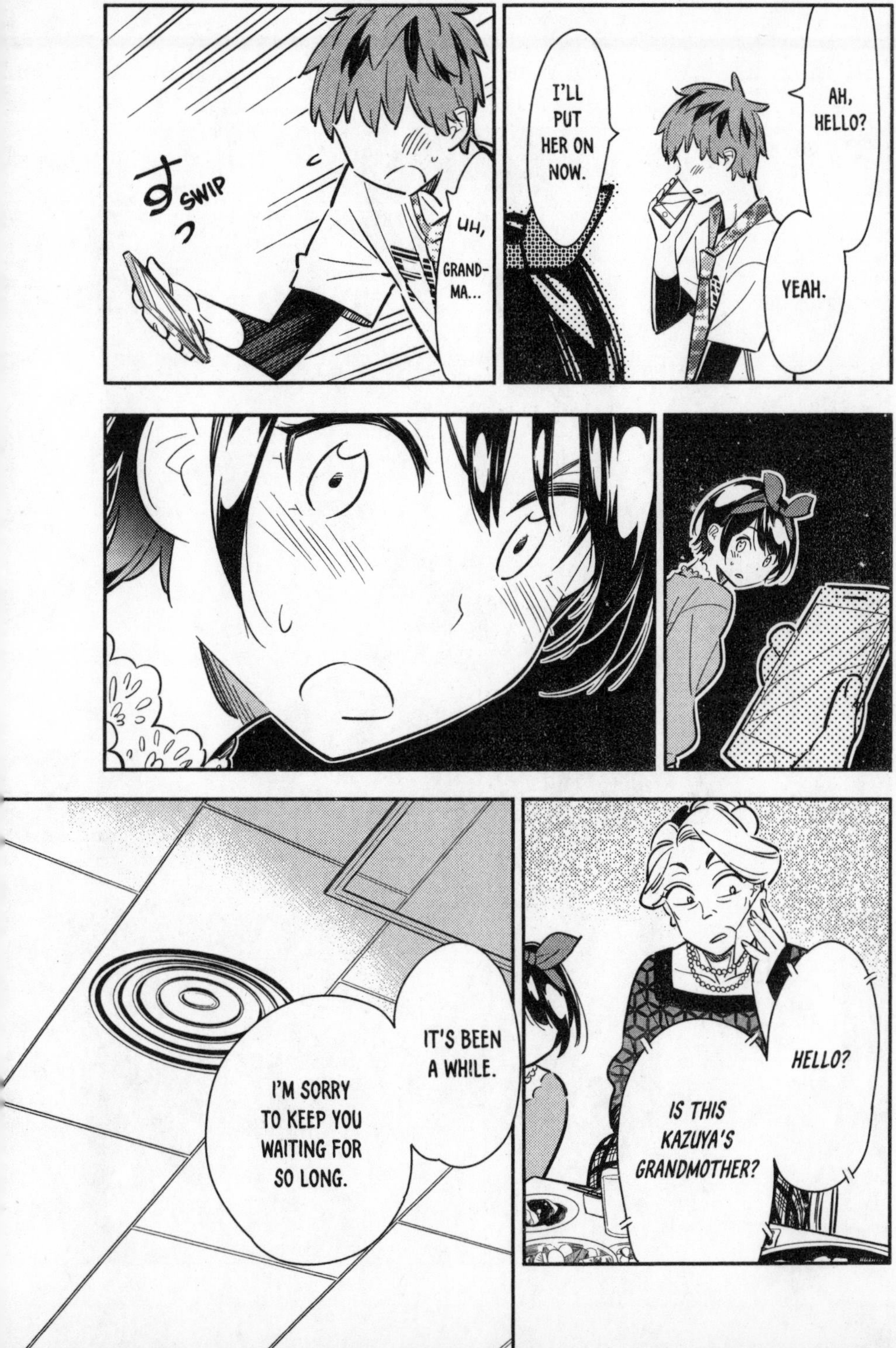
AH, HELLO?
YEAH.
I'LL PUT HER ON NOW.
すSWIP
UH, GRANDMA...
HELLO?
IS THIS KAZUYA'S GRANDMOTHER?
IT'S BEEN A WHILE.
I'M SORRY TO KEEP YOU WAITING FOR SO LONG.

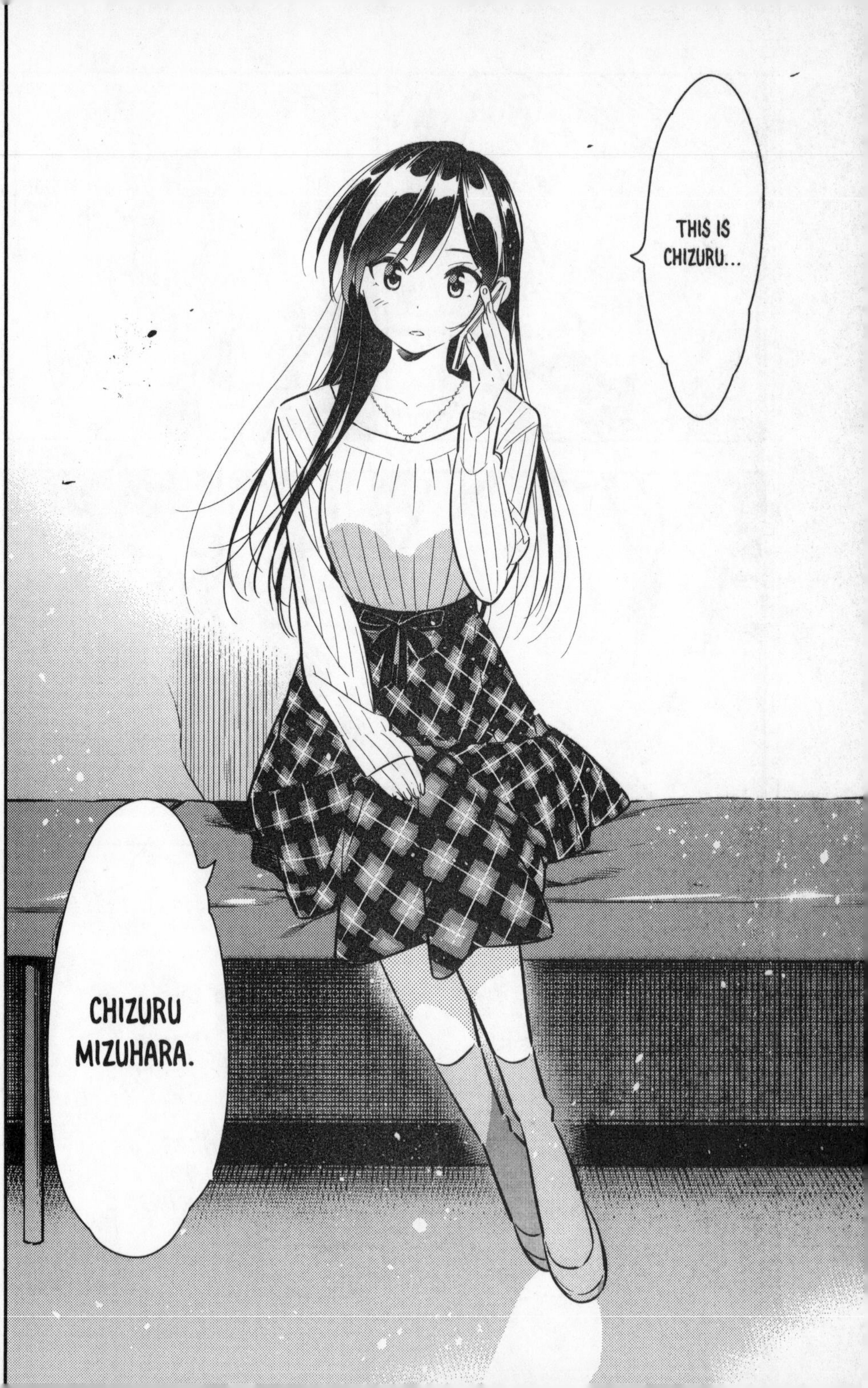
THIS IS CHIZURU...
CHIZURU MIZUHARA.

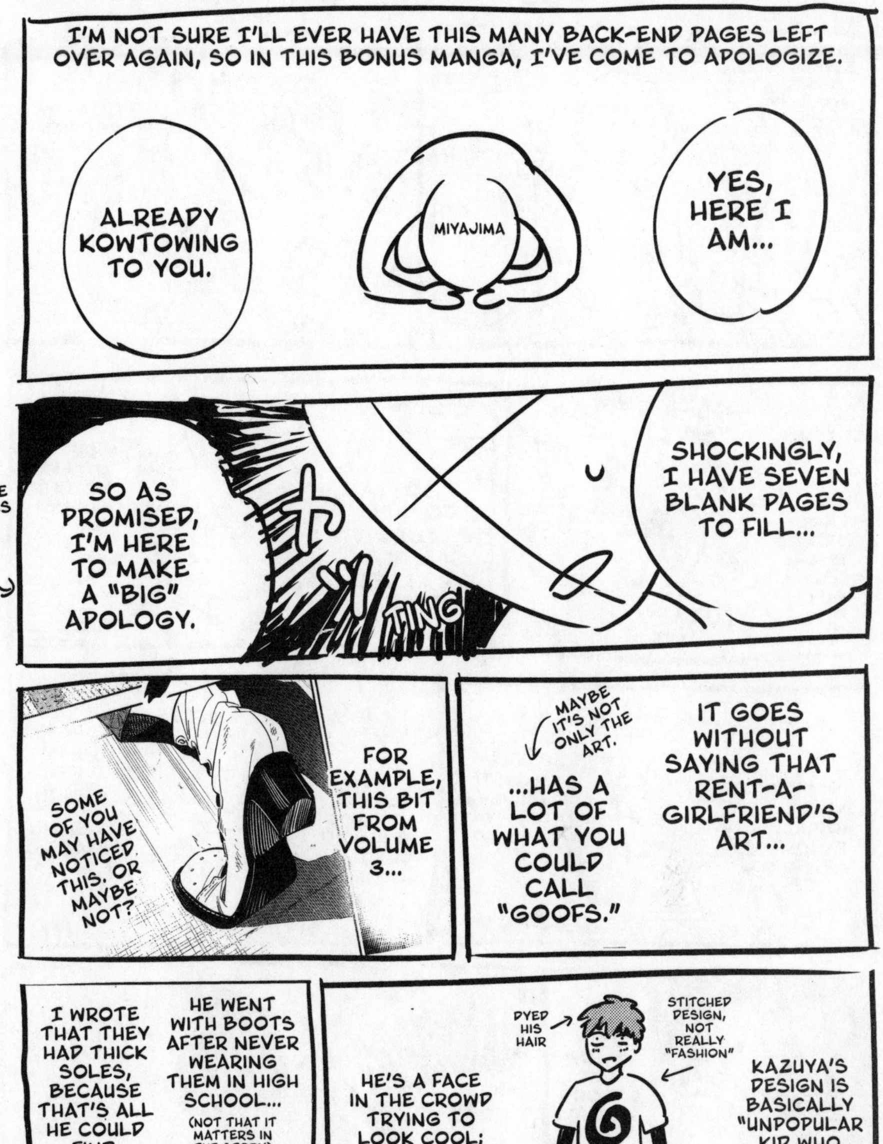
I'M NOT SURE I'LL EVER HAVE THIS MANY BACK-END PAGES LEFT OVER AGAIN, SO IN THIS BONUS MANGA, I'VE COME TO APOLOGIZE.
YES, HERE I AM...
MIYAJIMA
ALREADY KOWTOWING TO YOU.
SHOCKINGLY, I HAVE SEVEN BLANK PAGES TO FILL...
TING
SO AS PROMISED, I'M HERE TO MAKE A "BIG" APOLOGY.
NOT THAT ANYONE RECALLS THIS.
IT GOES WITHOUT SAYING THAT RENT-A-GIRLFRIEND'S ART...
MAYBE IT'S NOT ONLY THE ART.
...HAS A LOT OF WHAT YOU COULD CALL "GOOFS."
FOR EXAMPLE, THIS BIT FROM VOLUME 3...
SOME OF YOU MAY HAVE NOTICED THIS. OR MAYBE NOT?
KAZUYA'S DESIGN IS BASICALLY "UNPOPULAR KID WHO TRIES TO REINVENT HIMSELF FOR COLLEGE".
STITCHED DESIGN, NOT REALLY "FASHION"
DYED HIS HAIR
HE'S A FACE IN THE CROWD TRYING TO LOOK COOL; THAT'S THE ROOT OF IT.
THINKS CROPPED PANTS ARE COOL
POINTLESS FASHION POUCH
HE WENT WITH BOOTS AFTER NEVER WEARING THEM IN HIGH SCHOOL...
(NOT THAT IT MATTERS IN THE STORY)
I WROTE THAT THEY HAD THICK SOLES, BECAUSE THAT'S ALL HE COULD FIND.
THEY SHOULD LOOK LIKE THIS
FLAT HEEL

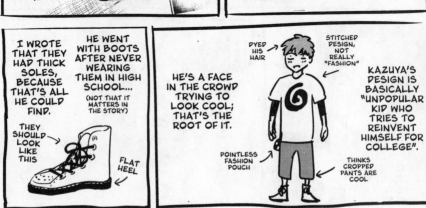

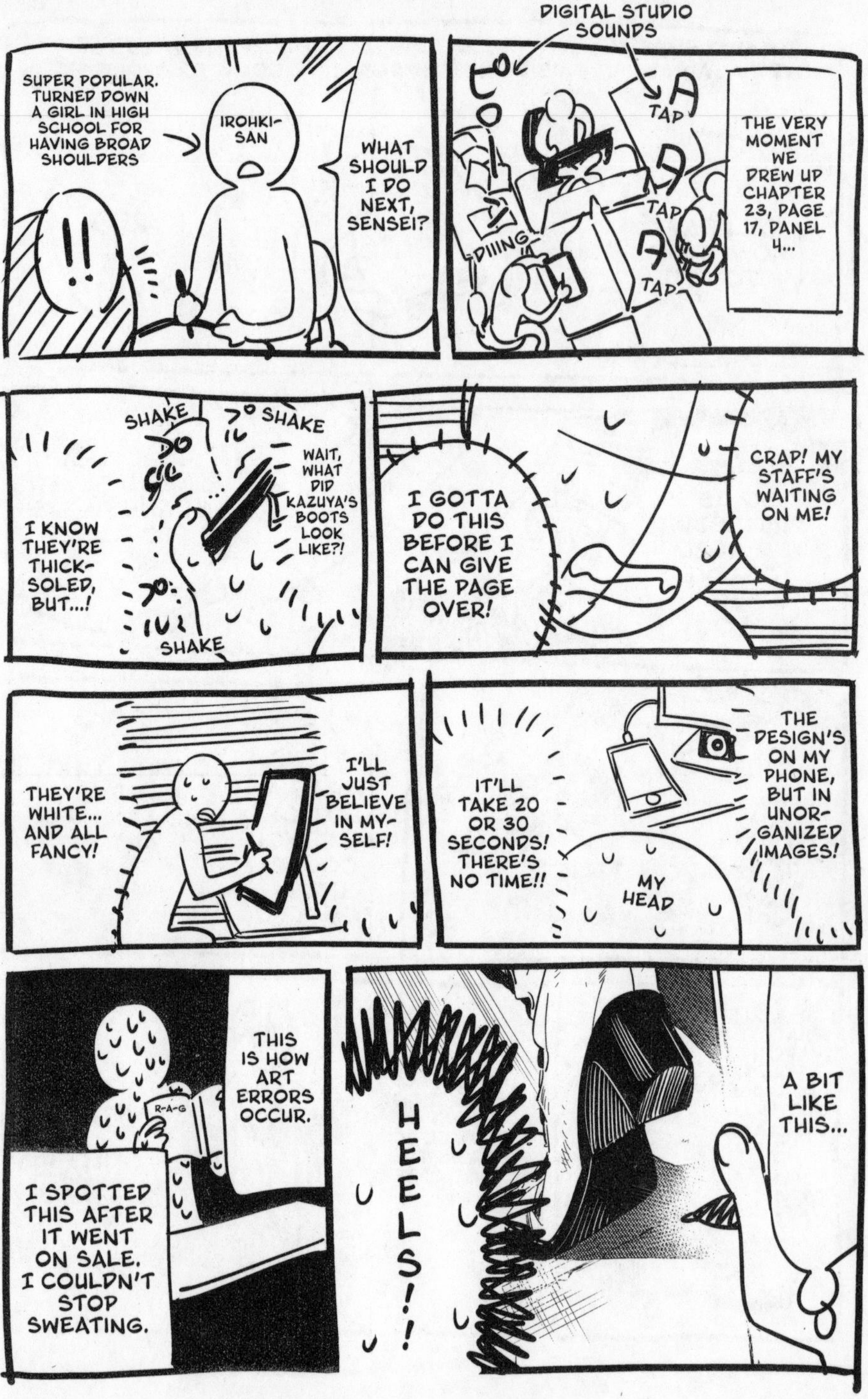
DIGITAL STUDIO SOUNDS
THE VERY MOMENT WE DREW UP CHAPTER 23, PAGE 17, PANEL 4...
TAP
TAP
TAP
DIIING
WHAT SHOULD I DO NEXT, SENSEI?
SUPER POPULAR. TURNED DOWN A GIRL IN HIGH SCHOOL FOR HAVING BROAD SHOULDERS
IROHKI-SAN
CRAP! MY STAFF'S WAITING ON ME!
I GOTTA DO THIS BEFORE I CAN GIVE THE PAGE OVER!
SHAKE
SHAKE
WAIT, WHAT DID KAZUYA'S BOOTS LOOK LIKE?!
I KNOW THEY'RE THICK-SOLED, BUT...!
SHAKE
THE DESIGN'S ON MY PHONE, BUT IN UNORGANIZED IMAGES!
IT'LL TAKE 20 OR 30 SECONDS! THERE'S NO TIME!!
MY HEAD
I'LL JUST BELIEVE IN MYSELF!
THEY'RE WHITE... AND ALL FANCY!
A BIT LIKE THIS...
HEELS!!
THIS IS HOW ART ERRORS OCCUR.
R-A-G
I SPOTTED THIS AFTER IT WENT ON SALE. I COULDN'T STOP SWEATING.

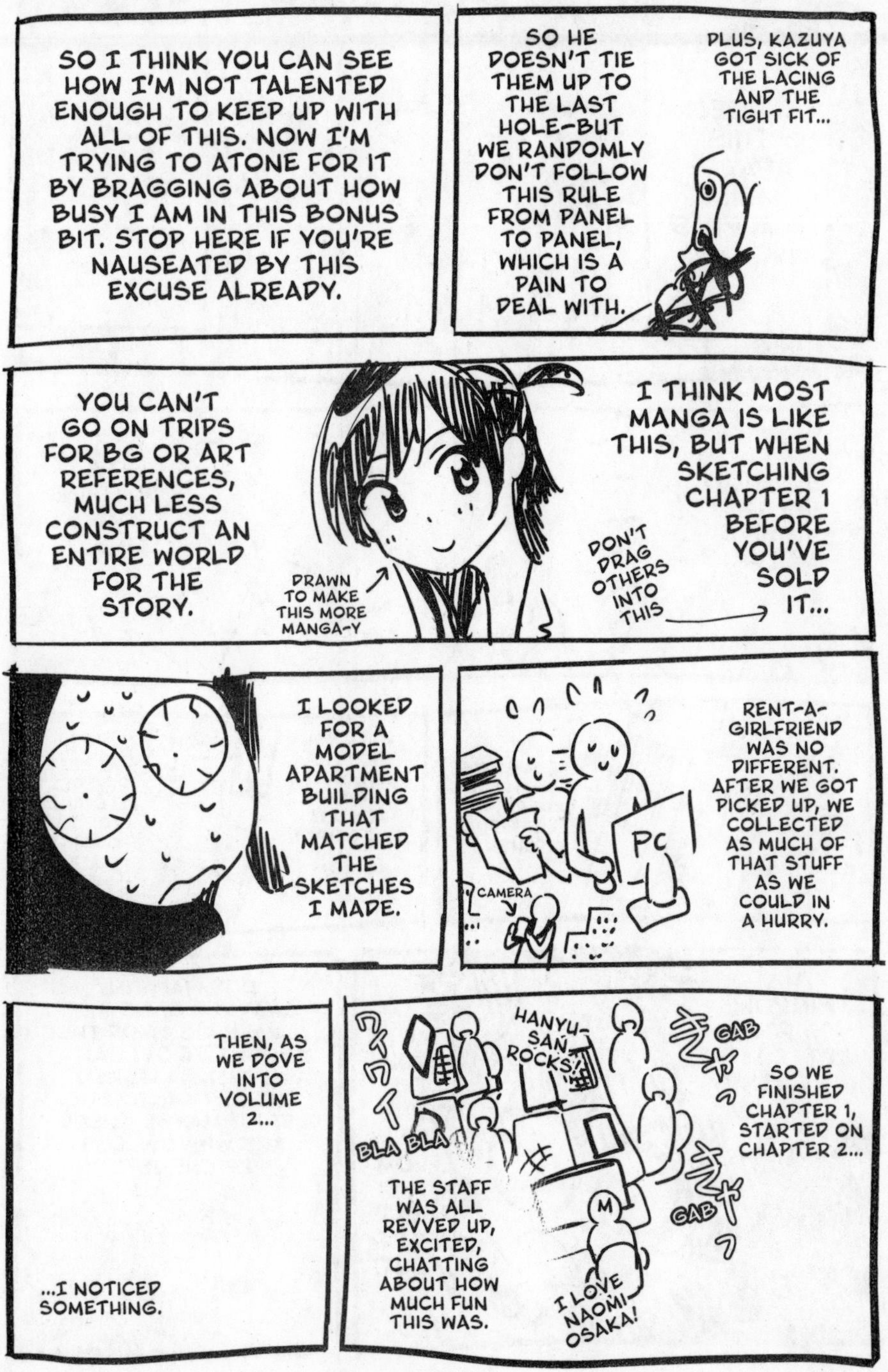
PLUS, KAZUYA GOT SICK OF THE LACING AND THE TIGHT FIT...
SO HE DOESN'T TIE THEM UP TO THE LAST HOLE—BUT WE RANDOMLY DON'T FOLLOW THIS RULE FROM PANEL TO PANEL, WHICH IS A PAIN TO DEAL WITH.
SO I THINK YOU CAN SEE HOW I'M NOT TALENTED ENOUGH TO KEEP UP WITH ALL OF THIS. NOW I'M TRYING TO ATONE FOR IT BY BRAGGING ABOUT HOW BUSY I AM IN THIS BONUS BIT. STOP HERE IF YOU'RE NAUSEATED BY THIS EXCUSE ALREADY.
I THINK MOST MANGA IS LIKE THIS, BUT WHEN SKETCHING CHAPTER 1 BEFORE YOU'VE SOLD IT...
DON'T DRAG OTHERS INTO THIS
YOU CAN'T GO ON TRIPS FOR BG OR ART REFERENCES, MUCH LESS CONSTRUCT AN ENTIRE WORLD FOR THE STORY.
DRAWN TO MAKE THIS MORE MANGA-Y
RENT-A-GIRLFRIEND WAS NO DIFFERENT. AFTER WE GOT PICKED UP, WE COLLECTED AS MUCH OF THAT STUFF AS WE COULD IN A HURRY.
PC
CAMERA
I LOOKED FOR A MODEL APARTMENT BUILDING THAT MATCHED THE SKETCHES I MADE.
SO WE FINISHED CHAPTER 1, STARTED ON CHAPTER 2...
GAB
GAB
HANYU-SAN ROCKS!
BLA BLA
I LOVE NAOMI OSAKA!
THE STAFF WAS ALL REVVED UP, EXCITED, CHATTING ABOUT HOW MUCH FUN THIS WAS.
THEN, AS WE DOVE INTO VOLUME 2...
...I NOTICED SOMETHING.

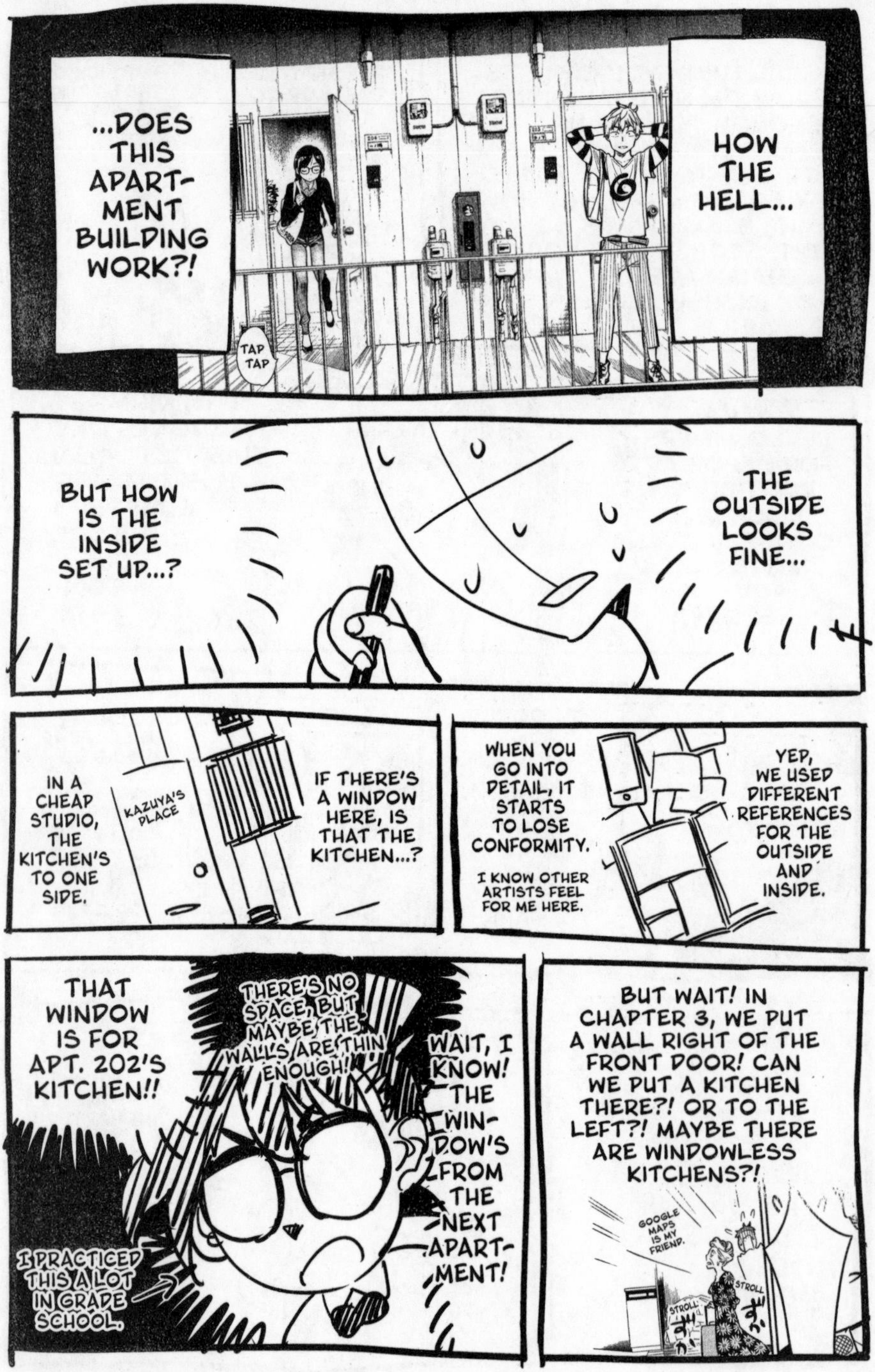
HOW THE HELL...
...DOES THIS APARTMENT BUILDING WORK?!
TAP TAP
THE OUTSIDE LOOKS FINE...
BUT HOW IS THE INSIDE SET UP...?
YEP, WE USED DIFFERENT REFERENCES FOR THE OUTSIDE AND INSIDE.
WHEN YOU GO INTO DETAIL, IT STARTS TO LOSE CONFORMITY.
I KNOW OTHER ARTISTS FEEL FOR ME HERE.
IF THERE'S A WINDOW HERE, IS THAT THE KITCHEN...?
KAZUYA'S PLACE
IN A CHEAP STUDIO, THE KITCHEN'S TO ONE SIDE.
BUT WAIT! IN CHAPTER 3, WE PUT A WALL RIGHT OF THE FRONT DOOR! CAN WE PUT A KITCHEN THERE?! OR TO THE LEFT?! MAYBE THERE ARE WINDOWLESS KITCHENS?!
GOOGLE MAPS IS MY FRIEND.
STROLL
STROLL
WAIT, I KNOW! THE WINDOW'S FROM THE NEXT APARTMENT!
THERE'S NO SPACE, BUT MAYBE THE WALLS ARE THIN ENOUGH!
THAT WINDOW IS FOR APT. 202'S KITCHEN!!
I PRACTICED THIS A LOT IN GRADE SCHOOL.

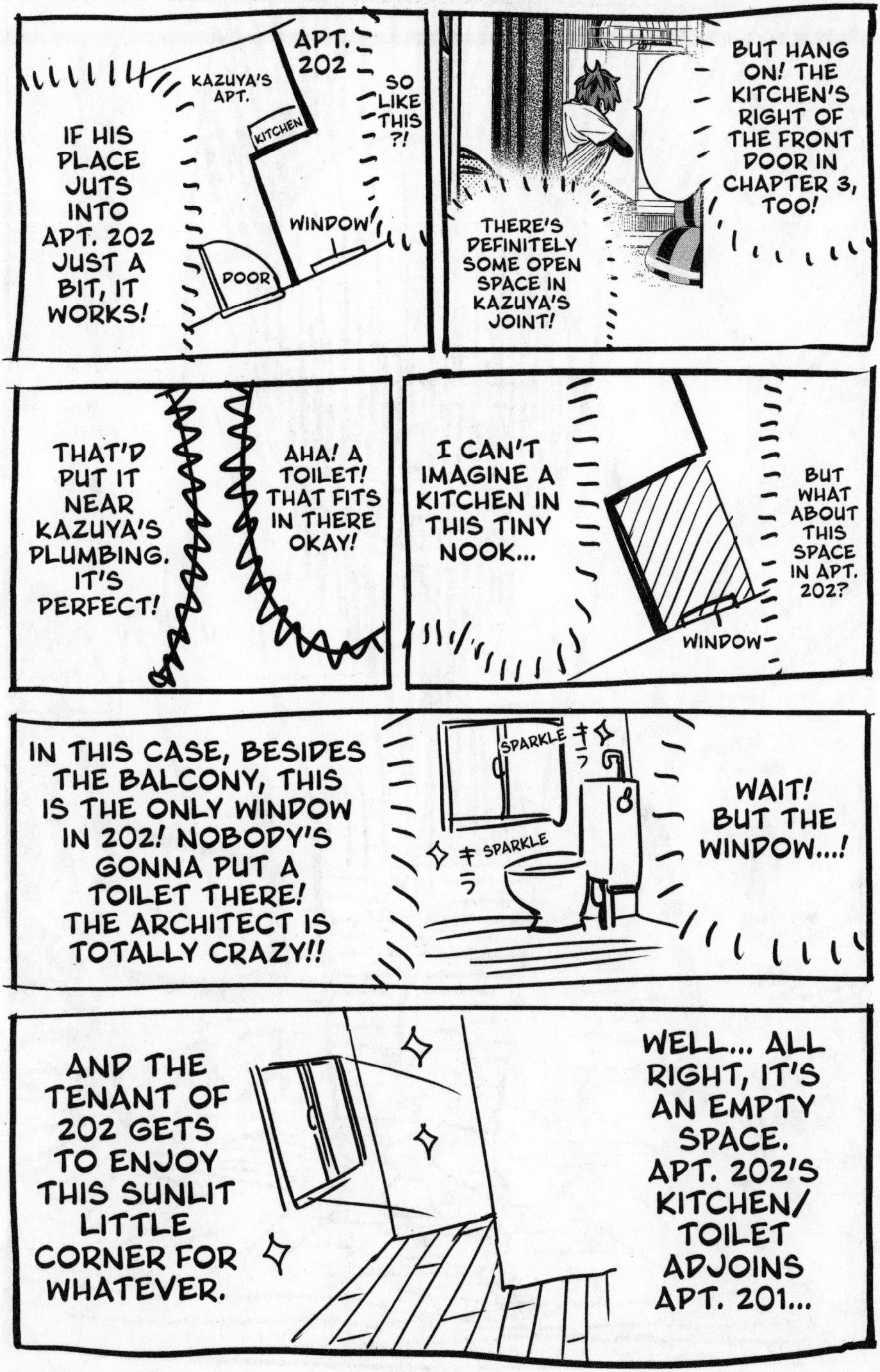
BUT HANG ON! THE KITCHEN'S RIGHT OF THE FRONT DOOR IN CHAPTER 3, TOO!
THERE'S DEFINITELY SOME OPEN SPACE IN KAZUYA'S JOINT!
SO LIKE THIS?!
APT. 202
KAZUYA'S APT.
KITCHEN
WINDOW
DOOR
IF HIS PLACE JUTS INTO APT. 202 JUST A BIT, IT WORKS!
BUT WHAT ABOUT THIS SPACE IN APT. 202?
WINDOW
I CAN'T IMAGINE A KITCHEN IN THIS TINY NOOK...
AHA! A TOILET! THAT FITS IN THERE OKAY!
THAT'D PUT IT NEAR KAZUYA'S PLUMBING. IT'S PERFECT!
WAIT! BUT THE WINDOW...!
キラ SPARKLE
キラ SPARKLE
IN THIS CASE, BESIDES THE BALCONY, THIS IS THE ONLY WINDOW IN 202! NOBODY'S GONNA PUT A TOILET THERE! THE ARCHITECT IS TOTALLY CRAZY!!
WELL... ALL RIGHT, IT'S AN EMPTY SPACE. APT. 202'S KITCHEN/ TOILET ADJOINS APT. 201...
AND THE TENANT OF 202 GETS TO ENJOY THIS SUNLIT LITTLE CORNER FOR WHATEVER.

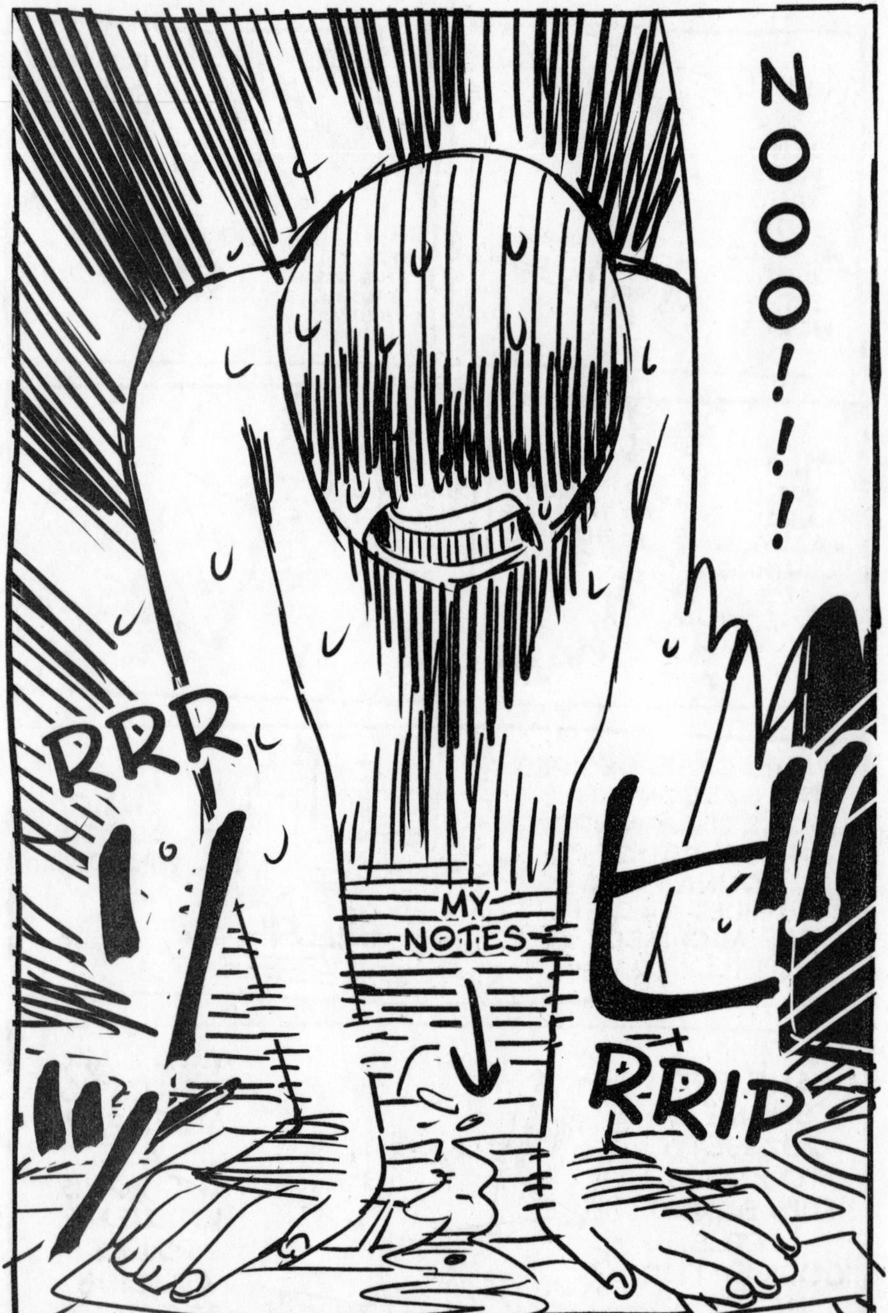
NOOO!!!
RRIP
MY NOTES
RRR

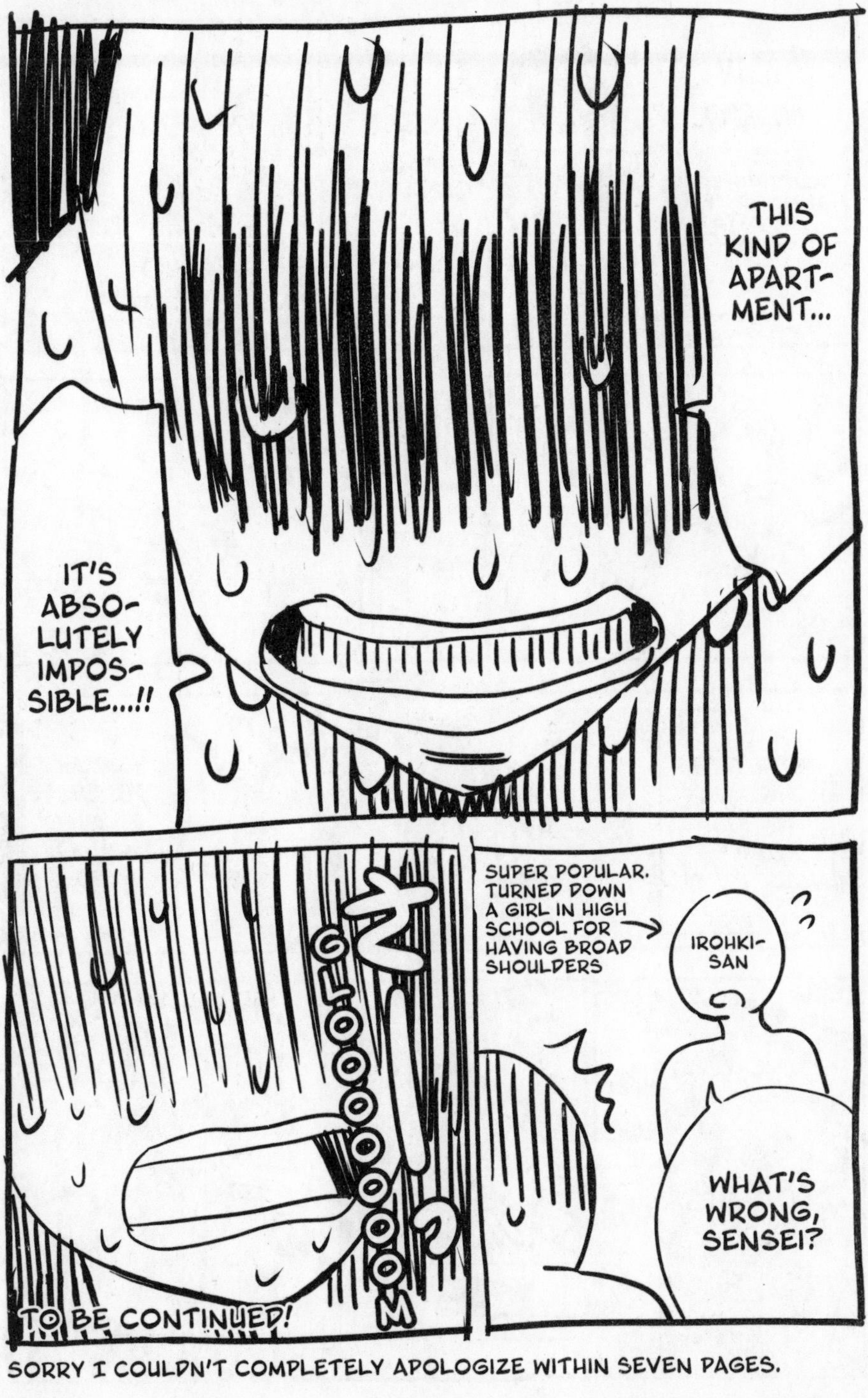
THIS KIND OF APART-MENT...
IT'S ABSO-LUTELY IMPOS-SIBLE...!!
WHAT'S WRONG, SENSEI?
SUPER POPULAR. TURNED DOWN A GIRL IN HIGH SCHOOL FOR HAVING BROAD SHOULDERS
IROHKI-SAN
GLOOOOOOOM
TO BE CONTINUED!

SORRY I COULDN'T COMPLETELY APOLOGIZE WITHIN SEVEN PAGES.

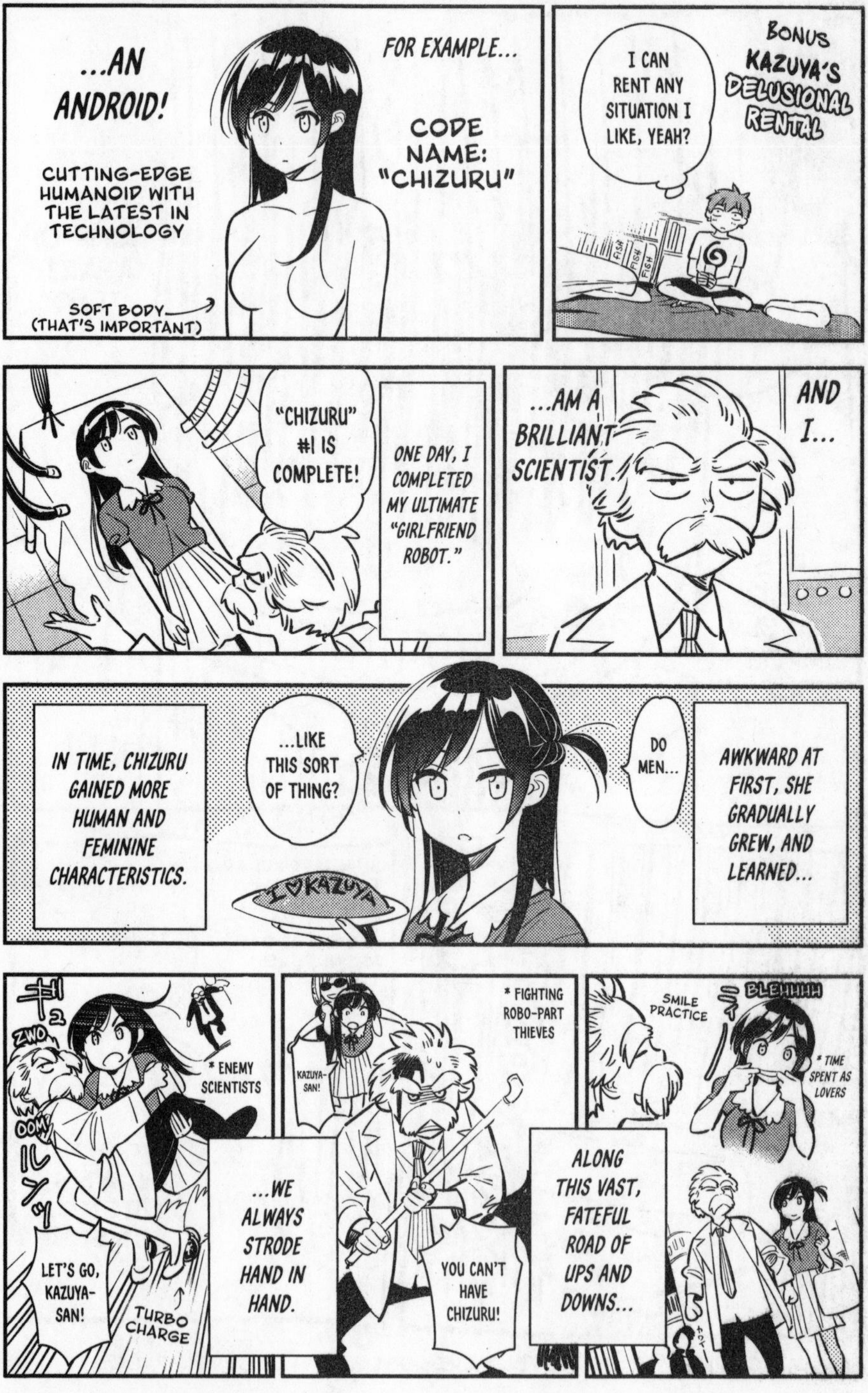
BONUS
KAZUYA'S
DELUSIONAL
RENTAL
I CAN RENT ANY SITUATION I LIKE, YEAH?
FOR EXAMPLE...
CODE NAME: "CHIZURU"
...AN ANDROID!
CUTTING-EDGE HUMANOID WITH THE LATEST IN TECHNOLOGY
SOFT BODY (THAT'S IMPORTANT)
AND I...
...AM A BRILLIANT SCIENTIST.
ONE DAY, I COMPLETED MY ULTIMATE "GIRLFRIEND ROBOT."
"CHIZURU" #1 IS COMPLETE!
AWKWARD AT FIRST, SHE GRADUALLY GREW, AND LEARNED...
DO MEN...
...LIKE THIS SORT OF THING?
I♡KAZUYA
IN TIME, CHIZURU GAINED MORE HUMAN AND FEMININE CHARACTERISTICS.
BLEHHHH
SMILE PRACTICE
* TIME SPENT AS LOVERS
ALONG THIS VAST, FATEFUL ROAD OF UPS AND DOWNS...
* FIGHTING ROBO-PART THIEVES
KAZUYA-SAN!
YOU CAN'T HAVE CHIZURU!
...WE ALWAYS STRODE HAND IN HAND.
* ENEMY SCIENTISTS
ZWO
DOM
LET'S GO, KAZUYA-SAN!
TURBO CHARGE

RENT-A-GIRLFRIEND STAFF: A, IROHKI, TEMAENO, KUSUMI, MITSUKI, MINATO

EDITORS: HIRAOKA-SAN, HIRATSUKA-SAN, HARA-SAN, CHOKAI-SAN. ALSO THANKS TO EVERYBODY WHO PICKED UP THIS BOOK!! SEE YOU SOON! ♡

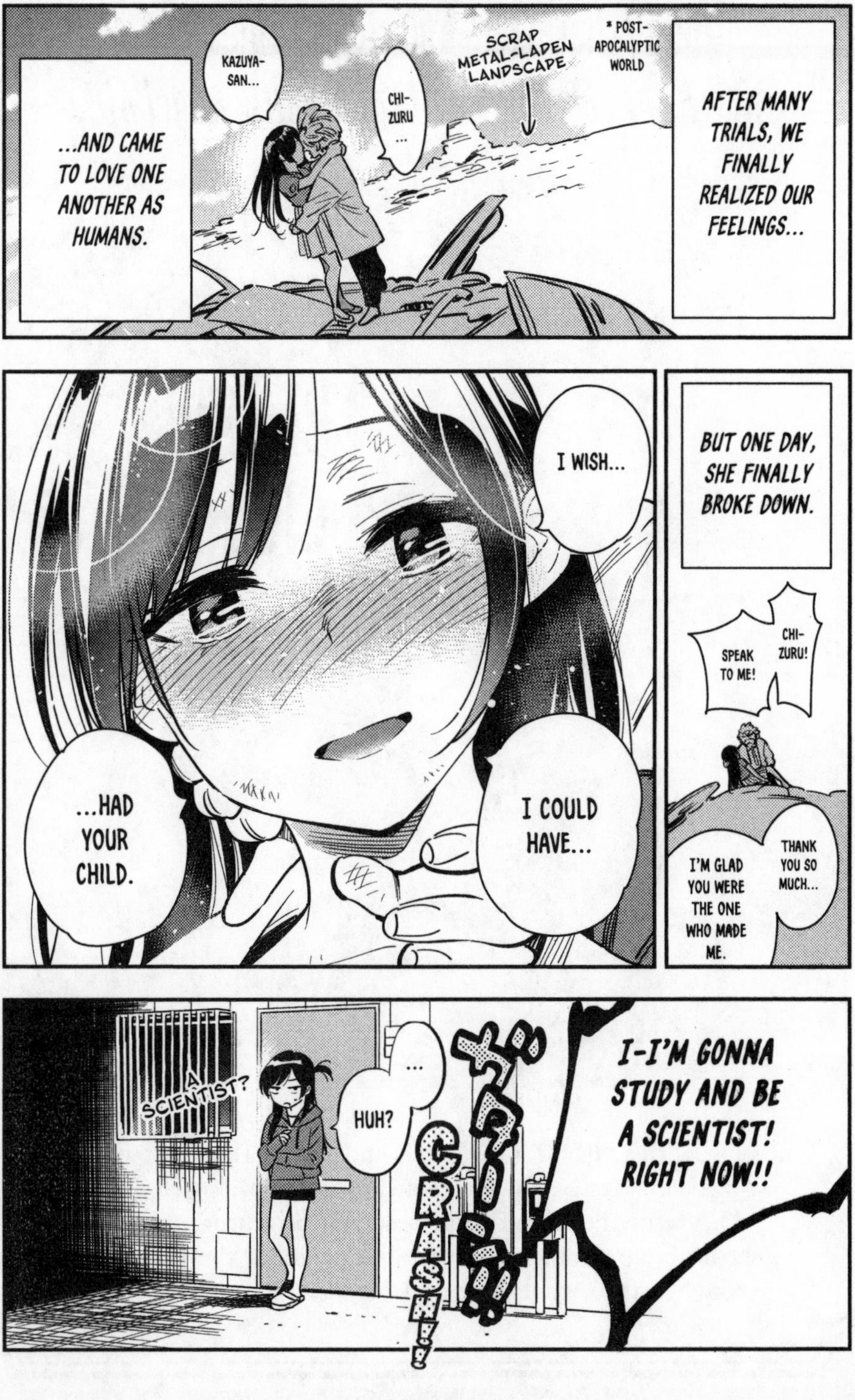
AFTER MANY TRIALS, WE FINALLY REALIZED OUR FEELINGS...
* POST-APOCALYPTIC WORLD
SCRAP METAL-LADEN LANDSCAPE
CHI-ZURU...
KAZUYA-SAN...
...AND CAME TO LOVE ONE ANOTHER AS HUMANS.
BUT ONE DAY, SHE FINALLY BROKE DOWN.
CHI-ZURU!
SPEAK TO ME!
THANK YOU SO MUCH...
I'M GLAD YOU WERE THE ONE WHO MADE ME.
I WISH...
I COULD HAVE...
...HAD YOUR CHILD.
I-I'M GONNA STUDY AND BE A SCIENTIST! RIGHT NOW!!
CRASH!!
...
HUH?
A SCIENTIST?

Young characters and steampunk setting, like *Howl's Moving Castle* and *Battle Angel Alita*

Beyond the Clouds © 2018 Nicke / Ki-oon

A boy with a talent for machines and a mysterious girl whose wings he's fixed will take you beyond the clouds! In the tradition of the high-flying, resonant adventure stories of Studio Ghibli comes a gorgeous tale about the longing of young hearts for adventure and friendship!

Knight of the Ice ©Yayoi Ogawa/Kodansha Ltd.

Yayoi Ogawa

SKATING THRILLS AND ICY CHILLS WITH THIS NEW TINGLY ROMANCE SERIES!

A rom-com on ice, perfect for fans of *Princess Jellyfish* and *Wotakoi*. Kokoro is the talk of the figure-skating world, winning trophies and hearts. But little do they know... he's actually a huge nerd! From the beloved creator of *You're My Pet* (*Tramps Like Us*).

Chitose is a serious young woman, working for the health magazine *SASSO*. Or at least, she would be, if she wasn't constantly getting distracted by her childhood friend, international figure skating star Kokoro Kijinami! In the public eye and on the ice, Kokoro is a gallant, flawless knight, but behind his glittery costumes and breathtaking spins lies a secret: He's actually a hopelessly romantic otaku, who can only land his quad jumps when Chitose is on hand to recite a spell from his favorite magical girl anime!

KC KODANSHA COMICS

A SMART, NEW ROMANTIC COMEDY FOR FANS OF *SHORTCAKE CAKE* AND *TERRACE HOUSE*!

Living-Room Matsunaga-san © Keiko Iwashita / Kodansha Ltd.

A romance manga starring high school girl Meeko, who learns to live on her own in a boarding house whose living room is home to the odd (but handsome) Matsunaga-san. She begins to adjust to her new life away from her parents, but Meeko soon learns that no matter how far away from home she is, she's still a young girl at heart — especially when she finds herself falling for Matsunaga-san.

PERFECT WORLD

Rie Aruga

A TOUCHING NEW SERIES ABOUT LOVE AND COPING WITH DISABILITY

An office party reunites Tsugumi with her high school crush Itsuki. He's realized his dream of becoming an architect, but along the way, he experienced a spinal injury that put him in a wheelchair. Now Tsugumi's rekindled feelings will butt up against prejudices she never considered — and Itsuki will have to decide if he's ready to let someone into his heart...

"Depicts with great delicacy and courage the difficulties some with disabilities experience getting involved in romantic relationships... Rie Aruga refuses to romanticize, pushing her heroine to face the reality of disability. She invites her readers to the same tasks of empathy, knowledge and recognition."
—Slate.fr

"An important entry [in manga romance]... The emotional core of both plot and characters indicates thoughtfulness... [Aruga's] research is readily apparent in the text and artwork, making this feel like a real story."
—Anime News Network

KC
KODANSHA
COMICS

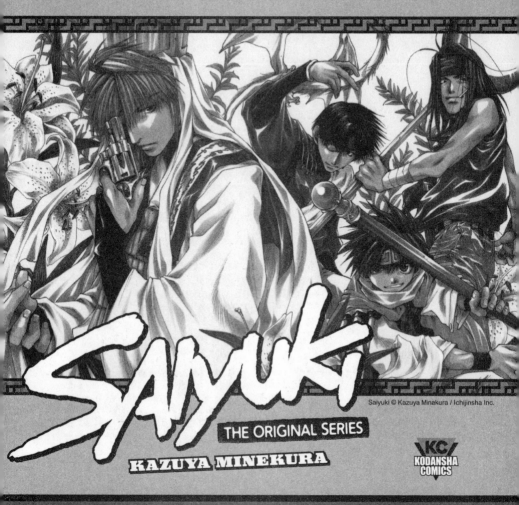

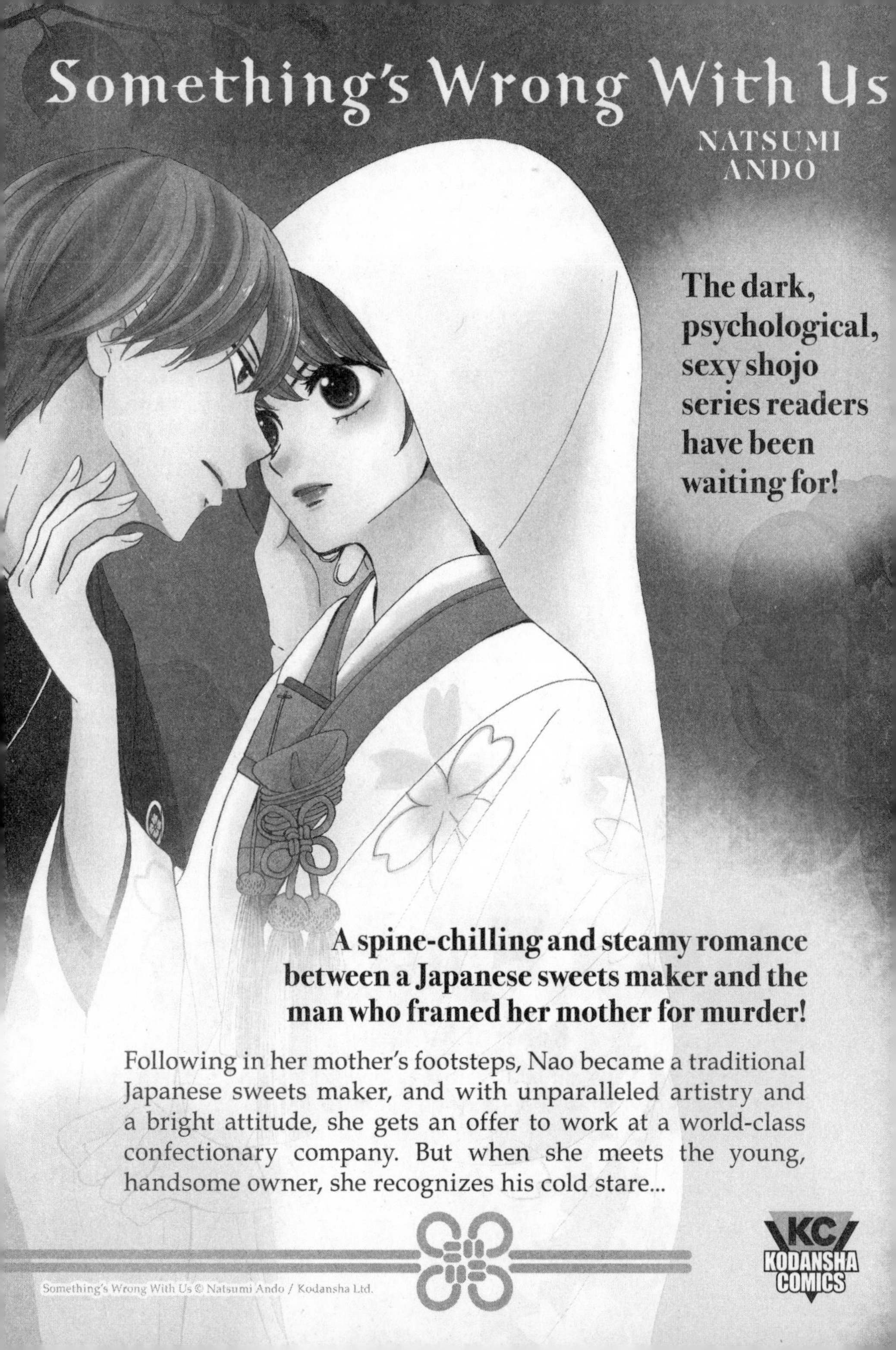
Something's Wrong With Us
NATSUMI ANDO
The dark, psychological, sexy shojo series readers have been waiting for!
A spine-chilling and steamy romance between a Japanese sweets maker and the man who framed her mother for murder!
Following in her mother's footsteps, Nao became a traditional Japanese sweets maker, and with unparalleled artistry and a bright attitude, she gets an offer to work at a world-class confectionary company. But when she meets the young, handsome owner, she recognizes his cold stare...
KC KODANSHA COMICS
Something's Wrong With Us © Natsumi Ando / Kodansha Ltd.

The adorable new odd-couple cat comedy manga from the creator of the beloved *Chi's Sweet Home*, in full color!

Sue & Tai-chan

Konami Kanata

Sue is an aging housecat who's looking forward to living out her life in peace... but her plans change when the mischievous black tomcat Tai-chan enters the picture! Hey! Sue never signed up to be a catsitter! *Sue & Tai-chan* is the latest from the reigning meow-narch of cute kitty comics, Konami Kanata.

KC
KODANSHA
COMICS

THE SWEET SCENT OF LOVE IS IN THE AIR! FOR FANS OF OFFBEAT ROMANCES LIKE *WOTAKOI*

Sweat and Soap © Kintetsu Yamada / Kodansha Ltd.

In an office romance, there's a fine line between sexy and awkward... and that line is where Asako — a woman who sweats copiously — meets Koutarou — a perfume developer who can't get enough of Asako's, er, scent. Don't miss a romcom manga like no other!

KC KODANSHA COMICS

CUTE ANIMALS AND LIFE LESSONS, PERFECT FOR ASPIRING PET VETS OF ALL AGES!

YUZU THE PET VET

1

BY
MINGO ITO

In collaboration with
NIPPON COLUMBIA CO., LTD.

Yuzu the Pet Vet © Mingo Ito / NIPPON COLUMBIA CO., LTD./ Kodansha Ltd.

For an 11-year-old, Yuzu has a lot on her plate. When her mom gets sick and has to be hospitalized, Yuzu goes to live with her uncle who runs the local veterinary clinic. Yuzu's always been scared of animals, but she tries to help out. Through all the tough moments in her life, Yuzu realizes that she can help make things all right with a little help from her animal pals, peers, and kind grown-ups.

Every new patient is a furry friend in the making!

One of CLAMP's biggest hits returns in this definitive, premium, hardcover 20th anniversary collector's edition!

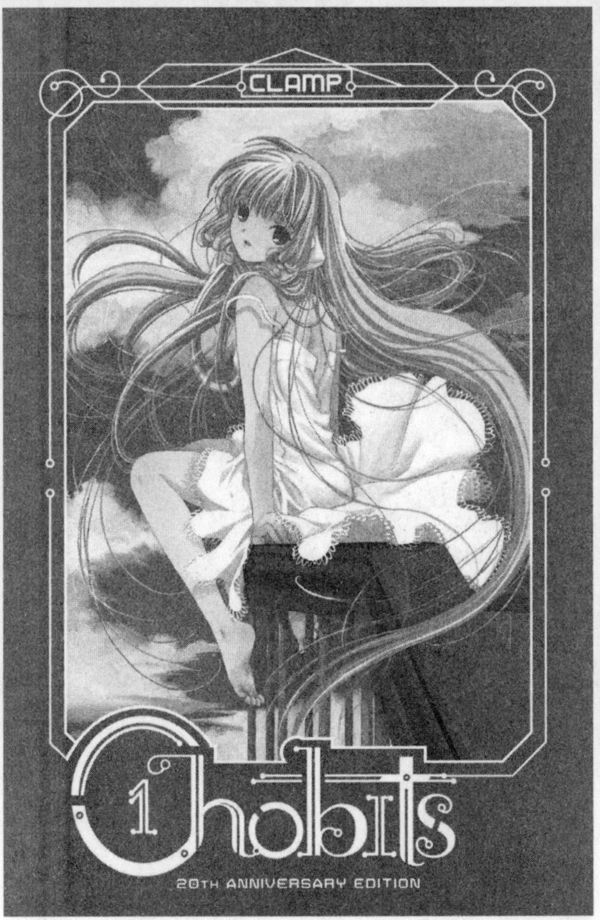
CLAMP
1
Chobits
20TH ANNIVERSARY EDITION

"A wonderfully entertaining story that would be a great installment in anybody's manga collection."
— Anime News Network

"CLAMP is an all-female manga-creating team whose feminine touch shows in this entertaining, sci-fi soap opera."
— Publishers Weekly

Poor college student Hideki is down on his luck. All he wants is a good job, a girlfriend, and his very own "persocom"—the latest and greatest in humanoid computer technology. Hideki's luck changes one night when he finds Chi—a persocom thrown out in a pile of trash. But Hideki soon discovers that there's much more to his cute new persocom than meets the eye.

KC
KODANSHA COMICS

THE WORLD OF CLAMP!

Cardcaptor Sakura
Collector's Edition

Cardcaptor Sakura:
Clear Card

Magic Knight Rayearth
25th Anniversary Box Set

Chobits

TSUBASA Omnibus

TSUBASA WoRLD CHRoNiCLE

xxxHOLiC Omnibus

xxxHOLiC Rei

CLOVER Collector's Edition

Kodansha Comics welcomes you to explore the expansive world of CLAMP, the all-female artist collective that has produced some of the most acclaimed manga of the century. Our growing catalog includes icons like *Cardcaptor Sakura* and *Magic Knight Rayearth*, each crafted with CLAMP's one-of-a-kind style and characters!

The art-deco cyberpunk classic from the creators of *xxxHOLiC* and *Cardcaptor Sakura!*

"Starred Review. This experimental sci-fi work from CLAMP reads like a romantic version of *AKIRA*."
—Publishers Weekly

CLOVER © CLAMP·ShigatsuTsuitachi CO.,LTD./Kodansha Ltd.

Su was born into a bleak future, where the government keeps tight control over children with magical powers—codenamed "Clovers." With Su being the only "four-leaf" Clover in the world, she has been kept isolated nearly her whole life. Can ex-military agent Kazuhiko deliver her to the happiness she seeks? Experience the complete series in this hardcover edition, which also includes over twenty pages of ravishing color art!

KODANSHA COMICS

The beloved characters from *Cardcaptor Sakura* return in a brand new, reimagined fantasy adventure!

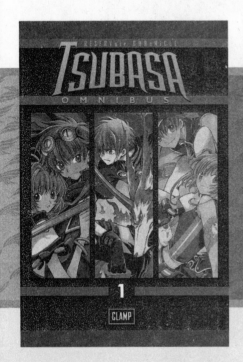

"[*Tsubasa*] takes readers on a fantastic ride that only gets more exhilarating with each successive chapter." —Anime News Network

In the Kingdom of Clow, an archaeological dig unleashes an incredible power, causing Princess Sakura to lose her memories. To save her, her childhood friend Syaoran must follow the orders of the Dimension Witch and travel alongside Kurogane, an unrivaled warrior; Fai, a powerful magician; and Mokona, a curiously strange creature, to retrieve Sakura's dispersed memories!

KODANSHA COMICS

"Clever, sassy, and original....*xxxHOLiC* has the inherent hallmarks of a runaway hit."
—NewType magazine

Beautifully seductive artwork and uniquely Japanese depictions of the supernatural will hypnotize CLAMP fans!

xxxHOLiC
OMNIBUS 1
CLAMP

1
xxxHOLiC
Rei
From the creators of *Tsubasa* and *Chobits*
CLAMP

Kimihiro Watanuki is haunted by visions of ghosts and spirits. He seeks help from a mysterious woman named Yuko, who claims she can help. However, Watanuki must work for Yuko in order to pay for her aid. Soon Watanuki finds himself employed in Yuko's shop, where he sees things and meets customers that are stranger than anything he could have ever imagined.

KC KODANSHA COMICS

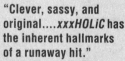

A Kodansha Comics Trade Paperback Original
Rent-A-Girlfriend 10 copyright © 2019 Reiji Miyajima
English translation copyright © 2021 Reiji Miyajima

Published in the United States by Kodansha Comics, an imprint of Kodansha USA Publishing, LLC, New York.

Publication rights for this English edition arranged through Kodansha Ltd., Tokyo.

First published in Japan in 2019 by Kodansha Ltd., Tokyo as *Kanojo, okarishimasu*, volume 10.

ISBN 978-1-64651-094-8

Original cover design by Kohei Nawata Design Office

Printed in the United States of America.

www.kodansha.us

1st Printing
Translation: Kevin Gifford
Lettering: Paige Pumphrey
Editing: Jordan Blanco
Kodansha Comics edition cover design by Phil Balsman

Publisher: Kiichiro Sugawara

Director of publishing services: Ben Applegate
Associate director, publishing operations: Stephen Pakula
Publishing services managing editors: Madison Salters, Alanna Ruse
Production managers: Emi Lotto, Angela Zurlo
Logo and character art ©Kodansha USA Publishing, LLC